FAMILY, RELIGION AND LAW

Family, Religion and Law: Cultural Encounters in Europe *offers a most timely, rich and much needed body of comparative work which presents discerning insights into the challenges of legal pluralism and the ways in which cultural and religious minorities in a range of European contexts navigate the legal system. This book fills a critical gap in current research, offering lawyers, academics, judges, parliamentarians and many others unique and critical insights into the key questions they ought to be asking.*
    Puja Kapai, Associate Professor of Law, Director of the Center for Comparative and Public Law, The University of Hong Kong

The views expressed during the execution of the RELIGARE project, in whatever form and or by whatever medium, are the sole responsibility of the authors. The European Union is not liable for any use that may be made of the information contained therein.

Cultural Diversity and Law in Association with RELIGARE

Series Editor: Prakash Shah, Queen Mary University of London, UK

RELIGARE is a project on Religious Diversity and Secular Models in Europe funded by the European Commission under the Seventh Framework Programme. The project brings together an interdisciplinary team of high profile researchers and 13 academic institutions to collaborate on examining how existing policy and practice is suited to the demands of religious diversity within Europe and what legal models can be recommended to accommodate such diversity in future. More details on the project can be seen at its website: http://www.religareproject.eu/. 'Cultural Diversity and Law in Association with RELIGARE' provides an outlet for the results of specific research undertaken within the RELIGARE project.

Other titles in this series:

The Burqa Affair Across Europe
Between Public and Private Space
Edited by Alessandro Ferrari and Sabrina Pastorelli

Religion in Public Spaces
A European Perspective
Edited by Silvio Ferrari and Sabrina Pastorelli

A Test of Faith?
Religious Diversity and Accommodation in the European Workplace
Edited by Katayoun Alidadi, Marie-Claire Foblets and
Jogchum Vrielink

Family, Religion and Law
Cultural Encounters in Europe

Edited by

PRAKASH SHAH
Queen Mary University of London, UK

with

MARIE-CLAIRE FOBLETS,
Max Planck Institute for Social Anthropology, Germany

and

MATHIAS ROHE
University Erlangen-Nürnberg, Germany

ASHGATE

© Prakash Shah with Marie-Claire Foblets and Mathias Rohe, and the contributors 2014

All rights reserved. No part of this publication may be reproduced, stored in a retrieval system or transmitted in any form or by any means, electronic, mechanical, photocopying, recording or otherwise without the prior permission of the publisher.

Prakash Shah with Marie-Claire Foblets and Mathias Rohe have asserted their right under the Copyright, Designs and Patents Act, 1988, to be identified as the editors of this work.

Published by
Ashgate Publishing Limited
Wey Court East
Union Road
Farnham
Surrey, GU9 7PT
England

Ashgate Publishing Company
110 Cherry Street
Suite 3-1
Burlington, VT 05401-3818
USA

www.ashgate.com

British Library Cataloguing in Publication Data
A catalogue record for this book is available from the British Library

The Library of Congress has cataloged the printed edition as follows:
Shah, Prakash.
  Family, religion and law : cultural encounters in Europe / By Prakash Shah with Marie-Claire Foblets and Mathias Rohe.
        pages ; cm -- (Cultural diversity and law in association with religare)
        Includes bibliographical references and index.
        ISBN 978-1-4724-3315-2 (hardback) -- ISBN 978-1-4724-3316-9 (ebook) -- ISBN 978-1-4724-3317-6 (epub) 1. Domestic relations--Europe. 2. Legal polycentricity--Europe. 3. Minorities--Legal status, laws, etc.--Europe. 4. Religion and law--Europe. I. Foblets, Marie-Claire, 1959- II. Rohe, Mathias, 1959- III. Title.
        KJC1105.S53 2014
        346.401'5--dc23
                                                                                        2013043994

ISBN: 9781472433152 (hbk)
ISBN: 9781472433169 (ebk – PDF)
ISBN: 9781472433176 (ebk – ePUB)

Printed in the United Kingdom by Henry Ling Limited,
at the Dorset Press, Dorchester, DT1 1HD

Contents

Notes on Contributors		*vii*
Preface: Family, Religion and Law in Europe: Embracing Diversity from the Perspective of 'Cultural Encounters' by Marie-Claire Foblets		*xi*
Acknowledgements		*xvii*

1	Distorting Minority Laws? Religious Diversity and European Legal Systems *Prakash Shah*	1
2	Plurality-Conscious Rebalancing of Family Law Regulation in Europe *Werner Menski*	29
3	Family and the Law in Europe: Bringing Together Secular Legal Orders and Religious Norms and Needs *Mathias Rohe*	49
4	On the Cooperation between Religious and State Institutions in Family Matters: Nordic Experiences *Maarit Jänterä-Jareborg*	79
5	The Uniformisation of Family Law in Europe and the Place of Ethnic Minorities *Domenico Francavilla*	103
6	Defending the Family Treasure Chest: Navigating Muslim Families and Secured Positivistic Islands of European Legal Systems *Federica Sona*	115
7	Cross-border Family Cases and Religious Diversity: What Can Judges Do? *Maarit Jänterä-Jareborg*	143
8	Secrets and Lies: When Ethnic Minority Youth Have a *Nikah* *Anika Liversage*	165
9	'Without Our Church We Will Disappear': Syrian Orthodox Christians in Diaspora and the Family Law of the Church *Annika Rabo*	181

| 10 | Religious Divorce in England and Wales: Religious Tribunals in Action
Gillian Douglas, Russell Sandberg, Norman Doe, Sophie Gilliat-Ray and Asma Khan | 195 |
| 11 | Kurdish 'Unofficial' Family Law in the *Gurbet*
Latif Taş | 209 |

Index   *237*

Notes on Contributors

Norman Doe is a Professor of Law and director of the Centre for Law and Religion at Cardiff Law School. He has written several books on canon law and law and religion, including *Canon Law in the Anglican Communion* (Oxford, 1998) and *Christian Law: Contemporary Principles* (Cambridge, 2013). He has acted as a consultant to the Primates Meeting of the Anglican Communion, the Lambeth Conference 2008 and the Anglican Communion Covenant Design Group. In 2010 he was president of the European Consortium for Church and State Research.

Gillian Douglas is Professor of Law at Cardiff University, having previously lectured at the University of Bristol and the National University of Singapore. She has written extensively on Family Law and is the co-author of the leading text, *Bromley's Family Law* (Oxford University Press) and co-editor of the *Child and Family Law Quarterly*. She has conducted a range of empirical research projects into aspects of the family justice system and the impact of law on family life, including the consequences of divorce for children, the position of separated cohabitants, and public attitudes to the rules on inheritance.

Marie-Claire Foblets was the head of the RELIGARE project. Since 2012, she has been the Head of a new department on Law and Anthropology at the Max Planck Institute for Social Anthropology in Halle a/d Saale (Sachsen-Anhalt). Her research areas include Europe and the Magreb, and her research is focused on various fields including social anthropological analysis and legal practice, religious diversity in secular contexts, European migration and asylum policy, transnational citizenship and human rights protection, Islam in Europe and international family law. For more than 20 years she taught social and cultural anthropology in the universities of Antwerp and Brussels, and was most recently ordinary professor at the Catholic University of Leuven, heading the Institute for Migration Law and Legal Anthropology. She is a member of various networks of researchers, focusing either on the study of the application of Islamic law in Europe, or on law and migration in Europe, including the Association Française d'Anthropologie du Droit (AFAD), of which she served as co-president for several years.

Domenico Francavilla is Associate Professor of Comparative Law at the Department of Law, University of Turin, where he teaches the courses on Comparative Legal Systems and Indian Law. He is also a Research Associate at the School of Law, SOAS, University of London, and a fellow of the Centre for Comparative and Transnational Law, Turin. He holds a Laurea in Giurisprudenza (Catholic University, Milan) and a doctorate in Philosophy of Law (University of Padova). His main areas of research are comparative legal systems, Indian law, classical and modern Hindu law, European legal systems and ethnic minorities.

Sophie Gilliat-Ray is Reader in Religious and Theological Studies at Cardiff University, and Director of the Islam-UK Centre. She has published a number of books, journal articles and edited book chapters on Islam and Muslims in Britain, religion in public life, and publicly funded chaplaincy. Most recently, she has published *Muslims in Britain: An Introduction* (Cambridge University Press, 2010) and, with S. Pattison and M. Ali, *Understanding Muslim Chaplaincy* (Ashgate, 2013).

Maarit Jänterä-Jareborg took her LLM at Helsinki University, qualified as a judge in Finland and defended her LLD thesis at Uppsala University where she has held the Chair of Private International Law with International Civil Procedure since 1998. Between 2004 and 2008 she was Dean of the Faculty of Law. She has acted as an expert member in numerous law commissions and working parties, in Sweden and abroad. She is the Deputy Director of the multidisciplinary research programme The Impact of Religion: Challenges for Society, Law and Democracy (Uppsala University 2008–2018) and is in charge of supervising the programme's research on religion and family law.

Asma Khan, previously a researcher at Cardiff University, is now studying towards an MSc in Social Change at Manchester University and is Director of Total Transcriptions, a company providing freelance qualitative research services. She is co-author of *Muslim Childhood* (Oxford, 2013).

Anika Liversage is a senior researcher at SFI, the Danish National Centre for Social Research in Copenhagen, Denmark, where she heads the programme area on ethnic minority research. Her studies focus on immigrant family relations, attending specifically to issues of gender and power. Among the Centre's areas of interest are the consequences of the strict Danish rules of family migration on ethnic minorities' family formation and Turkish immigrants in Denmark. Anika Liversage uses her ability to speak Turkish fluently in her qualitative studies, and has been investigating divorces among Turkish immigrants in Denmark.

Werner Menski, MA PhD, is Professor of South Asian Laws at SOAS, University of London, and writes on South Asian laws, Hindu law and Muslim law, comparative law and ethnic minority legal issues. His major books are: *Comparative Law in a Global Context: The Legal Systems of Asia and Africa* (Cambridge University Press, second edition, 2006); *Hindu Law: Beyond Tradition and Modernity* (Oxford University Press, 2003); *Modern Indian Family Law* (Curzon Press, 2001); *Muslim Family Law* (with David Pearl; Sweet & Maxwell, 1998); and *South Asians and the Dowry Problem* (Trentham Books, 1998). He also edits *South Asia Research* (New Delhi: SAGE).

Annika Rabo is a Professor at the Department of Social Anthropology, Stockholm University. She has conducted fieldwork in the Middle East since the late 1970s, mainly in Syria, focusing on a variety of topics related to state–citizen relations. She is currently involved in projects focusing on transnational connections and has recently finished a study on transnational Syrian families and family law.

Prof. Dr Mathias Rohe, MA (Islamic studies), is Chair for Civil Law, Private International Law and Comparative Law at the University of Erlangen-Nürnberg, Germany, and Director of the Erlangen Centre for Islam and law in Europe. He has been a judge at the court of appeals Nürnberg (retired), a member of the German Islam Conferences (Ministry of the Interior) and the Austrian Islam Dialogue Forum (State secretary). He has produced numerous publications and lectures on Islamic law in the past and present, private international law, comparative law and legal issues related to Muslims in Europe.

Dr Russell Sandberg is Lecturer in Law at Cardiff University where he researches at the Centre for Law and Religion. He is author of *Law and Religion* (Cambridge University Press, 2011) and has written extensively in the field of law and religion for a wide range of journals including *Law Quarterly Review*, *Modern Law Review*, *Cambridge Law Journal*, *Oxford Journal of Legal Studies*, *Public Law*, *Family Law* and the *Ecclesiastical Law Journal*.

Dr Prakash Shah has research interests in legal pluralism, religion and law, ethnic minorities and diasporas in law, immigration, refugee and nationality law, and comparative law. He joined Queen Mary University of London, in 2002, where he is now a Reader in Culture and Law and Director of GLOCUL: The Centre for Culture and Law. He was part of the RELIGARE project.

Federica Sona is a PhD candidate at SOAS, University of London. She recently obtained her Renato Treves International Research Doctorate in Law and Society, University of Milan. Federica was the researcher responsible for the London area in the inquiry commissioned by the Ministry of Justice: 'A study of Sharia Councils in relation to family law matters in England and Wales'. Since 2005, Federica has been providing legal consultancy to diplomatic personnel, individuals and lawyers involved in family law matters, predominantly those regarding Muslim majority countries' nationals settled in Italy and the UK.

Dr Latif Taş was a Rechtskulturen Fellow and legal researcher at the Faculty of Law, Humboldt University, in Berlin, Germany, in 2012–2013. He was awarded a doctorate in Law at Queen Mary University of London, in August 2012. He holds a first degree and Masters in Journalism from Marmara University, Istanbul. He also holds a Masters by Research at the School of Law, Queen Mary University of London. His research interests include socio-cultural legal studies, legal pluralism, philosophy of law, multiculturalism, ethnic minorities, diaspora identity, transnationalism and conflict resolution.

Preface
Family, Religion and Law in Europe: Embracing Diversity from the Perspective of 'Cultural Encounters'

Marie-Claire Foblets

This volume has a twofold origin: the underlying idea – set out in this brief preface – is identical for all the contributions it contains, although the papers were commissioned for different gatherings (see Acknowledgements). However, the idea underlying the meetings was the same: the aim of the organisers of each meeting was to convene researchers who, in various countries in Europe, are looking for keys to understanding some of the current developments in the various ways people organise their family relationships in a context where they are faced with the challenge of embracing diversity from the perspective of 'cultural encounters': civil versus religious law, majority versus minority practices, and so forth, with a particular focus on challenges related to religion and law. The participants were given free rein, so to speak, as to the particular topic they wished to consider in this context.

What gives the volume its coherence is the concern, shared by all contributors to the work, to demonstrate, by way of concrete illustrations taken for the most part from first-hand observation, the urgency, multiplicity and above all complexity of the questions having to do with the search for justice in the domain of family life in the Europe of today, especially when issues also involve religious convictions. It has long been thought that by opting for a secularisation of the law (i.e. of official state law), national legislators in Europe have found a solution to the problems raised by the coexistence of laws derived from religious inspiration with state law. In fact, this was a serious error, as is evident from the various illustrations provided in this volume. Each of these illustrations, without exception, is drawn from actual situations, and thus they must be seen and interpreted as integral parts of contemporary reality in European societies.

One could of course argue that the situation today is not substantially different from that of the past, and in any case the secular civil law is the only one that is granted recognition by the state authorities. In the event of a conflict between loyalty to state law and religious or confessional commitments, the problem is deemed resolved by virtue of the separation of law and religion.[1] In Europe today, with the exception of a few very specific regulations,

---

1 On this separation, which is in fact quite recent in the history of democratic societies, see especially Motzkinn G. and Fischer Y. 2008, *Religion and Democracy in Contemporary Europe*, London: Alliance Publishing Trust; Bader V. 2007, *Secularism or Democracy? Associational Governance of Religious Diversity*, Amsterdam University Press; Dierkens A. and Schreiber J.-Ph. (eds) 2006, *Laïcité et sécularisation dans l'Union européenne*, Brussels, vol. XVI, Ed. de l'Université libre de Bruxelles ('Problèmes d'Histoire des religions'); Grimpret, M. 2007, *Dieu est dans l'isoloir*, Paris: Presses de la Renaissance; Lambert, Y. 2000, Le rôle dévolu à la religion par les européens, *Sociétés contemporaines*, 37, 11–33; Larouche G.J. and Maesschalck, M. 2006, La religion dans l'espace public,

state law is most often the only formal source that applies in matters regarding family law. This response strikes us, however, as too categorical, as is shown in different contributions throughout this volume. Not only because it overlooks a major difficulty, namely, the close connection which many people – not just members of minority groups and communities – continue to make between law and religion, but also because it fails to explore alternative pathways that may be available for dealing with family issues through non-state approaches.

The principal aim of this volume is *not* to provide an inventory of the various analyses published in recent years on the way religion is handled in family matters within the domestic law of European countries – seen mainly through the prism of private international law – whether concerning the application of conflict of law rules by judges or the reception in one country of situations created abroad and of personal statuses governed by religious law. Several authors have, in the past few years, analysed the various solutions offered by case law or legal theory to the most common problems encountered in practice. These studies for the most part present an admirable analysis of private international law on questions relating to personal statuses governed by religious law in particular: filiation, naming, conditions for a valid marriage, the rights and obligations of the spouses, the relations between parents and children, the dissolution of marriage through divorce and, finally, the status of property as well as its distribution upon death.[2]

Université Laval, Ed. Liber, 8, 60–70; Massignon, B. 2007, L'Union européenne: Ni Dieu, ni César, *Esprit (special issue on 'Effervescences religieuses dans le monde')*, March–April, 104–11; Milot, M. 2002, *Laïcité dans le nouveau monde, le cas du Québec*, Turnhout: Brepols; Monod, J.-C. 2007, *Sécularisation et laïcité*, Paris: PUF ('Philosophies'); Milot, M., Portier, P. and Willaime, J.-P. (eds) 2009, *Pluralisme religieux et citoyenneté*, Rennes: Presses Universitaire de Rennes; Portier, P. 1998, Les laïcités dans l'Union européenne: vers une convergence des modèles?, in *La Tolérance* (Colloque international de Nantes, May 1998, Fourth centenary of the Edict of Nantes), edited by G. Sauin, R. Fabre and M. Launay. Presses Universitaire de Rennes; Portier, P. 2007, La critique contemporaine du religieux. Essai d'interprétation,, in *La liberté de critique*, edited by D. Carsin, Paris: Lexis-Nexis, 67–85; Randhaxe F. and Zuber, V. (eds) 2003, *Laïcités-démocraties: des relations ambigües*, Turnhout: Brepols ('Bibliothèque de l'Ecole des Hautes Etudes, Sciences religieuses'), 11–22; Tawil, E. 2005, *Norme religieuse et droit français*, Aix-en-Provence: Presses Universitaire d'Aix-Marseille; Torfs, R. 2004, Models of Freedom of Religion in the European Union and in the United States, in *Between Caesar and the Lord – Relation between Religion and the State in the countries of Asia and Europe*, Beijing: Kungcki Cultural Group, 225–52; Willaime, J.-P. 2006, Religion in Ultramodernity, in *Theorising Religion: Classical and Contemporary Debates*, edited by J.A. Beckford and J. Wallis, Aldershot: Ashgate, 73–85; Willaime, J.-P. 2007, Reconfigurations ultramodernes, *Esprit* (special issue on 'Effervescences religieuses dans le monde'), March–April, 146–55.

2 See, among others: Buechler, A. 2011, *Islamic Law in Europe? Legal Pluralism and its Limits in European Family Laws*, Farnham: Ashgate; Carlier, J.-Y. 2003, La reconnaissance mesurée des répudiations par l'examen *in concreto* de la contrariété à l'ordre public, *Revue trimestrielle du droit de la famille*, 35ff; El Husseini Begdache, R. 2002, *Le droit international privé français et la répudiation islamique*, Paris: LGDJ; Foblets, M.-Cl. and Carlier, J.-Y. 2005, *Le Code marocain de la famille. Incidences au regard du droit international privé en Europe*, Brussels: Bruylant; Gannagé, L. 2001, *La hiérarchie des normes et les méthodes du droit international privé. Etude de droit international privé de la famille*, Paris: LGDJ; François, L. 2002, La Convention européenne des droits de l'homme est-elle supérieure aux conventions bilatérales reconnaissant les répudiations musulmanes? *Recueil Le Dalloz*, 178, 2958–2962; Gaudemet-Tallon, H. 2004, Nationalité, statut personnel et droits de l'homme, in *Mélanges dédiés à E. Jayme*, Munich: Sellier, 219ff; Gaudemet-Tallon H. 2005, Le pluralisme en droit international privé: richesses et faiblesses (Le funambule et l'arc-en-ciel), *Recueil des Cours* 312, I; Gaudemet-Tallon, H. 2005. De nouvelles fonctions pour l'équivalence en droit international privé, in *Le droit international privé: esprits et méthodes, Mélanges en l'honneur de Paul Lagarde*, Paris: Dalloz, 302ff; Kinsch, P. 2005, Droits de l'homme, droits fondamentaux et droit international privé,

The techniques of private international law, however, offer only a partial response to the question of how, within the legal framework in force in Europe, one can develop an openness in which, while fully respecting freedom of belief and non-discrimination in matters of religion, the demands of civil law can be reconciled with the desire of individuals to continue to observe the rules of conduct dictated by their religious convictions. This desire gives rise to a legal pluralism that is in turn a reflection of the new configuration of contemporary European society. The question that arises is therefore how to go beyond the framework of private international law, strictly speaking, while remaining within the confines of secular civil law.

This volume therefore takes a different approach, focusing on empirical research rather than on theory. The contributions for the most part go *beyond* the limits of private international law as well as beyond the assumption that civil state law applies to all without distinction. Those observations show that one should not take comfort too readily in the argument that religious communities living in Europe today must necessarily accept the separation of law and religion. This normative stand, that takes secularisation for granted, does not evacuate or dissolve the close, not to say inseparable, link that members of various religious communities continue to make between (family) law and religion: it often happens that belief is treated by them as the principal, if not sole, source of law.³ One may obviously

---

Recueil des Cours, 318; Lagarde, P. 2005, Différences culturelles et ordre public en droit international privé de la famille, *Annuaire IDI*, 71(I), 7–115; Lequette, Y. 2005, Le conflit de civilisation à la lumière de l'expérience franco-tunisienne, in *Mouvements de droit contemporain, Mélanges offerts au Professeur Sassi Ben Halima*, Tunis: Centre de publication universitaire, 175ff; Lequette, Y. 2006, Le droit international privé et les droits fondamentaux, in *Libertés et droits fondamentaux*, edited by R. Cabrillac et al., Paris: Dalloz; Najm M.-Cl. 2005, *Principes directeurs du droit international privé et conflits de civilisations. Relations entre systèmes laïques et systèmes religieux*, Paris: Dalloz; Mahieddin, N.M. 2006, La dissolution du mariage par la volonté unilatérale de l'un des époux en droit musulman et en droit algérien, *Revue internationale de droit comparé*, 58(1), 73–100; Mezghani, A. 2003, Le juge français et les institutions du droit musulman, *Journal du Droit International*, 721–65; Niboyet, M.-L. 2006, Regard français sur la reconnaissance en France des répudiations musulmanes, *Revue internationale de droit comparé*, 58(1), 27–46; Witte, Jr, J. (ed.) 2011, Sharia, Family, and Democracy: Religious Norms and Family Law in Pluralistic Democratic States, *Emory International Law Review* (Special Issue), 25(2); Zaher, K. 2009, *Conflit de civilisations et droit international privé*, Paris: L'Harmattan.

3 On this link, see Cesari, J. and McLoughlin, S. (eds) 2005, *European Muslims and the Secular State*, Aldershot: Ashgate; Cesari, J. 2004 (2nd ed. 2006), *When Islam and Democracy Meet: Muslims in Europe and in the United States*. New York: Palgrave; more recently: Cesari, J. (ed.) 2009, *Muslims in the West after 9/11*, London: Routledge; Bader V. (ed.) 2007, Governing Islam in Western Europe. Essays on Governance of Religious Diversity, *Journal of Ethnic and Migration Studies,* 33(6); Klausen, J. 2005. *The Islamic Challenge: Politics and Religion in Western Europe*, Oxford: Oxford University Press; Marechal, B., et al. (eds) 2003, *Muslims in the Enlarged Europe: Religion and Society*, Leiden: Brill; Nielsen, J.S. 2004 (1992), *Muslims in Western Europe*, 3rd ed., Edinburgh: Edinburgh University Press; Nielsen, J.S. 1999, *Towards a European Islam?* London: Macmillan; Rohe, M. 2006, Muslims between Qu'ran and Constitution – Religious Freedom within the German Legal Order, in *'East is East and West is West'? Talks on Dialogue in Beirut*, edited by L.A. Tramontini, Beiruter Texte und Studien 80, Beirut: Orient-Institut Beirut, 151–76; Rohe, M. 2008, Islamic Norms in Germany and Europe, in *Islam and Muslims in Germany*, edited by A. Al-Hamarneh and J. Thielemann, Leiden: Brill, 49–81; Shadid W.A.R. and Van Koningsveld P.S. (eds) 2002, *Intercultural Relations and Religious Authorities: Muslims in the European Union*, Leuven: Peeters; Shah, P. 2006, Thinking beyond Religion: Legal Pluralism in Britain's South Asian Diaspora, *Australian Journal of Asian Law*, 8, 237–60; Shah, P. 2009, Transforming to accommodate? Reflections on the *shari'a* debate in Britain, in *Legal Practice and Cultural Diversity*, edited by R. Grillo, et al, Farnham: Ashgate, 73–92.

obscure this reality by giving a response from a strictly secularised legal perspective to any question regarding religious family law. Evidently, in practice, not everyone's perspective is the same, and the reference to religion will not be of equal importance to each person. But as various case studies in this volume show, in situations where the common reference to religion is an important, if not the main, source of regulation of family relationships, people will continue to seek a sort of compromise or reconciliation between the requirements of their religion and those of civil (state) law. The success of various alternative dispute resolution mechanisms among some communities in particular might be interpreted as an indication of this.

To refuse to take this endeavour into account may, in the long run, very well elicit reticence on the part of the communities concerned. In practice, such reticence with regard to the requirements of civil (state) law is indeed perceptible. It manifests itself in various forms, as the case studies elaborated in particular by Annika Rabo and Latif Tas in this volume show. At times this reticence can go so far as to simply displace civil law and set up a parallel legal regime within the religious community, without seeking recognition under civil law for the situation thus created: religious marriage, for example, may be celebrated without any concern for entering first into a civil contract, even if the law requires that this be done. In other cases, individuals return to their country of origin to seek justice, availing themselves of the rules of conflict of laws which, in private international law, allow them to have recourse to those countries' domestic laws regardless of the number of years a person has lived abroad.[4] In legal terms, and in particular from the perspective of legal certainty, both forms of behaviour raise serious concerns: informal marriage will not be recognised by the authorities of the country of habitual residence, leaving the spouses without protection under domestic (state) law and hence vulnerable. As for the solutions reached in the country of origin, these create a legal privilege that is reserved to the nationals of countries which confer upon religious (Islamic) law the status of personal law: religious law prevails over secular law exclusively in the case of those who have retained the nationality of the country in question. Moreover, one might wonder what justifies such a solution, in particular when, in practice, the factual connection between a person and the law of the country of his or her habitual residence has over the years grown strong through, among other things, acquisition of citizenship and/or long-term residence. Can such a person still be permitted recourse to the rules of private international law?

As we have argued elsewhere,[5] in light of these observations a search for alternatives is warranted, not to say becoming ever more urgent. At least three ways of embracing law and religion may – potentially – be envisaged: (1) allowing rules based on religion to be granted effect under civil law – this could, notably, take the form of a (civil) contract, as in the case of marriage; (2) allowing the autonomy of the person to become the basic principle for regulating family relationships under state law; (3) recourse to religious arbitration for certain disputes. These pathways draw inspiration from legal doctrine and,

---

4 Charfi, M. 1987, L'influence de la religion dans le droit international privé des pays musulmans, RCADI, 203-III, 321–454, 414ff; Ewan, O. 1992, L'Islam et les systèmes de conflits de lois, in J.-Y. Carlier and M. Verwilghen (eds), *Le Statut personnel des musulmans*, Bruylant: Brussels, 313–41; Berger, M. 2002, Conflicts Law and Public Policy in Egyptian Family Law: Islamic Law through the Backdoor, *American Journal of Comparative Law*, 50(3), 555–94.

5 Foblets, M.-Cl. 2013, Accommodating Islamic Family Law(s). A Critical Analysis of Some Recent Developments and Experiments in Europe, in *Applying Shari'a in the West. Facts, Fears and the Future of Islamic Rules on Family Relations in the West*, edited by M. Berger, Leiden: Leiden University Press, 207–26.

in part, from case law. Obviously, none of these are easy to put into practice. On the one hand, the contractual definition of certain aspects of religious law raises difficulties that cannot be neglected: to what extent are certain obligations, rooted in religious law, 'fit' to be the subject of a civil contract? On the other hand, in order for autonomy of the person to become a principle of regulation in family relationships, several conditions need to be met simultaneously – something that will rarely be the case in practice. So, for example, all persons involved should be informed of the legal/contractual options open to them, as Maarit Jänterä-Jareborg underscores in her analysis in this volume (see Chapter 4). But, above all, they should agree between them on the exact content of the additional protections they envisage for their own particular situation. They should also know how important it is to them to protect themselves against certain risks that are characteristic of the law by which they are bound as a result of their relationship and which may leave one of them more unprotected than the other. Furthermore, this approach is a proactive one. Unfortunately, in practice spouses do not see any immediate benefit from such agreement at the moment they contract a marriage; on the contrary, they are prepared to take a risk. Is it not asking too much (from them) that they should also consider, preferably before initiating the relationship or at the latest when they enter into their marriage, future difficulties and possible clashes of interests between them and possibly also with other kin? One could of course take the view that a contract might well be signed by them later on, after a few years of marriage, or that the marriage contract might be amended afterwards, but in such cases it is necessary to do so before any serious disagreements arise between them, for otherwise it will be too late to negotiate with due serenity.

The aim of this volume is to invite reflection. Some approaches adopted in the contributions here are ethnographically rooted, and some are, as mentioned above, also *exploratory*: addressing particular questions that are linked to the treatment, in civil (state) law, of practices and institutions in the domain of family relationships that are religious in nature, and weighing the pros and cons of various more or less technical ways to accommodate them. Despite the numerous obstacles, several of the illustrations brought forward here show that some communities would have much to gain from a (state) legal framework – legislative and/or judicial – that would entrust them with more responsibility with a view to finding out, for themselves, how to best bring norms imposed by their religious convictions into harmony with the requirements of civil law, and to then grant formal recognition to the solutions they privilege. It is true, however, that many questions remain unresolved, and therefore professional and detailed guidance in these matters may be necessary, in practice, with a view to offering kin the greatest possible protection (under state law) with regard to the rights and obligations they have taken on in their mutual relationships.

It is too soon to draw concrete lessons from the observations and analyses selected for this volume, yet it would be very instructive to conduct similar ethnographic research in various other settings. The benefit to be gained from this type of meticulous field observation is undeniable, all the more so since the question of accommodation of rules of conduct drawn from religion(s) is a lively one throughout Europe. Family law is a particularly sensitive domain of law, especially when it is closely linked to a religion or belief. This makes the handling of family matters from a civil (state) legal perspective all the more intricate. Religion in the vast majority of the case studies presented here functions as a complex normative framework of rules and principles that regulate family relationships (among other things) by offering a comprehensive vision of life for its adherents. Only time will tell which forms of accommodation (under state law) can serve as a path to be followed. In a context in which religion is returning to the forefront,[6] responses from state law should preferably embrace diversity from the perspective of 'cultural encounters', with due respect for freedom of religion and belief as well as for the principle of non-discrimination, both guaranteed as fundamental rights of individuals. The challenge is all the greater since, at an empirical level, religious demands are very often clearly connected with those relating to identity.[7]

---

6   Roy, O. 2008, *La sainte ignorance: Le temps de la religion sans culture* (English translation *Holy Ignorance: When Religion and Culture Part Ways*, trans. Ros Schwartz Hurst), Paris Seuil: Columbia University Press; Boeglin J.-G. 2006, *Etats et religions en Europe* (2 vols), Paris: L'Harmattan; Cane, P., Evans, C. and Robinson Z. (eds) 2008, *Law and Religion in Theoretical and Historical Context*, Cambridge: Cambridge University Press; Goris, H. and Heimbach-Steins, H. (eds) 2008, *Religion in Recht und politischer Ordnung heute*, Würzburg: Ergon; Lehmann H. (ed.) 2003, *Multireligiosität im vereinten Europa: historische und juristische Aspekte*, Göttingen: Wallstein; Norgren, J. and Nanda, S., 2006 *American Cultural Pluralism and Law*, 3rd ed., Westport: Praeger Publishers; Richardson, H.S. and Williams, M.S. (eds) 2009, *Moral Universalism and Pluralism*, New York: New York University Press; Sarat, A. and T.R. Kearns (eds) 1999, *Cultural Pluralism, Identity Politics, and the Law*, Ann Arbor: University of Michigan Press; Wagner, A. and Bhatia, V.K. (eds) 2009, *Diversity and Tolerance in Socio-legal Contexts: Explorations in the Semiotics of Law*, Farnham/Burlington: Ashgate; Eid, P., Bosset, P., Milot, M. and Lebel-Grenier, S. 2009, *Appartenances religieuses, appartenance citoyenne. Un équilibre en tension*, Québec: Presses de l'Universitaire Laval.

7   See especially: Dassetto, F. 2000, *Paroles d'Islam: individus, sociétés et discours dans l'Islam européen contemporain*, Paris: Maisonneuve; Sinno A.H. (ed.) 2009, *Muslims in Western Politics*, Bloomington: Indiana University Press; Tietze, N. 2001, *Islamische Identitäten: Formen muslimischer Religiosität junger Männer in Deutschland und Frankreich*, Hamburg: HIS Verlag.

Acknowledgements

The research leading to this book was partly performed within the framework of the RELIGARE project, or was brought together in meetings and workshops organised under the auspices of that project. The RELIGARE project received funding from the European Commission's Seventh Framework Programme (FP7/2007–2013) under grant agreement number 244635. Some chapters here emerged from a RELIGARE seminar on The Judiciary Facing Religious Pluralism in Family Matters, held in Brussels in December 2011 at the Institut de Formation Judiciaire and the Centre for Policy Studies (CEPS), and RELIGARE workshops held at the University of Erlangen in March 2012 and at Queen Mary University of London in September 2012. They were all supported by the RELIGARE project. Previous versions of some chapters were presented in June 2010 at a workshop organised at the International Institute for the Sociology of Law (IISL), in Oñati, Spain, and thanks are due to the IISL for providing premises and financial support, the British Academy for a conference grant, and the IMISCOE network for further supporting funds. The views expressed here are the sole responsibilities of the author(s). The European Union is not liable for any use that may be made of the information contained therein.

The editors would also like to acknowledge the considerable assistance towards the preparation of this book provided by Nevena Ilic and Kiran Morjaria.

Chapter 1
Distorting Minority Laws? Religious Diversity and European Legal Systems

Prakash Shah[1]

The contributors to this book examine how European legal systems have received aspects of diverse family life and accompanying legal institutions in the context of increasing religious diversity and transjurisdictionalism among Europe's populations. This context-setting chapter draws mainly on evidence of legislation, case law and fieldwork collected within the context of the RELIGARE Project, which was funded by the European Commission (2010–2013).[2] The RELIGARE Project surveyed legal developments within 10 countries (Belgium, Bulgaria, Denmark, England, France, Germany, Italy, the Netherlands, Spain and Turkey), as well as supranational case law from the European Court of Human Rights, with respect to how the various legal orders cope with aspects of religious diversity. Although the RELIGARE project research concerned the 10 countries listed, this book benefits from drawing into its scope material from other, primarily Euro-American, jurisdictions.

When considering family laws and religious diversity, at least three major factors constituting the wider backdrop have to be borne in mind. First, as with many branches of law in European legal systems, the roots of concepts and institutions within family law lie within the Christian religion. However much they may be secularised today, as several contributors to this book point out (see Rohe, Chapter 3, and Jänterä-Jareborg, Chapter 4), we can find traces of Christian religious presuppositions which lie behind contemporary legal rules and institutional arrangements. This does not mean that change has not been an ongoing process; it most certainly has. While differences among European legal systems remain quite visible, a trend in more or less the same direction has been taking place. As the comparative family lawyer Masha Antokolskaia (2003: 58) notes of divorce laws, 'There is an undeniable movement in the same direction: the divorce law in every European country, despite temporary periods of retroactive movement or stagnation, is moving from more restrictive to more permissive divorce law.'[3] Secularisation remains a significant factor shaping Europe's official family law systems and, in cases such as Bulgaria, the process

---

   1   Particular thanks are due to Professor Veit Bader and Professor Werner Menski for helpful discussions and comments about this chapter, to the various national RELIGARE project teams who have done the hard ground work to produce the results that have gone into this chapter, and to Manprit Kaur Virdi and Alberto Horst-Neidhardt, the RELIGARE postgraduate researchers, for their hard work compiling the research results.
   2   The research leading to these results has received funding from the European Commission's Seventh Framework Programme (FP7/2007–2013) under grant agreement number 244635. The views expressed during the execution of the RELIGARE project, in whatever form and or by whatever medium, are the sole responsibility of the author. The European Union is not liable for any use that may be made of the information contained therein. For further information about the research produced by the RELIGARE Project see http://www.religareproject.eu [last accessed 14 December 2013].
   3   For marriage laws, see Antokolskaia (2006) and Witte (2012).

appears to have gone very far indeed. Over time, dominant religions have had to give way to the state taking over responsibility from the Churches for supervising family life and enacting generalised rules for the population at large. This has created its own problems since, while once the Churches' canon law regarding the family could be seen as a set of personal law systems alongside those other systems followed by people of minority religions and traditions, a homogenised structure of family law poses the risk of overriding or covering up differences in a variety of cultures, religions and traditions and imposing a uniform set of solutions upon them. Besides that, the deeper the state became involved in the job of social engineering the more it risked interference in intimate areas of family life.

Second, Europe has indeed always remained plural despite historical attempts at homogenisation and penalisation of differences. It has also always contained minorities of different sorts. Jews, a long-standing historical and internally diverse minority population in Western and Eastern Europe and in the Ottoman Empire, remain a significant part of that diversity. During the period of legal homogenisation over the last 200 or so years they were subsumed under frameworks of uniform family laws (Schechter 2003, Schwarzfuchs 1979, Finestein 1993, Bayır 2013). They have not, however, lost their religious laws, and communities remain all over Europe seeking to maintain Jewish life. This entails that they continue to pose questions of official legal systems and courts (Herman 2011, and Rohe, Chapter 3). In various parts of Europe, Roma people have also maintained their customs and traditions and have often come into contact with official laws because many have refused to succumb to pressures for modification of their lifestyles (Weyrauch 2001). European countries have also long had Muslim populations, with different areas having different concentrations. Countries in south-eastern Europe have significant and long-present Muslim minorities, while Turkey is a Muslim majority country. Until about a century ago, Muslim family law was the official law enforceable in courts in many parts of the Ottoman Empire, its former territories and those states emerging from it (e.g., Karčić 2008). With the phasing out of this official Muslim personal law in most parts of south-east Europe, it applies only in Western Thrace, Greece, today (Tsitselikis 2012).

Third, the settlement of new minority populations from both outside and within the European Union (EU) has considerably added to the diversity and made legal systems face new challenges. Continuing transjurisdictional activities among people who include old and new citizens of the EU complicates this. All the authors writing in this book address these dimensions in one way or another. The older securities of gradual but inevitable secularisation and uniformisation are no longer guaranteed in the family law field. New diversities are emerging and challenging decision-makers to provide appropriate solutions. Customs and religious practices among more recent settlers and their descendants have not been altogether abandoned as a consequence of arrival and living in Europe. Under the homogenous official legal orders, customs and religious practices have in many cases simply gone 'underground' and survive, sometimes very vibrantly, but unofficially, as Sona (Chapter 6), Rabo (Chapter 9) and Taş (Chapter 11) confirm. As Francavilla (Chapter 5) discusses using different terminology, such 'subalternisation', or what are effectively forced navigational strategies, are a flip-side consequence of pursuing uniformistic legal regimes. This does not avoid official bodies facing circumstances for which they have to find accommodations and solutions, as Menski (Chapter 2) highlights for judges in particular. Meanwhile, contact with European societies and legal systems has provided opportunities for new hybrid laws to emerge which, on the one hand, provide opportunities and further legal options to people and, on the other hand, defy easy classification (Foblets 1994: 373, Pearl and Menski 1998: 74–80, Macfarlane 2012). Liversage (Chapter 8) shows how the inevitable changes have to be managed within families to 'keep up appearances' and not to reveal too much about how much has changed. Therefore, no clear framework has yet emerged as to how the legal issues brought by new diversities, combined with the ongoing older diversities, should be approached, although some 'typical' problems can be identified towards the continuing job of finding more suitable accommodations (Shah 2013a).

In matters of family law the dividing line between private and public international law is reduced for some countries where bilateral instruments with former colonies or third countries have been adopted to deal with the choice of law in matrimonial cases, notably in cases involving European nationals who also hold the nationality of third countries. The same applies in cases of adoption where the third country's family law system is based on Islamic law. However, in general the involvement of non-Western countries in private international law agreements which concern family relations, for example, in the context of the Hague process, is patchy. This may not be surprising, first of all, given that Western countries appear to have largely succeeded in getting their priorities included in such agreements, but there is scant recognition of non-Western legal forms of conducting family relations. Western legal forms of conducting family relations, for instance in the areas of marriage, divorce and adoption, are mostly premised on state involvement at crucial points in the process. These tend to get prioritised, whereas non-state law forms of managing family relations, which are predominant for many non-Western countries, appear to be ignored and, in the practice of private international law by European courts, very often rejected as inappropriate.

These features of private international law making, whether on the part of individual European courts or through international conventions, therefore appear strongly characterised by unilateralism and, one might say, chauvinism. In a judgment of 29 October 1948 concerning a unilateral divorce made in Syria, the Appeals Court of Rome refused to recognise the legal effects of repudiation on the grounds that 'it is abhorred by the moral and legal mentality of the peoples who have reached a higher degree of civilisation, and who have a far more advanced ethical and social concept of marriage than Eastern peoples'. A more recent example is shown in a judgment from 1984 by the English Court of Appeal, where Cumming-Bruce LJ said: 'Pronouncement of talaq three times finally terminates the marriage in Kashmir, Dubai, and probably in other unsophisticated peasant, desert or jungle communities which respect classical Muslim religious tradition.'[4] While European courts may no longer adopt this language, the structures embedding the kind of sentiments expressed by the courts continue to disfigure European legal systems in their approach to alterity. Thus, a sanitisation of language itself does not make the underlying structures disappear and, while flexibility may be shown by some European judges today, boundaries are also hardening in other respects (see Menski, Chapter 2, Rohe, Chapter 3, Jänterä-Jareborg, Chapter 4).

Second, agreement over the (in)compatibility of legal concepts, which then impacts on mutual recognition, may be holding up the securing of agreements. Third, in many cases non-EU, third states are not actively involved in securing recognition for their nationals abroad and allow EU states to regulate matters according to their versions of private international law.[5] They may not even be well informed about the fate of their nationals in EU states, but evidence cited in this book, in particular by Sona (Chapter 6) and

---

4   *Chaudhary v Chaudhary* [1985] Fam. 19, at 38.

5   An exception is the Hague Convention on Jurisdiction, Applicable Law, Recognition, Enforcement and Co-operation in Respect of Parental Responsibility and Measures for the Protection

Jäntera-Jareborg (Chapter 7), indicates that diplomatic premises of foreign countries may well be active in formalising the making or breakdown of family relationships. We also saw this recently in the case of *Dukali v Lamrani* involving a marriage conducted in compliance with the requirements of Moroccan law at the Moroccan consulate in London, and subsequently dissolved in Morocco.[6] The former wife was told by the English court that she was not entitled to financial relief because her marriage was not recognised under English law.

Further, the old models now embedded in European legal systems are in question. While the taken-for-granted models of legal uniformity are unsuited for providing a justice-oriented framework for the socio-legal cultures that currently inhabit European jurisdictions, it is increasingly felt that private international law models do not adequately allow for contemporary transjurisdictionalism to be captured appropriately. In particular, there has been some debate about the connecting factors – nationality, residence, domicile – and their continued appropriateness in an age of migration and transnationalism, and there is a perception that new mechanisms need to be developed to accommodate the presence of new minorities in Europe (Strijbosch and Foblets 1999, Büchler 2011). In other ways, too, the authors represented here (Rohe, Chapter 3, Jäntera-Jareborg, Chapter 7) show that 'traditional' private international law paradigms are no longer adequate to the task of accommodating transnational minorities, and Rabo (Chapter 9) and Sona (Chapter 6) define this problem even more sharply when they switch focus by looking from the 'informal' perspective of transnational families.

In order to flesh out and substantiate the above observations, this chapter focuses on some of the main elements of family relations that the RELIGARE Project investigated and covers the following areas: (1) the making of marriage, which involves religious and customary solemnisation in interaction with the expectation of state legal systems that registration or an officially recognised religious ceremony be followed in one of a number of prescribed ways; (2) polygamous marriages in light of the restriction, either civil or criminal, which that form of marriage attracts within European jurisdictions; (3) the making of payments during or after marriage (chiefly the Islamic dower or *mahr*), and the 'fit' of such institutions with existing regimes of marital property or marriage as contract; (4) divorce through means which may circumvent official European legal procedures and sanctions, often through a reliance on non-European legal systems and non-state bodies in third states; and (5) the existence in European jurisdictions of non-state bodies which are often involved in facilitating religious divorces, sometimes discussed under the framework of alternative dispute resolution. In an effort to gain a better understanding of the wider comparative context, the material used includes the case law, legislation and the results of fieldwork collected within the RELIGARE Project, secondary sources which cover project countries as well as non-project countries, within and outside Europe, and the work of the authors in this volume.

Solemnisation of Marriage

In all countries under study, civil law regulates the recognition and validity of marriage. Over a long period of time state laws in Europe have either attempted to substitute Church

---

of Children of 19 October 1996, recognising the *kafala* (an Islamic institution of adoption without inheritance), and acceded to by Morocco.

6 *Dukali v Lamrani* [2012] EWHC 1748 (Fam).

laws (and other personal laws) for marriage solemnisation by introducing registration requirements or have co-opted the form of solemnisation of Church marriage by recognising it. The historical model of Church solemnisation as a form of 'official' marriage still exists in some countries (e.g. England, Denmark, Sweden), and it now exists alongside other mechanisms (generally a 'secular' form of registration) to accommodate diversity developed over time. Therefore, in England, a religious functionary or other person can be recognised as a 'celebrant' under the 'secular' form of marriage registration. A variation of that model, which co-opts religious bodies into the process of solemnisation or registration, ostensibly facilitates greater symmetry among religious communities by allowing the opting-in by religious functionaries of different faiths as forms of State marriage, although this is not without conditions stipulated by state law (Denmark, England, Italy, Spain, Sweden). In Belgium, France and Turkey, meanwhile, only a uniform method of state registration leads to officially valid marriage. From a formal viewpoint, in no country does the marriage acquire the legal dimension of being religious.

However, in all countries, socio-legal realities lead to all methods becoming pluralised in practice, certainly when viewed from the perspective of the participants in marriages. The 'hybrid' models mentioned above, which may have once looked like ideals of religion–state cooperation, are now under some pressure. This is so not only because of the demands of increased religious and cultural plurality, but also because of moves to persuade churches/religious bodies to accept gay marriage. The ensuing discussions may lead to the withdrawal of some, or parts of some, Churches from accepting a state-mandated form of marriage. In Sweden, such reforms have already been enacted in legislation. Consequently, as Rabo (Chapter 9) points out, the Syriac Church, in which the celebration of marriages would result in their official validity, has decided to withdraw from state recognition for marriage purposes and this is now leading to unregistered marriages among Syriacs in Sweden. Fieldwork evidence from England also revealed some nervousness about the current discussions on gay marriage and some uncertainty about whether all religious bodies will want to opt in to the state registration system which allows the official recognition of marriages.[7] The current debate in Denmark, which the fieldwork in that country makes especially visible, reveals similar tensions (Vinding and Christoffersen 2012: 49–52). The Danish fieldwork suggests that solutions could lie in accepting voluntarism among the religious institutions which are currently officially authorised to perform solemnisation or, alternatively, to make marriage a civil-only affair at official level, leaving the choice of religious solemnisation without any official consequences to the parties.[8]

Meanwhile, there is divergence in approach even within the same country about whether the religious or customary aspects of a marriage have any official legal relevance. This uncertainty occurs in a context where, often, the celebration of marriage involves more than one kind of rite in practice. As the fieldwork reported from France indicates, even when, in state law, only the civil wedding has legal value, the religious form attributed to it in each religion may count as much for believers as the resulting rights and obligations.

---

7   Under the Marriage Act 1949, non-Anglican Churches and places of worship of other religious bodies may opt in to have their premises registered for the purpose of marriage registration.

8   For the compromise to conscience in Sweden, see further Jänterä-Jareborg, Chapter 4. Plans for gay marriage announced in England and Wales also aim to prevent religious organisations from being obliged to perform same-sex marriages, and in some cases (the Church of England and the Church in Wales) will prohibit them from doing so: http://www.bbc.co.uk/news/uk-politics-20680924 [last accessed 14 December 2013]. The Marriage (Same Sex Couples) Act obtained royal assent in July 2013.

This finding is probably generalisable to other countries. While officials and judges become more aware that for many groups and communities it is common to have more than one type of celebration, the lack of such multiple forms of marriage, or even their existence, has occasionally been used to cast doubt upon official validity. In France, case law shows that a religious marriage has given rise to a civil claim for expenses of an 'engagement', albeit one that the French court rejected.[9] In Belgium, where a civil form of marriage is mandatory, case law suggests that a misunderstanding of the legal effects of such a civil marriage, which could have been understood or treated by the parties as an Islamic betrothal, may result in the marriage being declared void.[10] In a more recent Scottish case, the act of registration which would ordinarily be accepted as constituting a valid marriage was considered by a court to be eligible for a declarator of nullity because no further ritual recognised by Pakistani Muslims had preceded or followed it. The court reasoned that the parties could not have had the requisite intention to constitute a marriage according to the Scottish conception of marriage.[11] Much depends on the factual scenario before the judges, the appreciation of judges of those facts, and how lawyers are presenting the case. It is therefore difficult to draw out a consistent line of principle in the illustrative cases. For instance, in the Scottish case mentioned here, it appears that the 'groom' wanted to remain in the UK and the marriage was a way to secure his residence, while it was the woman and her family who sought a declarator of nullity. As often happens in marriage cases, the dimension of immigration control and its evasion are not far away (Sona, Chapter 6; Jänterä-Jareborg, Chapter 7; Liversage, Chapter 8; and, further, Shah 2011).

In countries where the national legal system is more allergic to religious notions of family life and law, or at least purports to ignore religions distinctions, civil registration must occur before the religious celebrations, and penalties may be brought to bear on the couple, on the religious functionary (priest, imam, etc.; Belgium, Turkey), or someone else (possibly a family member) helping with the marriage arrangements (Turkey). Thus, penal offences exist in some countries where the solemnisation of religious marriages takes place earlier than the civil registration. This suggests that state institutions see in the jurisdiction of religious authorities a direct threat to state power and to the exclusive jurisdiction of the state legal system in family matters. In other countries there is more tolerance towards religious forms of marriage, and there is greater liberty as to the order of the ceremony, whether the religious marriage occurs either before or after the civil registration. It may also be, as in the French case cited above, that parties to civil or matrimonial claims have an incentive to 'distort' the nature of their relationship because of the potential to attract penal sanctions.[12] This sort of 'disguised' claims-making, which is evidently not restricted to the sphere of marriage solemnisation, may be quite frustrating for judges who often have to pierce the veil. In Bulgaria, the Civil Code has been amended with effect from 2009 by removing the requirement that a religious ceremony may be performed only after the contraction of a civil marriage. The Bulgarian approach probably indicates the direction

---

9 Court of Appeal of Paris, 08-12-1992, n. XP081292X.

10 Civil Tribunal Brussels, 17 January 1984, RTDF 1986 28.

11 *H v H* [2005] Fam LR 80, [2005] SLT 1025. Interestingly, many Belgian cases also follow similar reasoning for voiding a marriage: Liège (1re ch.), 19 March 1996, Rev. trim. dr. fam., 1997, p. 323; Brussels, 17 June 2003, JT 2003 861 (idem). The lack of a marriage according to 'North African Muslim customs' was held not to be a defence to claim under Art. 215 of the civil code (by which spouses mutually oblige themselves to community of living) according to a ruling of the Court of Appeal of Versailles, 30-03- 1995.

12 Court of Appeal of Paris, 08-12-1992, n. XP081292X.

which reforms of marriage law should take, especially in those countries where penalties are still in place.

The question of unregistered marriage has come up twice in the past few years before the European Court of Human Rights. Unfortunately, the Court has returned inconsistent and, in both cases, not particularly illuminating or well-reasoned decisions. In *Muñoz Diaz v Spain* (Application no. 49151/07) a Roma widow, and mother of six children, was refused a survivor's pension after the death of her husband, who had paid some 19 years of social security contributions. The refusal, which was upheld by the Constitutional Court in Spain, was grounded on the fact that their marriage had not been registered in the Civil Register; they had married by Roma rites only. Before the European Court of Human Rights, Mrs Muñoz Diaz claimed that the denial of survivor's pension was discriminatory and an infringement of article 14 (discrimination) in conjunction with article 1 of Protocol 1 (right to property), ECHR, and also that under article 14 taken together with article 12 (right to marry and found a family) the non-recognition of the civil effects of her Roma marriage was a discriminatory breach of her right to marry. The Court adopted a relatively generous position and took into account several factors in favour of Mrs Muñoz Diaz: her belonging to the Roma community which was deeply rooted in Spain; that the denial to her of the pension did not take into account her good faith and the social and cultural specificities of the applicant; that she could not have married under canon law – which was the sole possibility in 1971 – without infringing her freedom of religion; and that it was disproportionate that the Spanish state granted the 'large family' status, provided health coverage, and collected Mr Diaz's social security contributions for over 19 years but then refused to recognise the effects of Mrs Muñoz Diaz's Roma marriage when it came to the survivor's pension. A majority of the Court held that there had been a violation of article 14 of the Convention taken together with article 1 of Protocol 1. However, it rejected the claim under article 14 taken together with article 12 as manifestly ill-founded on the grounds that civil marriage had been open to all in Spain since 1981. While the Court's appreciation of the importance of cultural background, the applicant's good faith and the state's inconsistent approach are all to be welcomed, its reasoning as to why the recognition of some types of marriage within a legal system but not others is justifiable is not particularly well grounded. This may indicate that the European judiciaries face problems in adequately justifying the unfair consequences of the state's privileging or authorising certain forms of marriage over others, a stance which European legal systems will find less sustainable given their ever-pluralising societies.

In the second case, *Şerife Yiğit v Turkey*,[13] non-compliance with the official formalities for marriage resulted in an unenforceable claim for transfer of the applicant's deceased husband's pension and health insurance benefits to her. The European Court in turn decided that the protection of property rights under article 1 of Protocol 1 combined with article 14 (non-discrimination) was not breached because there was an objective and reasonable justification of protection of public order (the civil marriage aiming in particular at protecting women) and of the rights and freedom of others pursued by the different treatment of those who do not go through a civil marriage. The Court further held that article 8 of the ECHR could not be interpreted as obliging the State to recognise the religious marriage and hence enforce a specific regime for a particular category of non-married couples. In particular, the reasoning of the Court regarding the claim under article 1 of Protocol 1 appears to be based on shaky ground.

---

13   *Şerife Yiğit v Turkey* (Application no. 3976/05).

It justified treating different marriages differently on grounds of protecting women and the rights of others. However, in so holding it could be argued that these are the very threats that the applicant widow in the *Şerife Yiğit* case was exposed to because of the denial of the pension rights to her.

With respect to the Islamic form of marriage, the approach of the majority of the Court drew sharp criticism from the Russian Judge Kovler, who noted:

> I think it would have been wiser to refrain from making any assessment of the complexity of the rules of Islamic marriage, rather than portraying it in a reductive and highly subjective manner in the short section entitled 'History' ... where what is left unsaid speaks louder than what is actually said ... I would like to see the European Court of Human Rights take a more anthropological approach in the positions it adopts, by 'not just exploring difference, but exploring it differently' ... Otherwise, the Court is in danger of becoming entrenched in 'eurocentric' attitudes.

Whether the answer to the knotty problems of comparing different traditions of marriage is to not have a discussion about them at all is by no means the conclusion to be drawn from Judge Kovler's criticism, which in this respect is better read rhetorically. Rather, the salient point he makes is that a domestic and European-level court must address such issues but in a more informed manner than the Court in the *Şerife Yiğit* case appeared to be able or willing to do. Certainly, the evidence from Turkey reveals that there is a fairly high proportion of unregistered marriages, and non-accommodation could affect some ethnic groups within society (including Roma in Turkey) more than others.[14] The issue is all the more relevant where a large section of the population in Europe is of Muslim faith and the practise of marriage customs specific to Muslims from different parts of the world is palpable.

In England, there is evidence in the case law of some openness to recognising de facto and bona fide marriages.[15] Notably, this is not conditioned on their solemnisation in a religious ceremony (although that may constitute evidential support), but is dependent on a long-term and exclusive relationship. The general principle used to confer recognition to such long-standing relationships is the 'presumption of marriage' deriving from the canon law, and more recently borrowed by English judges from judicial practice in Scotland.[16] It is interesting to note, however, that, in Scotland, that principle was abolished by legislation in 2006 by section 3 of the Family Law (Scotland) Act 2006. It may be that it needs to be revived in some way and could also provide grounds for judiciaries in other European jurisdictions who face similar cases. The principle of presumption of marriage is actually also recognised in a wide range of legal systems outside Europe. In Turkey, meanwhile, one approach has been to periodically regularise unregistered marriages. Here, the state

---

14 This draws upon evidence of the Turkish team in the RELIGARE project and on evidence submitted by Derya Bayır, 'Unregistered Marriages as a Challenge to Turkish Law': paper presented at the Religare Expert Seminar, Queen Mary, University of London, 4 September 2012. For the podcast of the proceedings, see http://www.law.qmul.ac.uk/events/podcasts/religare2012/index.html [last accessed 14 December 2013].

15 Prakash Shah, 'Unregistered Marriages in the English Courts': paper presented at the Religare Expert Seminar on Unregistered Marriages and Alternative Dispute Resolution, Queen Mary, University of London, 4 September 2012. For the podcast of the proceedings, see: http://www.law.qmul.ac.uk/events/podcasts/religare2012/index.html [last accessed 14 December 2013].

16 *Chief Adjudication Officer v Bath* [2000] 1 FLR 8.

takes an activist approach by bringing those affected within the official realm, and this could also be a method to be adopted in other countries where the phenomenon may be significant. Another suggestion which appears in fieldwork in both Turkey and England is that imams be empowered to act as registrars for marriage. This may be a reform worthy of consideration; in England this is already possible but may be less effective because of the current need to celebrate the marriage in a registered building. Formal rules allowing imams to issue certificates already appear to be in place in Italy (see Sona, Chapter 6), Spain and Sweden (Jänterä-Jareborg, Chapter 4). However, Sona and Jänterä-Jareborg respectively show that in Italy and Sweden the take up of such facilities by imams is low. In Spain, Italy and Sweden, the rules also contemplate that the religious celebration of marriage be subsequently registered again, leaving scope for problems requiring further research. Fieldwork in England revealed that while imams report telling couples to register their marriages, many couples do not do so in practice, while a recent case shows that even where a mosque was registered for marriage, the celebrants did not follow the rules applicable, attracting criticism from the court.[17]

Another popular argument is to consider whether cohabitation laws can address the situation of people who consider themselves married under a religious or customary form of solemnisation. It would have to be borne in mind that, as with the presumption of marriage, such laws would also not cover a whole swathe of people who think they are married, and also that cohabitation without being married may not be the ideal for people who cannot say consistently with their ethical framework that they merely cohabit without marriage. The *Şerife Yiğit* ruling also underlines the added risk of religious-only marriages in a jurisdiction where a status akin to marriage is not extended to cohabitees. The European Court should perhaps have taken into account the lack of recognition of cohabitee status, unlike in other European legal systems where cohabitees are given some protection (Antokolskaia 2006: 367–441).[18] Such a lack in a legal system like Turkey's means that those who do not register their marriages with official authorities are also not able to avail of certain welfare benefits, even though contributions in anticipation of those benefits may have been made in good faith during the lifetime of the deceased family member.

Besides the question of marriage within a jurisdiction, it is not unusual for European judges to encounter problems of recognising a marriage which has some connection with a non-European jurisdiction. The general principle can be stated that when assessing foreign marriages European courts try to uphold the validity of the relationship. Polygamy may cause problems which are illustrated further below, and there may well be other qualification issues, like age or other factors affecting capacity, which differ in European legal systems. Difficult issues of evidence may be involved and may require expert evidence to help the courts ascertain the law and practice in any particular country abroad (Menski, Chapter 2, and Holden 2011). The problem of ascertaining the foreign law applicable in any particular case evidently goes far beyond the sphere of marriage.[19] In general, there can be problems of recognition when the type of marriage ceremony is said to depart from European norms.[20]

---

17 *MA v JA and the Attorney General* [2012] EWHC 2219 (Fam).

18 Evidence from Bulgaria reveals that cohabitation is increasingly common, while religious celebrations are declining in popularity.

19 At a RELIGARE seminar in Brussels, 5–6 December 2011, judges present emphasised the need for more discussions and better information and training about other legal systems.

20 Poulter (1986: 8) noted in what now seems like a classic statement: 'English law may only be prepared to accord that status to a foreign union if it displays a clear resemblance to the English conception of marriage.'

Telephonic marriages and proxy marriages are such types of marriage which appear to be common among some groups, and they often come before judges.[21] In one such case, on the basis that a telephone marriage between two Pakistanis was validly celebrated in the eyes of Pakistani law (which was the law of the common nationality of the spouses and the law of the place of celebration), the Court of Appeal of Milan declared the marriage valid. In so doing, it annulled the decision by which the Italian Embassy in Pakistan had denied an entry visa to a woman and held that the spouses were entitled to family reunification.[22]

In a case dealt with by the Court of Appeal in England,[23] the question of capacity to contract a marriage came up (see in more detail Menski, Chapter 2). In that case, a man with severe mental impairment was married over the telephone with a woman in Bangladesh, his consent given by his parents who helped arrange the marriage. As part of an action to prevent his travelling to Bangladesh, the local authority applied to the court for a declaration as to whether he had capacity to contract the marriage. The first instance court held that he was domiciled in England and had no capacity to consent to the marriage. On appeal, one of the judges in the Court of Appeal agreed that he had no capacity to contract into that marriage, notwithstanding its validity, according to expert evidence, in Bangladeshi law and Muslim law. Another judge held that under the rule of public policy the marriage could not be recognised in English law. The same case also raised the issue of telephonic marriages, but the judges did not feel they could deal with the matter squarely as it had not been argued fully. However, remarks they made may be indicative of the possibility that, in a future case, a narrow view would be taken of the validity of marriages by telephone and, presumably, other contemporary telecommunications. A restrictive approach here would parallel that taken by the British and other courts in cases of 'transnational' divorces, where the act of divorce itself crosses jurisdictional boundaries (Pearl and Menski 1998: 92–5).

Polygamy

Monogamy is claimed to be, and certainly remains, a basic principle of matrimonial law in the official legal systems of all RELIGARE countries. This is another instance where the Christian prohibitions on multiple spouses, however secularised they have become today, maintain their long shadow. Responses of the legal systems studied evidently vary. Polygamous marriages conducted within the jurisdictional territory are normally prohibited from having validity with specific legislative provisions to that effect (Denmark, Italy, Turkey, Spain, England) and may even be criminalised (England, Turkey, Italy). From a cursory look at the domestic laws dealing with cases concerning polygamy, whether with a 'foreign' element or not, there is great diversity in legal practice concerning the recognition of some effects of polygamous marriages, but one can also say that even where recognition is forthcoming there is a degree of ambiguity and hedging about with restrictions in all jurisdictions which may create problems in individual cases. Partial recognition is either granted in the context of claims for matrimonial relief or pension schemes (Spain, England,

---

21 Court of Appeals of Milan, 24 September 2003, although, at the same time, the court appeared not to want to rule on the question of validity of the marriage itself and approved the refusal of a visa on grounds that there did not appear to be any substance to the marriage because the parties had never been together and had possibly never met.
22 Court of Appeals of Milan, 2 February 2007.
23 *KC and NNC v City of Westminster and IC* [2008] EWCA Civ 198.

Belgium and France, on the condition that it is demonstrated that it is a bona fide marriage), or even providing a ground for divorce (Turkey, Denmark).[24] This latter solution is intriguingly similar to one adopted in various branches of Islamic law.

The grounds on which classification of cases as having a 'foreign' element is made are themselves not very clear or consistently applied. Usually judges refer to nationality, although residence and domicile are also relevant depending on the country concerned. However, in many cases, cultural factors, often ranging across jurisdictional boundaries, may be important, but tend to be overridden or even ignored, at least in the formal reasoning of the courts.[25] This underlines the fact that private international law more generally creates confusion or obfuscates about which indices of belonging are more important and, as in other areas of law, legal systems have not yet developed refined notions of socio-legal culture to work with. The example of polygamy most starkly illustrates that private international law is stuck within the 'methodological nationalism' it inherits. In cases which are thought to involve a 'foreign' element, the spectre of public policy, although it is not always applied consistently, looms large so as to reinforce, in secularised form, the basic assumptions of European Christian culture that polygamy is to be rooted out.

In cases where a 'foreign' element is combined with a strong European connection, polygamous relationships are very likely to be caught up in a jurisdictional tussle as to whether judges should respect the foreign law which allows polygamy or apply the stricter standards of the European legal system. This is starkly illustrated in Belgium, where the status of foreign polygamous marriages is disputed because of a difference of opinion between the Supreme Court of Cassation and the Constitutional Court.[26] Dutch courts have meanwhile adopted the position that the public policy rule can be used to deny recognition where the circumstances make it clear that the marriage is closely linked to the Netherlands.[27] This complex scenario of partial recognition also holds in cases concerning children: there are cases of family reunification where the second wife is allowed a residence permit in order to look after the children, even though the second marriage is not formally recognised. One of the frequently encountered issues in cases before European courts concerning polygamy is whether pensions or other social security entitlements of widows should be given to one surviving wife, shared among more than one wife, or not be provided to any of them. Courts in Spain have tended to say that there should be a division between the wives, although this view is not unanimously shared among them.[28]

---

24 For example, the decision of the Western High Court of Denmark, 2 September 2003, where a wife wanted a marriage annulment because her husband had a prior wife to whom he was religiously wed in Turkey. While not acknowledging the first marriage on grounds that it was solely a religious marriage and not the norm in Turkey, the court granted the second wife the right to divorce.

25 For a discussion and critique along these lines of an English Court of Appeal case, *Abbassi v Abbassi & Another* [2006] EWCA Civ 355, see Shah (2013b: 144–5).

26 See, respectively, the Supreme Court of Cassation (Cass. 3 December 2007, indirectly confirmed by Cass. 14 February 2011) and the Constitutional Court (CC 4 June 2009).

27 District court, Utrecht, 21 January 2009, rechtspraak.nl BH 3029, where a woman resident in the Netherlands who acquired Dutch nationality and then married a man in Morocco who already had a wife was refused a divorce because her marriage was considered as being so connected to the Netherlands that it was contrary to Dutch public policy and therefore could not be recognised. A similar statement of principle leading to non-recognition was made on grounds of close connection with the Belgian legal order by the Labour Court, Brussels (17 February 2011, JT 2011 383) when interpreting the General Convention on social security between Belgium and Morocco.

28 For cases advocating equal division, see the Superior Court of Justice of Galicia (TSJ de Galicia, Sala de lo Social, April 2, 2002); Superior Court of Justice of Madrid (TSJ de Madrid, Sala

It is notable that in some countries (France and Turkey) there tends to be less recognition of polygamy despite the reportedly high number of second wives who may require access to legal protection.[29] The Turkish legal system leaves open the possibility for civil actions against the husband and the second wife.[30] In such countries, polygamy also constitutes a criminal offence when the second marriage involves nationals. In so far as the question is one of criminalisation because of a religious-only marriage, the Bulgarian example may be worthy of note since the legal provision prescribing that any religious ceremony must occur only after the civil one has been scrapped, although polygamy itself appears to be disappearing in that country. In England and Spain, criminal liability can be circumvented because it is known in both countries that a second marriage by religious rites may be conducted within the jurisdiction without attracting a penalty, although the offence remains on the statute book and, certainly in England, prosecutions are known to take place, sometimes because of confusions on the part of the prosecuting authorities or the individuals concerned (Menski 2012b). On deeper examination these cases often turn out to be cases of private revenge with state backing and it is difficult to see what public interest is being served in pursuing prosecutions. The maintenance of criminal sanctions for polygamy should be seriously reconsidered, as with the criminalisation of family relations generally.[31] The Turkish solution of leaving open the route to civil action against a husband or second wife may yet be an alternative where it is thought that polygamy affects the interests of the first wife, although here too it is not evident what underlying concern would be served except personal revenge.

In several European countries the second wife is not allowed a marriage visa, and this leads to the split of families across legal frontiers (UK, Italy, Spain). The legitimacy of this position has been confirmed by the Council Directive 2003/86/EC of 22 September 2003 on the right to family reunification. According to Article 4§4 of that Directive, in the event of a polygamous marriage, where the sponsor already has a spouse living with him in the territory of a Member State, the Member State concerned is required not to – 'shall not' – authorise the family reunification of a further spouse. Member States may also limit the family reunification of minor children of a further spouse and the sponsor. Not all states have followed this suggestion, and children of a wife other than one who is already on

---

de lo Social, July 29, 2002); Superior Court of Justice of Andalusia (TSJ de Andalucía, Málaga, January 30, 2003). It has helped that in Spanish law each surviving divorced spouse is entitled to the deceased's pension in proportion to the respective periods of their marriage with the deceased. However, the Supreme Court of Justice of Catalonia (TSJ de Cataluña, July 30, 2003) has held that only the first spouse should be assigned the claimed pension.

29   See Freedman (2004: 114) on the impact of polygamy-related restrictions in immigration law imposed since 1993 which have an adverse impact on the situation of immigrant women even though the ostensible justification for the introduction of the laws was a defence of women's rights.

30   T.C. Yargıtay (Court of Cassation, case no 2006/2-558, decision no 2006/568, 20.9.2006), a case where a woman who married through a religious ceremony and effectively became a second wife opened a civil suit against the husband who had not informed her that he was already married. The Yargıtay suggested that she open a case in a general court because the family court was not the suitable forum.

31   For a softer approach at one end of the judicial spectrum in England one may cite Munby J's remark made while he allowed a claim for ancillary relief: 'An important "mitigating factor" ... is that the parties' contemporaneous religious marriage, which was obviously a matter of importance for each of them, was valid. So, whatever view the law of England may take, in their own eyes and in the eyes of their god, the husband and the wife were indeed just that – husband and wife.' *Ben Hashem v Ali Shayif and Others* [2008] EWHC 2380 (Fam), [2009] 1 FLR 115, [2008] Fam Law 1179 at para 321.

the territory may be admitted (Italy).[32] It is regrettable that Member States are *required* to refuse a residence permit to polygamous spouses where one spouse is already on the territory of that Member State. As with other legal restrictions on polygamy, it is unclear what public policy this serves and such a provision clearly discriminates against the choice of family form of an EU residence permit holder.[33] While giving the impression of a Europe protective of globalising influences which include traditions of family that accept, if not encourage, polygamy, it does not correspond with the fact that other varieties of family form are increasingly recognised both in the family law systems and in the immigration laws of EU Member States.

Dower or the *Mahr*

One of the best instances of a requirement of marriage derived from a religious institution is that of *mahr* (Islamic dower, also referred to as *sadaq* in some jurisdictions, notably Morocco).[34] This is a payment, or a promise of payment pending some future occurrence (e.g. divorce), which accompanies a Muslim marriage. It is clear that the question of *mahr* arises in many Western countries, including those in Europe with varied approaches taken by the legal systems and courts (Fournier 2010, Mehdi and Nielsen 2011). Previously, the UN Committee on the Elimination of Discrimination Against Women (CEDAW) had taken a stereotyped opinion on *mahr* as representing the ethos of sale of women and their treatment like chattels (Løvdal 2011: 81–2). This is similar to the view taken in the case of an Indian Muslim couple by a civil court and a court of appeal in France which held that the *mahr* represented the price (*prix de vente*) of the woman to marry and went against French *ordre public*, which could not tolerate the sale of human beings. These rulings were eventually overturned by the Court of Cassation.[35]

More recently, the Higher Regional Court of Hamm, Germany, held that a 'bride price' (*başlık parası* in Turkish) is contrary to public policy and need not to be paid back after the separation of the spouses. The court felt that payment in the form of a bride price as a compulsory requirement for marriage violates the freedom of entering a marriage and human dignity, and held the bride price agreement as being against public policy and therefore void in law.[36] While not considered 'Islamic', arrangements like the bride price are fairly widespread in the world, and it could be said that the German court took a rather narrow approach in this particular case based on its own stereotyped idea of a foreign custom. Institutions like 'bride price' also remind us that gifts and payments made upon marriage according to custom or convention occur in various directions and between different in-laws among various ethnic groups, and care should be taken not to have regard only to the 'Islamic' institution of *mahr*. An open, though not necessarily uncritical, approach should

---

32   Court of Appeals of Turin, decree of 18 April 2001; Court of Bologna, ordinance of 12 March 2003.

33   Again, see Freedman (2004: 114) on the socio-economic impact upon women and their children of such restrictions in France, and, in more detail with case studies, Raissiguier (2010: 80–90).

34   The institution of *mahr* or *sadaq* is often translated in English as dowry, which is incorrect because dowry represents another set of gifts moving from the bride's family to her or to her husband's family. Each cultural context will have its specificities in this regard.

35   Court of Cassation, 22-11-2005, n. 03-14.961, discussed further by Løvdal (2011: 91–2) and Bouillier (2011: 55–8).

36   Higher Regional Court of Hamm, 13.01.2011, I-18 U 88/10.

therefore be maintained as to the intricate relationship between religious obligations and the conduct of affairs arising from customs and conventions. More research is therefore needed which goes beyond the currently narrower focus on *mahr*.

Meanwhile, the CEDAW's view has been revised and *mahr* is now regarded as part of the tool kit available to ensure the protection of women in Muslim contexts (Løvdal 2011: 81–2). It is important that such a view does not in turn give rise to further stereotypes, and policymakers, judges and other officials will always have to keep in mind that practices around *mahr* vary considerably in Muslim-majority countries and, likewise, within Muslim communities in Europe (Fournier 2010: 29–33, Mehdi and Nielsen 2011). Depending on the amount of payment involved, a woman's pre-marriage bargaining position (Fournier 2010: 24–9), her socio-economic situation, as well as a range of other factors surrounding a marriage and its breakdown, it may or may not provide an appropriate safety mechanism for women. Legal officials will also rightly be concerned about the take up of social welfare as in other marital breakdown situations.

Fournier (2010) breaks down the policy concerns and outcome of *mahr* adjudication in Canada, France, Germany and the United States. Her results indicate, first, that the *mahr* and its claim outcomes vary both within and across jurisdictions and, second, that there is a significant distancing of *mahr* from its original conceptualisation. Four possible approaches to *mahr* were apparent in judicial practice within our research countries: (1) to consider it in the context of the law of contract or as a gift (Denmark, England); (2) as subject to the domestic matrimonial property and matrimonial relief regime (England, France, the Netherlands); (3) as a general effect of marriage (Germany); and (4) as part of maintenance (the Netherlands, Germany). The discussion of *mahr* often gets mixed up with issues such as whether the matrimonial regime in the relevant country observes the principle of common or separate matrimonial property. It is arguable, however, that *mahr* claims will be looked at more seriously if the applicable regime allows either a choice of law to the spouses as to whether a foreign legal regime applies or it simply assumes, whether by treaty or conflicts of law principles, that a foreign law regime applies. This is indicative of the larger point that European judges tend to find domestic equivalents for a foreign legal institution like *mahr*, preferring to deal with the institutions they know, thereby dismissing claims involving 'foreign' institutions which they do not understand or when they cannot figure out how those institutions fit within the applicable family law regime in their courts. This phenomenon of distortion, which Fournier refers to as a 'loss in transplantation', raises important discussion points of more general interest and relevance for the reception of 'foreign' family law concepts more widely.

Given these findings, it cannot yet be said that one European view as to *mahr* has developed. Variations exist among spousal property regimes, post-divorce financial payments regimes, and the application of domestic or foreign regimes in the various countries concerned. If there is a European point of departure, it is that *mahr* is not a legal institution of any European legal system but may seep in within a claim invoking the application of 'foreign' legal rules through private international law. As for claims where no such foreign legal regime is held to be operating, the courts will have to experiment to assess, for example, whether contract is the correct interpretation or whether a *mahr* payment should be subsumed within the general powers allowing financial payments to the spouses upon marriage breakdown and, perhaps, during the subsistence of a marriage. It should be noted that in some European legal systems, such as Turkey, property matters may be taken care of by agreement of the parties as long as they are evidenced in writing. In Turkey, the Court of Cassation has accepted that *mahr* can form an enforceable part of such an arrangement.[37] In other countries, the autonomy of parties to make pre- or post-nuptial agreements regarding property matters is increasingly endorsed by the judiciary.[38] Treating *mahr* as a contract (or as part of a contract) may be deemed appropriate for marriages which have not been registered. Non-registered marriages now appear to be a significant part of the practice of marriage, particularly among Muslims.[39]

Finally, it should be considered whether the variations among and within the different legal systems as to the classification of *mahr* are also, in part, a function of the ways claims-making occurs. It is not always the case that women ask for the *mahr* to be enforced by a European court. In some cases, men may also insist before a court that *mahr* be granted because this avoids an ex-wife potentially having access to the more beneficial post-divorce maintenance provisions of domestic European systems. In the case concerning the Indian Muslim couple cited above, the Court of Cassation in France was eventually convinced by the man's argument that the court follow the separate marital property regime and that the *mahr* therefore represented the limit of his obligation to her.[40] Such an argument would probably not have been accepted in an Indian court then or today since Indian law imposes upon a Muslim ex-husband the obligation to maintain his ex-wife for a reasonable period after divorce and therefore goes beyond merely the *mahr* (Pearl and Menski 1998: 201–22, Menski 2012a: 248–9). Nevertheless, the main lesson here would be that each case should be examined on its own facts and its own cultural context, and no general rule can realistically be set out for the recognition or otherwise of the dower or, indeed, any other payment on marriage.

Divorce

European family law systems have moved historically in terms of their attitude and stance towards divorce. This movement has occurred from a position where divorce was not countenanced, under the canon law, to one where divorce is allowed in every official legal system under study (Antokolskaia 2003, 2006: 360–61).[41] This has occurred particularly since family laws have been co-opted by the state and since it became accepted that state-assisted social engineering goals could be tried through the manipulation of family law.[42] The degree to which that occurs varies – in some countries waiting periods are applicable

---

37 For example, Yargıtay, 1. Hukuk Dairesi, E.2009/4577, K.2009/6090 (27.05.2009). The writer is grateful to Derya Bayır for this information on *mahr* in the Turkish courts.

38 See *Radmacher v Granatino* [2010] UKSC 42, where the UK Supreme Court endorsed the general principle that parties to a marriage may agree as to disposition of property. Interestingly, the case involved an agreement between the wife, who was a German citizen, and the husband, who was French, and the agreement had been drawn up in Germany by a notary.

39 This seems clear from the evidence from various countries presented at the Religare Expert Seminar on Unregistered Marriages and Alternative Dispute Resolution, Queen Mary, University of London, 4 September 2012. For the podcast of the proceedings, see http://www.law.qmul.ac.uk/events/podcasts/religare2012/index.html [last accessed 14 December 2013].

40 Court of Cassation, 22-11-2005, n. 03-14.961.

41 At the time Antokolskaia wrote, Malta was the one exception among European jurisdictions, but Maltese law changed in 2011 allowing divorce.

42 Although we have not researched this to any depth, it appears that Churches have in turn adapted to the fact that couples divorce more frequently and that divorce is now widely available. In particular, the use of concepts like nullity by canon lawyers as de facto recognition of broken marriages can be noted. Some *ulema*, meanwhile, take the position that the issue of a 'secular' divorce means

prior to being able to seek divorce, and reliance on establishing fault to secure divorce is diminished everywhere. In many cases, divorce has now become reduced to a procedural matter, although courts may still be involved, particularly where the terms of divorce are contested. A development linked to social engineering aspects of law is the bid to enable gender equality to be realised through family law reform. International instruments concerned with gender equality have also focused on inequalities within family laws.[43]

When it comes to the encounter between European legal systems and couples from ethnic or religious minorities wishing to secure their divorce or to have a divorce recognised, the above factors constitute the general background and may also become hurdles to ensure the necessary flexibility. The premises upon which the rules on divorce, as with all other areas of family law, have been based are to be found within European culture, prior to its recent unprecedented pluralisation. As in other areas of family law, European legal systems still generally regard minority legal orders and perspectives as irrelevant to the formulation of formal rules. In particular, the role of the State as guarantor of equality of arms in the breakdown of marriage is held up as the key benchmark to test whether 'foreign' rules live up to those standards. It remains difficult for legislators or judges to be convinced that these foreign legal rules, not necessarily designed with the same objectives or foundations as the ones applicable in European divorce laws, should yet be accepted as leading to valid divorce. A key difference between, on the one hand, many Asian and African legal systems (not just Islamic law), and European legal systems on the other, is that the non-European State may not play a critical role, or indeed any role, in effecting divorce, although it may yet offer options for effecting formal divorces.

All countries under study have rules in place to ensure that divorce occurring within the jurisdictional territory of a European state should be obtained through the official means available for divorce. This means that a non-State divorce between foreigners or nationals is not given legal effect or recognition.[44] This mirrors the situation with marriage; neither informal marriages nor divorces tend to gain recognition in European official legal systems.[45] Such 'territorialising' attempts have the converse effect in that the official legal discourse as reflected in the case law shifts to the recognition of divorces linked to a foreign, non-European legal order, with the dominant question being whether those foreign procedures measure up to European standards. This should be read with the fact in mind that actual cases often present themselves to European courts involving a complex mix of transnational, or non-state, socio-legal developments within the jurisdiction, which defy classification according to the terms established by a European legal system. As with other areas of family law, there is a 'translation exercise' involved in more than one sense: first, there is the effort of knowing enough about the foreign rule in the context of the foreign legal system; and second there is the job of enabling the European court to understand the

---

that a marriage is either dissolved or that the grounds for divorce in Islamic law have been met. See Douglas et al., Chapter 10.

43 See article 5 of Protocol 7 to the ECHR and article 16 of the Convention on the Elimination of Discrimination Against Women.

44 A local religious divorce between foreigners or Belgians is therefore deprived of any civil effect or recognition under the Belgian Code of International Private Law, Art. 32. For England and Wales, the Domicile and Matrimonial Proceedings Act, 1973, section 16(1) was introduced to prevent divorces being pronounced in the United Kingdom in purported reliance on foreign legal systems. Only divorces that go through British court procedures were to be recognised hence.

45 This is subject to what is said above about the recognition of some marriages in English law where there are irregularities in solemnisation or the couple has been cohabiting for a long period.

legal institution in the terms that it is familiar with. Both processes are bound to and do create distortions.

Cases have arisen in Germany where the courts have noted that a Jewish *get* (a document presented by a man to his wife to effect a divorce) cannot be accepted as such since it is a private document even if supervised in Israel by a rabbinical court. A German court can issue a divorce only if the requirements of the German law on divorce are met.[46] Mathias Rohe (Chapter 3) discusses a similar situation in France where courts may refuse to recognise a *get* on account of it being a religious matter and therefore 'private'. Subject to some further developments noted below, this is illustrative of the standard line in the jurisdictions studied where the validity of a 'private' act of divorce, particularly when 'gendered', is regarded with a high degree of scepticism or rejection. In such cases, litigants are faced with a set of mixed signals within the same jurisdiction, or even contradictory signals sent by different parts of a legal system in the very *same* case, thus creating confusions and havoc in family and private lives.[47] Naturally, they can often lead to 'limping' situations, meaning that in one legal system a marriage may have come to an end while in the European legal system it is not considered as such.[48]

Looking closely at some other cases, one may look in vain to find a consistent line of thinking even where the same set of principles ostensibly applies. In a case involving an Algerian couple, one German court considered a *talaq* divorce – a unilateral divorce normally issued by a man unless stipulated otherwise – to be against the principle of German *ordre public* since it is the right only of the man.[49] In so doing, it opened the way for the woman to claim divorce under German law. In another case, involving a *talaq* issued by a Greek Muslim, a German court noted the possibility of exceptionally recognising the divorce. The context of the case should be borne in mind: in the Western Thrace region of Greece the application of *shari'a* rules in family law matters is recognised as part of the Lausanne agreement of 1923 (Tsitselikis 2012). While the court noted that the *talaq* violates the principles of gender equality and the protection of the family under German Basic Law, the result of applying this aspect of Greek law was held to be compatible with German law, especially as the couple had lived apart for one year.[50]

Ambivalence about the *talaq* pronounced in non-European countries where *shari'a* rules allow it ranges across the European countries studied. French courts have denied recognition to a *talaq* even in situations where the woman has been heard during the religious proceedings and received financial compensation. In so doing, French courts have relied in

---

46 Federal Court of Justice, 02.02.1994, XII ZR 148/92; Federal Court of Justice, 28.05.2008, XII ZR 61/06. In a similar decision by the Higher Regional Court of Oldenburg, 07.03.2006, 22 UF 125/05, the rabbinical court's involvement was not considered relevant despite the fact that a husband can be penalised by those courts under Israeli law for withholding a *get*. For an earlier Belgian ruling recognising an Israeli Jewish religious divorce between two Belgian citizens, see Court of Appeal Brussels, 12 December 1974.

47 Concerning a Hindu law divorce case, see Menski (2007). An updated discussion of the same case is in Menski (2011). For a discussion of some Muslim law cases, see Shah (2011). Both writers also highlight the role played by foreign law experts in such cases.

48 In the decision by the Higher Regional court of München, 12.09.2002, 3Z BR 136/02, a consensual Muslim divorce which would be valid in Jordan was not accepted and the court insisted that only German law would be applied.

49 Higher Regional Court of Rostock, 07.11.2005, 10 WF 69/05.

50 Higher Regional Court of Hamm, 07.03.2006, 7 UF 123/05.

part on the precedence of article 5 of Protocol 7 to the ECHR (equality between spouses).[51] Italian courts have tended to refuse recognition to the unilateral repudiation or *talaq*.[52] A revision to Belgian law in 2005 provides against the recognition of Muslim *talaq* except in cases where there is no proximity to Belgium and the same law states that an act abroad recognizing the decision of the husband to dissolve the marriage may not be recognised in Belgium, unless the woman benefits from the same right, effectively derecognising *talaq*.[53] Therefore, rather than allowing for judicial recognition in appropriate cases, the legislator has deemed to oblige judges to refuse it. This leaves it open for further legally imposed harm in individual cases where a marriage may have de facto broken down and no real purpose, except some symbolic posturing, will be served by denying recognition. Such decisions go against what Rohe (Chapter 3) argues should be the preferred approach – an examination of the concrete outcome in each case.

Another line of cases, which is mirrored in various project countries, is concerned with the refusal of men to cooperate in granting a divorce, a situation encountered because of the specific consensual nature of divorce in Jewish law, and the refusal of men to grant the type of divorce – *talaq* – that enables a Muslim woman to retain her rights with respect to *mahr* or maybe because a woman is unable to access a religious divorce by another means. In such cases European judges are starting to take a more activist line and are less concerned about the 'contamination' of their national legal systems with the rules of Jewish or Islamic law but they are actually assisting in enforcing them. The question was raised as involving human rights law in Holland. A refusal by a man to give a *talaq* divorce was considered by a Rotterdam court as unacceptable behaviour violating his wife's rights under ECHR, article 8 (family and private life) and 12 (right to marry and found a family), and the court obliged the man to issue a *talaq* divorce on pain of a fine.[54] A case in England shows some similar features, although it is somewhat clearer in that case that the woman, who was Iranian and had started divorce proceedings in Iran, could have lost out on the *mahr* had her husband not pronounced a *talaq*. The judge proceeded to require the husband to pronounce a *talaq* within a specified time and compensate the wife the promised dower by a reduced amount

---

51 Court of Cassation, 17 February 2004, No. 01-11.549, and No. 02-11.618; Court of Cassation, 3 January 2006, no. 04-15.231. In the latter case the court gave precedence to the ECHR over the Franco-Moroccan Agreement of 10 August 1981, and it appears that it has held its position despite the revision of the rules on divorce in the Moroccan family law made in February 2004. For further comment on these developments, see Fulchiron (2010).

52 We found only one case in which, due to the presence of particular circumstances, a court recognised the *talaq*: Court of Appeals of Cagliari, judgment no. 198, 16 May 2008. The grounds were that the wife had been notified of her husband's intention to divorce; the repudiation procedure was not restricted to the mere repetition of 'I shall repudiate you' three times in a row; the court had verified the impossibility of the couple living together and had safeguarded the wife's right to defence and, after the divorce pronouncement, her right to alimony. In so doing, the court also took notice that Egyptian civil law recognises the wife's equal right to unilateral divorce (without her husband's consent). The court must have had in mind the Egyptian law of 2000 allowing a woman to apply to a court for a *khul* divorce on the condition that she gives up any financial claim.

53 Belgian Code of International Private Law, Art. 57 § 1 and 2. Belgian courts have tended to follow the same principles: Civil Court Liege, 26 June 2009; Labour Court Brussels, 27 May 2010; Court of Appeal Mons, 20 December 2007.

54 Rb Rotterdam 8-12-2010.

or, failing that, make a payment for the full dower. The judge did so explicitly under the applicable English domestic legislation allowing distribution of property and maintenance.[55]

Such cases have also arisen among Jewish couples where the man refuses to cooperate in issuing the *get*. In English cases, judges have tended to 'persuade' men by imposing some 'disadvantages' in divorce proceedings where a *get* is unreasonably withheld.[56] French cases show the same trend.[57] England is the only jurisdiction under study where legislative action in the form of the Divorce (Religious Marriages) Act 2002 has resulted in empowering official courts to withhold a decree finalising a divorce on condition that a religious divorce has been secured. Although there is not as yet unequivocal evidence of its 'success', in the interviews in England, Jewish respondents tended to express satisfaction about the existence of this legislation designed to offer some help to the Jewish chained wife (*agunah*) to ensure that a religious divorce is in place prior to the finalisation of an official divorce. No major demand seems forthcoming for the legislation, which currently applies to Jews only, to be extended to Muslims.[58] England, however, is not the only jurisdiction where such legislation exists, and it is probable that the 1990 amendments to Canada's Divorce Act adding section 21.1, provided the basic model for the English legislation. South Africa also introduced an amendment in 1996 to its Divorce Act (section 5A) to allow a court to withhold an official divorce where the lack of a religious divorce prevents one party from marrying again.[59] While the English (and other) legislation could be analysed and discussed as illustrating several points of relevance, for present purposes it is worth pointing out that in various jurisdictions, and even in Western jurisdictions, there are some ways in which legislation specific to an ethnic or religious group can intervene after evidence of persistent problems in families. Although Western legal systems largely deny the application of personal law systems, this legislation demonstrates that some kind of specific response to particularistic problems can indeed be made.[60]

---

55   *NA v MOT* [2004] EWHC 471 (Fam), also reported as *A v T (Ancillary Relief: Cultural Factors)* [2004] EWHC 471 (Fam), [2004] 1 FLR 977, [2004] Fam Law 404.

56   *N v N (Jurisdiction: Pre Nuptial Agreement)*, also known as *N v N (Divorce: Judaism)* [1999] 2 F.L.R. 745, [1999] 2 F.C.R. 583, [1999] Fam. Law 691; *O v O (Jurisdiction: Jewish Divorce)* [2000] 2 FLR 147.

57   In several judgments French courts have held that a refusal by the husband to deliver a *get* after the final judgment granting the divorce may constitute an abuse of law and give rise to damages: Court of Appeal of Paris, 19 December 2007, n.07/00609, B. M. / M.; Court of Appeal of Lyon, 9 March 2006, H. c/ M.; Court of Appeal of Versailles, 16 February 2012, No. 10/04809X / Y. See also the prominent Canadian case *Bruker v Marcovitz* [2007] 3 SCR 607, 2007 SCC 54, where a husband was held liable for damages for failing to appear before the rabbinical authorities for the purpose of obtaining the *get* as stipulated in the marriage agreement.

58   There is indeed provision in the act to have it extended by Ministerial statutory instrument to 'any other prescribed religious usages'. One challenge resulted in a rejection by the court of the demand that the legislation be extended to Muslims: *Kandeel v Hands* [2010] EWCA Civ 1233.

59   The English or South African legislation does not allow a husband to plead 'genuine grounds of a religious or conscientious nature' as the Canadian legislation does.

60   Indeed, it is generally the case that such legislation is made on a restrictive basis but the example here illustrates the application of a more facilitative principle, albeit with some penalty involved.

Unofficial Legal Fora

Concerns about religious divorce within Muslim communities in particular have led to the relatively recent development of unofficial legal fora in Britain. While Jews have established rabbinical courts wherever there was a substantial Jewish community, their self-organisation does not appear to have been an attractive subject for study within European academic circles. If it is so now, it is because of the increasing attention paid to Muslim dispute resolution fora (see Douglas et al., Chapter 11). It may be that Christian ecclesiastical courts attract increasing interest for the same reasons (again Douglas et al., Chapter 11), although in Catholic majority countries their role is often discussed in the context of a feeling of incomplete secularisation within family law.

Unlike in other European countries, demands for the official recognition of *shari'a* had indeed been made in the UK as far back as the early 1970s, but they were inevitably met with rejection by the government (Nielsen 1993, Poulter 1998: 195–236). The emergence of *shari'a* councils since then is seen by Menski (in Pearl and Menski 1998: 74–80) as part of the rise of *angrezi shariat*, which is a wider concept incorporating the whole range of unofficial legal practices among British Muslims, and which has even been taken notice of in the British parliament.[61] As Menski notes (in Pearl and Menski 1998: 80), 'these semi-official Muslim bodies are pursuing a strategy of operating *angrezi shariat*, aspiring for its eventual official recognition without claiming this as a definite right at the present time and lobbying vigorously for it.'[62]

While there is little doubt that, as in Britain, elsewhere in Europe too there have been individual processes of reconstruction and adjustment, a question that remains difficult to answer is why the pattern of institution building has occurred in Britain to the extent that it has. John Bowen (2010: 417–18), who distinguishes French and British postcolonial arrangements in light of the backdrop of their colonial settings, provides a possible explanation. In the French case, he argues that the civil law tradition has remained influential among postcolonial North Africans. The British case, notably in colonial India but also elsewhere, was characterised by a policy of recognition of religion and personal status law, and this finds echoes in the British post-colonial diasporic context (see also Rohe 2007: 93). An extension of this argument could be made with respect to migrants originating in Turkey, and their descendants, who constitute a substantial proportion of the ethnic minority and Muslim population in Western Europe today.

The prevailing view regarding Turkey is that there is already a fairly long history of living with civil law in family matters, once *shari'a* was officially 'abolished', and that may mean that *shari'a* is seen as an ethical issue to be dealt with by oneself or within one's social circle, but which one does not expect to be recognised in the courts of the state. It is well known that political parties in Turkey running on a platform for the resurrection of personal law have been closed down, and that this has meant a much more cautious strategy being followed by the proponents of reform along Islamic lines. The decision of

---

61 See Lord Lester, *Hansard, Lords Debates*, cols. 1246–1247 (30 Jun 2000).

62 A.H. Thomson, a barrister, is quoted in Ameli et al. (2006: 81) as saying: 'In fact the various UK Shari'a Councils are the precursors of what will eventually become Shari'a courts, insh'Allah – but they need to be improved and unified.' An important recent development is the proposal to legislate against certain activities of *shari'a* councils and similar bodies by the introduction of a Private Member's Bill by Baroness Cox in the House of Lords. The Arbitration and Mediation Services (Equality) Bill had its second reading in the House of Lords on 19 October 2012.

the European Court of Human Rights in the *Refah Partisi* case[63] has been much discussed in European legal circles.[64] Rohe (2007: 93–4) has furthermore noted that migrants and their descendants originating in Turkey would reject the re-introduction of Islamic law rules in European countries. However, the role of secularisation within the Turkish legal system should not be exaggerated. The extent to which Islamic norms were expelled from the legal system in Turkey is debatable. The transplantation of the Civil Code of Switzerland during the early years of the Republic was done only after changes adapting that code to pre-existing understandings of family relations (see Miller 2000), while custom is generally placed in a more prominent position in the Turkish legal system than is the case for Western countries. We have also had occasion to note (above) that legal institutions like the *mahr* are explicitly accepted by the higher courts in Turkey. A lack of attention to such features often results in an exaggerated evaluation of the secularisation of the Turkish legal system.

An additional explanation for why other European countries remain relatively shielded from the kind of semi-public profile *shari'a* institutions in Britain have is that, because of the importance of nationality as a 'connecting factor', Islamic law already has a strong position, especially within the areas of family and inheritance law (Rohe 2007: 19, 90, Büchler 2011: 27–34). In other words, the maintenance, through the principles of private international law, of the rule that the law of one's nationality is to be applied in court cases, which can mean a version of *shari'a*, could mean a more diminished perception of the necessity for *shari'a* fora than in Britain. In that sense, the default assumptions of courts in many continental European countries may effectively be more legally pluralistic than the British application of the *lex loci* or the Swiss application of the law of residence. However, a hypothesis based on the structure of private international law rules may also not be entirely satisfactory. For instance, RELIGARE fieldwork results showed that interviewees, among which were included many representatives of religious organisations, were largely ignorant of the rather technical rules of private international law. While advocating some accommodation within the framework of state law, this group could not have acted as spokespersons to argue for their preservation or otherwise. We cannot, at the same time, deny the evidence that in some Western European countries other than Britain, researchers have noticed the presence of non-state dispute resolution fora (Foblets 1994: 379–82). Research projects in these countries may in the near future reveal some interesting results.[65]

As for Muslim institutional structures in Britain, it is known that they have been operating since the 1980s (Pearl and Menski 1998: 74–80, Shah 2010). Since their emergence, their work has tended to concentrate on matrimonial issues and, notably, the issuance of divorces for Muslim women (Badawi 1995, Shah-Kazemi 2001, Bano 2007). Such bodies are established according to the various segments of Islam represented in Britain, including

---

63 *Refah Partisi (Welfare Party) and others v Turkey*, Application nos. 41340/98, 41342/98, 41343/98 and 41344/98, judgment of 13 February 2003. The case followed the closure of the political party by Turkey's Constitutional Court on the ground that the party's programme of establishing a plurality of legal systems in conformity with religious beliefs was in conflict with the constitutional principle of secularism (*laiklik*).

64 In *Fazilet Partisi and anor v Turkey* [2006] ECtHR 488, Application no. 1444/02, 27 April 2006, that political party had been closed down by the Constitutional Court on the ground that it offended against the secular nature of the Turkish Constitution. The European Court formally struck out the case after the party withdrew the application alleging bias of the Court in *Refah*.

65 Note the BEPULEX project on dispute resolution in immigrant communities in Belgium and research by Latif Taş in the Rechtskulturen programme in Berlin.

Barelwi, Deobandhi or Salafi, Ahmadiyya,[66] and various Shia groups,[67] and are often linked to mosques which may refer questions to those bodies which mosque personnel do not feel able to handle. Not all such bodies may refer to themselves as *shari'a* councils, although that is the most generally used designation in the literature (the more popular press has tended to use '*shari'a* law courts', '*shari'a* courts' or 'Islamic courts'). Some have taken on a more formalised structure with established and evolving procedures, websites, record keeping, form-filling, and a panel of *ulema* (learned men, scholars) who can consult each other, sometimes across *maddhab* (school of law) lines, before making decisions.

Douglas et al. report in Chapter 10 about their study on the procedures of case handling and decision-making by the Birmingham Shari'a Council, the London Beth Din and the Catholic Tribunal for Wales. Their findings with respect to the Birmingham Shari'a Council confirm the observations here, although they cannot necessarily be generalised for other Muslim bodies. *Shari'a* councils tend to be run on a voluntary basis and charge minimal fees, especially when compared to the costs involved in going to official courts. Besides lawyers and official courts being seen as too expensive, they may also not necessarily be regarded by the clients as capable of understanding or responding to their problems. This is particularly so if a marriage is not registered or it is a case of enforcing the terms of a *nikah* (Islamic marriage contract) which the courts have not regarded as binding (see discussion above). Similar reasons are reported by Bunting (2009: 84–9) for Canadian Muslims opting out of official family law.

The establishment of a network known as the Muslim Arbitration Tribunal (MAT) excited some additional interest, particularly following the speech of the Archbishop of Canterbury in February 2008. Some reporting in the European press has mentioned that the MAT is recognised as capable of delivering *shari'a*-compliant decisions enforceable in English law,[68] while some legal scholars have also received the same impression.[69] According to English law, if the parties to a dispute want to agree to a binding arbitration it could be enforceable under the Arbitration Act 1996. This practice is already well established among the Jewish *Batei Din*, and appears to be in use among the Ahmadiyyas

---

66   See the case *Bhatti v Bhatti* [2009] EWHC 3506 (Ch) for a reported instance of the Ahmadiyya dispute resolution mechanism which has a transnational dimension linking Pakistan and the UK. Ahmadiyyas are regarded by other Muslim groups as being outside the fold of Islam, and being an Ahmadi is unlawful in many Muslim-dominated countries.

67   *Jivraj v Hashwani* [2011] UKSC 40 is a case involving the Ismaili Conciliation and Arbitration Boards which also have a transnational dimension. The case of Masuma Jariwala, discussed *Hansard*, HC Deb, cols. 255WH–261WH (10 June 2009) House of Commons, concerned the Shia Dawoodi Bohra community where a former husband apparently withheld the pronouncement of *talaq* (divorce) for some 14 years after they had been divorced officially, while the leaders of that Bohra community could not do anything about it. The case shows that the general appeal to *shari'a* councils for the issuance of Islamic divorces does not hold in all cases.

68   See, e.g., K. Gelinsky, 'Deutsche Gerichte wenden die Scharia an', *Frankfrter Allgemeine*, 29 December 2012, who notes, 'The arbitrations of MAT are enforceable in court, unlike the decisions of the informal Sharia councils, which conduct mediations on Islamic marriage contracts or settle family disputes.' Translation by this writer. For another case of misreporting, see, A. Taher, 'Revealed: UK's first official sharia courts', *The Sunday Times*, 14 September 2008.

69   Witte and Nichols (2010: 123) state: 'English courts have regularly upheld the arbitration awards of Muslim tribunals in marriage and family disputes, so long as all parties consent to participate and so long as all arbitration takes place without physical coercion or threat. The same deference is accorded to the marital arbitrations of Jewish, Christian, Hindu, and other peaceable religious authorities.'

and Ismailis.[70] However, such agreements have tended to apply to non-family disputes (the exception being inheritance[71]) and are better known in business rather than family practice. So, in fact, English law already mirrored the situation in Ontario *since* its passing of the Family Statute Law Amendment Act, 2006, requiring that only family arbitration decisions made in accordance with Ontario and Canadian laws could be enforced in official courts (Bunting 2009: 80–84, Korteweg and Selby 2012).

Notwithstanding these lines which seek to draw a boundary around the jurisdictional scope of non-state fora, Menski's discussion (Chapter 2) of a case which touches on aspects of divorce and child care, with both transjurisdictional and non-state law elements involving a Beth Din in New York, shows the trust-conferring role judicial activism can play.[72] It remains to be seen how much of such 'interlegality' is adopted by the courts across Europe, and to which groups it is extended. Meanwhile, the discussion by Latif Taş (Chapter 11) of the case of the Kurds in London shows the religious dimension of law is not decisive and that non-state fora may yet be developed under a different umbrella. It is important to note that prior to this study by Taş, there was no public mention of the framework used by Kurds. It is also of concern that the more institutional appearance of dispute resolution attracts study; as Taş's work on Kurds and the work on Sikhs by Jhutti-Johal (2013) show, the role of kinship structures in acting as first-order dispute-solving mechanisms merits serious attention. By contrast, the overwhelming focus of public discussion and research in Britain, especially since the Archbishop of Canterbury's speech of February 2008 (Williams 2008), indicates that organisations based on explicitly Islamic lines tend to encourage much more scrutiny than do other institutions. This skewed research focus obviously needs addressing further.

Concluding Points

While we have acquired specifically legal information across a range of topics and are able to make some comparisons, we still lack anything like a comprehensive picture of how European legal systems are dealing with alterity in family life, especially if we consider the impact of European legal rules at the socio-legal level. Not only is there a lack of knowledge about the precise distribution of minority populations across European jurisdictions, not enough research exists to shed light on the variety of family practices in existence and the experience of these diverse families and their members with official legal systems. Some limited suggestions benefitting from the comparative research undertaken can be made despite the obvious gaps in knowledge.

Our study backs up the claim that, while ostensibly laudable and possibly widely supported common principles may be expressed in domestic and international laws and judicial rulings, legal practice across Europe often reveals some divergences depending on individual and institutional ethos and other factors. There is, however, no particular emphasis on being aware of, or for examining, how social and legal policy affects the diversity of families, especially given the common European legal space. The tendency of many scholars and policy advocates to assume that top-down legislative reform will result

---

70 See *Bhatti v Bhatti* [2009] EWHC 3506 (Ch) (for Ahmadiyyas) and *Jivraj v Hashwani* [2011] UKSC 40 (for Ismailis).

71 *Al-Midani v Al-Midani* [1999] 1 Lloyd's Rep. 923 concerning what was described by the judge as the division of the deceased's 'great estate'.

72 *AI v MT* [2013] EWHC 100 (Fam).

in the kind of social engineering they support is far from substantiated. Therefore, any socially beneficial impact occurs largely 'accidentally' and actually remains hypothetical at this stage. In future, policymaking should build in, possibly by mainstreaming, any impact factor upon the undeniable diversity of European family life.

Our evidence confirms that the existing critiques, highlighting the inadequacy of private international law models, which have hitherto been a key method in capturing alternative family forms within legal systems, can be supported, although further research to examine the range of problems which are either caused, or not addressed, by existing legal structures needs to be conducted. It already seems clear, however, that European legal systems are not yet adequately equipped to face the demographic changes that have already occurred over the past few decades and that will continue as a consequence of globalisation. Evidently, many people across Europe engage in and navigate through 'transnational social fields' and 'transnational legal fields'. Conversely, existing methodologically nationalist legal models are fairly simplistic and tend to operate on the basis of 'either-this-or-that-jurisdiction'. A better understanding is required of the complexity of family life and of the socio-legal cultures existing in Europe connected, as it is, to other parts of the world through these social fields.

European private international law rules and the hybridising rules of the domestic legal orders, as also reflected in some rulings by judges, tend to back up the critiques of unilateralism, and even chauvinism, when it comes to dealing with minority family practices. It is possible that further exchange of information and judicial training, which European judges appear to support, can address some of the existing constraints, but a continuous attention to researching the problems will also assist in highlighting problems. The underlying structural deficit can partly be put down to the emphasis in European legal cultures on 'sameness' and this undermines the valuing of and attention to 'differences'. Further, much of what goes under the name of policy and scholarly approaches towards diversity within family life is actually grounded in the assumptions of one dominant culture about others, which can often result in stereotyping, or lead to 'grandstanding' about the superiority of the principles proclaimed within one culture over those in others. Such an agonistic approach is not appropriate for a plural Europe of the present or the future.

In all areas of family law examined, there is a 'translation exercise' in more than one sense involved: first, there is the effort of knowing enough about the 'foreign' legal institution or rule in the context of the foreign legal system; and second there is the job of enabling the European court to understand the legal institution in terms that it is familiar with. Both processes create distortions. Further work needs to be devoted to working out an ethos within official legal systems so that each case can be examined on its own facts and its own micro-cultural context. Much more work therefore needs to be done about judging cases in diverse contexts with ease and effectiveness. Particular emphasis needs to be focused on judicial discretion and the possibility of judicial activism whereas, hitherto, legislation has often intervened as a brake on the kind of judicial creativity which may be required to respond to the requirements of diverse family contexts in Europe. When stating this, it is recognised that the dominant paradigm of judging within European legal systems is that of certainty within the framework of the rule of law, and what is called for here is nothing short of a paradigm shift which calls for empowerment of judges, enabling them to make context-relevant problem-solving decisions, rather than mere application of abstract principles.

Bibliography

Ameli, S.R., Faridi, B., Lindahl, K. and Merali, A. 2006. *Law and British Muslims: Domination of the Majority or Process of Balance?* London: Islamic Human Rights Commission.

Antokolskaia, M. 2003. The search for a common core of divorce: State intervention vs spouses' autonomy, in *The Role of Self-determination in the Modernisation of Family Law in Europe*, edited by M. Martín-Casals and J. Ribot. Girona: Documenta Universitaria, 33–58.

Antokolskaia, M. 2006. *Harmonisation of Family Law in Europe: A Historical Perspective: A Tale of Two Millennia*. Antwerp: Intersentia

Badawi, Z. 1995. Muslim justice in a secular state, in *God's Law versus State Law*, edited by M. King. London: Grey Seal, 73–80.

Bano, S. 2007. Muslim family justice and human rights: The experience of British Muslim women. *Journal of Comparative Law*, 2, 38–67.

Bano, S. 2012. *Muslim Women and Shari'ah Councils: Transcending the Boundaries of Community and Law*. Basingstoke: Palgrave Macmillan.

Bayır, D. 2013. *Minorities and Nationalism in Turkish Law*. Farnham: Ashgate.

Bayır, D. and Shah, P. 2012. The legal adaptation of British settlers in Turkey. *Transcultural Studies*, 1. [Online]. Available at: http://archiv.ub.uni-heidelberg.de/ojs/index.php/transcultural/article/view/9268 [last accessed 14 December 2013].

Bouillier, V. 2011. French law courts and South Asian litigants, in *Cultural Expertise and Litigation: Patterns, Conflicts, Narratives*, edited by L. Holden. London: Routledge, 53–70.

Bowen, J. 2010. How could English courts recognize Shariah? *University of St. Thomas Law Journal*, 7, 411–35.

Büchler, A. 2011. *Islamic Law in Europe? Legal Pluralism and its Limits in European Family Laws*. Farnham: Ashgate.

Bunting, A. 2009. Family law's legal pluralism: Private 'opting-out' in Canada and South Africa, in *Multijuralism: Manifestations, Causes, and Consequences*, edited by A. Breton, A. D. Ormeaux, K. Pistor and P. Salmon. Farnham: Ashgate, 77–97.

Douglas, G., Doe, N., Gilliat-Ray, S., Sandberg, R. and Khan A. 2011. *Social Cohesion and Civil Law: Marriage, Divorce and Religious Courts: Report of a Research Study Funded by the AHRC*. [Online: Cardiff: Cardiff Law School]. Available at: http://www.law.cf.ac.uk/clr/Social%20Cohesion%20and%20Civil%20Law%20Full%20Report.pdf [last accessed 14 December 2013].

Finestein, I. 1993. *Jewish Society in Victorian England*. London: Vallentine Mitchell.

Foblets, M.-C. 1994. Community justice amongst immigrant family members in France and Belgium, in *Law and Anthropology*, edited by K. Rene and R. Pötz. Dordrecht: Nijhoff, 371–85.

Fournier, P. 2010. *Muslim Marriage in Western Courts: Lost in Transplantation*. Farnham: Ashgate.

Freedman, J. 2004. *Immigration and Insecurity in France*. Aldershot: Ashgate.

Fulchiron, H. 2010. The French family judge encounters cultural pluralism, in *Cultural Diversity and the Law: State Responses from around the World*, edited by M.-C. Foblets, J.F. Gaudreault-DesBiens and A.D. Renteln. Brussels: Bruylant, 613–34.

Griffith-Jones, R. (ed.) 2013. *Islam and English Law: Rights, Responsibilities and the Role of Sharia*. Cambridge: Cambridge University Press.

Grillo, R., Ballard, R., Ferrari, A., Hoekema, A.J., Maussen, M. and Shah P. (eds) 2009. *Legal Practice and Cultural Diversity*. Farnham: Ashgate.

Herman, D. 2011. *An Unfortunate Coincidence: Jews, Jewishness, and English Law*. Oxford: Oxford University Press.

Holden, L. (ed.) 2011. *Cultural Expertise and Litigation: Patterns, Conflicts, Narratives*. London: Routledge.

Jhutti-Johal, J. 2013. How parties to Sikh marriages use and are influenced by the norms of their religion and culture when engaging with mediation, in *Managing Family Justice in Diverse Societies*, edited by M. Maclean and J. Eekelaar. Oxford: Hart, 203–220.

Karčić, F. 2008. The reform of Shari'a courts and Islamic law in Bosnia and Herzegovina, 1918–1941, in *Islam in Inter-War Europe*, edited by N. Clayer and E. Germain. London: Hurst and Co, 253–70.

Korteweg, A.C. and Selby J.A. (eds) 2012. *Debating Sharia: Islam, Gender Politics and Family Law Arbitration*. Toronto: University of Toronto Press.

Løvdal, L. 2011. *Mahr* and gender equality in private international law: The adjudication of *mahr* in England, France, Norway and Sweden, in *Embedding* mahr *(Islamic Dower) in the European Legal System*, edited by R. Mehdi and J.S. Nielsen. Copenhagen: DJØF, 77–112.

Macfarlane, J. 2012. *Islamic Divorce in North America: A Shari'a Path in a Secular Society*. Oxford: Oxford University Press.

Mehdi, R. and Nielsen J.S. (eds) 2011. *Embedding* mahr *(Islamic Dower) in the European Legal System*. Copenhagen: DJØF.

Menski, W.F. 2007. Dodgy Asians or dodgy laws? The story of H. *Journal of Immigration, Asylum and Nationality Law*, 21, 284–94.

Menski, W.F. 2011. Life and law: Advocacy and expert witnessing in the UK, in *Cultural Expertise and Litigation: Patterns, Conflicts, Narratives*, edited by L. Holden. London: Routledge, 151–71.

Menski, W.F. 2012a. Ancient and modern boundary crossings between personal laws and civil law in composite India, in *Marriage and Divorce in a Multicultural Context: Multi-tiered Marriage and the Boundaries of Civil Law and Religion*, edited by J.A. Nichols. New York: Cambridge University Press, 219–52.

Menski, W.F. 2012b. Punishing polygamy in multicultural Europe: Public prosecution policies and private problems. Paper delivered at the Workshop on Applied Legal Anthropology, Max Planck Institute for Social Anthropology, Halle, Germany, 13 September 2012.

Miller, R.A. 2000. The Ottoman and Islamic substratum of Turkey's Swiss Civil Code. *Journal of Islamic Studies*, 11(3), 335–61.

Nielsen, J.S. 1993. *Emerging Claims of Muslim Populations in Matters of Family Law in Europe*. Birmingham: Centre for the Study of Islam and Christian–Muslim Relations.

Pearl, D. and Menski, W. 1998. *Muslim Family Law*. London: Sweet and Maxwell.

Poulter, S.M. 1986. *English Law and Ethnic Minority Customs*. London: Butterworths.

Poulter, S.M. 1998. *Ethnicity, Law and Human Rights: The English Experience*. Oxford: Clarendon.

Raissiguier, C. 2010. *Reinventing the Republic: Gender, Migration, and Citizenship in France*. Stanford: Stanford University Press.

Rohe, M. 2007. *Muslim Minorities and the Law in Europe: Chances and Challenges*. New Delhi: Global Media Publications.

Schechter, R. 2003. *Obstinate Hebrews: Representations of Jews in France, 1715–1815*. Berkeley and Los Angeles, CA: University of California Press.

Schwarzfuchs, S. 1979. *Napoleon, the Jews and the Sanhedrin*. London: Routledge.

Shah, P. 2010. Between God and the Sultana? Legal pluralism in the British Muslim diaspora, in *Shari'a as Discourse: Legal Traditions and the Encounter with Europe*, edited by J.S. Nielsen and L. Christoffersen. Farnham: Ashgate, 117–39.

Shah, P. 2011. When South Asians marry trans-jurisdictionally: Some reflections on immigration cases by an 'expert', in *Cultural Expertise and Litigation: Patterns, Conflicts, Narratives*, edited by L. Holden. London: Routledge, 35–52.

Shah, P. 2013a. Transnational family relations in migration contexts: British variations on European themes, in *The Ashgate Research Companion to Migration Law, Theory and Policy*, edited by S.S. Juss. Farnham: Ashgate, 599–616.

Shah, P. 2013b. Judging Muslims, in *Islam and English Law: Rights, Responsibilities and the Role of Sharia*, edited by R. Griffith-Jones. Cambridge: Cambridge University Press.

Shah-Kazemi, S.N. 2001. *Untying the Knot: Muslim Women, Divorce and the Shariah*. London: Nuffield Foundation.

Strijbosch, F. and Foblets M.-C. (eds) 1999. *Relations familiales Interculturelles/Cross-cultural Family Relations*. Oñati papers no. 8. Oñati, Spain: International Institute for the Sociology of Law.

Tsitselikis, K. 2012. *Old and New Islam in Greece: From Historical Minorities to Immigrant Newcomers*. Leiden: Brill.

Vinding, N.V. and Christoffersen L. 2012. *Danish Regulation of Religion, State of Affairs and Qualitative Reflections: A Report on 20 Qualitative Elite Interviews*. [Online: Centre for European Islamic Thought, Faculty of Theology, University of Copenhagen]. Available at: http://www.teol.ku.dk/ceit/religare/Danish_WP7_report_10_05_2012.pdf [last accessed 14 December 2013].

Weyrauch, W.O. (ed.) 2001. *Gypsy Law: Romani Legal Tradition and Culture*. Berkeley, CA: University of California Press.

Williams, R., The Rt Revd 2008. *Civil and Religious Law in England: A Religious Perspective*. Speech given at the Royal Courts of Justice, 7 February 2008. [Online]. Available at: http://rowanwilliams.archbishopofcanterbury.org/articles.php/1137/archbishops-lecture-civil-and-religious-law-in-england-a-religious-perspective [last accessed 14 December 2013].

Witte, J. Jr and Nichols, J.A. 2010. Faith-based family laws in Western democracies? *Fides et Libertas: The Journal of the International Religious Liberty Association*, 122–35.

Witte, J. Jr 2012. *From Sacrament to Contract: Marriage, Religion, and Law in the Western Tradition*. Louisville, KY: Westminster John Knox Press.

Chapter 2

Plurality-Conscious Rebalancing of Family Law Regulation in Europe

Werner Menski

This chapter argues that the challenges of diversity management in post-modern Europe are now more visibly pushing us all to acknowledge that simplistic, state-centric methods of handling difference and diversity are no longer sufficient. Research shows how continuing reluctance to embrace pluralist methodologies for rebalancing family law regulation in Europe risks leading to deeply messy scenarios, in which states risk losing credibility, control and power, unless they learn to improve their handling of such complex new conflicts. Examples are given of how this subtle rebalancing may work, and what the reservations against such manipulation continue to be. At the end of the day, there seems to be no feasible way to avoid the pluralising challenges posed by the new super-diversities, which include legal pluralism. If states wish to keep control in such messy scenarios, they have to learn about 'the other' in the law itself. This chapter seeks to reassure nervous practitioners and politicians that plurality-consciousness is not a deadly disease, but a necessary tool to handle the growing challenges in today's world.

Pluralist Struggles in Legal Theorising

The main line of argument was indicated above. It still seems necessary though, on many occasions, to highlight the critical relevance of legal pluralism to our lives.[1] Ultimately, we assess here specifically how legal practice and state policy seem to be slowly shifting now in Europe into a more sophisticated plurality-conscious mode, specifically in handling 'ethnic' and religious differences. The synergies of the RELIGARE network,[2] the Halle MPI developments and several related initiatives and conferences[3] have been quite instrumental,

---

1 I dedicate this article to the memory of Professor Franz von Benda-Beckmann (1941–2013), whose sudden death on 7 January 2013, while I was drafting this article, deeply shook me, especially as we had just begun to work together more closely on the Halle Project (http://www.eth.mpg.de [last accessed 14 December 2013]). His wonderfully worded inaugural lecture at the University of Leipzig on 3 February 2004, given in German, so fittingly started with the words: 'We all live with law, whether we wish to or not. We are legal personalities'. Soon thereafter, he continued that, especially in the countries of the Third World, life involves living with legal pluralism, it is 'a life with several legal orders at the same time'. What more does one need to say? This profound statement clearly applies not only in Asia and Africa, but also among us in Europe.

2 On the background of RELIGARE, see specifically Foblets in Ferrari and Pastorelli (2012: 1–21) and http://www.religareproject.eu [last accessed 14 December 2013].

3 For Halle, see http://www.eth.mpg.de [last accessed 14 December 2013]; also *Recht als Kultur* in Bonn, http://www.recht-als-kultur.de [last accessed 14 December 2013], and the Uppsala Religion and Society Research Centre (CRS), with its focus on the impact of religion (2008–18), under http://www.crs.uu.se [last accessed 14 December 2013].

and many of these initiatives have involved judges from various jurisdictions. There have been some eye-opening events for those who are still able to listen and learn, for we are all under enormous pressure to relearn quite a few 'standard' types of knowledge as the world around us keeps changing.

I argue here that judges are maybe faster learners than academic participants in such conferences, especially academics who seem to lose the plot when pursuing political agendas or specific hobby horses. Overall, there is manifestly a real sense of progress now in bringing together theory and practice to achieve a deeper understanding of the processes involved in various related legal industries concerning the better management of normative and legal pluralities in multicultural Europe, and especially in the UK.

This challenge to navigate diversity and difference has been there all the time (see note 1), but the intensity of the pressures has probably become more evident. It is no longer simply possible – nor fiscally advisable in view of resource crunches throughout the Eurozone – to assume that complete, direct state control of all legal processes is the most suitable management strategy. States and their judiciaries are becoming more sophisticated in maintaining claims of state supervision and ultimate legal control, while devising numerous strategies and mechanisms to virtually 'let go' and in effect delegate the often arduous and costly task of settling messy disputes and sorting out doubts over precise socio-legal, financial and supervisory arrangements to informal dispute settlement mechanisms. There are disparities, but there is a clear trend in this direction. All along, state-centric arguments have accompanied this process, desperately claiming that formal legal supervision and control remain of utmost importance. However, doubts are surely in order whether such state-centric claims are always matched by lived reality and, more crucially, by due responsibility when states take on such onerous tasks.

Both in theory and practice, such contested pluralising developments undermine and challenge traditional state-centric assumptions and standard rule of law models. Hence there is much unease and discomfort, not to speak of uncertainty and doubt, about the direction in which these manifestly pluralising developments are now going. What wider consequences will result? Are we going to see *shari'a* law as law in the UK? Do we not have it already? Clearly, a lot depends on a – simply non-existent – agreement about the basic definition of 'law'! Bowen (2012: 54) observes that 'Europe is already a plural society' and reminds us of 'the emergence in Western Europe of the kind of social diversity that has long been a matter of pride in the United States' (Bowen 2012: 19). Highlighting 'social diversity', not legal pluralism, this seems to suggest that we get our assessment of the role of *shari'a* in this context wrong if we talk about legal pluralism. Instead, there is simply a disingenuous tendency of blaming Islam for our own confusions (Bowen 2012). While this most valuable analysis plays very cleverly with key words, most significantly, it does not tell us enough about the deeply contested meaning of 'law'.

As one of few people writing, long before the Archbishop of Canterbury spoke, that social plurality will result in a scenario of legal pluralism, I hold the position that pluralisation is inevitable if you invite migrants of different kinds to your shores. Elements of other normativity-related orders, not just social systems, will of necessity make themselves felt over time and demand more and more official, and hence legal, recognition and acknowledgement. It matters a lot how we handle such challenges. That one gets pilloried for such views is most obvious from how Rowan Williams, then Archbishop of

Canterbury, was treated by the press.[4] But Dr Williams has now been cited with approval in *AI v MT* [2013] EWHC 100 (Fam), reported while I was completing this chapter. A familiar academic dilemma arose: should I build this new case into the analysis? I could not resist, for this perfectly confirms what I was going to argue anyway.

It was evident long before *AI v MT* [2013] EWHC 100 (Fam) that examination of recent semi-hidden developments in the interface of public/private and formal/informal legal regulation benefits from wider theoretical enquiry. This may be perceived as redundant and repetitive, since we know so much about legal theory. Yet legal theory, too, remains a highly dynamic field, full of conflicts and contradictions, unsurprising as the meaning of 'law' itself remains contested. Presently, both theory and practice are recalculating their paths and approaches, partly adjusting their methodologies and underlying presumptions. This confirms law as a living entity, subject to changes in time, place, context and supervening agenda, highly dynamic and constantly 'on the move'. This scenario may remind us of the stern voice of the invisible satnav lady, who gives directions and speaks up when we change the direction of our car journey, and then justifies her temporary silence by announcing the process of 'recalculating'. Presently, we are recalculating how to assess various key factors in the socio-cultural and legal environments around us when it comes to accounting for ethnic minorities' presence and diverse legal orders.

I was planning to discuss earlier cases and their semi-hidden implications on the gradual pluralisation of English domestic law, mainly related to family law. Islamic finance law is, of course, part of English law in the new millennium – England did co-opt Islamic norms as law because failure to do so would damage our financial self-interest and standing. There seemed no progress at all in other fields, only bad politicking, while some of the most relevant cases remained unreported. *AI v MT* [2013] EWHC 100 (Fam) now clearly brings out that the judges of England and Wales actually know well what they are doing when they accept certain decisions made outside their courtrooms and build them into the formal structures of the national legal system. Earlier decisions gave away growing awareness of the fuzzy boundaries between official and unofficial laws and highlighted the existence of quite different normativity-related systems displayed before judges. I write 'normative systems', as the definition of law remains, as noted, deeply contested. We tend to forget this, though, and always slip back into positivism-centric presumptions that are just partial theorising, at best, if we care to think more deeply.

Such observations indicate that the ongoing journey of law is, like *shari'a*, the following of a path. Whether this gets us to the right destination is a different matter. I maintain, though, that a more suitable image for legal development is the silent flight of a kite in the air. I have proposed and suggested this in the past few years to explore the finer details of such processes of skilful legal navigation, everywhere an inevitable part of life.[5] Judges, as the most directly involved decision-makers in such potentially dangerous navigations, seem to be acutely aware now of their huge responsibilities as navigators in this virtually limitless sky. This could be because members of the judiciary attended recent academic conferences – perhaps we may even claim 'impact', a prized element craved for in British academia these days. Remarkably, though, many legal scholars continue to struggle with

---

4 This Foundation Lecture was delivered on 7 February 2008. See Williams, R. (2008) 'Civil and religious law in England: A religious perspective', *The Guardian*, 7 February 2008. See http://www.guardian.co.uk/uk/2008/feb/07/religion.world2 [last accessed 14 December 2013] and Williams (2008).

5 On the kite image, see various recent articles of mine in the references.

acknowledging that law and life are as closely related as they manifestly are. Academics often seem light years behind the judiciary (and some excellent practising lawyers, by the way) in terms of awareness of the absolutely critical role of plurality-consciousness in decision-making.

The Key Element of Religion in Relation to Law

Faced with the manifest pluralities of life, one is really saying nothing new today if one observes that the categories of analysis and practice are now including more specific attention to matters of religion, often prominently in connection to Islam and Muslims (Joly 2012). This goes also for relations to law. We should not forget that Glenn (2000: 47) observed that 'there are a number of globalizations going on. It is not just the spread of western technology, open markets and human rights. There is also, for example, globalization in the form of islamization'. Unsurprisingly, there is now a virtual global war of competing convictions, though hardly a new phenomenon (Menski 2010a). Today, as soon as one opens the computer, reams of newsprint scream about the urgent need to ban religion of all kinds, and to protect 'our' heritage against invasions of ideological and cultural bugs eating away at the most basic foundations of human progress. Similarly aggressive culture wars are presently witnessed, prominently in Britain itself, over the extent of formal recognition of different sexualities and various gender-based marriage-like arrangements.

Compared to this, recent census news that Polish is now the second most prominent language in the UK, as it is in Norway (Friberg 2012), Ireland (Krings et al. 2013) and maybe elsewhere by now, does not lead to aggressive hate mail, but nicely phrased comments about assimilative strategies by Eastern European migrants. One wonders what people make of information that the next prominent languages in Britain remain Punjabi, Urdu, Gujarati and Bengali, apart from French. Do we register that these 'others' probably do not just speak different languages? They may also organise their lives largely 'on their own terms' (Ballard 2007 [1994]). As we are increasingly superdiverse now (Vertovec 2007), in more and more parts of the Eurozone, concurrently global and local, hence glocal, to presume that Poles and other East Europeans just blend into new environments without deeper changes, maybe even invisible legal implications, seems unwarranted. Much relevant research simply does not exist yet.[6] Specific glocal patterns everywhere challenge academic analysts by their complexities, upsetting presumed standard perceptions of how the world of law should develop. While we all react to various aspects of this increasing diversity in different ways, questions about whether to privilege legal assimilation or diversification remain heavily contested. The basic view that once you come to 'my country', you should also follow 'my law' remains strong everywhere, judging by innumerable bloggers' comments on various issues and the hate mail I get myself.

But this does not reflect people's real lives as plural legal personalities. The RELIGARE project clearly identified that different forms of Christianity dominate specific European jurisdictions. Nothing is really 'neutral'; there is no escape from such conclusions. Various traditional forms of natural law are now rediscovered in deeply stressful relationships with state laws, competing also with 'new' forms of natural law (Menski 2006: 168–73), prominently human rights jurisprudence. Different European states have chosen specific

---

6 See now Bayır and Shah (2012) on British migrants in Turkey.

methods to incorporate such new expectations into their jurisprudence, generating sometimes quite specific turbulences over identity formation and multicultural management.

Various manifestations of fears about loss of 'our' identity as somewhat unsurprising outcomes are reflected today when politicians and other public figures, who may need the bloggers' votes, go public. Selected scaremongering and targeted stirring of emotions is strategic, so easy, and frequently indulged in,[7] assisted not only by an often self-interested press with an eye on circulation figures, but by science in various names. Social science in this context may appear relatively enlightened and harmless. However, every conflict now offers the potential to be milked to exhaustion.[8] It has become an 'amplified industry' (Bowen 2012: x) not only in relation to Muslims and MILLI,[9] as Ralph Grillo (2012: 204–5) perceptively notes. Much recent writing on this growth industry produced a rich bibliography,[10] but do not expect to find emerging consensus on more than that we live in 'interesting', contest-ridden times and that there is growing diversity all around us, raising the temperatures of the multiple boiling cauldrons of contests.

Cool, calm analysis becomes difficult in a climate of nervousness about the manifest resurgence of religion (in effect natural law principles), in our era of post-positivistic legal rationality, now with strong human-rights-centred orientation. This reshifting of balances within the kite structure of law still far too often leaves out acknowledgement that social norms are also an ancient well-known form of law that cannot just be brushed aside. The kite model of law explicitly recognises the four key elements of that subtle structure: natural law/ethics/morality, and thus prominently psychology in corner 1 at the top, social norms (including economic considerations) in corner 2 at the right, state laws and politics in corner 3 at the left, and human rights and international norms/laws, and thus also international relations, at the bottom in corner 4.[11] That these four corners represent different perceptions and incorporate quite varied academic disciplines in evidently law-related discourses is further spelt out here to achieve more clarity: corner 1 concerns interconnected individuals and their handling of philosophy, ethics/religion and psychology; it thus also highlights law-related strains over the scope for autonomous, individualised perceptions and perspectives. Corner 2 is more the societal level of such perceptions and perspectives, and incorporates a rich variety of internally diverse norm systems based on socio-legal processes, economic arrangements and cultural influences in their widest sense. Corner 3 concerns everything related to politics and the state, but is much more than classic positivist law. Importantly, it includes even those religious and social norms (elements originating in corners 1 and 2 respectively) which have been accepted and co-opted by state law

---

7   Significant examples are the speeches by the leaders of Germany, the UK and France on multiculturalism in 2010/11, picked up by Bowen (2012: 17–18), who seeks to provide some intellectual correctives. See also Joly (2012: 484).

8   Most recent examples from the UK include the tracing of horsemeat in beefburgers, which then boosts arguments against consumption of any red meat, and DNA traces of pork found in supposedly *halal* prison food, which then justifies claims to abolish provisions allowing *halal* meat altogether. All along, evidence of growing numbers of migrants in our midst, not to mention Muslims, allegedly engaged in various 'forced' practices, has never lost momentum as a catalyst of legal reforms widely sold as recipes for making the world a better place.

9   This clever acronym stands for 'Muslims, Islam and the Law, a Legal Industry'. Remarkably, Professor Grillo came to law late in life, in fact post-retirement, and is thus able to maintain a healthy distance to its shenanigans and inflated claims.

10 The most recent additions are Bowen (2012), Bano (2012), Mehdi, Menski and Nielsen (2012) and Sonneveld (2012).

11 For further details, see Menski (2012b: 181 and 2013: 26).

(Chiba 1986). Corner 4, highly visible and prominent today, comprises everything related to global and international dimensions. It concerns international relations, and underpins the 'new natural law' (Menski 2006: 168–73), which now fiercely clashes with corner 1. Readers should appreciate one further highly relevant dimension of this kite image, namely that all these four corners coexist. One type of law has not replaced or substituted the other; their competition has simply become more intense. To cut out any of these corners, denying it the right to a voice in the chorus of legal pluralism, will be perceived as violence, not to say terrorism.

Decision-making processes, we realise with increasing clarity, start with the actor's positioning from within a particular angle of the kite, then moving to other kite corners. What one likes least comes last, but cannot be cut off completely, since to eliminate a whole corner would make the whole structure crash. This is how judges decide, as *AI v MT* [2013] EWHC 100 (Fam) now confirms: the state-centred judge in corner 3 considers first corner 4, basic human rights like the best interests of the child, and then notes that corner 2, the extended Jewish families, were deeply involved in the navigational process. Corner 1, within the secular context of modern state law, certainly comes last. It is not outlawed, however, but subtly incorporated. Positioned close to corner 3 of the kite, judges act as highly skilful navigators, evidently much more alert to underlying theories than many legal scholars. The RELIGARE events with judges from various jurisdictions confirmed impressively that professional decision-makers simply cannot sit on the fence on such highly contested issues. Professional ethics mean they may not talk much about this. Silence, we learn again, does not signify ignorance or lack of understanding; it is strategic.

So 'religion' has definitely come back into the field of law, which sought to expel it on well-argued policy grounds, while facing similar problems about how to handle ethics and morality as alternative law-related entities. This development is now strongly reflected in a virtual avalanche of new publications on religion and law (see Ferrari and Cristofori 2010; Ferrari and Pastorelli 2012), on the public/private navigation of fuzzy boundaries (Bhamra 2011) and also specifically on Muslims and Islamic law (e.g. Büchler 2011). This healthy situation shows that activist publishing on pluralism is now possible in Europe, unlike some places in the world that steadfastly refuse to discuss such issues of crucial national importance in barely disguised efforts to protect fictions of scholarly progressiveness.[12] Now also in North America, significant new initiatives elaborate and update existing studies on legal and other pluralisms, recalculating how to deal with conflict situations.[13]

Academic discussions among social scientists, in particular, seem to lag behind the activism now identifiable in the Eurozone's increasingly plurality-conscious legal networks and courtrooms. Introducing a recent Special Issue, Brubaker (2013: 1) notes 'the surge of interest in religion on the part of students of ethnicity, race and nationalism' and finds this a striking trend. Scholars working on legal pluralism, especially through the RELIGARE project, probably no longer bat an eyelid. Many social scientists, however, continue to perceive law merely as state law and remain oblivious of intense legal debates about growing pluralisation. Regarding Muslims, awareness of different types of Muslims everywhere is hardly new in the twenty-first century, though there is continued need for better analysis.

---

12 Surprisingly, on Indian family law, see Parashar and Dhanda (2008), critiqued by Menski (2010b). Signs of progress are seen in Huda (2011) on Bangladesh.

13 On America, the network of scholars around John Witte at Emory has been most active (see now Nichols 2012); earlier see Estin (2008).

Social scientists do know that various identification processes are going on at the same time and compete with each other, especially in diaspora (Knott and McLoughlin 2010). Such processes are also known from numerous studies of 'ethnicity', a term which itself, like religion, became a dirty word for many scholars, while for others it constitutes the foundation for critical reflections on skilful cultural navigation (Ballard 2007 [1994]).

So we know quite well today that '[t]he interplay between self-identification and other-identification is not simply an interplay between Muslims and non-Muslims; it is also an interplay among Muslims themselves' (Brubaker 2013: 3). That such interplay between self-identification and other-identification will change the quality of self-identification as a Muslim is, one might uncharitably say, equally trivial today. So what is the point of restating the reality of pluralism? Brubaker (2013: 6) explains:

> My argument is not about what categories we should use; it is about how we should use them. We may have no good alternative to using analytical categories that are heavily loaded and deeply contested categories of practice; but as scholars we can and should adopt a critical and self-reflexive stance towards our categories. This means, most obviously, emphasizing that 'Muslims' designates not a homogenous and solidary *group* but a heterogenous *category*. Beyond this, and more substantively, it means focusing on the changing ways in which the category 'Muslims' works, both as a category of analysis and as a category of self- and other-identification in practice.

Such well-worded academic fine-tuning of what I now call 'pop', the plurality of pluralities all around us, reminds us again of the satnav lady's recalculating announcement. How long are we going to struggle with laborious differentiations before we arrive at the destination? Do we really not know, or do we not want to know?[14]

More Pluralities and Turbulences

The closely connected, parallel misconception that custom is not (or should not be) law, and simply does not exist anymore in modern jurisdictions, also turns out to be make-believe, delusion or *maya*, as the ancient Indians called it, just a pious hope. We learn again – whether we call this postmodernity or not seems irrelevant – that law remains in lived reality internally plural and dynamically capable of growth. State law, if it wishes to control such developments, is simply forced to engage with such competing elements of its own other. It should particularly account for the socio-cultural needs of individuals and whole communities to avoid massive evasive action through people's informal arrangements beyond the radar of state law. Individuals and communities in kite corner 2 retain the agency to bypass state law. As one cannot jail everyone who resorts to informal arrangements, it seems increasingly recognised today that delegation of many tasks to informal processes is actually sustainable and cost-effective.[15]

---

14 See Menski (2011). More evidence of academic obfuscation strategies is found in Knop, Michaels and Riles (2012: 651).

15 Many Southern legal systems know this very well, leading to the observations recorded in note 1 above.

If state law wants to lead and retain control, it must exercise its functions responsibly and, as recent discussions on the Pluri-Legal Network identified, intelligently.[16] The simplistic vision that one can outlaw 'religion' or 'social norms' is just positivist 'baloney', as Bowen (2012: 51) puts it, quite passé now, but also evidence of 'the persistent racism that plagues the continent' (Bowen 2012: 53). Notably, in today's world we would not find it politically correct to outlaw human rights concerns in the same way as we treat some ethnic minority customs. Why and how did so many scholars follow the pied pipers who whistled the tempting, still audible tunes of state-centricity and its shriller tones of legal centralism?

Becoming wiser, we realise not only that we are all pluralists today, as David Nelken famously suggested a while ago. Somehow, we have to become still more plurality-conscious, whether we like it or not, if we want to cultivate the ultimate aim of justice. Achievement of justice, like enlightenment, remains an arduous process, a desirable aim, not a guaranteed fact. However, plurality-conscious analysts who express their convictions about the need to listen to a range of plural voices face grave penalties, as the Archbishop of Canterbury found out (see note 4 above). Pope Benedict and Jürgen Habermas engaged in discussions about such issues at the start of the twenty-first century, too, only to be reviled by many commentators (see Habermas 2006). I would have much to say on this myself. The pluralist *madhab* that Prakash Shah (2005: 357) finds established in London, followed now by innumerable scholars and students all around the world, remains evidently an irritant to legal scholars who do not share a plurality-conscious perspective. It seems that arguing for legal pluralism is still often portrayed today as fuzzy-headed confusion-mongering or, worse, a devious attempt to deny the critical importance of basic human rights, the widely accepted dominant expectation of our day and age.

Worrying reflections of fierce power struggles in academia arise, with many young scholars seeking guidance on how to navigate such roadblocks of political correctness, recalculating their routes to sharing insights about the potential for pluralist navigation without endangering their future prospects and careers. Such evidence makes it necessary to assert here that activist engagement in pluralist analysis by academics cannot be portrayed as an automatic contradiction of basic human rights. These, too, are outdated thought patterns now (Shah 2007).

While I am getting tired of repeatedly using the kite image to analyse legal management, we observe presently much rebalancing of kites, yet again, to ensure safer journeys and avoid violent crashes, especially in matters of family law, often a battleground for ideology, a borderland between private and public law in the global Bukovina (Hertogh 2009). In the search for 'the right law' in such contested arenas, to be told that pluralism theory is 'too loose' is quite understandable from the perspective of those who prefer (or simply have been taught) to see law as a strong tool of control.[17] However, such perspectives ignore the fact that legal centralism, as an extreme form of state centrality of law, is not only a fiction (Griffiths 1986), but suffers from the potentially fatal virus of circularity: if law simply becomes what a strongman (or the state) says it is, we are thrown back to risking most terrible abuses. While no German can ever brush this issue off completely, current events in the Middle East and Northern Africa confirm that the search for pluralist solutions in various

---

16 The link for this is PLURI-LEGAL@JISCMAIL.AC.UK, and the anchor is Dr. Prakash Shah (at prakash.shah@qmul.ac.uk).

17 Notably, this objection was still raised at the legal pluralism conference in Cape Town in autumn 2011.

respects is extremely hard, but essential for progress. There is no room for complacency: tragic injustices happen also in European courtrooms, mostly behind closed doors.

To be faced with comments that pluralistic theorising is 'partial theorising' simply shows that the commentator makes a political statement and fails to understand what pluralist methodology seeks to achieve. Pluralist reasoning is exactly opposing various forms of partial theorising by showing the connectivities of the many law-related elements – indeed the different types of law – involved in the kite's journey. It seems now that pluralist methodology, as a strong metatheory, upsets certain types of political correctness and risks being misunderstood and deviously misrepresented as making aggressively exaggerated and inflated moral claims to superiority and normative upper caste status. This of course challenges legal positivist claims that the state alone, on our behalf, must retain authority and ultimate discretion for decision-making. We saw that this is merely quite partial theorising. Moreover, since we cannot be sure that states exercise their prerogatives responsibly and intelligently, it appears that state bureaucracies – just like human rights rationalities and various connected entities – must also remain accountable to higher forms of justice. Critical analysis cannot merely be directed at religions and customs, corners 1 and 2 of the kite; all kite elements must be open to scrutiny.

However, opponents of pluralist methodology find themselves justified in using various devious rhetorical devices to support plainly partial theorising. The simple statement that law is internally plural is turned on its head by insinuating that the speaker is a nihilist or an unconstructive anarchist, whose fuzzy mind prevents clarity and legal certainty. But when cherished legal certainty results in manifest illegality, as it would have done in the highly significant case of Mrs Bath before the English courts, this needs to be challenged, and equitable solutions must result.[18] Otherwise we are simply thrown back to the Hitler problem of law's circularity, which manifestly the world has not completely overcome. This pungent issue needs to be scrutinised more intensely if legal scholarship wants to match the increasingly impressive achievements of judicial activism worldwide in recognising various forms of legal pluralism. Instead, so-called progressive scholars, positivists at heart, quite like their famous predecessor Hart, tend to hide behind smokescreens of officialdom and obfuscate enlightenment when it comes to plurality-conscious analysis.

Of course, a 'pure' legal positivist will *per definitionem* only wish to grant the coveted title of 'law' to state law. But how long will we go on arguing that this is appropriate legal methodology in today's globalising and increasingly interconnected world? It is indeed tiresome. It might admittedly generate well-worded intellectual debates, virtually deifying Hart and Kelsen and other intelligent theorists, as happens so prominently in Indian law schools. However, such sterile exercises in a putatively value-neutral intellectual playground devoid of morality and anxious to avoid reference to any conviction, as this supposedly pollutes 'pure' legal debates, have become almost pointless. Such exercises may have pedagogical skills-related value, but waste much precious time, better spent on other forms of legal education.

---

18   This case confirms that courts, but not even specialist family law scholars, are able to generate 'the right law'. In *Chief Adjudication Officer v Kirpal Kaur Bath* [2000] 1 FLR 8 CA, a feisty Sikh widow, party to an unregistered Sikh marriage in London in 1956, forced the Court of Appeal to apply a presumption of marriage in her specific scenario, more than 40 years later, as to deny her a widow's pension would have been blatant injustice. Significantly, this case is not treated as a precedent, as to do so would challenge the predominance claims of English marriage law, which demands formal registration of marriages conducted in England and Wales as a basis for legal validity.

If 'law' is indeed everywhere situation-specific and differs from place to place, over time and depending on who is involved in a specific scenario, it should be almost axiomatic to acknowledge, argue and teach that legal pluralism is all around us. Uncomfortable questions arise whether much law teaching has actually lost its sensitivity to common sense and has strayed too far into indoctrination or devious induction for legal industries that thrive on bureaucratisation, complexity and much skullduggery. Even if this may be a harsh assessment, how do we manage to pull ourselves out of the collective black hole of excessive worship of positivist law and precedent to recover sensitivity to situation-specific justice? The most interesting aspect of teaching about precedent might become how to get around precedents, cultivating awareness of scenarios in which strict adherence to *stare decisis* would lead to injustice. This is not deviousness. Learning to be critical and to question the status quo does not produce confused law students or wishy-washy pluralists for whom anything goes, but empowers them to become better lawyers. That such skills may be abused is neither here nor there.

My key argument remains, then, that legal management is almost everywhere a pluralistic endeavour. Law needs non-legal or so-called 'extra-legal' assistance to become 'good law', or 'the right law' (Menski 2006: 133–4), as the German jurist Rudolf Stammler (1856–1938), forgotten by most lawyers today, found in a different age of legal scholarship. That perceptions of the right law constantly change confirms that law is everywhere situation-specific and dynamic. Refusing or failing to study or teach law as a context-sensitive interdisciplinary discipline thus offers only half-baked methodologically deficient education, which often conflates the critical difference between 'is' and 'ought'.[19] How to break this deadlock of deficient doctrinal dependency and instruction may well be the million-dollar question for legal education management. That, however, is not the focus of the present chapter. We need to turn now to less depressing evidence, namely academic discussions that suggest solutions and actual case samples, to assess what kinds of progress have been made, mainly in Britain, to handle the challenges of pluralist legal navigation.

Evidence of Progress

There is now indeed much activist scholarship that challenges and interrogates state-centric myopia. Amien (2010) persuasively discusses the heavily contested issue of the long overdue formal recognition of Muslim law in South Africa. What she calls GNI, Gender-Nuanced Integration, constitutes a viable methodology to enhance women's human rights claims, which are never simple to assess (see also Howard 2012). Using different images, pluralist scholarship seems to express common concerns, while scholars devise their own terminology and memorable catchphrases. In Canada, reflections on new modes of managing inclusive citizenship and governance generated the notion of 'joint governance' (Shachar 2005: 87). Rethinking the boundaries of state-sponsored accommodation of diversity then leads to warnings about 'privatizing diversity' (Shachar 2008). When Shachar (2008: 577) refers to 'embedded individuals' she comes pretty close to identifying that there are four elephants in the room of law, or roaming in the global Bukovina (Hertogh 2009), just as there are four corners of the kite of law. More recently, Maleiha Malik (2012) perceptively recommends deeper analysis of 'cultural voluntarism' as a technique to avoid parallel legal systems. *AI v*

---

19   Notably, Habermas (2006: 13) argues that '[e]very "ought" presupposes a "can"'.

MT [2013] EWHC 100 (Fam) now confirms that we need sensible and somewhat altruistic state agents to manage such plural scenarios.

Another concept debated in RELIGARE proceedings brought significant advances in understanding. Matthias Rohe's 'open hierarchical system' seemed at first another example of deliberately positivist Eurocentric myopia when it elegantly argued against the notion of legal pluralism as a kind of superfluous irritant. While Rohe's model admits the presence of multiple normativities, it reserves the label 'law' to state law. This approach, rehearsed in the 2011 Erlangen RELIGARE conference, portrays the German post-war Constitution as an excellent example of positive law. It is good law because, having learnt from history, it assiduously takes account of various values and ethics, accounts for local people's social norms through the strong federal system and, of course, respects human rights and international law (see Menski 2013: 29).

The hidden message, however, is quite Hartian in effect: good state law actually needs these legal 'others', whatever we call them, to generate 'the right law'. Good governance critically depends on intricate pluralist navigation; it becomes a matter of justice-conscious public interest, not merely self-protection of 'law'. The Erlangen conference confirmed the futility of engaging in polemics over nomenclature. It was agreed that given the multiplicity of interacting entities, normative pluralism was a fact. Hence legal pluralism was impliedly accepted to a certain extent. The boundary was drawn with the familiar expectation of good governance, based on ultimate state control and supervision. What we did not address in that conference was what should happen if a state or its institutions make wrong decisions. That issue swiftly came up in recent discussions about the proposed ban on male circumcision in Germany, which focused the mind on state responsibility and the need for plurality-consciousness. The rest is indeed rhetoric.

In retrospect, the RELIGARE seminars brought out that some rapprochement can be reached between maintaining a positivistic emphasis and altruistic plurality-conscious perspectives. Rohe's 'open hierarchy' model is constructive and positive. The key question becomes to what extent states will be able and willing to listen to other claimants' voices. Just banning discordant voices goes too far, subjecting them to intelligent scrutiny seems the way forward. Such plurality-conscious approaches may make constructive integration of a legal 'other' more digestible to state-centric secular legal systems that are otherwise prone to simply disregarding or overlooking minority claims of various kinds, treating them as 'extra-legal'. The law-related others, namely values/ethics/religions, social norms and international law and human rights principles, are given a voice, but each have to prove their capacity to deliver and strengthen just outcomes. As the recent circumcision debates confirmed, a state law that blocks reason, forgets history and fails to listen to the voices of 'others' loses credibility very fast.

There is indeed, then, a price to pay in this open yet hierarchical arrangement. Somewhat indirect formal legal recognition of the legal 'other' means that this other type of law will then also claim some recognition as a form of 'law'. This particular problem of fuzziness will never go away. Assessments depend on different perspectives and convictions, as a religiously committed individual or community may well perceive that it, rather than state authorities, is the dominant element in any pluralist navigation. This confirms that the starting point in the sequencing of decision-making processes involving kite corners is a crucial aspect. Power struggles over this can be anticipated, but if everyone concerned is willing to cooperate with the 'other' in a spirit of constructive altruism, viable multilevel solutions may indeed be found. Toleration of the other may be secured as long as none of the four corners is completely cut out – one simply keeps the least liked last.

While problems of legal navigation are everywhere multiplied for communities and individuals who are not part of the mainstream of a specific national legal culture, the extent of involvement in negotiations of boundaries and cross-boundary cooperation clearly also depends on available resources. Most people of any national or ethnic background, including members of majorities, simply cannot afford protracted litigation and international litigation tourism, often connected to multijurisdictional arbitration mechanisms as witnessed again so impressively in *AI v MT* [2013] EWHC 100 (Fam). Less advantaged people faced with legal problems are simply left without assistance in clarifying fine points of legal navigation. They are regularly forced to 'lump it', even rudely told not to bother courts (Menski 2007a). Legal systems today struggle with plurality-conscious recognition of less resourceful claimants because expectations and benchmarks about the extent of non-formal navigations have been raised to completely unrealistic levels for people of moderate means. Those levels also seem higher for certain minorities than others.

A significant reflection of such socio-economic imbalances is that major textbooks on family law tell us much about so-called 'big money cases',[20] but leave researchers, lawyers and the public almost clueless about smaller claims that still have the potential to harm people's lives and ruin the mental peace of whole extended families, even communities. Some litigants will bring fake cases, or may be exploited by ruthless lawyers attracted by extra easy fees, even for hopeless cases. When devious claims are put forward, just to harass others and/or to make extra profit, bad legal developments may easily result.

To illustrate this, imagine that in the unreported case of *Ali v Ali* (Menski 2002, see also further below), the devious husband might have escaped from the liability to pay the agreed *mahr* of £30,001 to his divorced wife if the judge had not had expert guidance. The intelligent decision to make the husband pay £30,000, the claimed sum minus one symbolic pound, clearly avoided lurking conflict scenarios and served as guidance for subsequent *mahr* cases. It meant that a Muslim husband cannot simply avoid Islamic contractual obligations because he is now in England, before an English court. My interpretation of this case suggests that the learned Judge knew exactly what he was doing when he gave the wife one pound less than stipulated in the *mahr* contract (Menski 2002). Notably that case was not reported.

In retrospect, this important decision appears like a critical building block in current judicial strategies to take more explicit account of ethnic minority facts. The case probably tested the waters. It also shows how much the fate of legal development, or lack of it, depends on litigation tricksters and *mala fide* actions and petitions, which need to be stopped in their tracks by alert interventions. *AI v MT* [2013] EWHC 100 (Fam) gave rise to much scrutiny, but was ultimately found an agreeable case for pluralist compromise. All participants had, albeit with difficulty, engaged in protracted informal negotiations to reach agreeable settlements.

Such plurality-conscious decisions indicate that basic fears of the polluting effects of legal pluralism can be overcome in the interest of better governance and development of best practice. Shachar (2008: 577) observes that the multiplicity of affiliations needs to be built into formal adjudication processes, as not to do so 'misses the mark for these embedded individuals'. I could not agree more, but am not convinced that courts are always so open-minded. However, if states simply look the other way in such scenarios, they are effectively letting down the most vulnerable participants in these potentially violent struggles over

---

20 More recent writing focuses on landmark cases such as *Radmacher v Granatino* (2010) UKSC 42. See, to a lesser extent, *Uddin v Choudhury* (2009) EWCA 1205 (Civ).

resources, involving also ownership of the label 'law'. It is precisely when the best interests of children and the legitimate claims of divorced and otherwise disadvantaged women are concerned that our courts are called upon to take action, to protect basic rights rather than the positivist concept of law. Shachar (2005: 86) asks in this context for acknowledgement 'that individuals may perceive themselves as authors and subjects of more than one legal and cultural system'. State-sponsored legal activism should thus be open-minded towards 'joint governance' (Shachar, 2005: 87), quite altruistic in pluralist scenarios, even to the extent of partly renouncing its own superiority claims. This was clearly done in the *Bath* case (see note 18), where this does not mean irresponsible opening of floodgates, or pluralist messiness, but brings significant advances in situation-specific justice, indeed progressing from case to case.

The Cases

While legal scholarship remains dominated by modernist paradigms of state-centric positivism, judges in England and Wales (and elsewhere) have increasingly faced tricky pluralist legal scenarios in their courtrooms. Being put on the spot in terms of decision-making, they have evidently become more alert to the resulting challenges than most academics. Additionally, judges have sought help from experts on specific jurisdictions or areas of expertise, a well-established method especially in English law (Holden 2011), but also by attending seminars on pluralism.

State-centric perspectives suggest that the state and its agents, ultimately judges, should hold the strings of the kite of law, supervise and manage the recalculation of navigational tools and also oversee (and thus control) any actions to publicise these balancing acts. It is well-known, however, that most cases do not get published and that most civil law cases tend to be cryptic. Hence one sometimes wonders whether there is something to hide or whether the shadows of the law hide also its own practices. In pluralist legal scenarios, too, some state authority should officially have the final say. The state-centric Eurozone's presumptions of 'one law for all' (Menski 2007b: 254), a prominent consequence of modernist nationalism, treats this as axiomatic. As David Nelken (in Hertogh 2009: 240) rightly observes, '[t]he state may not dictate everyday life, but its importance should never be underestimated'. However, there are indeed significant limits to state authority (see note 1).

In most European jurisdictions, there is significant room for discretion and making certain targeted exceptions. When transnational disputes arise, a national legal system may be bound by what another state has accepted as law. In such contexts, the standard management tool of classical conflict of laws methodology or private international law requires states and state authorities as partners in various legal matching exercises. This methodology does not always work, however, specifically if Muslim law and Jewish law are presented as religious legal systems (Shachar 2008: 593). There is increasing evidence today that the laws of another state are found deficient in securing justice. Some English cases have been remarkably aggressive in rejecting other systems of law.[21]

Decision-making is often extremely difficult, and different legal cultures and wider policy concerns may be involved. When expert evidence is involved, some case scenarios

---

21 A particularly unpleasant example is *Chaudhary v Chaudhary* [1984] 3 All ER 1017, which speaks of 'jungle law'.

involve head-on clashes of basic concepts, such as consent to marriage, the best interests of a child, immigration concerns, and the extent of state responsibility for vulnerable adults. In one extremely difficult case,[22] a severely autistic Bangladeshi male, aged 25 years with a mental age of three, had been married over the phone to a cousin in Bangladesh. The legal validity of this marriage was challenged on several grounds by various state agents. Islamic law permits such marriages and treats them as legally valid, basically as family-based care arrangements for individuals who would otherwise be stranded. Under a modern state's social welfare system, state claims to supervening control were bound to arise. Lord Justice Thorpe thus held that '[t]he role of marriage in the life of one so handicapped is inconceivable in our society. Furthermore as a matter of law marriage is precluded. IC lacks the fundamental capacity to marry. However the marriage is not precluded in Bangladesh'.

This clearly identifies the huge conflict, justifies the judiciary as state agent to hold the marriage void under English law, but also refuses to acknowledge the family's arrangements for the presumed best interests of this vulnerable child. Obviously the family was unhappy with that decision. Judicial navigation of this problematic case started from kite corner 3 and then incorporated corner 4 through the best interests of the child principle. Somewhat reluctant acceptance of the Islamic legal position acknowledged kite corner 1, but in the judges' eyes, this case scenario failed the public policy test. That the family concerned had apparently made a skilfully negotiated private care arrangement for their severely disabled son by finding a cousin to join the family from Bangladesh, thus using kite corner 2, did not persuade the Court. The case has to be viewed in the wider context of deeply problematic evidence about the negative effects of cross-cousin marriages among Asians (Hasan 2009). Accepting this marriage as legally valid would surely have given wrong signals to a whole community. Yet the refusal also left this troubling scenario and a simmering conflict legally unresolved.

The cases selected for brief discussion here demonstrate that the process of skilful judicial navigation and experimentation with the limits of pluralism has been going on longer and much more intensely than we realise or are officially told. However, at earlier stages, even in *Ali v Ali* in 2000 (Menski 2002), as indicated above, nervousness about accepting the legal 'other' prevented an opening up of the legal arena to explicit pluralist navigation.[23] In *Ali v Ali* (typically unreported), the 'case of the missing pound', a dower of £30,001 had been agreed for a Bangladeshi Muslim marriage contracted in London, both under *shari'a* and in English law. When this marriage soon broke down, the husband's instant *talaq* divorce was followed by his English divorce proceedings. However, since he refused to pay the *mahr*, claiming this was merely a 'cultural' and not a 'legal' matter, the wife cross-petitioned and asked the English court for an order to secure her *mahr*. The Judge held that the wife should be paid £30,000, not £30,001, which would have meant recognising the Muslim law contract. If the wife had been denied *mahr*, she would surely have gone to a *Shari'a* Council. While the judge was probably concerned to avoid this, his intelligent use of the traditional English concept of equity indicated growing judicial

---

22   *Westminster City Council v IC* [2007] EWHC 3096 (Fam) and *KC and NCC v City of Westminster* [2008] EWCA Civ 198.

23   In *Qureshi v Qureshi*, [1971] 1 All ER 325, a Muslim husband had divorced his wife in the UK by *talaq*, but refused to pay her *mahr*. Through some legal gymnastics, it was held that this *talaq* in England was legally valid. Depriving the wife of her *mahr* would have been an evident rights deprivation. However, the unpalatable effect of recognising a *talaq* in England was rapidly remedied by the *Domicile and Matrimonial Proceedings Act* of 1973 to leave no doubt that state law expects formal divorces (see Pearl and Menski 1998: 92).

awareness at that stage that a total refusal to formally recognise ethnic minority law would create blatant injustice.

Earlier key cases show that in the 1970s activist judicial intervention did not yet occur explicitly in human rights terms. More recently, courts still seem to avoid open expressions of strategic interventions based on human rights considerations, but the underlying rights-based agenda and gender sensitivity are increasingly evident now. Faced with strong evidence of continuing self-regulatory mechanisms 'in the shadow of the law' everywhere, and parallel evidence that recourse to state law does not necessarily guarantee 'justice', state legal systems find themselves under intense pressure to prove that they are able to develop superior mechanisms to uphold the basic rights that rightful bona fide claimants are seeking. One could in fact portray such cases as public interest cases.

In some scenarios, judicial navigation today involves avoiding the costly process of adjudicating such matters *de novo*. Thus, even if the competing expectations are negotiated and managed by agents other than state courts, such outcomes are now capable of official recognition, as *AI v MT* [2013] EWHC 100 (Fam) confirms. Significantly, this case involved Jewish parties. Not only *The Times* (1 February 2013) trumpeted immediately that such decisions also open the doors for formal recognition of Muslim arbitration mechanisms. What should matter most is clearly whether the transnational legal/cultural negotiation processes achieve a good result, Stammler's 'right law' (Menski 2012a). Glimpses of such cases were indeed available earlier, significantly also in cases involving Muslims.[24]

If this chain of observations is correct, then not only countries all over Asia and Africa, but now also some European states are becoming more sophisticated at co-opting management systems for legal disputes that result in appropriate outcomes. To some extent this is indeed still different from Asian/African models, as the state clearly remains the final decision-maker for cases that go to court. But increasing recognition that family law issues are private matters first and may never reach state courts is also present. The key issue is thus a subtle balancing act between less state involvement and more state engagement, or *Entstaatlichung* and *Verstaatlichung*. While careful alertness about the potential for rights abuses by non-state bodies remains acute, assertion of state supremacy in rule of law mechanisms continues, but is now subjected to 'right law' scrutiny in some revised balancing acts. That such circumspect state authorities may then virtually adopt a rather close approximation of the pluri-legal model of the rule of law cultivated in places like India, South Africa and many other jurisdictions of the global South, however, is a message that will probably hurt Eurocentric pride.[25] One hopes that this will not prevent justice-focused recalculation.

Postscript and Conclusions

The synergies of the RELIGARE network, the Halle MPI developments, and related projects and conferences are remarkable. There is a real sense of progress now in bringing together theory and practice to achieve a deeper understanding of the processes involved in various

---

24 Pluralistic sophistication appears in the comments by Lady Justice Arden in paragraphs 46–48 of *Khan v Khan* [2007] EWCA 399 (Civ), which suggest the potential for acceptance of Asian joint family arrangements.

25 For illustrations of different models of legal management worldwide, see Menski (2009 and 2012b).

related legal industries concerning better management of normative and legal pluralities. It is the privilege of academics to argue forever about the impossibility of finding any middle ground in pluralist navigations (Knop, Michaels and Riles 2012: 652). Judges do not enjoy that privilege; they are paid to make decisions, aware that making mistakes may be costly in several respects. Top-notch practising lawyers face similar pressures.

This chapter sought to take a constructive theoretical perspective, facing the simmering conflicts rather than denying that they exist as legal contests and shooting them into an imagined 'extra-legal' space. It was argued, following important advice from other jurisdictions,[26] that in multicultural Europe today, it is in the long run impossible and dangerous to cut corners, figuratively and quite literally in terms of kite methodology, by pretending that states alone can regulate the complexities of law. As an internally plural field, marked out by interconnected corners of a kite-like structure, law today needs to relearn constructive management of its own pluralistic connectivity. One key problem of pluralist recognition of 'the other' within the law will then be posed by challenges to state law's customary monopoly claims. Forcing state law to share the high table with other forms of law indeed risks spoiling the appetite of legal positivists for pluralist engagement: it becomes a bitter pill. However, this is the price to pay for progress in fine-tuning justice consciousness in intensely plural contexts. Surely, this is more important than protecting the ideological supremacy of state law?

State-centric law clearly struggles, thus, with managing various challenges thrown to it by the complexities of daily life. The instinctive desire to maintain order and to preserve certainty suffers turbulences from the pluralities of the lived daily experience. The kite of law seems constantly challenged by turbulences, but the image itself works, as law is manifestly highly dynamic. Legal professionals, ultimately those on whom we put the burden of judging, have to struggle with managing those dynamic challenges. They may indeed find it difficult to offer new directions, as there will never be total agreement about any decision made. This is a natural consequence of the 'pop' nature of life as a plurality of pluralities, nerve-rackingly messy and atrociously chaotic if left to itself.

Intriguingly, this chaos scenario was experienced by ancient Indians, thousands of years ago. They observed nature and thought of 'shark rule', a scenario where the bigger fish eat all the smaller ones until nothing is left and even the sharks starve (Menski 2010a). They sought to avoid such disastrous chaos by stressing the value of open-minded common sense, situation-specificity and, above all, the principle of self-controlled ordering. Most importantly for the present discussion, they placed those who sought to lead and govern under an all-encompassing duty to do the right thing (*dharma*), not by giving them authority to make laws, but by supervising what people did, privileging situation-specific self-controlled ordering. Providing rather vague guidance about balancing good and evil, this ancient methodology seems nevertheless far more aware than we are today of the so-called 'limits of law' (Allott 1980), the power of negotiated informal settlements and the potential advantages of private arrangements.

AI v MT [2013] EWHC 100 (Fam) now confirms that our courts are rediscovering such ancient wisdoms. It also shows how cautious and alert judiciaries have to be today when they venture into the stormy zones of recognition of pluralism. In this case, the notable efforts to protect and hide the personal identity of the real people who became the reactive agents through whom legal development may occur are highly significant, evidently as a

---

26   As indicated, especially Amien (2010) for South Africa and Shachar (2005 and 2008) for Canada.

matter of professional ethics. Rather than being conducted and securely kept behind closed doors, though, proceedings such as those approved in *AI v MT* are now reported, as a matter of public interest, perhaps also to educate a suspicious and nervous public about the urgent need to move beyond petty legal politics. It seems at long last recognised that, led by judges rather than scholars, we must collectively strive to find sustainable solutions that allow more people to live in peace and to avoid trouble. *AI v MT* is indeed not a judgment in the conventional sense, but driving instruction for navigators and sailing guidance for kites of law. It offers insights into the methods that may be legitimately chosen to make the right decision, or at least to come close to 'best practice', which can only ever be a partial recognition of 'the other' in the law itself. When Mr Justice Baker characterises the case report as 'an explanation of the court's approach to the process of arbitration chosen by the parties', this provides a highly significant and indeed innovative practice statement, acknowledgement that law is internally plural, and thus can never only be state law alone, to become Stammler's 'right law'.

One remarkable consequence of this new variety of judicial activism is that it leaves prima donna-like scholars peeved for not being cited, deprived of the coveted 'impact' element so craved in British academia these days. Remarkably, however, judge-scholars receive those coveted citations abundantly from their own brethren. This raises questions whether there is another conspiracy going on here, when judges as closet academics claim the fruits of wisdom that plurality-conscious academia offered them in the first place, perhaps all too readily, in recent years. It is indeed remarkable that a public figure such as Dr Rowan Williams, the Archbishop of Canterbury (as he then was) is referred to in the judgment of *AI v MT*. But perhaps scholars in the RELIGARE network should actually be relieved about this, as the emerging storms over *AI v MT*, brewing in numerous anguished and angry web comments, shield activist scholars from yet more hate mail and worryingly aggressive vituperations by status quo-ists. If this most recent case means that in due course even Muslims (and others) will be officially trusted to sort out their own affairs informally and have them endorsed by state courts, we would see real progress in multicultural plurality-conscious management of such conflicts and tensions. Presently, it seems, some communities are trusted more than others to handle such challenges. But if one can accept Islamic finance (Menski 2013), then why not other aspects of the same law, too?

Since we surely do not want a full-fledged system of personal status laws, though, the realisation is growing that maintaining the fiction of legal uniformity in Western legal systems does require constant careful navigation around all sorts of supposedly fixed structures like national jurisdictions, local laws, precedent, and even in some cases custom. Federica Sona in this volume elaborates on this by devising her own imagery of a multiplicity of legal islands. I am not saying that this island imagery does not make sense, but hope to have demonstrated here that the image of law as kite-flying continues to make equally good sense in several respects, especially for judges. We are not sailing in water, afraid of drowning, but floating in the air, and thus scared of crashing. Up in the air, there are certainly even fewer assumed or actual fixed boundaries or prescribed roads, dynamism becomes super-dynamism, and subtle changes of navigational guidance may bring truly significant changes of direction. Whichever image we use, real fears of crashing seem to motivate the current plurality-conscious rebalancing of family law regulation in Europe.

There is thus some hope in a possible final conclusion that British judges today seem to be bold enough to face the cacophony of the music of legal pluralism, because they have devised strong public policy reasons for why it is in the best interests of the public and the system itself that judges should be creative and even activist. The present shift of concern towards substantive justice rather than stubborn reliance on positivist dogma and nervousness about procedural propriety and mistrust of the 'ethnic other' may be read as real signs of progress. As gender concerns and consideration of the best interests of children remain centre-stage in such scenarios, we also need to highlight, however, that such human rights concerns are not focusing on the autonomous individual that legal modernity so assiduously sought to protect, but shift instead towards recognition and acknowledgement of the continued relevance of community-based considerations and socio-ethical considerations. From that angle, too, the new developments are highly significant and, I submit, very intelligent. Still, some positive decisions do not mean that all is well or unproblematic, but there is reason for upbeat analysis.

The alternative interpretation, that such a decision as found in *AI v MT* [2013] EWHC 100 (Fam) only exists because of a disingenuous alliance of religious leaders, Jewish lobbyists and Muslim fundamentalists has evidently much less appeal. It also does not do justice to the evidence of enormous efforts undertaken by the judiciary everywhere, not only in the UK, to act as final guardians of justice. Scholars may be complaining about juridification and increasing evidence of juristocracy worldwide, but then questions must be asked why more scholars are not cultivating the analytical skills that top-quality judges so evidently possess. It appears that an increasing number of judges are not merely doing rather well what they have been appointed to do, namely protecting justice. Probably at times they do so despite the formal legal education they received. They seem to have been recalculating their navigational tools. After all, this subtly flavoured ephemeral entity called justice, as leading thinkers from all over the world, including Ashoka, the Prophet Mohammad, Derrida, Habermas, Amartya Sen and many others have brought out, poses a never-ending situation-specific experience, a challenge that state-centric positivist indoctrination seeks to deny and often defines away. The rather evidently plurality-conscious judicial navigation displayed by some recent judgments indicates that there is unlimited mileage in the journey of the pluralistic kite of law. The kite model, I suggest finally, also comes out as a better image than the satnav picture, as the legal field is not just a network of pre-formed roads, but more like an open sky in which all kinds of navigational manoeuvres are indeed possible.

Bibliography

Allott, A. 1980. *The Limits of Law*. London: Butterworths.

Amien, W. 2010. A South African case study for the recognition and regulation of Muslim family law in a minority Muslim secular context. *International Journal of Law, Policy and the Family*, 24(3), 361–96.

Ballard, R. 1994 [2007]. *Desh Pardesh: The South Asian Presence in Britain*. London: Hurst.

Bano, S. 2012. *Muslim Women and Shari'ah Councils. Transcending the Boundaries of Community and Law*. Basingstoke: Palgrave Macmillan.

Bayır, D. and Shah, P. 2012. The legal adaptation of British settlers in Turkey. *Transcultural Studies*, 1, 43–76. [Online]. Available at: http://archiv.ub.uni-heidelberg.de/ojs/index.php/transcultural/article/view/9268 [last accessed 14 December 2013].

Bhamra, M.K. 2011. *The Challenges of Justice in Diverse Societies. Constitutionalism and Pluralism*. Farnham: Ashgate.

Bowen, J.R. 2012. *Blaming Islam*. Cambridge, MA: MIT Press.

Brubaker, R. 2013. Categories of analysis and categories of practice: A note on the study of Muslims in European countries of immigration. *Ethnic and Racial Studies*, 36(1), 1–8.

Büchler, A. 2011. *Islamic law in Europe? Legal Pluralism and its Limits in European Family Laws*. Farnham: Ashgate.

Chiba, M. (ed.) 1986. *Asian Indigenous Law in Interaction with Received Law*. London and New York: KPI.

Estin, A.L. (ed.) 2008. *The Multi-cultural Family*. Farnham: Ashgate.

Ferrari, S. and Cristofori, R. (eds) 2010. *Religion and Law in the 21st century. Relations between States and Religious Communities*. Farnham: Ashgate.

Ferrari, S. and Pastorelli S. (eds) 2012. *Religion in Public Spaces. A European Perspective*. Farnham: Ashgate.

Friberg, J.H. 2012. Culture at work: Polish migrants in the ethnic division of labour on Norwegian construction sites. *Ethnic and Racial Studies*, 35(1), 1914–33.

Glenn, H.P. 2000. *Legal Traditions of the World*. Oxford: Oxford University Press.

Griffiths, J. 1986. What is legal pluralism? *Journal of Legal Pluralism and Unofficial Law*, 24, 1–56.

Grillo, R.D. 2012. In the shadow of the law, in *Interpreting Divorce Laws in Islam*, edited by R. Mehdi, W. Menski and J.S. Nielsen, Copenhagen: DJØF, 203–33.

Habermas, J. 2006. Religion in the public sphere. *Philosophy and Social Criticism*, 32(5), 35–47.

Hasan, K. 2009. The medical and social costs of consanguineous marriages among British Mirpuris. *South Asia Research*, 29(3), 275–98.

Hertogh, M. (ed.) 2009. *Living Law. Reconsidering Eugen Ehrlich*. Oxford: Hart.

Holden, L. (ed.) 2011. *Cultural Expertise and Litigation: Patterns, Conflicts, Narratives*. London: Routledge.

Howard, E. 2012. Banning Islamic veils: Is gender equality a valid argument? *International Journal of Discrimination and the Law*, 12(3), 147–65.

Huda, S. 2011. *Combating Gender Injustice. Hindu Law in Bangladesh*. Dhaka: South Asian Institute.

Joly, D. 2012. Race, ethnicity and religion: Emerging policies in Britain. *Patterns of Prejudice*, 46(5), 467–85.

Knop, K., Michaels, R. and Riles, A. 2012. From multiculturalism to technique: Feminism, culture, and the conflicts of laws style. *Stanford Law Review*, 64(3), 589–656.

Knott, K., and McLoughlin, S. (eds) 2010. *Diasporas. Concepts, Intersections, Identities*. London and New York: Zed Books.

Krings, T., Bobek, A., Moriarty, E., Salamoniska, J. and Wickham, J. 2013. Polish migration to Ireland: 'Free movers' in the new European mobility space. *Journal of Ethnic and Migration Studies*, 39(1), 87–103.

Malik, M. 2012. *Minority Legal Orders in the UK. Minorities, Pluralism and the Law*. London: The British Academy.

Mehdi, R., Menski, W. and Nielsen, J.S. (eds) 2012. *Interpreting Divorce Laws in Islam*. Copenhagen: DJØF.

Menski, W. 2002. Immigration and multiculturalism in Britain: New issues in research and policy. *KIAPS: Bulletin of Asia-Pacific Studies (Osaka)*, XII, 43–66.

Menski, W. 2006. *Comparative Law in a Global Context. The Legal Systems of Asia and Africa*, 2nd edition. Cambridge: Cambridge University Press.

Menski, W. 2007a. Dodgy Asians or dodgy laws? The story of H. *Immigration, Asylum and Nationality Law*, 21(4), 284–94.

Menski, W. 2007b. Law, religions and South Asians in diaspora, in *Religious Reconstruction in the South Asian Diasporas*, edited by J.R. Hinnells. Basingstoke: Palgrave Macmillan, 243–64.

Menski, W. 2008. Law, religion and culture in multicultural Britain, in *Law and Religion in Multicultural Societies*, edited by R. Mehdi, H. Petersen, E.R. Sand and G.R. Woodman, Copenhagen: DJØF, 43–62.

Menski, W. 2009. Indian secular pluralism and its relevance for Europe, in *Legal Practice and Cultural Diversity*, R. Grillo, R. Ballard, A. Ferrari, A. Hoekema, M. Maussen, and P. Shah. Farnham: Ashgate, 31–47.

Menski, W. 2010a. *Sanskrit Law. Excavating Vedic Legal Pluralism*. [Online: SOAS School of Law Research Paper, No. 05-2010]. Available at: http://ssrn.com/abstract=1621384 [last accessed 14 December 2013].

Menski, W. 2010b. Slumdog law, colonial tummy aches and the redefinition of family law in India. *South Asia Research*, 30(1), 67–80.

Menski, W. 2011. Islamic law in British courts: Do we not know or do we not want to know?, in *The Place of Religion in Family Law: A Comparative Search*, edited by J. Mair and E. Örücü. Mortsel: Intersentia, 15–36.

Menski, W. 2012a. Plural worlds of law and the search for living law, in *Rechtsanalyse als Kulturforschung*, edited by W. Gephart. Frankfurt am Main: Vittorio Klostermann, 71–88.

Menski, W. 2012b. The uniform civil code debate in Indian law: New developments and changing agenda, in *The Many Faces of India. Law and Politics of the Subcontinent*, edited by M. McLaren. Delhi: Samskriti, 136–82.

Menski, W. 2013. Law as a kite: Managing legal pluralism in the context of Islamic finance, in *Islamic Finance*, edited by V. Cattelan. Cheltenham: Edward Elgar, 15–31.

Nichols, J.A. (ed.) 2012. *Marriage and Divorce in a Multicultural Context*. Cambridge: Cambridge University Press.

Parashar, A. and Dhanda A. (eds) 2008. *Redefining Family Law in India*. London: Routledge.

Pearl, D. and Menski, W. 1998. *Muslim Family Law*. London: Sweet and Maxwell.

Shachar, A. 2005. Religion, state, and the problem of gender: New modes of citizenship and governance in diverse societies. *McGill Law Journal*, 50, 49–88.

Shachar, A. 2008. Privatizing diversity: A cautionary tale from religious arbitration in family law. *Theoretical Enquiries in Law*, 9(2), 573–607. [Online]. Available at: http://ssrn.com/abstract=1151234 [last accessed 14 December 2013].

Shah, P. 2005. Globalisation and the challenge of Asian legal transplants in Europe. *Singapore Journal of Legal Studies*, 348–61. [Online]. Available at: http://law.nus.edu.sg/sjls/articles/SJLS-2005-348.pdf [last accessed 14 December 2013].

Shah, P (ed.) 2007. *Law and Ethnic Plurality*. Leiden and Boston: Martinus Nijhoff Publishers.

Sonneveld, N. 2012. *Khul' Divorce in Egypt. Public Debates, Judicial Practices, and Everyday Life*. Cairo: The American University in Cairo Press.

Vertovec, S. 2007. Super-diversity and its implications. *Ethnic and Racial Studies*, 30(6), 1024–54.

Williams, R. 2008. *Civil and Religious Law in England: A Religious Perspective*. [Online]. Available at: http://rowanwilliams.archbishopofcanterbury.org/articles.php/1137/archbishops-lecture-civil-and-religious-law-in-england-a-religious-perspective [last accessed 14 December 2013].

Chapter 3
Family and the Law in Europe: Bringing Together Secular Legal Orders and Religious Norms and Needs

Mathias Rohe

Introduction

Should religious norms or state rules govern the personal and legal status of families and their members? Both spheres feel responsible and competent for doing so. In Europe, there was a century-long, bitter struggle on the right of decision between religious and secular institutions. In the end, a solution was found which seems to grant considerable stability: whereas personal attitudes and behaviour may be ruled by religious norms – including religious ceremonies – state law has the exclusive right to govern worldly legal aspects. Delegating legal competences, for example in marriage issues, to religious institutions is but a confirmation of this principle, since legal effects depend on state recognition of such institutions.

While this is true for the Christian and non-religious majorities of the European population, there are some particularities regarding religious minorities. Jews, for example, have established Beth Din courts in various European countries, dealing with several issues including divorce, which is governed by Jewish religious rules and differs from contemporary standards of equal treatment of the sexes.[1] Interestingly, these institutions attracted neither broad public interest nor in-depth scientific research.[2] The contrary is true for the pursuit by Muslims of legal-religious rules in matters of personal status and family. While focusing on religious topics, we have to discern religion from broader cultural phenomena and social issues influencing the opinions and acts of the persons involved. This is particularly true for patriarchal family structures.

Nevertheless, the main needs with regard to rethinking European legal practice concern religious minorities, particularly in connection with migration phenomena. Whereas the laws in Europe have developed widely accepted regulations concerning established

---

1   Cf. Freeman 2001: 365, 377ff, with further references; Gärtner 2008: 110ff with further references. A certain difference, however, is that a 'Get' can only be personally pronounced, whereas the 'Talaq' can be substituted by a judicial decision; for the problem of a forced 'Get', cf. Biale 1984: 97ff. Moreover, there seem to be social pressure mechanisms – e.g., women's demonstrations before the office of the unwilling husband with the aim of causing him to pronounce the 'Get'; cf. Atlan 2002: 236. Tellingly, in the UK, the introduction of a religious law of divorce was also demanded by Jews; cf. Berkovits 1993: 119ff, 141ff.

2   State courts had to deal with such institutions from time to time; cf., e.g., the judgment of the German Imperial Court (Reichsgericht) of 16.02.1904, RGZ 57, 250; Court of Appeals Oldenburg FamRZ 2006, 950ff.

religions – being based in part on Christian rules[3] – there are considerable challenges, such as religiously-based Islamic or Jewish rules, which in their more or less traditional form stick to systems of gender disparity (patriarchal structures) and disparity of religions (for example, interdiction of inter-marriage).

The Framework: European Legal Traditions

How European Legal Orders Organise Unity in Diversity

The primary aim of legal orders is to maintain peace in society by providing mechanisms for avoiding or resolving conflicts. There is no doubt that, caused primarily by developments of broad globalisation and migration, the ideas concerning the structure and tasks of legal orders have diversified among the European population. Therefore, we should first examine the possible models of regulating the existing competition between normative systems, since very often debates on rethinking or reform of the existing orders suffer from different pre-understandings, which are not always taken into consideration. In principle, the relation between the necessary amount of normative unity and diversity for a particular society has to be defined and possibly adjusted. Various models have emerged for tackling this issue. This chapter focuses on the European perspective, without neglecting models from other parts of the world.

In addition, there is a considerable difference between the sociological and legal perspectives regarding the scope of relevance and the tasks of legal orders for broader society. The different models can be visualised by the following schemata.

1. Sociological Perspective

From a sociological point of view, the legal order is but one out of several normative settings that regulate communication and coexistence within society (Figure 3.1). This point of view is perfectly acceptable for lawyers who know that the law is neither capable nor entitled to regulate all normative aspects of human life. At the same time it is clear that all of the normative subsystems influence each other, and the legal orders are exempt from this interaction.

Nevertheless, from time to time sociological criticism is directed against the law or its interpreters, accusing them of ignoring the facts of life on the ground and claiming superiority over all other normative orders ('the law is the boss'). However, the truth is that neither the law nor (most of) its interpreters ignore this. Instead they simply confine their activities to the very tasks the legal order has to fulfil; this is to maintain peace in society by:

- defining a necessary minimum of common standards and sanctions for violations of rights;
- providing model rules for efficient interaction in the field of private autonomy; and
- maintaining institutions for securing an equally efficient and reliable implementation and enforcement of the rules agreed upon.

---

3 Cf. Dilcher and Staff 1984 – Dilcher: 304–59 and Coing: 360–75 in particular.

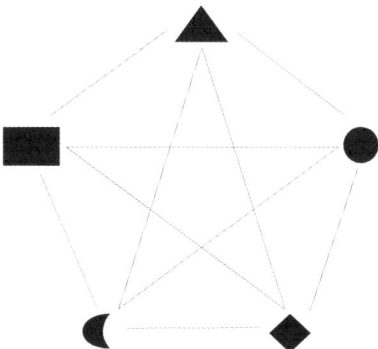

Index: Explication of symbols

legal order

other normative systems (religion, belief, ethics, ...) ▲ ● ◆ ☾

Figure 3.1 Relationship of legal and other systems from a sociological perspective

Thus, the lawgiver has to weigh up possibly conflicting interests within society and define measures for granting unity or diversity in the various fields of the law. Here, the issue of accommodation of individuals and groups belonging to minorities comes into focus and three main models of regulating unity and diversity can be discerned.

2. Legal Perspectives

This model is of considerable age, going back to the Roman *ius gentium*, early medieval European legal orders, but is also still in practice in parts of Africa, India and vast parts of the so-called Islamic world. In Britain, certain Muslim groups have sought the introduction of a general system of religious law in matrimonial, family and succession matters according to such traditions.[4] Such a model might be described as a system of respectful distance between members belonging to different legal orders (Figure 3.2). It potentially allows the continued existence and cultural identity of organised religious minorities within the Islamic world and elsewhere.

Figure 3.2 Model 1 – Parallel legal orders

---

4 Cf. Poulter 1993: 147 with further references.

In medieval Europe, besides the different tribal legal orders, the Jews and the Slavs had their particular legal systems for a long time.[5] However, this does not necessarily reflect the idea of equality of different legal orders. On the contrary, Jews and Slavs were taken to belong to an inferior culture and were thus prevented from participating in a more advanced legal system. Consequently, such legal models tend to segregate different groups within society with, for example, provisions banning inter-marriage bilaterally or unilaterally, as was the case in Europe in the past[6] and is still the case in Islamic family law today.[7]

Such systems certainly do not facilitate the application of the law, particularly in mixed cases. Thus, in Europe there was a century-long development from such personal law systems to unified territorial legal orders granting more or less *internal* freedom. Besides that, when accepting parallel legal orders, in cases where members of different orders are involved, a decision has to be made which order shall prevail, or a third 'neutral' order[8] has to be developed for such cases. Usually, the legal order of the politically dominating part of the population will prevail. In Egypt, for example, this leads to the strange result that Islamic law, which is generally dominant in family law, prevails even in family law disputes between Christians belonging to different denominations.[9] It would be impossible to establish such an ultimate right to adjudicate within the framework of European constitutional law. Interestingly, in states sticking to mandatory religious systems in personal status like Lebanon or Israel, initiatives to establish at least optional secular systems are increasing. Furthermore, freedom of religion contains the freedom to change one's religion or not to belong to any religion. This freedom would be unduly constrained by forcing people into a legal regime defined by religion.

In the field of private law, mainly in the UK,[10] a broader discussion has emerged among Muslims on the (optional) introduction of a Muslim law of personal status and inheritance. Regarding such demands, it has to be taken into consideration that there is no uniform Islamic legal system of substantial rules to be identified. There is a considerable variety among the existing legal orders in Islamic states. The Turkish Republic and the Balkan states, being the regions of origin of many Muslims in Europe, have completely abolished legal Sharia rules and the vast majority among them would heavily reject the re-introduction of such rules in European countries. Obviously, there are no homogeneous group interests, neither among religious minorities nor within society as a whole.

---

5   Cf. Rohe 1994b: 16–32 with further references.

6   For example, according to § 64 of the Austrian ABGB, marriages between Christians and non-Christians were interdicted until 1938; since 1868, only a 'Notzivilehe' (emergency civil marriage) could be concluded. In addition, non-Christians were prevented from witnessing wills of Christians (§ 593 ABGB) until 1860, and apostasy from Christianity resulted in disinheriting the apostate (§ 768 Z 1 ABGB) until 1868.

7   Cf. Rohe 2011: 82f., 210. Whereas according to Twelver-Shi'i law marriages between Muslims and non-Muslims are generally forbidden, Sunni law permits marriage between a Muslim male and a non-Muslim Jewish or Christian female.

8   An example of this may be found in the Indian Special Marriage Act 1954. Cf. Rohe 2011: 304; Werner Menski characterises this legislation as part of an 'artificial uniformisation' (Menski 2006: 252).

9   Cf. Bergmann et al. 1952: 8; Wähler 1981: 163. Regarding the self-conception of Islamic law as the governing law concerning family relations, see Demosthenous-Pashalidou 1999: 315. It should be mentioned that in certain cases Christians seek the application of Islamic rules, especially if their own religious law prevents them from being divorced.

10 Cf. Nielsen 1993; Pearl and Menski 1998: 51ff, 73ff; Shah-Kazemi 2001; Shah 2013: 58–75; Klausen 2007: 190f.; Malik 2010; Bano 2007: 38–66.

Taking religious affiliation as the basis for civil legal relations would raise other serious questions. Clearly, several aspects of, for example, Jewish or Islamic law – in its various existing forms – would not be acceptable within the European legal-political context. Despite widespread tendencies to improve women's rights in the Islamic world,[11] many legal orders in this region are still far from the legal standard of equality of the sexes and religions achieved in Europe.[12] For example, polygamous marriages contracted in Europe, the guardianship powers of male legal representatives of the bride, the husband's unilateral right to divorce, the general assignment of a duty to care for a minor's property and the relatively strict assignment of custody of minor children to the father or the mother according to the child's age, as well as the legal inequality of male and female heirs (corresponding to different maintenance obligations within a social framework of a relatively strict separation of sexes in all spheres of life) conflict with the principles of European legal systems.[13] It would simply be unacceptable to implement such rules into the existing systems. This is true in any case for compulsory laws, but also regarding forms of *official* recognition as a possible option.

In sum, European legal systems are fundamentally different from parallel legal systems based on religious, ethnic or other distinct affiliations. Considering the (re-)introduction of such systems would seriously infringe the fundamental principle of secularity, which has to be taken seriously in all considerations. This model should not be considered further in developing realistic options of accommodation of religious minorities in the field of family law. Instead, appropriate solutions 'within' the system have to be sought.[14]

The model shown in Figure 3.3 describes the opposite of Model 1. One unified legal order deeply governs all aspects of societal interaction. It is the model of intense external and internal assimilation, leaving neither scope for competing normative orders nor for broad choice *within* the system. No present European legal order has adopted this model, and it certainly does not meet the basic requirements of human rights standards, including the provisions of the ECHR. Nevertheless, it is true that from time to time court or administrative decisions seem to implicitly follow this 'model' anyway, by disregarding different cultural convictions and attitudes that are not necessarily in conflict with the law of the land. Such approaches will lead to serious conflicts and alienation of minority groups from the legal order and its institutions.[15] They are neither inclusive nor even-handed.

Instead, a model based on European experiences of the technical and institutional instruments and the legal-political culture is needed, which is at the same time able to react to new developments by granting inclusive even-handedness. Comparative law impressively demonstrates the failure of attempts to impose foreign legal systems on

Figure 3.3 Model 2 – Full hierarchical system

---

11 Cf. Rohe 2011: 53.
12 Cf. Shah-Kazemi 2001; Freeland and Lau 2008: 331–47 (340ff. in particular); Bano 2012; Malik 2012.
13 This is overlooked by Yilmaz 2000: 357.
14 Cf., e.g., the findings and reflections of Estin 2012: 92ff.
15 Cf. Saris et al. 2007: 44.

societies whose legal traditions differ considerably from these systems.[16] Legal export or import is only successful in cases of comparable political, social, economic and cultural environments. Thus, genuine solutions for new challenges are preferable. Equally, tools for granting inclusive even-handedness for migrants or minorities are and have to be sought 'within'. This is the only realistic way to gain broad acceptance for any kind of formal or informal legal adjustment.[17] Given the fact that a considerable section of the European public is suspicious of religion in general, and minority religions in particular, inclusive even-handedness is required to de-problematise religion by equal measure. This means a non-biased weighing up of conflicting interests (including human rights, which freedom of religion and belief is a part of) according to the established European legal practice.

On the other hand, we have to bear in mind that the existing rules can create limping situations – legal relationships being recognised in one state but not in others. In addition, direct or indirect discrimination may easily result from unreflective continuation of traditions under changing factual circumstances.

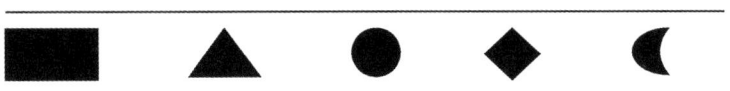

Figure 3.4 Model 3 – Open hierarchical system
Note: The line indicates the restrictive degrees of legal interferences in fields of dispositive law (private autonomy, including freedom of religion). The limits are drawn by public policy/ordre public in a broad sense (defining the necessary degree of unity to protect the weak and to preserve peace in society).

The model shown in Figure 3.4 by and large reflects existing European legal systems. The law claims a core sphere of intense regulation (left part of the figure), particularly in public law including penal law. In the field of private law (right part of the figure), far-reaching private autonomy is only limited by compulsory rules aiming at protective measures and granting an indispensable minimum of common legal standards, which undergoes constant reflection and reform. European traditions of regulating the applicability of rules concern citizens as well as residents, the predominant idea behind legislation being to grant individual diversity in secular unity. This is reflected in the thoughtful lecture on the relationship between civil and religious law in England given by the then Archbishop of Canterbury, Rowan Williams, in February 2008. In that speech, he spoke of the need to subject private ordering to a measure of protection to that part of human nature which corporate belonging may not be able capture.[18]

A characteristic of contemporary European family law is that relatively strong states are now taking intense responsibility in family matters, particularly for protective reasons. Families are no longer perceived to be a private circle beyond states' rights and interests to

---

16   Cf. Menski 2006: 252.
17   This insight is the result of more than two decades of research and practice by the author in this field.
18   Available at http://www.archbishopofcanterbury.org/articles.php/1137/archbishops-lecture-civil-and-religious-law-in-england-a-religious-perspective#Lecture [last accessed 13 December 2013].

interfere. This is not restricted to cases of domestic violence or neglect of children, but also covers the protection of the weaker parties (particularly children or spouses without their own income) in regulating financial and other family matters. This system considerably differs from the situation in vast parts of Asia and Africa where personal law systems are still operating. Attempts at unification have not found enough support in such different countries as India, Lebanon and Egypt.

In contrast, European traditions of regulating the applicability of rules concerning citizens and residents can be characterised as a model of individual diversity in secular unity. Regarding civil law issues, as was mentioned above, Europe has undergone a centuries-long development from personal law systems differentiating along ethnic or religious lines towards territorially unified national (or partly regional) laws granting individual choice by dispositive rules within a clear common framework. Thus, legal pluralism is accepted to a certain extent, but not on the level of the final decision in case of conflict as it is upon the secular national/regional law to define the scope of pluralism 'within'.

The Basis of European Family Laws

EU family law systems are secular. The systems of regulation in the member States range between laic, religiously open secular and state church orders. But in the field of family law, the Christian legal tradition has been broadly secularised; the legal and the religious aspects and effects of marriage, divorce and family relations have been almost totally separated. Nevertheless, given the historical development of European family laws, their Christian heritage is undisputed.[19] In substantive family law, some important legal institutions like marriage are certainly based on Christian convictions (for example, the. monogamous lifetime marriage between one male and one female partner), and on the procedural level religious bodies are involved at least optionally (for example in the UK, Spain and in Nordic countries). Moreover, possible conflicts between secular and religious laws are restricted to the 'internal' religious sphere: the applicability of European secular family laws does not create obstacles to the conditions of living of the parties. As long as state law does not interfere in the solely religious aspects of institutions like marriage, freedom of religion is not threatened.[20] Only in Italy[21]

---

19 Cf. Dilcher and Staff 1984, in particular the contributions of Dilcher: 304–59 and Coing: 360–75; Sörgjerd 2012: 23ff.

20 Cf. the judgment of the Italian Court of Cassation of 16.11.2006 (no. 24494) regarding the law no. 898 of 1 December 1970, which empowers a civil court to declare the ceasing of legal effects (divorce) of concordatarian marriages (celebrated according to the Concordat between the Italian Government and the Holy See of 18 February 1984). By this regulation, the state did not regulate marriage as understood in Canon Law (indissolubility), but only civil legal effects.

21 According to Art. 8 § 2 of the Concordat between the Italian Government and the Holy See of 18 February 1984, ecclesiastical courts' judgments of nullity of marriage may be recognised as having legal effects by the competent civil Court of Appeals under some conditions, among them the compatibility with public policy/ordre public. Thus, the Court of Cassation decided on 20.01.2011 (judgment no. 1343) that nullification on grounds of mere 'simulation of consent' after 20 years of cohabitation would breach public policy/ordre public.

and Spain[22] can problems in marriage arise pertaining to the civil law recognition of a religious declaration of nullity.[23]

Thus, one major concern that comes with this specific cultural heritage is how to address issues of religious minorities in the field of family law. Such minorities are mostly non-Christian, but in some aspects Christian minorities are also affected. For example, in some member States divorce is granted on the grounds of fault of one of the spouses. Can a (minority) religious practice constitute a 'fault'? It should be clear that such an approach would contradict freedom of religion and constitute discrimination against the spouse who adheres to a religious minority. French courts have thus decided that belonging to the Jehovah's Witnesses[24] or to a 'sect'[25] cannot constitute a 'fault' as such. Good practice would rather weigh up the concrete exercise of one's religion with the concrete family duties to be fulfilled by the spouses.[26] The same principles would apply in custody cases (see further below).

Reasonable accommodation has to be sought by clarifying misunderstandings and false conflicts in cases where legal institutions are in fact not contradictory, and to examine to what extent party autonomy opens space for private choice in arranging marriage, in cases such as matrimonial property, for example. There is indeed a trend towards increasing autonomy. In family law, usually no free choice is granted (as opposed to contract law) but several options (appropriate connecting factors) are formulated (mostly either habitual residence or nationality) concerning, for example, maintenance, matrimonial property and divorce.[27]

In Europe, religion and belief can become relevant on three main legal levels:

---

22 According to the Agreement between the Holy See and the Spanish State on Legal Issues, 3 January 1979, Art. VI and Art. 80 of the civil code, canonical marriages have civil effect once registered in the Civil Registry. Judicial annulments by the ecclesiastical courts or Papal dissolutions of non-consummated marriages have civil effect in Spanish law, upon request of any of the parties, when those decisions have been declared 'adjusted to the State law' by the competent civil court. RELIGARE's Spanish country team expressed the need for further legal clarification of the criteria for such declaration. While similar agreements were concluded in 1992 with the Jewish and Muslim communities, no serious claims have arisen.

23 In Italy there is a rich and not totally consistent jurisprudence on the relationship between ecclesiastical judgments of nullity and civil court jurisdiction on civil law aspects like marital property, maintenance claims, etc. These issues seem to be restricted to Italy and certainly deserve further research on an Italian level.

24 Court of Appeal Bourges 20.03.1996 (Juris-Data no. 043754).

25 Court of Cassation, 2. Civ., 08.11.1995 (Bull. Civ. II, no. 271; RTD civ., 1996, p. 369).

26 Cf. Court of Cassation 09.10.1996 (Juris-Data no. 003682); Court of Appeal Nancy 23.02.1996 (Juris-Data no. 044054) concerning Jehovah's Witnesses (one may doubt whether the religiously based refusal to participate in family celebrations such as children's birthdays or Christmas parties reaches the degree of a serious or continual violation of the duties and obligations of marriage which render intolerable the continuation of communal life, as regulated in Art. 242 CC); Court of Appeal Aix-en-Provence 21.01.1997 (Juris-Data no. 040044) concerning Muslims (the husband insisted his wife wear a veil, and forbade her to work and leave the house). The Court of Appeal Versailles (30.03.1995) granted a divorce to a wife under Art. 215 CC – breach of the obligation to community of living, whereas the husband claimed that according to North-African Muslim custom he was not entitled to share the marital home before the Islamic marriage which was planned for six months after the civil marriage. The courts seemingly ignored the possible religious implications by simply saying that religious marriage was not a condition of validity for civil marriage, and foreign customs were not to be invoked.

27 Cf. Kruger 2010: 5.

- On the basis of private international law, courts within the EU are obliged to apply religiously formed laws in family matters to the extent that the public policy/ordre public permits.
- In some member States like Denmark, Italy, Spain and the UK, registration of marriages can be performed by religious institutions according to the legal prerequisites of the respective member State.
- Religious convictions may play a role in formulating matrimonial contracts or other arrangements under the substantive family law of the member States. In most countries court cases have predominantly concerned members of minority religions, Muslims in particular, but there have also been cases involving Jews and others. Most of the cases reported deal with the prerequisites of legally valid marriages and their recognition if concluded under religious laws abroad, including some specific concerns such as dower payment obligations and divorce issues (recognition of foreign decisions made according to religious laws) and the limits of the applicability of such foreign laws according to internal private international law provisions (application of public policy/ordre public against religious laws treating sexes or religions/beliefs unequally). In addition, Christian minorities or members of 'sects' sometimes lack equal treatment in custody and divorce cases.

In general, among the 'majority' population in Europe, including lawyers, there is relatively little awareness of the fact that European family law derives from a Christian background and has been turned into secular forms. Thus, specific needs of religious minorities, which are not equally covered by the legal structure, should be appropriately considered through the approach of inclusive even-handedness. Whereas public policy/ordre public has to maintain human rights standards irrespective of the parties involved, feasible solutions for religious minorities should be sought under the applicable law, including aspects of recognition of decisions in the countries of origin of migrant religious minorities. A main concern is to de-ideologise the debate on religious aspects of family life. Difference in attitudes is not necessarily dangerous, but also not necessarily acceptable in all respects. Thus, possible tensions between individual or collective religious rights and convictions on one side and the principles of secular legal orders have to be addressed in a neutral and fair way. This goes beyond formal equality and falls under material inequality.

The formal neutrality-only approach comes down to ignoring the concrete impact that formal neutrality on the part of the state authorities may – or may not – have on people's concrete family situation. It may well be, for example, that neutrality impacts differently on majority and minority groups of the population creating internal tensions in society, for some groups do in fact feel that they are not treated equally by the law. Second, state law can offer space for the development of interpretations and applications of the relevant rules that aim at inclusive even-handedness. Inclusive even-handedness stands for an approach on the part of state law that strives at accommodating minority legal practices to the extent possible, in this case in the field of family law, by granting them recognition under state law. A reservation about this approach, however, is that this should not result in granting special rights to specific groups in society. 'Even-handedness' means that the state legal orders refrain from granting unjustified advantages to any community, group or religion. The starting point is the observation that in all EU Member States – with the exception of

Greece, for historical reasons[28] – no personal law systems are applied separately to particular religions or ethnicities. Instead, inclusive even-handedness confirms the principle that state family law applies to all, while allowing space for a considerable degree of individual choice and thus leaving room for religious or cultural needs.[29]

In the following section, the two main levels of normative conflict will be discussed. First, private international law has to decide on the applicable laws in cross-border cases, thus leading to the application of foreign religiously driven laws to a certain extent, which might cause tensions regarding conflicting contents. Second, domestic law is usually applicable to all citizens irrespective of their religious affiliation. Nevertheless, it opens up the space for individual regulations, which might meet religious needs of the parties or which would enable tailored solutions for 'hybrid' perspectives of life, for example due to circular migration.

Private International Law and Substantive Domestic Law (Contract Law)

General

The bulk of the case law collected within the framework of the project reveals that the main legal conflicts revolving around issues of religious diversity and the family arising in recent decades relate to private international law (PIL). In consequence, it is PIL and its techniques that have for the most part been invoked to govern this coexistence, in particular when linked to situations involving families with migrant backgrounds (in EU terminology, these are 'third country nationals' or TCNs).

PIL is the branch of law that deals with situations (private relationships) that are connected with more than one legal order. This connection may result from the mixed nature of the relationship between parties who, for instance, do not share the same nationality. Or it may arise from a situation of cross-border mobility, meaning that the parties (or one of them) are living in a country other than that of their nationality – whether temporarily or on a long-term basis – and reside there as foreign nationals. This field is of prime importance for the EU, since it concerns the obligation of mutual recognition of legal decisions, including large parts of family law.[30]

The techniques of PIL therefore continue to be important for all types of questions relating to the reception, within the domestic law of the country of the parties' habitual residence, of situations relating to personal status that have arisen in a foreign country: marriages celebrated abroad, divorces granted by foreign judges, etc.[31] As we focus on conflicts arising from religious diversity and confessional heterogeneity, of most relevance are cross-border family situations involving members who come from countries where religious law constitutes a major source of law, particularly on matters of personal status. It regularly happens that questions relating to these matters continue to be governed by religiously inspired law even if the parties reside in Europe.[32] The aim of the project has

---

28 Cf. Tsitselikis 2004: 402, 417ff; id. 2012: 367ff. For a critical report on the current situation, see Papadopoulou 2010.
29 Cf., e.g., Witte Jr 2010: 279–92; Waldron 2010: 103–13; Hoekema 2009: 177–98.
30 Cf. inter alia Mansel 2008: 137, 181ff. in particular.
31 Jänterä-Jareborg 2003: 185–385.
32 See especially Carlier and Verwilghen 1992.

therefore been to examine such situations closely, for they are widespread and pose the problem of reconciling, on the one hand, the requirements of State law, and on the other, a number of norms that are connected to religious convictions and that are often seen by groups and individuals as equal to, if not of greater standing, than official (State) law.

In practice, interactions with religious family laws and hence the accompanying questions of PIL appear to remain the particular concern of people who have settled in Europe on a more or less permanent basis, but who nevertheless retain connections with their country of origin. They thus look for solutions that would allow them to live a harmonious family life with international status, i.e., enjoying equal recognition under civil (in Europe) and possibly religiously inspired law (in the country of origin). Their situation is 'transnational'.[33] The difficulty in their case lies in articulating their (personal) status in such a way that it can be effectively received in both legal orders involved: on the one hand, that of the country of emigration (i.e., of origin), and on the other hand, that of their habitual residence.[34] Today it seems that it is primarily Muslims who – in various parts of Europe – are faced with the difficulty of combining respect for the laws enacted by the (secular) State in their country of residence with the laws that apply in their countries of origin. The values of the latter are often endowed, in their view, with particular legitimacy.[35] According to RELIGARE and other sociological data,[36] this seems to be the case particularly among Muslims living in the UK (cf. below), but is obviously not restricted to them. For example, among Jews seeking divorce, the religious aspect of the delivery of the 'Get' to the divorced wife can play an important role.[37]

The research on family issues provides an inventory of the main conflicts that have occurred in recent years between civil/state and religious family laws and how these conflicts were handled in the different PIL systems of the 10 countries under scrutiny. Among the issues most frequently submitted to the courts are: the prerequisites for legally valid marriages and their recognition if concluded under religious laws abroad, some specific concerns like dower payment obligations and divorce issues, in particular the recognition of foreign divorces performed according to religious laws and the limits of the applicability of such laws under PIL provisions. In the latter case, the invocation of public policy/ordre public appears to be the most recurrent argument: religious laws are disposed of for treating sexes or religions/beliefs unequally. The case law significantly differs, however, from country to country.

Key Observations

The correct application of foreign law is based on two indispensable prerequisites. First, sound knowledge of the foreign law, as applied by its relevant institutions, is needed. Second, since the application of foreign norms might cause tension in broader society, especially if the outcome of their application fundamentally contradicts the law of the land, society is in need of basic information about the reasons and the functions of such application. Nevertheless, there is little information about the specific function of PIL in

---

33 See especially Bramadat and Koenig 2009.
34 See Foblets and Carlier 2005.
35 See especially Asayyad and Castells 2002; Benhabib 2007; Cesari 2005; Coward 2000; Erdemir 2008; Ross 2009; Levey and Modood 2009; Nielsen and Allievi 2002; Yazbeck 2002.
36 Cf. Shah-Kazemi 2011; Bano 2012; Malik 2012: 17–19, 28–30 in particular; Klausen 2007: 190. For Denmark see also Vinding and Christoffersen 2012: 124–7.
37 Cf. Wegner 1982: 1ff; Freeman 2001: 365, 377–85.

broader society, as our sociological data clearly demonstrate.[38] According to a widespread (and wrong) supposition, only the (substantive) law of the land has to be applied. The idea of granting predictability in private cross-border cases for the parties involved, and consequently accepting legal diversity to a certain extent (within the limits of public policy/ ordre public) is not very well known – even among some lawyers.

One other main finding regarding family issues worth mentioning here is the striking lack of information on issues of application of religiously inspired family laws by secular courts. 'Religious law' may possibly be a misleading term. In single cases, courts rejected the application of foreign religiously inspired law because being secular institutions they felt unable to decide on religious matters.[39] This reveals a profound misunderstanding of Jewish or Islamic legal rules as they are also part of state law and enforced by state institutions.

In many cases, courts have to deal with institutions of foreign laws, including, for example, Sharia law or Jewish law, with which they are not familiar. The RELIGARE project collected testimonies of judges from various member States[40] who expressed the urgent need for accurate information about the specificities of religious family laws, and in particular of those laws they encounter in their daily practice. There is a serious risk of misinterpretation on account of the lack of easily accessible expertise. This might occur both in the application of foreign law according to PIL rules as well as under domestic law regarding, for example, marriage agreement cases.

Contractual conditions regulating the payment of dower (Mahr or Sadaq)[41] in Muslim marriages in particular, have been judged by courts all over the EU.[42] It should be noted that such payments are due to the bride,[43] not to her father/family as is the case in other customary law practices among Kurds,[44] or in countries such as Yemen, Afghanistan or Pakistan, which are not recognisable under European laws,[45] including in Turkey.[46] Such payments would be considered as the sale price for the bride, which would challenge her human dignity as well as her free will to decide whether or not to marry. According to research done by the Turkish Hacettepe University,[47] such payments (*başlık parası*) were given for more than two million women in Turkey. To the contrary, Mahr claims would only improve the legal situation of the bride, and thus cannot be considered to violate her rights.[48]

---

38 Cf. Vermeulen and Bader 2012: 7: 'Our respondents did not address issues of *international private law* due to their complexity and people's own lack of relevant first-hand information.'

39 In 2000, the court of appeals in Berlin rejected (reversed by the German Federal Supreme Court in 2004, FamrZ 2004, 1952) the application of Iranian divorce law which was applicable according to German private international law, because it held this law to be *religious as opposed to worldly*, and thus *not applicable in a secular court*; a similar decision is *Kaddoura v Hammoud* (1998), 168 D.L.R. (4th) 503 (Ont. Gev. Div.), 507, based on poor 'advice' by imams.

40 In the RELIGARE seminar held in Brussels on 5–6 December 2011 with judges from several member States.

41 For details, see Rohe 2011: 85ff.

42 On the application of Mahr provisions in Western courts: Fournier 2010: 35–100; Mehdi and Nielsen 2011; Shah 2013: 58–75; Jones-Pauly 2008: 299–330.

43 This was stressed by the French Court of Cassation, November 22, 2005, No. 03-14.961: Therefore, the Mahr cannot be qualified as a 'prix de vente'.

44 Cf. Rumpf 2004: 118.

45 Cf., e.g., Court of Appeals Hamm, 13.01.2011 (I-18 U 88/10).

46 The Court of Cassation has rejected a *başlık parası* claim due to a 'breach of the law and ethical values' of the country; T.C. Yargıtay (19. Civ) no 2009/6565; decision no 2010/4421.

47 Aslan 2011.

48 The Mahr was misinterpreted in this sense by the Regional court of Köln IPRspr. 1980 no. 83; Court of Appeals Lyon, 2 December 2002, reversed by Court of Cassation (1ère civ) 22

On the other hand, taking the payment of Mahr as an indispensable prerequisite for a valid marriage could violate European public policy/ordre public, since this could contradict the principles of freedom of marriage and equality of the spouses.[49]

Two major legal questions have to be dealt with here. First, in cross-border cases the institution of Mahr has to be classified according to PIL rules, to fix the applicable PIL rule.[50] Here, European courts have found varying solutions, ranging from classifying it as a mere gift to regarding it as a part of the marriage contract, as a regulation of the matrimonial regime or as relating to maintenance. Second, when the applicable law is determined, it has to be examined whether the content of the agreement is in accordance with public policy/ordre public. This is the case irrespective of whether foreign or domestic substantive law has to be applied. In some cases, courts[51] have fundamentally misunderstood the Mahr to be a price to be paid for the bride, which would certainly contradict human rights and which does not discern even the basic facts of Mahr (cf. above).

Often the dower payment is divided into two parts. The first one, due at the time of the marriage, is only symbolic, whereas the second part is due at the time of (unilateral) divorce by the husband or at his death. This regulation can be an effective instrument of protection for wives who, according to traditional Islamic law, can only claim post-marital maintenance for three months, or as a tool for bargaining over the post-marital custody of children, which is generally distributed according to patriarchal principles – the wife can then waive her claim for the deferred Mahr in exchange for the husband's agreement to a favourable custody arrangement. In Britain, according to a court decision in 2010,[52] a pre-nuptial agreement was accepted, whereas before this, they were taken to be void for violation of the British public policy/ordre public.[53] Dutch,[54] French[55] and German[56] courts have similarly accepted these agreements in principle.

On the other hand, a Danish court[57] has qualified such agreements as simple donation promises, which are then usually in need of specific forms of contracting often unknown to the parties. This does not necessarily meet the complexity of such agreements, which could become meaningful for the couple when leaving for a country governed by Islamic

---

November 2005, no 03-14.961.

49 Cf. the relevant French decision by the Supreme Court (1ère civ) 4 April 1978 (Benziane), and the Belgian decision by the Court of Appeals Ghent 12 September 1994 (the lack of dower alone is no proof for the lack of consent between the spouses); but see also Court of Appeals Bruxelles 1 February 1994 (JLMB 1994, 599) and 10 May 1996 (RTDF 1998, 43), where the lack of dower was taken as evidence for the lack of consent, but only among other elements indicating a sham marriage.

50 Cf. Kruger 2010: 3

51 Cf. for France, Court of Appeal Lyon 2.12.2002 (thus declaring void a Mahr agreement, and instead applying French law on matrimonial property); but cf. Court of Cassation 22.11.2005, no. 03-14.961 correcting the misinterpretation and thus quashing the Court of Appeals' decision; for Germany, LG Köln IPRspr. 1980 No. 83.

52 *Radmacher v Granatino* [2010] UKSC 42. The prior decision approving Mahr (*Uddin v Choudhury* [2009] EWCA Civ 1205) concerned a case of informal marriage.

53 Information given to the author by Alberto Neidhardt from University of London/Queen Mary College in 2011.

54 Rb Alkmaar 16-10-2008; Rb Rotterdam 22-02-2010.

55 Court of Cassation, 02-12-1997, n. 95-20.026 and 22-11-2005, n. 03-14.961

56 Federal Supreme Court, NJW 1999, p. 574; Court of Appeal Celle FamRZ 1998, pp. 374; Court of Appeal Saarbrücken NJW-RR 2005, pp. 1306; Court of Appeal Stuttgart 29.01.2008, Az 17 UF 233/07.

57 Eastern High Court of Denmark, April 6, 2005; for possible functions of Mahr in Denmark cf. Vinding and Christoffersen 2012: 38.

family law, and clearly indicates the need for more in-depth information about Islamic law institutions in European courts.[58] This necessity was recognised by a Dutch court,[59] which asked the parties to bring forward evidence on the concrete meaning of Mahr according to their home law (of Bangladesh in this case). In fact, Mahr can be taken to be a mere formality when concluding the marriage contract, can deter from unilateral divorce if the payment is due precisely at this time (deferred Mahr), it can replace weak post-divorce maintenance rights of the wife, and can compensate for her lack of participation in acquiring property during marriage. In addition, Mahr provisions enforced may change their function within a European context as compared to when enforced in an Islamic law environment. In Europe, rights to post-marital maintenance can replace the financial function of deferred Mahr payments after divorce in part or totally. It might also be argued that a Mahr payment would amount to unjust enrichment of the wife, due to the fact that under European laws she can claim maintenance much longer than according to the maintenance provisions contained in the Islamic legal order under which the Mahr agreement was concluded.[60]

In sum, it is necessary to thoroughly examine each contract containing Mahr provisions on its own merits in the light of the parties' intentions. The same is true for the Jewish 'ketubah' with regards to its civil aspects such as matrimonial property.[61] In addition, customary practices which are relevant for the parties' express or silent intentions are of equal importance as far as legal relations rely on the party autonomy. They must not be neglected in favour of more abstract religious-legal interpretations.[62]

Changes in Applying Public Policy/Ordre Public: A Shift from Concrete Approaches to Abstract Control of Foreign Norms

The relative majority of case law revealing conflicts between religiously based laws (Islamic and Jewish laws[63] in particular) and secularised European family laws concern divorce. The different ways of reasoning within European legal orders shall be demonstrated using case law examples of repudiation (Talaq) according to Islamic law.[64] Similar problems may occur with regards to the 'Get' (divorce decree given by the husband, which is necessary for remarriage) according to Jewish law.[65]

---

58   In a seminar for European judges organised within the RELIGARE research framework in December 2011, the participants unanimously expressed the need for creating easily accessible information structures for courts and administrations. As an example of the necessity of detailed information, see Menski 2011: 151, 168ff. in particular.

59   Rechtsbank Haarlem March 9, 2004.

60   Cf. the cases decided by German courts: OLG Köln, IPRax 1983, 731983; OLG Celle, FamRZ 1998, 374.

61   Cf. French Court of Cassation 06.07.1988, no. 86-16.499 regarding a Moroccan Jewish couple.

62   Cf. Shah 2013: 58–75.

63   Cf. Freeman 2001: 365–85.

64   For studies concerning the application of Islamic legal provisions, see Foblets 2001: 33, 63 with numerous references, and id. 2007: 10–32; Gärtner 2008; Rohe 2011: 353; Koch 2012.

65   As case law shows, some husbands, once the civil divorce is pronounced, consider themselves free from the law, forgetting the religious aspect of their new situation, which places the ex-wife in a delicate situation of always being officially married in the eyes of Jewish law, although divorced in the eyes of the civil law of the French State. The French courts (Court of Cassation decision 'Levinçon', 29.05.1905; Court of appeal Paris 19.12.2007, no. 07/00609) have abstained from deciding on the wife's request for a Get, since it was of religious nature and thus not to be decided in a secular court. On the other hand, French courts have granted payments for damages to the wife in case of

Should such divorces be granted recognition in the internal legal order of European States?

According to traditional Islamic law, which is still in force in many countries applying Muslim family law despite a number of internal reforms in favour of women,[66] only the husband is entitled to terminate the marriage with a unilateral declaration of repudiation without having to give any reason. This has to be repeated two additional times. Attempts at reconciliation have to be made, but should it fail, the marriage is dissolved. Unilateral proceedings that are the exclusive right of the husband contradict the legal principle of equality between the sexes – since wives only have very limited rights to divorce,[67] as well as the principle of sustainable relationship, which is a characteristic of civil marriage under civil state law. According to unanimous regulations in European legal orders, a Talaq cannot be validly pronounced on European soil.[68] Moreover, the case law unanimously refuses to recognise Talaq procedures performed abroad as soon as an EU citizen or resident is involved. The refusal is grounded either on public policy/ordre public or by applying specific laws that explicitly state that a Talaq will in no way be granted recognition when a national is involved, or when the spouses are habitually residing in Europe (Belgium, England and Wales).[69] The same applies for such divorce procedures, which were started abroad, but partly performed in a member State.[70]

Nevertheless, how should a European legal system address a case where a Talaq has become valid abroad under another legal order?[71] The contentious question that plays in the background here, and that can be phrased in more general terms, is whether a legal proceeding that is in conflict with European human rights standards of protection should be rejected, integrally, or whether courts and administrations should instead focus on the concrete outcome and then decide, case by case, whether this concrete outcome is acceptable for the parties involved. Would European 'public policy/ordre public' prevent its recognition in any case (as opposed to Khul' or other forms of divorce[72]) or only in those cases where the wife was not able to defend her rights and did not agree to the divorce?

---

undue refusal of the husband to give the Get; cf. Court of appeal Paris 19.12.2007, no. 07/00609; Court of appeal Lyon 09.03.2006, H. c/M; Court of Appeal Versailles 16.02.2012, no. 10/04809. Cf. also Douglas et al. 2011: 22f., 25ff, 32ff, 39, and also the decisions of the German Supreme Court regarding the non-recognition of a Get-divorce according to Jewish law in a case where German law applied according to German PIL (28.05.2008, XII ZR 61/06), and of the Belgian Court of Appeal Antwerp 18.12.1981 (RW 1982-83. 453, conf. by Cass. 15.06.1982).

66 For new developments, see Mir-Hosseini 2009: 37–48 with numerous references; Rohe 2011: 182ff, 207ff; Voorhoeve 2012.

67 Cf. Rohe 2011: 93ff, 216ff. Courts usually differentiate between these forms of divorce. Foreign decisions are then recognised if the cases meet the prerequisites of an 'equal rights' divorce. Cf. the French Court of Cassation, February 23, 2011, No. 10-14.760.

68 Cf., e.g., Civil Court Brussels, May 26, 1978; House of Lords, *R. v Secretary of State for the Home Department ex p. Fatima Ghulam* [1986] AC 527 (HL). The reasoning and wording has certainly changed since the decision of the Court of Appeals Rome from 29 October 1948, 'it is abhorred by the moral and legal mentality of the peoples who have reached a higher degree of civilisation, and who have a far more advanced ethical and social concept of marriage than Eastern peoples'.

69 Cf. only Art. 46 Family Law Act 1986 of England and Wales; Art. 57 section 2.2., 2.3. Belgian PIL code 2004.

70 For the UK, cf. *R. v Secretary of State for the Home Department ex p. Fatima (Ghulam)* [1986] 2 W.L.R. 693 concerning an Islamic Talaq-divorce, and *Berkovits v Grinberg* [1995] 2 W.L.R. 553 concerning a Jewish Get-divorce.

71 For an overview, see Alidadi 2005: 1–80; Foblets 2007: 10–32.

72 Cf. French Court of Cassation 23.02.2011, no. 10-14.760, regarding a French-Moroccan case where the spouses had lived separately for three years and the divorce was not qualified as a unilateral

There has been a remarkable shift within European legal orders over the last decade. The traditional PIL approach, where the *outcome* of applying the respective foreign law is addressed, is increasingly challenged in favour of examining the foreign norm itself. German,[73] Italian[74] and Spanish[75] courts still broadly adhere to the traditional approach.[76] Thus, the recognition of Talaq would contradict public policy/ordre public in cases where the wife was not able to claim her legitimate interests or was not even informed about the divorce. In other cases, where the prerequisites for divorce according to the law of the land would be fulfilled in a comparable way,[77] or if the wife agrees, the legality of such a divorce would be accepted by the controlling legal authority. By the same token, the contractual delegation of the right to divorce by the husband to his wife (Talaq-e Tafwid) under Iranian law, has been accepted by German courts,[78] thus enabling the wife to apply for divorce without the husband's consent.

Belgium followed this way until after the enactment of the new law on PIL in 2005, when the courts began to adopt a stricter attitude to recognition.[79] The same development can be found in court decisions in France since 2004[80] and the Netherlands, where in the past the differentiation made by German courts equally applied.[81] In Austria, the Supreme Court[82] from the beginning refused to accept any kind of Talaq. There is an emerging trend in PIL to follow a policy of legal symbolism, which means to abstractly defend principles as such instead of deliberating the particularities of a case before the court.

---

divorce by the Moroccan court; Court of Appeals Versailles 25.03.2010 no. 08/08808; Dutch Supreme Court 13 July 2001, rechtspraak.nl LJN AB2623 (WPNR 2001 (6470)); Cour d'appel Antwerpen 30 June 1982, J.D.I. 1982, 740f.

73 Cf., e.g., Court of Appeals Düsseldorf, FamRZ 1998, 1113; Court of Appeals Köln, FamRZ 2000, 895; Court of Appeals Zweibrücken, NJW-RR 2002, 581; Court of Appeals Hamm 07.03.2006, BeckRS 2007, 00423; Court of Appeals Frankfurt a.M. 11.05.2009, 5 WF 66/09, BeckRS 2009, 24414; Court of Appeals Hamm NJW-RR 2010, 1090; Rohe 2003: 46, 50.

74 Cf. Court of Appeals Cagliari, Nay 16, 2008, No. 198.

75 Cf. Supreme Court, ATS 21.04.1998, RJ 3563.

76 The Court of Appeals Stuttgart is stricter in its rules; cf. the decisions in IPRax 2000, 427; FamRZ 2004, 25.

77 Only one recent French decision seems to follow this way: see French Court of Cassation 20.10.2010, no. 09-15.379, where in a Moroccan case (recognition of a Moroccan judgment) the court considered the failure of reconciliation efforts and the impossibility to maintain marital life due to the wife's adultery with her neighbour and the desertion of the marital home.

78 Supreme Court 6 October 2004, XII ZR 225/01, BeckRS 2006, 10621; Court of Appeals Koblenz 26 November 2008, 9 UF 653/06, BeckRS 2008, 24576.

79 Court of Cassation April 29, 2002; after 2005 cf. Court of Appeals Mons, December 20, 2007; Civil court Liège, June 26, 2009; Labour court Brussels, May 27, 2010; but also Labour court Brussels, January 12, 2011. Cf. Foblets 2007: 10–32; Koch 2012: 175–8.

80 Older decisions by the Court of Cassation from 2001, 2002 are now overruled following a turn of the same court in 2004 (February 17, 2004, No. 01-11.549, and No 02-11.618; Court of Cassation, January 3, 2006, No. 04-15.231; Court of Cassation November 4, 2009, No. 08-20.574). The decisions of 2004 were implicitly approved by the ECHR in the decision of 8 November 2005 (Affaire D.D. c France, no 3/02, available in French at the court's website http://hudoc.echr.coe.int), pointing at the relevant new French decisions.

81 The last decisions in this sense were Court of Cassation July 3, 2001, Rev. crit. int. privé 2002, 704 note Gannagé.

82 OGH decision of 31.08.2006 (6Ob189/06), Zeitschrift für Rechtsvergleichung 2007, 35; OGH decision of 28.06.2007 (3Ob130/07z); both decisions available at http://ris.bka.gv.at [last accessed 14 December 2013].

The crucial legal question is whether legislative bodies and the courts compare foreign legal norms categorically as with their normative domestic 'counterpart' in an abstract way, or whether the results of the strict application of foreign norms must be controlled in specific cases. Whereas the abstract 'human rights approach' leads to clear results – the rejection of Talaq in any case – the concrete approach lacks the same clarity. This might be one of the main reasons for the increasing popularity of the abstract approach in several European legal orders. In addition, it can be used as a political instrument to demonstrate European 'cultural self-defence' against Islamic law.

The concrete approach is worthy of consideration, since it might help the divorced wife in cases when she wishes to remarry and therefore needs the recognition of the previous Talaq, for example.[83] In case of principled non-recognition of the dissolution of marriage, women are forced to apply for divorce in European courts. This means that they have to divorce for a second time, which often turns out to be time-consuming and expensive, in particular in cases where the husband has moved and is living in a country that is not easily accessible for judicial correspondence, or if his address is unknown. If the residence permit for the woman is dependent on the new marriage, her need to have the Talaq recognised is even more pressing. Moreover, refusal to grant any recognition of Talaq, even in cases where the wife does not protest, creates limping marriages: in effect, the couple will be considered still married in the legal order of the European country where they habitually reside, even if they have formally divorced under the legal order of the country where the Talaq was performed. The abstract 'human rights approach' would thus turn itself against the person it intends to protect, and the woman would consequently be punished twice.

In practice, only a flexible approach to the Talaq gives precedence to the search for a fair and equitable outcome for women who consent to it[84] over abstract human rights reasoning, and thereby offers an illustration of inclusive even-handedness. The Belgian legislator has tried to formulate a balanced solution in Article 57 of the 2005 PIL code. In general, the declaration of the husband's will to dissolve the marriage abroad, without his wife having the same right, cannot be recognised (section 1). But according to the regulation in section 2 (2.4), a Talaq validly performed under certain circumstances can be recognised if the wife has accepted the dissolution of the marriage unambiguously and without any compulsion. If applied cautiously on the basis of the concrete approach, this regulation may serve as an example for good practice. Nevertheless, it should be amended for cases where the prerequisites for divorce are equally fulfilled under domestic law, thus leaving no space for the application of public policy/ordre public on the basis of the concrete approach.

The same systemic differences – abstract or concrete approach – are visible in polygamous marriages. Polygamy fundamentally contradicts European legal standards; it cannot be contracted legally in Europe and is even punishable under many European penal codes. Similarly, polygamous marriages by European citizens or domiciliaries that have been performed abroad are not recognised under different European legislations.[85] The question arises in other cases (where neither citizens nor domiciliaries are involved) as to whether the second wife or other wives are entitled to claim their rights to maintenance from

---

83   This was the case in the decisions of the German Supreme Court from 2004 (BGH FamRZ 2004, 1952) and from 2007 (NJW-RR 2007: 145, 148ff). The same policy seems to be followed in Denmark according to Nielsen 1997: 69–70.
84   Cf. n. 85.
85   Cf. the English Court of Appeal in *Hussain v Hussain* [1982] 1 All ER 369.

their husband, rights to participate in the estate of the deceased husband under succession law, or in social security claims he acquired during his time in employment.

In England, courts have rejected claims to a widow's pension by women who engaged in polygamous marriage, resulting in none of the wives in the marriage receiving a payment.[86] In 2009 a Dutch court rejected the request of a second wife for divorce, because the marriage itself was not recognised.[87] On the other hand, German social security laws treat polygamous marriages as legally valid, provided that the marriage contracts are valid under laws applicable to them at the time of their conclusion.[88] The legal reasoning is to ensure that women in polygamous marriages are not deprived of their marital rights, including maintenance. Thus, according to German[89] and Spanish[90] social security laws, widows' pensions are divided among widows who were living in polygamous marriages. In Belgium, widows' pensions generally have to be divided similarly to the way it is handled in Germany. Nevertheless, there are disputes between the courts[91] regarding whether, in cases where the first wife has the nationality of a country prohibiting polygamy, the second wife has to be excluded from widow pension claims. The underlying 'principle of proximity', which aims at granting the first wife the full rights available to wives in monogamous marriages, applies in France according to the Court of Cassation.[92] English courts[93] have granted a second wife dower payment agreed upon in the marriage contract under the law of contract, thus separating this particular provision from status issues.

The law differentiates between mainly private aspects of marriage and predominantly public ones, especially those relating to immigration law. Italian[94] and German[95] law, for instance, provide only the first wife in polygamous marriages with marital privileges within their scope of application, for example, regarding residence permits. Alternatively, a Dutch judgment[96] from 2009 accepted such a marriage for immigration purposes, but another

---

86   Court of Appeal in *Bibi v Chief Adjudication Officer* [1998] 1 FLR 375: none of the widows is accepted to be one legally; cf. the critical remarks of Pearl 2000: 14.

87   District Court Utrecht, January 21, 2009, LJN BH 3029.

88   Cf. Regional Court Frankfurt a.M.FamRZ 1976, p. 217; Regional Court Osnabrück NJW-RR 1998, p. 582; Local Court Bremen StAZ 1991, pp. 232, 233; Administrative Court of Appeals Kassel NVwZ-RR 1999, pp. 274, 275.

89   Cf. para 34 sect. 2 Social Code I.

90   Cf. Superior Court of Justice of Galicia (TSJ de Galicia, Sala de lo Social), April 2, 2002; Superior Court of Justice of Madrid (TSJ de Madrid, Sala de lo Social), July 29, 2002; Superior Court of Justice of Andalusia (TSJ de Andalusia, Sala de lo Social), January 30, 2003; Superior Court of Justice of Catalonia (TSJ de Cataluña, Sala de lo Social), July 30, 2003.

91   Cf. the Belgian Court of Cassation, December 3, 2007, and Constitutional Court, June 4, 2009. The latter equated the situation of simultaneous polygamy to the (well-established Belgian) successive polygamy (remarriage after divorce), which equally leads to shared claims in the public sector pension scheme. The same reasoning can be found in Spanish cases. Cf. also Labour Court Mons 25.06.2009 (decision in favour of second wife).

92   Court of Cassation, July 6, 1988, No. 85-12.743. On the other hand, a polygamous marriage valid under the domestic law of either spouse can be recognised according to Court of Cassation, September 24, 2002, No. 00-15.789.

93   Cf. *Shahnaz v Rizwan* [1964] 2 All E.R. 993; *Qureshi v Qureshi* [1971] 1 All E.R. 325.

94   Cf. Regional Administrative Court of Emilia-Romagna, December 14, 1994, No. 926; Court of Appeals Turin, April 18, 2001.

95   Cf. OVG Koblenz 12.03.2004 (10 A 11717/03), available at http://www.asyl.net/index.php?id=185&tx_ttnews[tt_news]=19684&cHash=e4a46e2d9a [last accessed 14 December 2013].

96   Rechtsbank Den Haag, November 23, 2009.

Dutch court[97] rejected in 2006 the possibility for the second wife to voluntarily participate in the social security scheme of her 'husband'. In 2011 the Spanish Supreme court[98] rejected a woman's application for citizenship for lack of integration, because she was living in a polygamous marriage. Thus, while private effects of polygamy such as the second wife's rights against the husband are recognised, polygamy cannot be supported by the expense of third parties or the state as a whole.

A Shift from Cross-border Cases to Internal Diversity beyond PIL

General

Over the years, the demographic profile of European communities of (im)migrant origin has undergone profound change. The presence of these groups and communities is no longer linked primarily to (im)migration, but now represents a permanent settlement in the country of habitual residence. In consequence, they obtain the citizenship of their country of residence in increasing numbers, not to forget the groups of citizens of the third, fourth or older generations of previous 'migrants'. The family relations of these groups are regularly governed by domestic law, irrespective of whether PIL relies on nationality or residence as the main connecting factor.

In addition, there is a consequent development in European PIL laws regarding connecting factors in international family and succession law (for example, on the EU level, the Rome III Regulation on divorce and legal separation [Regulation No 1259/2010][99] and on matters of succession [Regulation No 650/2012]). (Habitual) residence ever more frequently replaces nationality as the sole or prime connecting factor in international family law. This development demonstrates an increasing self-perception of being immigration countries. While countries with a relatively stable population tended to choose nationality as the prime connecting factor, which is easy to handle, immigration countries usually tend to 'homogenise' laws by preferring residence as the main connecting factor – granting normative plurality 'within' instead of applying foreign law.[100] In combination with the jurisdiction rules, domestic substantive law will in consequence mostly be applied irrespective of the nationality of the parties involved. Furthermore, practical aspects would corroborate such a development. As far as a choice of law (residence or nationality) is granted to the parties, legal advice will often be indispensable. In Germany, notaries would often have to be involved, because the relevant law requires notary registration. It cannot realistically be expected that notaries would tend to give totally 'open' advice whether to choose foreign or domestic law, since usually their knowledge of domestic law prevails over other legal orders, and their professional insurances only cover advice in domestic law, as opposed to foreign law.[101]

All these developments are changing the status quo. Matters of personal status become, in such cases, first and foremost matters governed by domestic law. Thus, the integration

---

97 District court Rotterdam 20 July 2006, Rechtspraak.nl LJN AY5484 concerning the application of the Treaty regarding Social Security between The Netherlands and Morocco.
98 Supreme Court, Chamber for Administrative Proceedings 30.06.2011, no. 3902/2008.
99 Cf., inter alia, Fallon 2012: 291–317.
100 Cf. Rohe 1994b: 1–39.
101 Information given by notary Prof. Dr Sieghörtner, Erlangen/Germany.

of former 'foreign' regulations into domestic contract law will gain even more importance, insofar as four major tasks have to be tackled.

First, former 'foreign' legal institutions have to be considered and (indirectly) implemented into domestic legal orders within the scope of dispositive contract law. Sound information about such institutions is then of prime importance. This is particularly true regarding institutions based on religious laws, which are bluntly taken to be contrary to European secular legal orders by the general public (especially Islamic law[102]). Since they will be measured according to the relatively strict internal public policy/ordre public (as compared to international public policy/ordre public), non-biased information based solely on facts is needed.

Second, as far as parties may choose between domestic and foreign law (of their nationality), informed consent regarding the implications of such choice has to be granted appropriately.

Third, circular migration and cross-border family life are creating increasingly legally hybrid situations. The parties affected are in need of recognition of their family regulations both in the state of actual residence and in the state(s) of future residence and/or residence of other relevant family members. Thus, they are virtually forced into finding solutions fitting into the legal framework of more than one state. Limping situations would infringe on their interests and thus their mobility even more than in cases of permanent immigration to a particular state. On the other hand, limping situations cannot be avoided in any case, if this means depriving parties of human rights; secular European family laws respecting the human right to marriage cannot recognise rules preventing marriages, for example between Jews and non-Jews, between Christians and non-Christians or between Muslim women and non-Muslim men according to Islamic law which is still in force in most Islamic states, and even preventing marriage between Shi'i and Sunni Muslims according to Shi'i law.[103] In such cases, the marriage has to be registered, but the parties should be well informed about the possible limping legal situation regarding the relevant foreign legal order.

Fourth, equal rights and duties in family issues have to be granted for members of religious minority groups and 'sects'. Case law indicates that, particularly in custody disputes and in cases of divorce for fault, the mere fact of adhering to a non-mainstream religion or belief must not work to the disadvantage of such persons.

RELIGARE sociological data reveals that the legal diversity within the EU is mirrored among the inhabitants of the member States.[104] The more religious institutions play a role in organising family status (marriage, divorce), the more equal treatment is required. On the other hand, there is no unanimous attitude regarding the importance of religious rules, whether in society as a whole or among members of certain religions. But it is clear that there is little or no awareness of the legal complexities regarding PIL and domestic law. In contrast, nearly all interviewees stressed the importance of creating legally valid marriages.

---

102 Cf. Rohe 2013.
103 Cf. the German cases Federal Supreme Court BGHZ 56, 180; Court of Appeal MünchenFamRZ 1970, pp. 408; Court of Appeal Hamm NJW 1977, pp. 1596; Bavarian Supreme Civil Court FamRZ 1970, pp. 656; Court of Appeal Koblenz FamRZ 1994, pp. 1262; an example of bad practice is Court of Appeal Oldenburg IPRspr. 1967 No. 68: the right to marriage was not considered even in a case where a child had been born. For Italy, see the relevant Ministry of Interior Affairs' circular no. 46 of 11 September 2007 and the court decisions Court of Reggio Emilia 09.06.2005, Court of Milan 14.03.2007, Court of Piancenza 05.05.2011. Cf. also Rohe 2011: 82f; 359f.
104 Cf. the relevant parts of Vermeulen 2012.

Key Observations

In the field of domestic civil law, including family law, internal public policy/ordre public applies (as opposed to international public policy/ordre public in cases where foreign law is applicable under PIL rules). This increases possible tensions between the substantive family law of the land and 'foreign' legal institutions. While international public policy would accept considerable differences in the outcome of decisions under foreign or domestic law, the more the cross-border aspect prevails and the less the forum state is concerned (weak 'Inlandsbezug'/relationship to the forum state), by contrast, internal public policy has to follow indispensible common minimum standards for civil life 'within'. Here, reasonable accommodation should be sought by increasing trust in state institutions/systems with regards to accommodating religious needs (review of interpretations of laws as to whether they impose limits on free choice for valid reasons, or whether they only reflect past historical developments). Thus, in particular regarding marriage contracts, the freedom of choice should be broadly granted within the necessary protective limits drawn by (appropriate) mandatory law.

Again, one of the most relevant and interesting examples are dower (Mahr) agreements as a part of Muslim marriage contracts. The function(s) of Mahr can indeed change in the context of migration. Treating Mahr as a contract (or as part of a contract) may be deemed appropriate, especially for unregistered marriages (see Chapter 1 by Prakash Shah). The principles developed by the UK Supreme Court in *Radmacher v Granatino* may serve as an example of good practice. According to that decision, a valid agreement has to meet the following minimum conditions:

- The husband and wife must enter into it out of their own free will, without undue influence and after being informed of its implications. Any standard contractual vitiating factors including duress, fraud or misrepresentation, as well as any pressures upon a party to agree, unstable emotional state, unworthy conduct, or exploitation of a position of authority may affect the weight of the agreement.
- Reasonable requirements of the children of the family must not be prejudiced by the nuptial agreement.

RELIGARE sociological data from Denmark reflects insecurities among Muslims themselves on whether Mahr is still necessary or recommendable in a migration context. This demonstrates that lawyers and also Muslims themselves are in need of more thorough information or advice on the issue.

The leading principle of contractualisation of former 'foreign' institutions could equally solve shortcomings of foreign legal orders, which do not recognise all religious groups equally. This concerns citizens of such countries resident in the EU. Under domestic contract law, such unrecognised groups would be equally able to organise their family affairs within the scope of dispositive substantive law, since recognition as 'foreign state law' would not be required. Nevertheless, for a complete understanding of the possible complexities (different functions) of the Mahr, is it absolutely necessary to examine the intentions of the concrete parties and thus the concrete function of Mahr for the case at stake. Superficial classifications (for example, categorising it as a gift which need not be restored after the breakup of the engagement or the marriage) should be avoided.

Besides cases of integrating former foreign legal institutions into the domestic contractual system, there are well-established institutions of family law like custody or divorce for fault where all kinds of religious minorities might face discrimination. Courts in the member States have had to repeatedly grant equal treatment to religious minorities, including Christian confessions[105] or 'sects',[106] due to biased decisions of administrations or lower courts. Case law is available regarding divorce for fault. French courts have thus decided that belonging to the Jehovah's Witnesses[107] or to a 'sect'[108] cannot constitute a 'fault' as such. Good practice would rather weigh up the concrete exercise of one's religion with the concrete family duties to be fulfilled by the spouses.[109]

A much greater number of cases concern custody and guardianship claims. Here again, bad practice would only stress possible abstract 'dangers of indoctrination' of the children or their alienation from mainstream society,[110] whereas good practice would respect freedom of (minority) religion and only look at the concrete, sufficiently proven circumstances of the case to provide the best support for the child.[111] In fact, according to the ECHR[112] and European constitutions, raising children and educating them is primarily the obligation and the right of the parents, whereas the role of the state is to protect children in cases of insufficient or even detrimental performance of the parents' obligations. The question of whether the integration into a religious community would serve the best interests of the child or not has thus to be answered first and foremost by the parents. The state and its institutions are not entitled to limit the interpretation of the best interests to 'secular' arguments (which would indeed turn out to be a new kind of 'state religion or belief'). In cases where some restrictive measures against possible indoctrination have to be taken, they still have to comply with the principle of proportionality.[113] Concretely, Belgian courts (shared by courts in other member States) have developed a three-stage test, which could serve as an example for good practice in many constellations:

---

105 In Belgium, 15 out of 45 published cases concern Jehovah's Witnesses.

106 Cf. the Danish decision of the Civil Law Directorate 10.04.2001 (CRD2001.1998-540-84-) concerning a parent adhering to Hare Krishna. The country report stresses the relevance of this decision (under former law of custody which regularly led to the sole custody of one parent) regarding the 'unease with new or smaller religious identities in the country'.

107 Court of Appeal Bourges 20.03.1996 (Juris-Data no. 043754).

108 Court of Cassation, 2. Cil., 08.11.1995 (Bull. Civ. II, no. 271; RTD civ., 1996, p. 369).

109 Cf. the cases cited above at note 26.

110 The Danish sociological team states: 'All religious interviewees warn against that the state misunderstand the role of religion in family life and only accepts secular family life.'

111 Cf., e.g., the Italian jurisprudence in Court of Velletri 20.12.1999 concerning a Jehovah's Witness mother, where no evidence was given for any detrimental impact on the children; in contrast, the Court for Minor Children of Genova (decree no. 504 f 16.08.1999) held that the mother belonging to the Lubavitch Movement subjected her daughters to an extremely strict style of life without their own or the father's consent. Other cases regarding Jehovah's Witness parents are less clear in their reasoning, e.g. Court of Appeals of Rome decided (judgment of 18.04.2007).

112 Cf. the custody case decided by the ECtHR on 3 May 2012 (İlker Ensar Uyanık v Turkey, application no. 60328/09).

113 Cf. the Spanish Constitutional Court 29.05.2000, no. 141/2000 concerning a father who was a member of the Universal Gnostic Church of Spain; the English decision in *Re S (A Minor) (Blood Transfusion: Adoption Order Conditions)* [1994] 2 F.L.R. 416 concerning a residence order to a Jehovah's Witness party, the court did not refuse the order and held that in case of necessity of a blood transfusion contrary to Jehovah's Witnesses' conviction, a specific order could be granted.

- The first test addresses stability/continuity: children should be raised in the religion/belief chosen by their parents at the beginning of their marriage.[114]
- The second test of increasing importance requires socio-political expertise of the children, in order to choose one out of the beliefs in dispute.[115]
- The third, most recent and most popular test looks at possible 'syncretic balancing' of the conflicting religions/beliefs, with, for example, mixed education, to provide children with free and informed choice during pre-adolescence.[116]

In addition, some custody (residence[117]) cases concern role conflicts due to religious-legal or cultural pre-understandings. In the sphere of PIL, child abduction cases relating to such conflicts are numerous. Many cases concern custody conflicts between European non-Muslim mothers and Muslim fathers maintaining family ties with their own or their ancestors' country of origin. According to states in which family laws are influenced by Islam, the best child welfare is sought only by abstract, gender-biased considerations despite recent reforms in some countries. They lead to the effect that in cases of custody in personal matters (Hadana), younger children usually stay with the mother (differences between boys and girls are made, leaving girls with the mother longer than boys), whereas older children will stay with the father. In addition, often only the father or other male relatives are entitled to guardianship (Walaya). Furthermore, it is the husband alone who may decide on the family's place of residence.[118] In contrast, European family law examines the best welfare of the child in a non-gender-biased way[119] weighing up all the circumstances of the concrete case. In addition, joint guardianship and custody has ever more frequently become the rule according to modern family laws, irrespective of the marital status of the parents. In cases where the fathers do not accept the decision of family courts in favour of the mother, child

---

114 Cf. Court of Appeal Mons 23.04.2002 (JLMB 2004, 205) concerning the baptism of a Catholic child. Cf. also the English Court of Appeal in *Re P. (A Minor) (Residence Order: Child's Welfare)* [1999] 2 F.L.R. 573 considering 'religious heritage' as relevant, but not paramount. In other cases, the factor of 'social integration' of the child in the environment of the parent with whom s/he is living has played an important role; cf. the English decision in *Re S (Change of Names: Cultural Factors)* [2001] 3 FCR 648 in a mixed Muslim and Sikh parents case concerning the child's name; German Court of Appeal Oldenburg 09.02.2010 (13 UF 8/10) in a mixed Catholic and Muslim parents case concerning baptism.

115 Cf. Court of Appeals Brussels 25.11.1999 (AJT 1999 771). Sound evidence on the alleged religious fanaticism of the former spouse is required (a case concerning a former Catholic convert to Islam).

116 Cf. Court of Appeal Liège 18.12.2000 (RTDF 2002, 118); Court of Appeal Liège 17.10.2000 (JLMB 2001, 946); Court of Appeal Brussels 05.07.2001 (RTDF 2002 499); a huge number of further cases is reported in the Belgian template on WP 3 issues: guardianship and custody. Cf. also the English case in *S (Children) (Specific Issue order: Religion: Circumcision)* [2004] EWHC 1282 (Fam) in a mixed Muslim and Jain parents case; *Re A (Local Authority: Religious Upbringing* [2010] EWHC 2503 (Fam) in a mixed Muslim and re-convert Catholic parents case; the German decision of the Court of Appeal Schleswig 08.05.2003 (13 UF 62/02) concerning a mixed Protestant and Muslim parents case regarding baptism; the Italian decision Court of Appeal Rome 04.04.2007 in a mixed Jewish and Christian parents case regarding religious education; cf. also Court of Tivoli 30.06.2009.

117 In England and Wales, the term of custody has been replaced by 'residence' (residential/non-residential parents).

118 Cf. Rohe 2011: 96f, 228f.

119 It cannot be excluded that in some cases there is a factual bias towards the mother, in particular in cases where mothers are nationals of the forum state in contrast to the fathers. Further research in this field would be desirable.

abduction has been known to take place. On the other hand, there are cases where mothers have tried to obtain sole custody by alleging that the fathers would abduct the children (by, for example, not returning them after holidays spent abroad),[120] and therefore prevent the children from visiting their relatives abroad.

In such conflicts, a neutral fact-based solution has to be sought before granting sole custody to one parent. The possibility of courts privileging their 'own' citizens should be taken into consideration. At the same time, efficient protection of the child is of prime importance, for example in cases where girls are in concrete danger of being mutilated (FGM) or abducted[121] in the country of the parents' or family's origin.[122] In such cases custody can be and has to be withdrawn.

In addition, creative solutions might be found to grant stability and the necessary amount of cooperation between the parents (one-sided decisions often lead to continuing conflicts at the expense of the children). Informal solutions might help here, but only under the condition of informed consent of the parties.[123] The same is true for international cases, if according to PIL rules foreign laws on custody or guardianship have to be applied. The public policy/ordre public test has to look only at the outcome regarding the best welfare of the child in question.[124]

A European Model for Unity and Even-handed Diversity

In sum, the following model discerns the different levels of legal action and the major aspects to be considered for reaching two essential goals: preserving the structure and basis of secular European legal orders by granting inclusive even-handedness for everybody.

In my opinion the solution has to be found in formulating common laws under the constitution as a result of debates in parliament and society. Common convictions are changing with respect to important parts of the legal order: European family law in force at present is fundamentally different from the respective rules 30 or 50 years ago. One of the most striking examples might be the change in law concerning homosexual life. Whereas 40 years ago such activities were punishable under German penal law even among adults, homosexual persons may now enter into a registered partnership granting them rights not far from those of marriage. Considering this fact, it is upon society as a whole to (often controversially) discuss these issues, thus enabling the legislator to legally define the fields where unity in standards and behaviour is necessary, and others, where diversity may take place and might even be desirable. The characteristics of the European legal system of managing diversity may be described firstly as granting diversity under the rule of a uniform law, which in every field of regulation has to decide whether unified standards have to be granted (e.g. in constitutional law, penal law, administrative law) and how far

---

120 Cf., e.g., the decision of the Danish Eastern High Court 18.08.2008 (OE2008.B-1005-08-) concerning a Pakistani Muslim father.

121 Cf. the Dutch Rechtsbank Den Haag 24.03.2003 in a case where the father expressly threatened to commit an abduction.

122 Cf., e.g., German Federal Court of Justice 15.12.2004 (XII ZB 166/03).

123 Cf. the Danish decision Eastern High Court of Denmark 21 February 2006 (OE2006.B-3980-05), rejecting a custody contract arranged by an imam for lack of information on the mother's side regarding the content of the agreement.

124 Cf., e.g., the contrasting cases decided by the German Federal Supreme Court in application of Iranian family law (14.10.1992, XII ZB 18/92; 24.04.1993, XII ZB 96/92).

the ruling law itself has to grant self-determination within a certain framework of options (private law).

In addition to that, the focus of self-determination lies in granting individual rights. In the field of legal norms, there is no option for claiming competing collective rights. The main reason for that is to be found in the European perception of the law itself. There is no sphere of law being restricted to group interests which could then be regulated autonomously by these groups; the law governing private aspects of family life may serve as an example. Certainly family life is primarily a matter concerning the persons involved. Nevertheless, the legal framing of family life is intrinsically linked to social cohesion.[125] The centralisation of power in the hands of the democratic legislator under the rule of law has replaced former weak political unities, which had to rely on far-reaching communitarian structures. The latter would create space for the exercise of collective rights at the expense of conflicting individual rights of the weaker members of the community, which would simply be unacceptable under a constitution demanding the efficient protection of human rights.

Bibliography

Ahdar, R. and Aroney, N. (eds) 2010. *Shari'a in the West*. Oxford: Oxford University Press.

Aldeeb, A.-S.S. and Aronovitz, A. (eds) 1999. *Le droit musulman de la famille et des successions à l'épreuve des ordres juridiques occidentaux*. Zürich: Schulthess.

Alidadi, K. 2005. The Western judicial answer to Islamic Talaq. *UCLA Journal of Islamic & Near Eastern Law*, 5, 1–80.

Aluffi Beck-Peccoz, R. and Zincone, G. (eds) 2004. *The Legal Treatment of Islamic Minorities in Europe*. Leuven: Peeters.

An-Na'im, A.A. 2008. *Islam and the Secular State. Negotiating the Future of Shari'a*, Cambridge MA/London: Harvard University Press.

Asayyad, N. and Castells, M. (eds) 2002. *Muslim Europe or Euro-Islam: Politics, Culture, and Citizenship in the Age of Globalization*. Lanham: Lexington Books.

Aslan, H. 2011. *kadın olmanın bedeli*. [Online: 11 April]. Available at: http://www.haberturk.com/yazarlar/huseyin-aslan/619693-kadin-olmanin-bedeli [last accessed 6 June 2013].

Austrian Association for the Middle East Hammer-Purgstall (ed.) 2009. *Family, Law and Religion. Debates in the Muslim World and Europe and their Implications for Co-operation and Dialogue*. Oberwart, Austria: Gröbner Druck.

Atlan, Gabrielle 2002. *Les juifs et le divorce: Droit, histoire et sociologie du divorce religieux*. Bern: Peter Lang.

Bakht, N. 2005. *Arbitration, Religion and Family Law. Private Justice on the Backs of Women*. Ottawa: National Association of Women and the Law.

Bano, S. 2007. Muslim family justice and human rights: The experience of British Muslim women. *Journal of Comparative Law*, 2, 38–66.

Bano, S. 2012. *An Exploratory Study of Shariah Councils in England with respect to Family Law*. [Online: University of Reading]. Available at: http://www.reading.ac.uk/web/

---

125 In my opinion, the Lebanese and other experiences show that separate systems of family law instead of a unified system granting a certain range of options can contribute to social tensions and lead to the emergence of exclusive self-definitions partly directed against other groups in society.

FILES/law/An_exploratory_study_of_Shariah_councils_in_England_with_respect_to_family_law_.pdf [last accessed 6 June 2013].
Von Bar, C. (ed.) 1999. *Islamic Law and its Reception by the Courts in the West*. Köln: Carl Heymanns Verlag KG.
Benhabib, S., Shapiro, I. and Petranovic, D. (eds) 2007. *Identities, Affiliations and Allegiances*. Cambridge: Cambridge University Press.
Bergmann, A., Ferid, M. and Henrich, D. 1952. *Internationales Ehe- und Kindschaftsrecht mit Staatsangehörigkeitsrecht*. Länderbericht Ägypten. Loseblattsammlung. Frankfurt a.M., Berlin: Verlag für Standesamtswesen.
Berkovits, B. 1993. Get and Talaq in English law: Reflections on law and policy, in *Islamic Family Law*, edited by C. Mallat and J. Connors. London: Graham & Trotman. 119–46.
Bernard-Maugiron, N. and Dupret, B. (eds) 2010. *Ordre public et droit musulman de la famille en Europe et en Afrique du Nord*. Bruxelles: Bruylant.
Biale, R. 1984. *Women and Jewish Law: The Essential Texts, their History, and their Relevance for Today*. New York: Schocken.
Boele-Woelki et al. 2003. *European Family Law in Action*. Antwerp: Intersentia.
Bowen, J. 2009. *Can Islam be French? Pluralism and Pragmatism in a Secularist State*. Princeton: Princeton University Press.
Bowen, J. 2012. *Blaming Islam*. Cambridge MA: Boston Review.
Bramadat, P. and Koenig, M. (eds) 2009. *International Migration and the Governance of Religious Diversity*. Montréal/Kingston: Metropolis.
Büchler, A. 2011. *Islamic Law in Europe? Legal Pluralism and its Limits in European Family Laws*. Farnham/Burlington: Ashgate.
Cadet, F. and Peruzzetto, S. 2005. *L'ordre public en droit international de la famille. Etude comparé France/Espagne*. Paris: L'Harmattan.
Carlier, J.-Y. and Verwilghen, M. (eds) 1992. *Le statut personnel des musulmans. Droit comparé et droit international privé*. Brussels: Bruylant.
Cesari, J. 2010. *Muslims in the West after 9/11: Religion, Politics and Law*. Abingdon/New York: Routledge.
Cesari, J. 2014 (in print). *Handbook of Islam in Europe*. Oxford: Oxford University Press.
Cesari, J. and McLoughlin, S. (eds) 2005. *European Muslims and the Secular State*. Farnham/Burlington: Ashgate.
Charnay, J.-P. 2001. *La Charia et l'Occident*. Paris: L'Herne.
Cilardo, A. 2002. *Il diritto islamico e il sistema giuridico italiano. Le bozze di intesa tra la Repubblica italiana e le associazioni islamiche italiane*. Napoli: Edizioni Scientifiche Italiane.
Connolly, A.J. 2010. *Cultural Difference on Trial. The Nature and Limits of Judicial Understanding*. Farnham/Burlington: Ashgate.
Conseil de la communauté marocaine à l'étranger (ed.) 2010. *Le statut juridique de l'Islam en Europe*. Acte du colloque international organize par le Conseil de la communauté marocaine à l'étranger Fès, 14 et 15 Mars 2009. Rabat: Marsam.
Coward, H., Hinnells, J.R. and Williams, R.B. (eds) 2000. *The South Asian Religious Diaspora in Great Britain, Canada and the United States*. New York: State University of New York Press.
Demosthenous-Pashalidou, A. 1999. Rechtskollisionen bei der Auflösung von Mischehen zwischen Muslimen und Andersgläubigen. *Der Islam*, 76(2), 313–33.
Dilcher, G. and Staff, I. (eds) 1984. *Christentum und modernes Recht: Beiträge zum Problem der Säkularisation*. Frankfurt a.M.: Suhrkamp.

Douglas, G. et al. 2011. *Social Cohesion and Civil Law: Marriage, Divorce and Religious Courts*. Cardiff: Cardiff University.

Erdemir, A., Rittersberger-Tiliç, H., Ergun, A. and Kahveci, H. (eds) 2008. *Rethinking Global Migration: Practices, Policies, and Discourses in the European Neighbourhood*. Ankara: KORA.

Estin, A.L. 2012. Unofficial family law, in *Marriage and Divorce in a Multicultural Context*, edited by J. Nichols. Cambridge: Cambridge University Press. 92–119.

Ferrari, S. and Bradney, A. (eds) 2000. *Islam and European Legal Systems*. Aldershot: Ashgate.

Fetzer, J.S. and Soper, C.C. 2005. *Muslims and the State in Britain, France, and Germany*. Cambridge: Cambridge University Press.

Foblets, M.-C. et al. (eds) 2001. *Convergences musulmanes. Aspects contemporains de l'islam dans l'Europe élargie*. Louvain la-Neuve: Acad. Bruylant.

Foblets, M.-C. 2001. Le statut personnel musulman devant les tribunaux en Europe: une reconnaissance conditionelle, in *L'étranger et le droit de la famille: pluralité ethnique, pluralisme juridique*, edited by P. Kahn. Paris: Documentation Française. 33–74.

Foblets, M.-C. and Carlier, J.-Y. 2005. *Le code marocain de la famille: Incidences au regard du droit international privé en Europe*. Bruxelles: Bruylant.

Foblets, M.-C. 2007. The admissibility of repudiation: Recent developments in Dutch, French and Belgian private international law. *Hawwa*, 5(1), 10–32.

Foblets, M.-C. et al. (eds) 2010a. *Cultural Diversity and the Law*. Bruxelles: Bruylant.

Foblets, M.-C. et al. (eds) 2010b. *Convictions Politiques et Religieuses et Droits Positifs*. Bruxelles: Bruylant.

Fournier, P. 2010. *Muslim Marriage in Western Courts. Lost in Transition*. Farnham: Ashgate.

Freeland, R. and Lau, M. 2008. The shari'a and English law: Identity and justice for British Muslims, in *The Islamic Marriage Contract. Case Studies in Islamic Family Law*, edited by A. Quraishi and F.E. Vogel. Cambridge MA: Islamic Legal Studies Program, Harvard Law School. 331–48.

Freeman, M. 2001. The Jewish Get and the state, in *Law and Religions: Current Legal Issues 2001*, vol. 4, edited by R. O'Dair and A. Lewis. Oxford: Oxford University Press, 365–85.

Fulchiron, H. et al. 1999. *L'étranger face et au regard du droit. Rapport du recherché*. Lyon III: Université Jean-Moulin.

Gärtner, V. 2008. *Die Privatscheidung im deutschen und gemeinschaftsrechtlichen Internationalen Privat- und Verfahrensrecht: außergerichtliche Ehescheidung im Spannungsfeld von kultureller Diversität und Integration*. Tübingen: Mohr Siebeck.

Grillo, R. (ed.) 2008. *The Family in Question: Immigrants and Minorities in Multicultural Europe*. Amsterdam: University of Amsterdam Press.

Grillo, R. et al. (eds) 2008. *Legal Practice and Cultural Diversity*. Farnham/Burlington: Ashgate.

Al-Hamarneh, A. and Thielmann, J. (eds) 2008. *Islam and Muslims in Germany*. Leiden/Boston: Brill.

Hellyer, H.A. 2009. *Muslims of Europe. The 'Other' Europeans*. Edinburgh: Edinburgh University Press.

Hoekema, A. 2009. Does the Dutch judiciary pluralize domestic law?, in *Legal Practice and Cultural Diversity*, edited by Ralph Grillo et al. Aldershot: Ashgate. 177–98.

Holden, L. (ed.) 2011. *Cultural Expertise and Litigation. Patterns, Conflicts, Narratives*. Abingdon/New York: Routledge.
Jayme, E. (ed.) 2003. *Kulturelle Identität und Internationales Privatrecht*. Heidelberg: Müller.
Jeldtoft, N. and Nielsen, J.S. (eds) 2012. *Methods and Contexts in the Study of Muslim Minorities*. Abingdon/New York: Routledge.
Jänterä-Jareborg, M. 2003. 'Matière préliminaire.' Foreign Law in National Courts: A Comparative Perspective. Collected Courses of the Hague Academy of International Law, vol. 304. Leiden/Boston: Martinus Nijhoff Publishers.
Jones-Pauly, C. 2008. Marriage contracts of Muslims in the Diaspora: Problems in the recognition of *mahr* contracts in German law, in *The Islamic Marriage Contract. Case Studies in Islamic Family Law*, edited by A. Quraishi and F.E. Vogel. Cambridge MA: Islamic Legal Studies Program, Harvard Law School, 299–330.
Kahn, P. (ed.) 2001. *L'étranger et le droit de la famille: pluralité ethnique, pluralisme juridique*, Paris: Documentation Française.
King, M. (ed.) 1995. *God's Law versus State Law. The Construction of an Islamic Identity in Western Europe*. London: Grey Seal.
Klausen, J. 2007. *The Islamic Challenge. Politics and Religion in Western Europe*. Oxford: Oxford University Press.
Koch, J. 2012. *Die Anwendung islamischen Scheidungs- und Scheidungsfolgenrechts im Internationalen Privatrecht der EU-Mitgliedstaaten*. Frankfurt: Lang.
Kruger, T. 2010. *State of the Art Report: The Family*. [Online: June]. Available at: http://www.religareproject.eu/content/state-art-report-family [last accessed 5 June 2013].
Laurence, J. 2012. *The Emancipation of Europe's Muslims. The State's Role in Minority Integration*. Princeton/Oxford: Princeton University Press.
Levey, G.B. and Modood, T. (eds) 2009. *Secularism, Religion and Multicultural Citizenship*. Cambridge: Cambridge University Press.
Malik, J. (ed.) 2004. *Muslims in Europe*. Münster: LIT.
Malik, M. 2010. *Anti-Muslim Prejudice: Past and Present*. Abingdon/New York: Routledge.
Malik, M. 2012. *Minority Legal Orders in the UK*. London. [Online: British Academy Policy Centre]. Available at: http://www.britac.ac.uk/policy/Minority-legal-orders.cfm [last accessed 6 June 2013].
Mansel, H.-P. 2008. Die kulturelle Identität im Internationalen Privatrecht, in *Pluralistische Gesellschaften und Internationales Recht*, Berichte DGVR Vol. 43, edited by G. Nolte et al. Heidelberg: C.F. Müller. 137–214.
Mehdi, R. and Nielsen, J.S. 2011. *Embedding Mahr (Islamic Mahr) in the European Legal System*. Copenhagen: DJOF.
Mehdi, R. et al. (eds) 2008. *Law and Religion in Multicultural Societies*. Copenhagen: DJOF.
Meeusen, J., et al. (eds) 2007. *International Family Law for the European Union*. Antwerp/Oxford: Intersentia.
Menski, W. 2011. Life and law: Advocacy and expert witnessing in the UK, in *Cultural Expertise and Litigation. Patterns, Conflicts, Narratives*, edited by L. Holden. Abingdon/New York: Routledge. 151–71.
Menski, W. 2006. *Comparative Law in a Global Context*. 2nd ed. Cambridge: Cambridge University Press.
Mir-Hosseini, Z. 2009. Islamic family law and social practice: Anthropological reflections on the terms of the debate, in *Family, Law and Religion. Debates in the Muslim World and their Implications for Co-operation and Dialogue*, edited by Austrian Association for the Middle East Hammer-Purgstall. Oberwart, Austria: Gröbner Druck. 37–48.

Murphy, J. (ed.) 2000. *Ethnic Minorities, their Families and the Law*. Oxford: Hart Publishing.
Nichols, J.A. (ed.) 2012. *Marriage and Divorce in a Multicultural Context*. Cambridge: Cambridge University Press.
Nielsen, J. 1993. *Emerging Claims of Muslim Populations in Matters of Family Law in Europe*. CSIC Papers No. 10. Birmingham: CSIC-MR.
Nielsen, J. and Allievi, S. (eds) 2002. *Muslim Networks and Transnational Communities in and Across Europe*. Leiden: Brill.
Nielsen, J. et al. (eds) 2009. *Yearbook of Muslims in Europe*, vol. 1. Leiden/Boston: Brill.
Nielsen, J. and Christoffersen, L. (eds) 2010. *Shari'a as Discourse. Legal Traditions and the Encounter with Europe*. Farnham: Ashgate.
Nielsen, P.A. 1997. *Internasjonal privat- og procesret*. Copenhagen: Gjellerup/Gad.
Nolte, G. et al. (eds) 2007. *Pluralistische Gesellschaften und Internationales Recht*. Heidelberg: C.F. Muller.
Panafit, L. 1999. *Quand le droit écrit l'islam*. Bruxelles: Bruylant.
Papadopoulou, L. 2010. Trapped in history: Greek Muslim women under the sacred Islamic law. *Annuaire International des Droits de l'Homme*, 5, 397–418.
Pearl, D. 2000. *Islamic Family Law and Its Reception by the Courts in England*. Cambridge MA: Harvard Law School Islamic Legal Studies program.
Pearl, D. and Menski, W. 1998. *Muslim Family Law*. Lahore: Brite Books.
Potz, R. and Wieshaider, W. 2004. *Islam and the European Union*. Leuven: Peeters.
Poulter, S. 1993. The claim to a separate Islamic system of personal law for British Muslims, in *Islamic Family Law*, edited by C. Mallat and J. Connors. London: Graham & Trotman. 147–66.
Poulter, S. 1998. *Ethnicity, Law and Human Rights*. Oxford: Clarendon Press.
Rohe, M. 1994a. *Zu den Geltungsgründen des Deliktsstatuts*. Tübingen: Mohr.
Rohe, M. 1994b. Staatsangehörigkeit oder Lebensmittelpunkt? Anknüpfungsgerechtigkeit im Lichte neuerer Entwicklungen, in *Festschrift für Dietrich Rothoeft zum 65. Geburtstag*, edited by C. Engel and H. Weber, München: Jehle-Rehm. 1–39.
Rohe, M. 2003. Islamic law in German courts. *Hawwa*, 1, 46–59
Rohe, M. (Guest ed.) 2004. Sharī'a in Europe. *Die Welt des Islams Special Theme Issue*, 44(3). Leiden: Brill.
Rohe, M. 2007. *Muslim Minorities and the Law in Europe. Chances and Challenges*. New Delhi: Global Media Publications.
Rohe, M. 2011. *Das islamische Recht: Geschichte und Gegenwart*. 3rd edn. München: C.H. Beck (English translation to be published by Brill).
Rohe, M. 2013. Sharia in Europe, in *The Oxford Handbook on Islam in Europe*, edited by J. Cesari. Oxford: Oxford University Press.
Roy, O. 1999. *Vers un islam européen*. Paris: Editions Esprit.
Rumpf, C. 2004. *Einführung in das türkische Recht*. München: Beck.
Saris, A. et al. (eds) 2007. *Étude de cas auprès de Canadiennes musulmanes et d'intervenants civils et religieux en resolution de conflits familiaux*. Montréal: Département des Sciences Juridiques UQAM.
Shachar, A. 2001. *Multicultural Jurisdictions. Cultural Differences and Women's Rights*. Cambridge: Cambridge University Press.
Shadid, W. and Van Koningsveld, P. (eds) 2002. *Religious Freedom and the Neutrality of the State: The Position of Islam in the European Union*. Leuven: Peeters.

Shah, P. 2013. In pursuit of the pagans: Muslim law in the English context. *Journal of Legal Pluralism*, 45, 58–75.

Shah, P. and Menski, W. (eds) 2007. *Migration, Diasporas and Legal Systems in Europe*. London: Routledge Cavendish.

Shah-Kazemi, S.N. 2001. *Untying the Knot. Muslim Women, Divorce and the Shariah*. London: Nuffield Foundation.

Silvestri, S. 2008. *Europe's Muslim Women. Potentials, Aspirations and Challenges*. Brussels: King Baudouin Foundation.

Sörgjerd, C. 2012. *Reconstructing Marriage. The Legal Status of Relationships in a Changing Society*. Cambridge: Intersentia.

Tsitselikis, K. 2004. The legal status of Islam in Greece. *Die Welt des Islams*, 3(44), 402–31.

Tsitselikis, K. 2012. *Old and New Islam in Greece: From Historical Minorities to Immigrant Newcomers*. Leiden: Martinus Nijhoff Publishers/Brill Academic.

Van Bruinessen, M. et al. (eds) 2011. *Producing Islamic Knowledge: Transmission and Dissemination in Western Europe*. London: Routledge.

Van der Ven, J.A. (ed.) 2012. *Empirical Research in Religion and Human Rights*. Leiden/New York: Brill.

Vermeulen, F. and Bader, V. 2012. *Reasonable Accommodation of Religious Claims in Europe? Basic Tensions and Socio-legal Debates*. Summary of results for Work Package 7 of the RELIGARE project, December 2012. Available at: http://www.religareproject.eu/?q=system/files/Summary%20WP7_FINALCONFERENCE_form.pdf [last accessed 12 January 2014].

Vinding, N.V. and Christoffersen, L. 2012. *Danish Regulation of Religion, State of Affairs and Qualitative Reflections*. Copenhagen: Centre for European Islamic Thought, Faculty of Theology, University of Copenhagen.

Voorhoeve, M. (ed.) 2012. *Family Law in Islam. Divorce, Marriage and Women in the Muslim World*. London: Tauris.

Waardenburg, J. 2003. *Muslims and Others. Relations in Context*. Berlin: de Gruyter.

Wähler, K. 1981. *Internationales Privatrecht und interreligiöses Kollisionsrecht*. Bielefeld: IPRax.

Waldron, J. 2010. Questions about the reasonable accommodation of minorities, in *Shari'a in the West?*, edited by R. Ahdar and N. Aroney. Oxford: Oxford University Press. 103–13.

Wegner, J. 1982. The status of women in Jewish and Islamic marriage and divorce law. *Harvard Women's Law Journal*, 5, 1–33.

Witte Jr. J. 2010. The future of Muslim family law in Western democracies, in *Shari'a in the West?*, edited by: R. Ahdar and N. Aroney. Oxford: Oxford University Press. 279–92.

Yazbeck Y.H. (ed.) 2002. *Muslims in the West: From Sojourners to Citizens*. Oxford: Oxford University Press.

Yilmaz, I. 2000. Muslim law in Britain: Reflections in the socio-legal sphere and differential legal treatment. *Journal of Muslim Minority Affairs*, 20, 353–60.

Zucca, L. 2012. *Law and Religion in the European Constitutional Landscape*. Oxford: Oxford University Press.

Chapter 4
On the Cooperation between Religious and State Institutions in Family Matters: Nordic Experiences

Maarit Jänterä-Jareborg

1. Prelude: Muslim Marriage Consultation in Sweden

In the spring of 2012 two women covered by *niqab* approached Sweden's 10 largest mosques under the pretext of consultation regarding marital problems between a Muslim couple in Sweden. One of the women presented herself as 'the wife of the marriage' whereas the other woman was presented as her 'supportive friend'. In reality she was a journalist carrying a hidden camera and a recorder. The consultation focused on what the wife should do given that her husband had other wives too, physically abused her and forced her into non-consensual sex. Two of the 10 consulted imams explicitly advised the wife to report her husband's domestic abuse to the police. The others advised against it and encouraged her to seek to solve the problems jointly with the husband, and by increasing her efforts to demonstrate her love to him. As regards the polygamous nature of the marriage, only one of the consulted imams argued that polygamy cannot be practised in Sweden whereas the others were of the opinion that polygamy is permitted for a man under certain conditions.

The recording was presented in *Mission Scrutiny*, a popular television programme in Sweden which strives to reveal various kinds of abuse in Swedish society, in particular among authorities. It received enormous media coverage in Sweden and also some attention abroad.[1] Attention came to focus on the alleged incompatibility of Islamic values with Swedish law and the existence of double Muslim agendas in Sweden – one for the public eye and another for the private sphere of life.

In the discussions following the TV programme, three aspects emerged which I find highly relevant also from the point of view of this chapter. First, attention was drawn to the fact that several of the consulted mosques were recipients of the Swedish state's special funding for religious communities, funding which is linked to the faith community's promotion of fundamental values of Swedish society, in particular the promotion of equal rights for men and women. By violating these values the mosques, according to critics, not only breached their undertakings in relation to the state but also confirmed Islamophobic prejudices in society. Only a few voices were raised in support of a more nuanced approach, *inter alia*, by pointing out that a consultation within a religious context reasonably follows the faith community's own faith-based teachings and not state law.[2]

Secondly, the chairman of Sweden's leading Islamic organisation, the Islamic Council of Sweden, and the chairman of the Swedish Imam Council, were quick to dissociate their organisations from the controversial statements made in the recording and wished to give

---

1 See, e.g., http://www.euro-islam.info/2012/05/21/page/2 [last accessed 14 December 2013].
2 See, e.g., Helmersson (2012).

a different version of the true content of Islam.³ A Muslim believer's duty, they pointed out, is to obey the laws of the country of residence. What makes this statement particularly important is that Muslim representatives themselves brought up the prospects of adapting Islam to the surrounding society and its laws, in full compliance with the intended universal message of Islam and human rights.

Thirdly, the need for a state-sponsored education for imams regarding Swedish society, its organisation, fundamental values and laws, in particular family law legislation, was once again brought to the agenda. Only in 2009, a Swedish investigation on the topic had concluded that special state-organised education of imams would amount to a state intervention in the Islamic communities' internal affairs (Swedish Ministry of Education 2009). The discussions showed that not only those who fear Islam's societal impact but also imams active in Sweden are positively inclined towards state-supported educational measures (Swedish Ministry of Education 2009: 45).⁴ Matters of confession should, obviously, fall outside any such commission.

2. The Nordic Paradoxes in Relation to Religion

Several paradoxes, i.e., apparently contradictory facts or ideas, emerge when approaching religion's role in the Nordic states of Europe, namely Denmark, Finland, Iceland, Norway and Sweden. These paradoxes, in turn, affect prospects of cooperation between the state and, in particular, the minority faith communities in each of the states.

2.1 Secular States but with a Privileged National Church

First, the Nordic states have a reputation of being among the most secular states in the world. This might also be taken to mean that churches play a very limited role in society. At a closer look, however, each state's posture towards religion appears far more complicated. To start with, each of the Nordic states has a *national church*, a 'Folk's Church' (i.e. Church of Denmark, Church of Finland,⁵ Church of Iceland, Church of Norway and Church of Sweden) of the Evangelical Lutheran faith, dating back to the Protestant reforms in the 1500s. This national church forms part of the state organisation and has special functions of its own in this context. Only Sweden has carried out (since 2000) a formal legal separation between the state and the national church.⁶

The national churches enjoy special privileges from the state, not least in terms of the funding of their activities. Generally speaking, however, the ties between the state and the national church have loosened in each of the states during the last two decades.

---

3 See Press Release, available at http://www.islamiskaforbundet.se [last accessed 14 December 2013].

4 This is in line with the 2009 investigation, above. Out of 121 (then) interviewed imams, 94 were positive towards the idea of special Swedish imam education, preferably within a state-funded university's regime (Swedish Ministry of Education 2009: 45). In Norway, special courses have been offered since 2007for religious leaders (other than the Church of Norway) by the Faculty of Theology at Oslo University, in cooperation with the Ministry of Labour and Inclusion. By 2009, 26 religious leaders had participated in such courses: 10 Muslims, 10 Christians (of various faith communities), one Rabbi, one Hindu and four Buddhist monks (Swedish Ministry of Education 2009: 74).

5 For historical reasons, the Greek Orthodox Church qualifies as Finland's other national church.

6 A corresponding reform has been under discussion in the other four states.

One result of this is the increased autonomy of the national church in relation to the state. Another result is that the other faith communities active in the state have gained a more equal footing with the national church. The still existing privileges are explained to be a necessary compromise, reflecting not only the states' history but also the dominance in terms of church membership compared to other denominations.

2.2 High Church Membership but with no Daily Engagement

Second, the high church membership rates in the national churches – somewhere from 70 percent to more than 80 percent of the total population depending on the state – also appear to contradict the secular image of the Nordic states.[7] The paradox is even more complicated. Members of the national churches do not participate in church activities on any regular basis. In Sweden, for example, only two percent of the members of the Church of Sweden[8] participate in church services daily or weekly. On the other hand, special church rites, such as church marriages, church funerals and baptism ceremonies, continue to be popular and are used by the majority of the church members. This contradiction might be difficult to combine with the notion of 'belonging without believing', frequently employed within the sociology of religion to describe the nature of membership in the Nordic Folk's Churches. According to this outlook, people belong to the national church for reasons of tradition, the public sector being in charge of the functions that traditionally belong to churches (health care, education, providing for the poor, etc.). Alternatively, or in addition, religion is seen as a totally private matter not to be manifested publicly. In respect of the most significant events of life, however, church members are willing to demonstrate 'the private' publicly.

A religious dimension may certainly lie behind the popularity of church weddings and church funerals. But there are also other explanations which a jurist finds natural to point out, namely the states' legislation on the concerned fields and the quality of the alternative services available on the market. All of the states follow a double-track system permitting both civil and religious marriages on their territories, as legally equal alternatives. The 'naked' civil marriage ceremony lacks the solemnity of a church ceremony. This might explain, to some extent, why most marriages taking place in these states are celebrated in a religious form. Civil funerals have only recently become a more available option to church funerals and a new market, specialising in such services, is slowly developing.[9] In 2006, eight percent of all funerals in Sweden were 'civil funerals'.

2.3 A Secular Law that Reflects the Values of the National Church?

Third, according to the more or less official self-image of the Nordic states their *legal orders* are not only confession-neutral (with certain privileges for the national church)

---

7 The lowest membership rates are found in Sweden, approximately 70 percent of the population (2011). There has been a decline of more than 10 percent since the separation between the state and the church.

8 See http://www.svenskakyrkan.se [last accessed 14 December 2013].

9 Even after the separation of the Church of Sweden from the Swedish state, the national church is in charge of most funeral activities in Sweden. It is, e.g., responsible for ensuring that everybody has access to a burial ground, irrespective of faith, and that there is access to premises which are free from religious symbols. Funeral activities are financed in the form of an income-based fee, which is compulsory for all. This fee is not linked to church membership. See Government Offices, *Fact Sheet*, February 2000: Changed Relations between the State and the Church of Sweden.

but also secular. The impact of the Nordic family law cooperation is well known in this context. In its early institutionalised form, starting in the beginning of the 1900s, the goal of this cooperation was, explicitly, to emancipate family law regulations from religion and traditional values, or to loosen such ties, and to promote in particular equality between men and women, within and out of marriage. The results of this cooperation brought Nordic family law into the forefront of modernity.

Nordic states transformed early into social welfare states, whereby society/state came to replace many of the traditional welfare functions of the family or the church.[10] The underlying idea is that the public (= state and municipalities) guarantee the basic needs of all residents, based on the ideology of solidarity and shared responsibility (Edgardh 2011: 38). Later on, we can perceive a development towards upgrading individual freedom and self-expression into core values of family law, an increasing emphasis on gender neutrality and, even, 'gender similarity', instead of the notion of 'gender complementarity' (Edgardh 2011: 42), traditionally endorsed by all world religions. This latter phase of development has been seen as a major source of value conflicts in Swedish society in relation to minority groups, which do not share the dominant Swedish values (Edgardh 2011: 42).

The latest pan-Nordic development is the removal of all legal differences of treatment on the basis of a person's sexual orientation. The institution of registered partnership as a legal tool for same-sex couples to formalise their mutual relationship was developed in the Nordic legal and religious environment towards the end of the 1980s.[11] Today, registered partnership is an established institution in numerous jurisdictions around the globe. Between the years 2009 and 2012, four Nordic states introduced legislation permitting same-sex marriages. The remaining state, Finland, can be expected to follow suit in the near future.

The paradox here is that it has been possible to reconcile these developments with the Evangelical Lutheran faith, as interpreted by the majority of both the members and the leaders of the Nordic Folk's Churches.[12] The new legislation and the majority faith might be claimed to be 'children of the same kind', promoting the same or similar values. An alternative and more cynical way of looking at this interrelationship is that a national church of the Nordic kind cannot maintain its social relevance unless it is willing to adjust to societal developments. This has happened earlier in relation to the outlook on divorce, remarriage, cohabitation and parentage out of marriage. On all these issues, the Nordic states' tolerant legislation has been approved of by the national church (or its majority). No corresponding link exits with the other world religions, present as minority faiths in the Nordic states. Their opposition to reforms risks being equated with 'expressions of

---

10 This development started already during the second half of the nineteenth century – the family continues to play a significant role in the individual's life, even when other actors are in charge of economic welfare functions. In the 2005 World Value Survey, 93 percent of the interviewed Swedes reported that they had full confidence in their family, whereas the corresponding figure for the USA was 72.5 percent, and for Germany 81.7 percent. In other studies too, 92 percent of Swedes are reported to value family and close relations as most important in life (see Westerlund 2012: 13–14).

11 A partnership registration was from the very beginning aimed as a purely civil (secular) ceremony, having regard to faith communities' freedom of religion.

12 An illustrative example is the reasoning of the Church of Sweden in relation to the Swedish government's plans to propose same-sex marriage legislation. The Church affirmed that the new marriage notion could be combined with its teachings. Same-sex marriage could, namely, be regarded as a good way for society to support people and be in line with the Lutheran understanding of the biblical commandment of love (Church of Sweden 2009: 14).

moral panic' and disregarded in any legal context.[13] As a result, family law legislation may endorse values that are in direct conflict with the doctrines of other faiths.

2.4 Religion's Expansion in a Diaspora Context

Fourth, religious affinity, traditions and customs tend to grow stronger in a diaspora context, and to become binding normative systems among people who find themselves to be in an 'ethno-religious' minority position in a totally different kind of social and legal environment.[14] Requests are made, explicitly or implicitly, for a public recognition of religion's normative force. Deep tensions arise: not only is the notion that religion should remain a private matter challenged, the representativeness of any such requests is equally questioned. Special attention is often drawn to the fact that not all 'newcomers' wish to live in accordance with the faith practised in their state of origin but wish to adjust to the lifestyle of their new state of residence.

These tensions form a particular challenge in the historically homogeneous Nordic states which, in international comparison, were late to transform into pluralistic multi-faith communities, mainly as major recipients of refugees from politically unstable states. What are the prerequisites of social inclusion and social coherence? Should the state engage in value debates including issues which may form a part of a faith, in order to make it plain to all residents that it cherishes certain fundamental values that all residents must respect?[15] Or should the state focus on the newcomers' integration as regards labour market, adequate housing facilities, education, and so forth, in addition to providing access to basic societal information?

In all of the states, different governments have taken different approaches to these issues. Whereas state-initiated value dialogues are often criticised as causing division among people, 'a we-and-them attitude' and a stigmatisation of minorities, *labour market integration* is expected to promote societal participation and, in the long run, social inclusion, in a much more concrete manner. Whatever strategies have been used, they have not been successful enough. In Sweden, for example, unemployment rates are highest among immigrants from the Middle East and Africa, groups within which many sympathise with Islam. The fact that people carry other normative systems with them and do not necessarily share basic Swedish values was evident in the incident of Muslim marriage consultation in Sweden described above. According to the Muslim organisations, mistakes happen when resources are extremely limited in relation to the high demand on religious consultation services in matters of the family.

2.5 Uncertainty Regarding the Scope of the Protected Freedom of Religion

Fifth, opinions differ regarding what freedom of religion should be regarded to entail. A lot of uncertainty appears to exist in this respect in the Nordic institutionalised and legal landscape. The European Convention on the Protection of Human Rights and Fundamental

---

13   This has repeatedly happened regarding law reforms on same-sex relationships.
14   Tariq Ramadan (1999: 4) mentions the following among explanations: 'Lack of Islamic knowledge, added to specific circumstances such as an often difficult exile, the feeling of being foreign, economic problems and so forth, lead to the reactive posture we are witnessing today.'
15   Scandinavians in general have faith in the state and its system, and accept state intervention in value debates. For the newcomers arriving from unstable non-democratic states, state intervention may appear far more questionable.

Freedoms (ECHR), to which all the Nordic states are parties, sets a minimum standard regarding conventional rights and freedoms. A popular notion in Nordic states appears to be that the concepts of Article 9 of the ECHR – freedom of thought, conscience and religion – should be interpreted with caution. It is emphasised that the Article does not aim to go further than to protect against violations regarding the central content of one's conviction or religion (Danelius 2012: 417).[16] And even when covered by the protection provided by the Article, the margin of appreciation granted to each contracting state may permit restrictions by the state.

In the Nordic states, the emphasis is on the protection of a personal conviction and the right to worship.[17] The explicit inclusion in Article 9 of the right to manifest a religion or belief, *inter alia*, through 'practice and observance' is regarded as an expression of the protection of religion or belief.[18] The divergent opinions of followers of a faith concerning what the faith stipulates or requires of them, as illustrated by the example of Muslim marriage consultation in Swedish mosques, adds to the uncertainty. After the broadcast of the TV programme, internal investigations were initiated in at least some of the consulted mosques, and in at least one case the person delivering the advice was reported by the mosque to be a visiting lecturer and not representative of its teachings! It is claimed that a Muslim residing in a Nordic state can always find an imam there who is willing to share the believer's understanding of Islam. It is also claimed that in particular Muslim women living in the Nordic states lack knowledge of their rights under Islamic law, which makes them vulnerable to abuse by others (Mehdi 2007: 140f).

A related matter is the alleged flexibility of a faith, depending on time and the surrounding society. Tariq Ramadan (1999: 3), in particular, has drawn attention to the risk that European Muslims confuse peculiar local traditions, as practised in a country of origin, with Islam and lack a clear understanding and knowledge of the true message of Islam and its adaptability in time and place. Similar concerns, focusing on the identity formation of a Muslim believer, have been expressed by Abdullahi Ahmed An-Na'im.[19] The essence is that a religious identity does not exclude a person from being a good citizen, and that fundamentalism, discrimination and extreme movements embracing violence do not qualify as religion.

---

16 In addition, freedom of religion and belief protects a person from legal persecution and discrimination, due to one's faith. It comprises the freedom not to cherish any faith at all.

17 Additional provisions set aims in particular for the protection of minority religions. In Sweden, the Constitution obliges the state to promote each person's inclusion, equal value and human dignity in society, to counteract all forms of discrimination, *inter alia*, on the basis of religious affiliation, *and to enable religious minorities to maintain and develop their community life*. See *Government Ordinance*, Ch. 1 § 2.5.

18 In Sweden, this has to do with the definition of freedom of religion in the national Constitution. The European Convention on Human Rights, however, provides the minimum standard for the rights covered by it.

19 'As a Muslim, I may assert an exclusive Islamic identity or emphasize Islamic tolerance and acceptance of religious differences, depending on whether I am a member of a majority or a minority and the prevailing political relations among the religious communities of my country ... In other words, identity formation and transformation is a dynamic procedure involving deliberate choices, not an immutable or inevitable condition' (An-Na'im 2008: 22).

2.6 Religion as a Societal Advantage?

Sixth, the Nordic states' transformation into multi-faith societies could be claimed to require an increased attention to religious voices in the public spheres of life. Such expectations are increasingly expressed by faith communities and their active members. It does also happen that the state refers to the societal advantage of faith communities' activities, for example, as a justification of the various available kinds of state support to those activities. For those who would wish a public recognition of religion's mission in society and an enrolment of faith communities in societal activities, acknowledgements of this kind remain too vague and count as little more than 'lip service'.[20] The dilemma for the faith communities and believers is not religious persecution but societal marginalisation of religion and faith.

Apart from crisis management where faith communities are actively enrolled by the state (see further, Section 3.4 below), religious actors are not perceived by the general public as the secular state's – or society's at large – first choice of partner. Many link them with intolerance and inequalities, as well as oppressive practices. Society's uneasiness with religion is not made less by the extensive and even alarming reports on extreme manifestations carried out in the name of religion globally and locally. To achieve societal recognition and influence it is necessary that faith communities not only know 'the laws of the state'[21] but venture 'coming out' by taking efforts to manifest where they stand in respect of fundamental issues. Giving a 'good impression' – which can be expected to contribute to a more general societal approval – is, ultimately, the responsibility of faith communities themselves.

3. Institutionalised Cooperation between Religious and State Bodies

3.1 Basic Similarities

The paradoxes described above apply to all the Nordic states and, naturally, have an impact on the prospects for and nature of cooperation between state institutions and religious bodies. In all of them, in matters of confession, the state identifies itself, primarily, with the national church,[22] even when claiming to be neutral in matters of confession. As the above-mentioned 'paradoxes' illustrate (Section 2.3), a special kind of kinship between the state and religion is identifiable in relation to family law legislation.

As mentioned above, the ECHR provides the minimum standard regarding access to and the content of the protected freedom of religion and conscience in each of the Nordic states. In spite of this, relevant differences exist among them regarding the forms through which

---

20 A series of seminars on the topic were held in Sweden in October 2012, mainly under the auspices of the Catholic Church. A point the organisers wished to raise was whether an increased role for religion was necessary to promote democratisation, peace and integration processes. Religion – privat terapi eller samhällsaktör? *Fyra seminarier om religionens roll i samhällsbygget*. Bilda 2012.

21 This raises the issue of the necessity of access to special education on the laws of the state. See Section 1 above.

22 In Sweden, after the state–church separation, a special enactment was found necessary to, separately, regulate the Church of Sweden, see *Act (1998:1591) on the Church of Sweden*. The country's other faith communities are, largely, covered by the *Act (1998:1593) on Religious Communities and the Ordinance on the Registration of Religious Communities*. A faith community is defined as a community for religious activities, which include organising divine services.

the state cooperates with religious communities. To avoid misunderstandings within this surprisingly little explored legal field and to be able to look at the issues more closely, I will in the following primarily focus on Sweden as the system with which I am best acquainted.

3.2   Focus on Sweden

In Sweden, state (or other public) support to religious activities finds expression, *inter alia*, in the following:

1. provision of state financing to faith communities for faith-related activities;
2. encouragement of inter-religious communication and cooperation;
3. delegation of state powers to faith communities to officiate in valid civil marriages through religious ceremonies;[23]
4. the public authorisation and funding of schools with a confessional orientation; and
5. collecting church taxes and membership fees on behalf of faith communities.[24]

These forms of public support are all linked with special conditions which a faith community must meet in order to qualify for the support in question. In the following, my focus shall be on the first three forms of state support. Due to the topicality of faith communities' delegated right to officiate legally valid marriages and the principle issues that this right raises, I will devote a full section to this issue alone (Section 4).

3.3   *Faith and its Manifestation as a Societal Advantage – State Financing of Faith Communities*

Since 1971, a special state body, called the Commission for Government Support to Faith Communities (*Nämnden för Statens Stöd för Trossamfund*, SST), has been in charge of distributing the Swedish state's financial support to faith communities in Sweden.[25] The Commission consists of nine members representing different (minority) faith communities in Sweden and is appointed upon proposal by The Islamic Council for Cooperation, The Jewish Central Council, The Ecumenical Council for the Orthodox and Oriental Churches, the Pentecostal Churches, The Roman Catholic Church in Sweden and The Swedish Mission Church.[26] In its activities the Commission must integrate perspectives of equality,

---

23   A school with a confessional orientation can qualify for public funding only on condition that the education it provides fulfils the same quality requirements that apply to public schools in Sweden. In that case, the school receives the same amount of public funding per student as applies to a public school education. Education in a confessional publicly funded school must, on the other hand, be open to a student irrespective of the student's faith (see Jänterä-Jareborg 2010: 683–5).

24   The collecting of church taxes and membership fees is carried out by the state in connection with general taxation, but only upon application by the faith community. This service was, initially, restricted to the national church (Church of Sweden). Upon state–church separation in 2000 it became available for other faith communities too, but only on condition that the faith community is organised as a so-called registered faith community in Sweden and wishes to take advantage of this assistance. Contrary to what applies to the Church of Sweden which receives this assistance free of charge, as the actual form of state financing of its activities, the other faith communities 'pay' for this service through a reduction of the state financing for which they otherwise qualify (see Lindqvist 2001: 29–30).

25   This body is currently organised under the Swedish Ministry of Civil Affairs.

26   The faith communities in Sweden consist of Christian, Jewish, Muslim and Buddhist faith communities. See the Commission's homepage, http://www.sst.a.se [last accessed 14 December 2013],

plurality and children's rights, in addition to promoting international and intercultural exchange and cooperation.[27]

The underlying ideology is that faith communities, as important actors in civil society, perform *functions that are advantageous for the society* and can contribute to strengthening the fundamental values of the society (Swedish Ministry of Education 2009: 88–90).[28] Therefore, the state should support faith communities to pursue long-term religious activities, such as the provision of worship services and the provision of spiritual guidance, education services and care. In 2011, altogether 22 faith communities active in Sweden received state financing in accordance with the 1999 enactments;[29] *in toto* 41 faith communities qualify for the support (Göransson 2011: 186). The model comes from the state's funding of political parties and the press, through special subsidies.[30] The Church of Sweden is not included, but is subject to another regime of state financing.[31]

3.4 The Promotion of Fundamental Societal Values

The funding is not automatic, but requires that the faith community in question meets the specific criteria established by the state.[32] A religious community must, *first*, contribute to maintaining and strengthening the fundamental values of society. This means that the community must be committed to counteracting all forms of racism and other discrimination as well as violence and brutality.[33] In particular, the community should in its activities contribute to equality between women and men. Its members and staff are to be guided by ethical principles which correspond to the fundamental democratic values of

---

which also includes information in English.

27 See 2a §, added in 2009 to the *Regulation (2007:1192) with Instruction for the Commission on Government Support to Faith Communities*.

28 The initiative for state funding came through proposals in Parliament. The justifications for state funding were elaborated by a committee in 1968. Basically, three arguments were considered to be in favour of state support: 1) *The service argument*, i.e., that it is a primary concern of society to meet the population's individual needs, including religious and cultural needs; 2) *The democracy argument*, i.e., that the vitality of Swedish society depends upon giving scope to and listening to different ideologies and faith orientations; and 3) *The value argument*, i.e., democracy is based on certain fundamental values which have developed under strong impact of humanist ideals, Christian ideologies and other religions or non-religious ideologies.

29 SST homepage, http://www.sst.a.se [last accessed 14 December 2013].

30 SST, *Uppföljning av trossamfundens användning av beviljade statsbidrag, Memorandum*, available at http://www.sst.a.se [last accessed 14 December 2013]. In the Nordic states, the Norwegian state financing of faith communities is by far the most comprehensive one. This has to do with the fact that a general church tax is levied in Norway, irrespective of a person's membership in any faith community. To compensate for this, all faith communities – as well as humanist life stance communities – receive subsidies based on the number of members. Whereas in Sweden the state subsidies are estimated to amount to 50 Swedish crowns per member, i.e. 6 Euros, in Norway they amount to 900 Swedish crowns per member, i.e. more than 100 Euros per member (see Lindqvist 2001: 30). In Denmark and Finland, on the other hand, state subsidies are reserved for the national churches. I have not been able to establish the position taken in Iceland.

31 Instead, it enjoys other kinds of economic support from the state, in particular in the state levying church taxes (membership fees) in connection with the general taxation. In economic terms, this support is considerable. This support is not subject to any kind of value-promotion test, contrary to what applies to the other faith communities' prospects of receiving state financing.

32 The requirements are stipulated in the *Act (1999:932) on State Support to Faith Communities* and the *Regulation (1999:974) on State Financing for Faith Communities*.

33 *Government Bill, Prop. 1998/99:124*, 64 and Swedish Ministry of Education (2009: 89–90).

society.³⁴ *Secondly*, a faith community must pursue its activities with stability and vitality. Stability and vitality require in this context that the community has been continuously active in Sweden for at least five years, that it has an organised structure, a solid economy and premises for its activities, at least 3,000 members, and activities in different parts of the country.

In Section 2 above, various kinds of paradoxes were identified regarding the state's posture towards religion. An additional paradox could be claimed to arise in respect of the instructions for state financing of faith-based activities. State funding is made dependent on the promotion of societal core values while, according to authoritative statements in a Government Bill, the body in charge (SST) is not to carry out any closer investigation regarding how a religious community's faith and teachings correlate with the society's value basis.³⁵ The contradictions in the instruction and the resulting uncertainty³⁶ may explain why many of Sweden's faith communities have abstained from applying for state funding. Another contributing explanation might be that the economic value of this kind of state financing remains limited in Sweden. In 2011, for example, it amounted to altogether around 50 million Swedish crowns, which corresponds to approximately 5.2 million Euros. From a faith community's perspective, making an application might not be worth the trouble in light of the modest amount of expected funds. No corresponding requirements apply concerning the state's funding of political parties or the media which, again, could be claimed to be a paradox.³⁷

In the introductory example of (fake) Muslim marriage consultation, five of the criticised imams represented faith communities receiving state funding for their activities. Much of the public concern focused on this fact alone and the alleged violation of the laws of Sweden. The issue at stake is, however, much more complicated. It raises concerns as to the scope of the protected freedom of religion as well as the ambiguity of the conditions for the funding. It follows that it cannot be expected of any faith community that its counselling in matters of faith should be in full compliance with state law. Thought-provokingly, however, within a week of the airing of the TV programme, the state body (SST) published its own comments on the incident, condemning the statements made by the representatives of the mosques.³⁸ Besides gathering the representatives of the concerned Islamic faith communities to discuss the incident and the measures they aimed to take, the SST announced that it planned to visit the concerned mosques.

What qualifies as a fundamental societal value can, generally speaking, be approached from different perspectives. In connection with Sweden's same-sex marriage reform, finally carried out in 2009, the faith communities' opposition to same-sex marriages was not considered to disqualify any of them for state funding or to prevent their continued

---

34 The SST is to conduct an ongoing dialogue with the faith communities concerning the prerequisites for state support.

35 *Government Bill, Prop. 1998/99:124*, 63.

36 *Government Bill, Prop. 1998/99:124*, 66. See also Swedish Ministry of Education (2009: 89–90) with further references.

37 Sweden is no longer protected from nationalist political parties. In the last parliamentary election in Sweden in 2010, a party – *Sverigedemokraterna* – which, according to its programme, aims to preserve the Swedish values in society – received more than seven percent of the vote and entered Parliament for the first time. This party is highly critical of Sweden's immigration policies and, according to public opinion, is regarded as having national-socialist ambitions.

38 SST: SSTs kommentar till Uppdrag Gransknings reportage Imamernas råd som sändes i SVT 16 maj, Stockholm 2012-05-22, available at http://www.sst.a.se [last accessed 14 December 2013].

authorisation by the state to officiate legally valid civil marriages (see Section 4.4.1 below). This demonstrates a balancing of interests, considering that at stake was an issue which, from the perspective of state law, was essentially a matter of combating discrimination (Swedish Ministry of Education 2009: 90, Hirschfeldt 2011: 141). In a report concerning the faith communities' use of state subsidies, the SST emphasises that, in its opinion, the values to be shared should be of a more universal and permanent character and not just values reflecting current opinions in Swedish society.[39] The requested contribution to these values by faith communities should, furthermore, be seen as an ongoing process, to be carried out in a *dialogue*.[40] In the opinion of the SST, the 'instrumental' outlook of the state in respect of faith communities' qualification for state financing should be reconsidered in favour of recognising the value of spiritual life as such.[41]

3.5 Promotion of Inter-religious Communication and Cooperation

The SST's functions include those of providing general assistance for faith communities in Sweden, and to be the Swedish government's expert body in matters related to religion and faith. It is also to provide a forum for value dialogues regarding, not least, how to counteract extreme movements employing violence and to contribute to societal democracy. It has recently also been proposed that the SST should be in charge of conducting a dialogue with faith communities and marriage officiators about child marriages and marriages against a person's will (Swedish Ministry of Justice Committee 2012: 39).[42]

The SST is also in charge of societal crisis management, by coordinating emergency actions between faith communities in situations of crisis when Swedish society is confronted or threatened by a local or global catastrophe.[43] The ideology is that churches and other sacred locations are self-evident places for people to seek comfort and support in difficult situations of life and that this function is to be recognised by the state without favouring any special faith community (Swedish Ministry of Education 2009: 93).

4. Marriage Celebration within Faith Communities' Regime

4.1 Religious Marriage as a Valid Civil Marriage

From a family law perspective, the most important form of interaction between state institutions and religious institutions relates to marriage celebration. In Sweden and the other Nordic states, a legally valid marriage may be celebrated in a religious ceremony alone, without any supplementary measures. The condition is that the state has authorised

---

39 SST, *Uppföljning av trossamfundens användning av beviljade statsbidrag, Memorandum*, 9.

40 SST, *Uppföljning av trossamfundens användning av beviljade statsbidrag, Memorandum*, 9–10. Several such dialogues have been initiated by the state, for example, for peace and tolerance, or regarding forced marriages and child marriages.

41 See also SST, *Uppföljning av trossamfundens användning av beviljade statsbidrag, Memorandum*, 10.

42 Previously, the government has granted special funds for the SST for dialogues with faith communities on issues related to equality and children's rights, and how to combat honour-related violence and coercion (Swedish Ministry of Justice Committee 2012: 274).

43 Crisis management is a traditional function of the Church of Sweden, now to be shared with other faith communities.

both the faith community, within which the ceremony takes place, and the person conducting the ceremony, to officiate marriages within its territory. In charge of the authorisations is a state body, called the Financial and Administrative Services Agency (*Kammarkollegiet*).[44] The authorisation amounts to *a delegation of public powers*, with the result that both the faith community and its officials act as state agents when exercising this power.[45]

To qualify as a marriage authority under state law, the activities of the faith community must be of a certain stability and vitality and organised in such a manner that there is reason to expect that the faith community – and the concerned officials – will follow Swedish law when making use of the authorisation (Swedish Ministry of Justice 2007: 269). This requires sufficient knowledge of the basic requirements of the Swedish Marriage Code in respect of obstacles to marriage,[46] the marriage ceremony procedure and the measures which the official must take after having solemnised a marriage. The spouses-to-be must be at least 18 years of age and unmarried, both must be present at the ceremony in addition to witnesses, and both must consent to the marriage. Once the authorised official has conducted the ceremony and declared the parties to be married to each other, the marriage is legally valid, even if it was concluded against a marriage impediment.[47] As part of the authorisation, the official has the duty to immediately inform the Swedish authority in charge of the population records of the marriage for registration. Swedish law contains no special requirements regarding which premises qualify for marriage solemnisation.

The control of the individual marriage official's knowledge of Swedish law and suitability to perform the functions concerned is, under the current system, normally delegated by the state to the concerned faith community.[48] This is not only a practical solution but implies a trust on behalf of the state towards the faith communities' ability to perform the delegated functions. Contrary to what (formally) applies in respect of state funding of faith communities' faith-based activities (see Section 3.4 above), marriage authorisation does not depend on any specific kind of 'value basis'. This might be regarded as an additional paradox considering that marriage solemnisation amounts to the exercise of public (state) powers.

4.2 The System's Origin and Current Figures

As a result of Nordic legal cooperation in the early 1900s, aiming to modernise family law in the Nordic states, a secular marriage ceremony was introduced in Sweden in 1908, as an alternative to the hitherto obligatory religious marriage ceremony, normally to be celebrated in the national church.[49] While the religious marriage ceremony maintained its

---

44 The *Kammarkollegiet* is in charge of assessing and granting the applications for authorisation. See *Act (1993:305) on the Right to Officiate at Marriages within Faith Communities*.

45 The legal ground follows from a special provision in the *Ordinance of Government (Regeringsformen)*, Ch. 11 § 6. This provision is a general clause concerning delegation of administrative duties of a public law nature from the state to other bodies.

46 See *Swedish Marriage Code (1987:230)*, Ch. 4 § 2 and §§ 5–8.

47 In this respect Swedish law is exceptional. It is not possible to declare the marriage void afterwards or to annul it, but the existence of the marriage impediment allows an *immediate divorce*. The public prosecutor may take court action to have the marriage dissolved by a decree of immediate divorce, Swedish Marriage Code Ch. 5 § 5.3.

48 Act (1993:305) on the Right to Solemnize Marriages within Faith Communities, § 2.2.

49 Roman Catholics were, however, permitted to form congregations in Sweden towards the end of the eighteenth century and also to officiate marriages within the congregation in accordance with Catholic rites. Jewish communities received similar rights. Intermarriage between Christians

position as the preferred form for the great majority, it became subject to the rules of civil law.[50] The double-track system still prevails in all of the Nordic states. From having been the sole right of the national church, numerous faith communities have during the course of the years received an authorisation to officiate marriages on the Nordic states' territories by the state in question. All faith communities enjoy an equal footing at the outset, but the national churches have retained certain privileges.

In Sweden, for example, until 2010 all ministers of the Church of Sweden were *ex lege*, through an explicit provision in the Swedish Marriage Code, authorised to conduct legally valid marriages. This competence followed from ordination as a priest of the Church and reflects the Church's former position as the state church. Since 2010, the Church's and its ministers' right to officiate at marriage ceremonies is subject to the same requirements of authorisation that apply to the other faith communities.

In 2011, 37 faith communities in Sweden (Evangelical Lutheran, Free Protestant, Muslim, Mosaic, Roman Catholic, Greek Orthodox, etc.) and almost 9,000 religious officials had state authorisation to solemnise legally valid marriages.[51] Of the religious officials, almost 6,000 were ministers of the Church of Sweden. The next group in size were ministers of the Mission Church (1,000 authorised ministers), followed by the Pentecostal Churches (650), the Baptist Church (250) and the Salvation Army (200). Among Sweden's Muslim communities, only 30 imams had state authorisation to solemnise marriages.[52] This is thought-provoking, having in mind that Muslims are reported to be Sweden's second largest faith group, after the Evangelical Lutheranism.

4.3 The Advantages of a Religious but Legally Automatically Valid Marriage

Ever since the introduction of the option of a purely secular marriage ceremony in the early 1900s, numerous proposals have been made in each of the states to make a purely civil, secular marriage ceremony obligatory. The double-track system has, however, been maintained, due to its popularity among the general public.[53] In each of the states, the majority of marriages continue to be celebrated in a religious ceremony alone, and approximately half of all marriages are celebrated within the national church.

A religious marriage ceremony solemnised under proper authorisations qualifies *ex lege* as a valid marriage under civil law. In addition, it is expected to qualify as a marriage under the faith community's own confession and, possibly, also in the spouse's country of origin when that jurisdiction requires that the marriage has been concluded in a religious ceremony or by a religious official of a certain faith. The special advantage of the system

---

and those of the Mosaic faith was forbidden under Swedish law until 1863, when a special 'non-religious' ceremony was introduced through a special ordinance for such couples. Another ordinance was adopted in 1873, to enable 'non-religious' marriage ceremonies for couples to whom the religious ceremony was unacceptable (for reasons of conscience) or not available (due to differences in faith).

50   'The priest is obliged to establish the marriage by means of a legally effective church wedding under such conditions and prerequisites for the marriage as are to be regulated solely in civil law' (Modéer 2005: 58f).

51   Information by the state body in charge (Financial and Administrative Services Agency), September 2011.

52   E-mail to the author, 13 February 2012, by Karin Granberg, legal official at the Financial and Administrative Services Agency.

53   In a survey carried out by Statistics Sweden in 2006, in connection with the same-sex marriage reform, 86 percent wished to retain Sweden's current double-track system of marriage conclusion (SOU 17, Annex 3).

is that the spouse needs to go through only one marriage ceremony, and yet acquires both a legal and confessional status for the marriage. Two norm systems meet, and the costs are reduced. In a multi-confessional society, this delegation of powers is, furthermore, one of the few examples of family law recognising the importance of a person's religious affinity (Jänterä-Jareborg 2011a: 866–7).

4.4 A System under Attack

4.4.1 The Aftermath of the Same-sex Marriage Reform

An exercise of state powers should be delegated only to a body willing to fully adjust to state law, respecting the equal value and dignity of all persons.[54] This became a particular concern in the Nordic states in connection with the same-sex marriage reform carried out in Norway and Sweden in 2009, in Iceland in 2010 and in Denmark in 2012, whereby the state made it plain that it alone decides what qualifies as marriage under state law.[55] After much hesitation and a split within their churches on the issue, the Church of Sweden, the Church of Iceland and the Church of Denmark have decided to marry same-sex couples. Each minister's personal conviction on the matter is, nevertheless, to be respected. Very few other faith communities marry same-sex couples. In Sweden, for example, the Mission Church officiates same-sex marriages, but subject to the right of each minister to refuse.

Before the same-sex marriage reform was carried out, Sweden's leading faith communities were consulted regarding the planned reform. With the exception of the Muslim faith communities, which chose to abstain by simply being absent, all invited religious communities participated as 'referee groups' in all of the meetings of the law commission in charge.[56] The results of the consultations are interesting, in two contradictory ways. First, the faith communities' opposition to the new marriage concept was overrun.[57] The law commissioner in charge of the proposal emphasised that only arguments of a *general validity* and *objectivity* can be taken into account, *not emotional reasons or religious outlooks* or concerns regarding homosexuality (Swedish Ministry of Justice 2007: 220–21). This outlook was shared by Parliament which, before passing the enactment, emphasised that religious doctrines and beliefs cannot be decisive in law-making.[58] Secondly, the state acknowledged that the freedom of religion, enjoyed by faith communities and their officials, must be interpreted to prevent the state from requiring them to officiate marriages which run counter to their faith, for example same-sex marriages.[59] Considering the popularity of marriages within

---

54 See, e.g., Sweden's *Ordinance of Government*, Ch. 1 § 2 and the legislation on anti-discrimination.

55 See Swedish Ministry of Justice (2007) and *Bet. 2008/09:CU19*, regarding Sweden.

56 It is an established practice in Sweden to consult directly concerned public and private bodies before the government proposes a bill to Parliament on any law reform. Sweden's main faith communities are included among the consulted bodies whenever a law reform might have an impact on their activities. In connection with the same-sex law reform, however, the religious communities formed a part of the law commission itself, which is a highly unusual solution even in a Swedish setting.

57 On the retreat and reconsideration by the Church of Sweden on this issue, see Jänterä-Jareborg (2011a: 861–5).

58 *Bet. 2008/09:CU19*, 10ff.

59 This is explicitly stated in the marriage legislation. In Sweden, see *Marriage Code*, Ch. 4 § 3.2.

faith communities and the advantages of the double-track system,[60] the faith communities' marriage solemnisation powers were left intact.

In comparison, no civil ceremony marriage official can refuse to marry any couple, fulfilling the marriage requirements of Swedish law, without risking dismissal from office. As a public agent fully covered by labour law, the marriage official has an obligation to perform all tasks included in the office, and cannot refer to a legally protected freedom of religion or conscience to do otherwise.

4.4.2 Multi-faith Concerns

More recently, religious marriages in a multicultural and multi-faith setting have become a public concern in the Nordic states. The reasons are manifold.

First, confusion appears to exist regarding the validity of certain religious marriages, both from a legal and a confessional point of view. Is the marriage aimed to be valid in both respects or only in one respect? What adds to the confusion is that religious marriages, for example in Sweden, are performed not only by religious officials with marriage authorisation by the Swedish state but also, and often within the same faith community, by religious officials lacking such authorisation. How can the couple to be married distinguish between one and the other?

Secondly, various kinds of malpractices have been reported, consisting of attempts to evade marriage requirements in Swedish law. Forced marriages and child marriages (defined under Swedish law as marriages where at least one of the parties is under 18 years of age) are extensively linked to religious marriage ceremonies within minority faiths in Scandinavia.[61] In recent years, different ways of combating such marriages have become a public concern and a legislative priority of several of the states.

Thirdly, it has turned out that confusion exists regarding the dissolubility of a religious marriage. From the point of view of state law in the Nordic states, divorce decrees belong to the exclusive jurisdiction of the state, irrespective of how a legally valid marriage was concluded. From the point of view of many minority faiths, on the contrary, a religious marriage can be dissolved only in an order recognised by the concerned religion.[62] These conflicting outlooks not only create 'limping' marriages and 'limping' divorces, but also cause confusion and a lot of practical and confessional problems for believers.

In the following, attempts will be made to evaluate the first two concerns. The third concern relating to the form of the marriage dissolution is not discussed.[63]

---

60 In particular, the need for publicly funded civil marriage authorities is much less when faith communities solemnise the majority of all new marriages.

61 An investigation carried out by a government body called the Swedish Youth Agency (*Ungdomsstyrelsen*) concerning all applications in Sweden for a dispensation to marry before the legal marriage age, i.e. 18 years of age, showed that 25 percent of the applicants were already 'married' in the form of a religious or other traditional marriage ceremony. See also Swedish Ministry of Justice Committee (2012: 262–4).

62 Consequently, a Swedish court dismissed a Roman Catholic woman's request to have her marriage annulled also in the form of a Swedish court decree, due to the fact that she had been forced into the marriage. The marriage had been annulled by the Roman rota and dissolved by a Swedish divorce decree. In Sweden, a marriage can be dissolved only by a divorce – or by the death of a spouse.

63 The reason for this delimitation is that marriage dissolution by divorce qualifies as an issue of fundamental importance in the Swedish legal system and would require a comprehensive analysis on its own. Of relevance is, e.g., the Swedish outlook on divorce as a fundamental unilateral and equal right of both men and women to freely dissolve a marriage through divorce, without a need to provide any kind of ground in support of the application. The applicable law to divorce leaves no scope for

4.4.3 Reported Abuses: Creating a False Impression and False Expectations

Some faith communities, authorised by the state to solemnise marriages, also perform ceremonies which aim to establish a purely religious marriage which does not qualify as a valid civil marriage under Swedish law. The reason for this may be the wish of the concerned parties to conclude an exclusively religious marriage, for example in order to avoid the legal effects of a marriage under Swedish law. The choice can also be motivated for other reasons, such as the existence of an obstacle to the marriage under Swedish law for reasons of age (i.e. so-called child marriages) or because one of the parties is already married to someone else (i.e. polygamy). In these cases, the parties need to have access to a religious official who is willing to conduct the ceremony.

The state body in Sweden in charge of the marriage authorisations has found reason to repeatedly remind certain faith communities that any marriage certificate issued by them must be explicit regarding the nature of the marriage. A marriage certificate may not falsely give the impression that the marriage qualifies as a marriage under the (Swedish) state law.

Example 1 An imam had solemnised a marriage in spite of the fact that the man at the time of the ceremony was married to another woman.[64] The marriage certificate issued by the imam gave the impression of a fully valid marriage. Both the faith community and the imam in question had the required state authorisation to solemnise marriages. When the couple wished to have the marriage registered in Sweden, the registration authority noticed the defects. The controlling state body was informed, and both the imam and the faith community were heard. The imam's explanation was that he had only conducted a blessing ceremony in accordance with Muslim rites, and that he had informed the couple that their marriage did not qualify as a marriage under Swedish law. The state body did not accept this explanation. In its opinion, the imam, by issuing the marriage certificate, demonstrated serious mismanagement in his exercise of state powers. The imam's marriage authorisation was cancelled.

The state body also found reason to question the concerned faith community's ability to follow Swedish law, after several similar incidents. Nevertheless, having regard to the fact that the faith community afterwards had taken educational initiatives comprising all its imams and including issues of marriage celebration, the faith community could in the future be expected to follow Swedish law. The faith community kept its authorisation. It should be emphasised that a religious official or a faith community which has lost its marriage authorisation can be re-authorised by the state body in charge when the shortcomings no longer exist.

Example 2[65] A marriage certificate issued by an imam active within a faith community (the same as in the previous example), authorised to solemnise marriages, was delivered for registration in Sweden by the parties. The registration official noticed that the imam had no personal authorisation and contacted the controlling state body. The faith community

---

any kinds of religious, moral or cultural concerns. On the other hand, it is not forbidden for spouses to supplement their divorce decree by a religious decree on marriage dissolution. For example, Jewish *bet-din* tribunals gather regularly in Sweden to facilitate religious divorces, after the parties' marriage has been dissolved by a Swedish civil divorce decree. The 'fundamental' nature of an equal right to divorce was the decisive reason for Sweden's objection to the EU's Regulation on the law applicable to divorce and legal separation (Rome III).

64 Financial and Administrative Services Agency, Decision 2008-12-19, Dnr 422-17334-08.
65 Financial and Administrative Services Agency, Decision 2011-01-28, Dnr 429-02354-2010.

explained that the couple and those present at the wedding ceremony had been informed that the issued marriage certificate was not an official document, but a purely religious document. The state body abstained from further actions.

It has been queried whether faith communities with authorisation to solemnise marriages under Swedish law *abuse* the confidence of the state by performing exclusively religious marriage ceremonies. From the point of view of state law no marriage has in such a case taken place. The parties may in practice, nevertheless, be just as bound by the 'marriage', and cannot freely leave it. Thought-provokingly, faith communities that apply for marriage authorisation normally state in support of their application that they will abstain from conducting purely religious marriage ceremonies, if their application is granted.[66] From the point of view of faith communities' protected freedom of religion it would, nevertheless, appear that no such commitment can be required of a faith community which regards a marriage to be a religious undertaking. Difficulties could also arise regarding how to distinguish marriage solemnisation within a faith community from a religious blessing of a marriage. Religious blessings are practised by all faith communities as part of their creed. From a faith community's perspective, marriage authority by the state may be a way of increased service to its members, and a way of gaining societal respect. From the state's perspective, entrusting a faith community with public powers is a way of promoting the community's societal integration.

Example 3 Numerous organisations and networks, working for the protection of women's rights in Sweden, reported in a law commission hearing in Stockholm in November 2011 on their experiences on both formal and informal religious marriages which the woman cannot leave against the man's will.[67] They wished to call attention to patriarchal oppression of women, supported by religious leaders who threaten women with divine sanctions if they are not willing to consent to a marriage or when they wish to leave a marriage. The concerned organisations pleaded for measures by the state to put an end to this form of 'religiously justified coercion'. In its own report, published in 2012, the law commission proposes, *inter alia*, the criminalisation of not only legally valid but also *informal marriages* when the marriage is forced, or whenever it involves a child under the age of 18 years.[68]

Example 4 Before the marriage solemnisation rights of the Church of Sweden and its clergy became subject to state authorisation (as of 1 May 2010), all ministers of the Church – those in office and those retired – were *ex lege* competent to officiate legally valid marriages. In anticipation of the reform, the Church applied for marriage authorisation for its priests in office. Retired priests continued to celebrate marriages, without having acquired a state authorisation and without the couples to be married being aware of this. These marriages were later on declared to be valid, by the Swedish Ministry of Justice, in the interests of the couples concerned and since there had been no intention to evade the law.

---

66 Oral information by legal officer Karin Granberg, Financial and Administrative Services Agency, Hearing 9 December 2011.
67 The hearing was organised by the Commission on Increased Protection against Forced Marriages and Child Marriages, under the auspices of the Swedish Ministry of Justice.
68 The Commission also proposed abolishing the current right under Swedish law to, exceptionally, marry under the age of 18 years after special permission by a competent authority (see Swedish Ministry of Justice Committee 2012: 44–7, summary in English).

This outcome was possible to achieve due to a special procedure, provided by law, enabling the government (in the form of the Ministry of Justice), upon application by a party, to afterwards declare that a marriage, which originally was not valid, be regarded as legally valid, due to extraordinary circumstances at the time of its conclusion. Normally, only a few such cases are decided each year in Sweden, and mainly regarding marriages concluded in a religious form.[69]

4.4.4 Evasion of Law?

Another source of criticism focuses on the alleged evasion of marriage law when the authorised official does not in advance check for the existence of obstacles to the marriage or conducts the marriage ceremony in spite of an obstacle. Swedish law, for example, requires any impediments to the marriage, as identified by the Swedish Marriage Code, to have been investigated in a special order not later than four months before the marriage. Where malpractices have been reported, the cause has been an insufficient knowledge of Swedish law or negligence, rather than an intention to evade Swedish law.

Example 5 An imam, belonging to a Muslim faith community authorised by the state to officiate marriages, solemnised the marriage of a Muslim couple without having investigated the impediments to the marriage in the order required by Swedish law.[70] This defect was noticed when the couple applied for registration of the marriage in the Swedish population records. As a defence, the imam submitted that he had relied on a German marriage certificate, believing it to be valid in Sweden. His marriage authority under state law was cancelled by the state body. In another case, an imam had falsely certified that impediments to the marriage had been investigated. That imam's authorisation to solemnise marriages was also cancelled by the state body.[71]

Even if most of the reported cases relate to shortcomings within Muslim faith communities, there is reason to emphasise that other faith communities have also been involved. An example is a minister of the Church of Sweden who after more than 30 years in office within the Church had married a couple without the required investigation of impediments to the marriage. Her marriage authorisation was cancelled.

As already indicated, an exclusively religious marriage may be chosen because of an existing impediment to the marriage under Swedish law. Such manoeuvres cast light on the coexistence of different notions of marriage. A Swedish law commission proposed in 2012 that the state authorisation of faith communities and their officials to solemnise marriages should be made dependent on whether they undertake *not* to perform religious marriages ('informal marriages') when one of the parties is under 18 years of age or when there is reason to suspect that the marriage is coerced (Swedish Ministry of Justice Committee 2012: 39, summary in English). The proposed limitations focused, in other words, on situations regarded as a clear evasion of Swedish law. A marriage authorisation

---

69 In 2012, however, the government decided to declare valid approximately 50 marriages concluded in Uppsala by a well-known politician, after her authorisation to officiate civil wedding ceremonies had expired. The politician had forgotten to check the date of expiry of her marriage authorisation, and the couples married by her had had no reason to believe that this popular politician's authorisation had expired.

70 Financial and Administrative Services Agency, Decision, 2011-05-02, Dnr 16.3.5-01783-2011.

71 Financial and Administrative Services Agency, Decision, 2010-12-16, Dnr 16.3.5-07121-2010.

should not, according to the Commission, depend on an undertaking by the faith community to abstain from officiating (in other cases) marriages aimed to be valid only 'in the eyes of the faith'.

4.5 Should the Validity of Religious Marriages be Reconsidered within State Law?

The state disposes of effective instruments of control. It has the right to choose whom to authorise to solemnise marriages. It also has the right to cancel any marriage authorisation previously granted. Normally it is the official found not to abide by the law who loses his authorisation. In more serious cases, however, the faith community's authorisation is also cancelled. In that case, all its officials also lose it (Swedish Ministry of Justice 2007: 267). In addition, disciplinary measures and even criminal law sanctions are available, in cases of serious malpractice.

Abuses and mismanagement of marriage authorisation within faith communities appear to be rare. During a 10-year period (2000–2011), the controlling state body cancelled, after notification of suspicions of malpractice, the marriage authorisation of altogether 36 religious officials, due to mismanagement of the delegated powers (Swedish Ministry of Justice Committee 2012: 258–9). The vast majority of these decisions, two-thirds, were taken during 2010, most likely as a result of the Church of Sweden coming in under the general scheme of state authorisations for each minister.[72] In 10 additional cases, the faith community itself applied for such cancellation, after it had been notified of serious defects related to marriages celebrated within its regime (Swedish Ministry of Justice Committee 2012: 259). During the same period, nine faith communities lost their authorisation, in two cases upon their own application and in seven cases on the ground that the faith community no longer fulfilled the requirements for authorisation, for example as regards organisation (Swedish Ministry of Justice Committee 2012: 258–9). These numbers need to be related to the figures mentioned above in Section 4.2. The comparison shows that very few religious officials have been involved in malpractices. On the other hand, strikingly many of the small minority faith communities have lost their marriage solemnisation powers, at least temporarily.

It has been indicated above (see Section 4.4.3) that child marriages and non-voluntary marriages are believed to take place mainly through religious ceremonies. The figures above do not support any theory of widespread abuse, even if it can be asked whether the control mechanism is effective enough. At present, state control focuses on observing whether any obstacles to the marriage have been taken into account and that the issued marriage certificate does not give a false impression of the nature of the marriage. In what form the ceremony itself takes place, in particular how the Swedish law's requirement of the spouses' joint presence in the ceremony is interpreted by faith communities, and how the solemnising official assures that both parties conclude the marriage of their own free will, are not controlled. A more comprehensive control would require increased accountability of faith communities' activities in Sweden which might be in conflict with their protected freedom of religion. The inquiry

---

72   This has to do with the fact that a very high number – i.e. the majority of all marriages – are celebrated within this Church (Swedish Ministry of Justice Committee 2012: 259). See also above, Section 4.2.

of a faith community's ability to follow Swedish law should, primarily, take place before its application to solemnise marriages is granted.[73]

Example 6 Is, for example, the requirement of both spouses' joint presence fulfilled when, during the marriage ceremony, the bride and the groom are in the same facility but in different rooms, the wedding official being in the same room as the groom but confirming the bride's consent through her positive answer delivered by telephone and a loudspeaker? The answer is not evident. If the answer is negative, thousands of marriages celebrated in a mosque might risk being regarded as invalid according to Swedish law, because an absolute form requirement has not been followed. This would result in an enormous hardship for the concerned parties, and special measures would be necessary to declare these marriages valid.[74]

As late as in 2009, preceding Sweden's same-sex law reform, the current double-track system of marriage solemnisation was regarded by Parliament to function sufficiently well. More recently, both public and private organisations have raised critical concerns in respect of faith communities' continued authority to officiate marriages (Swedish Ministry of Justice Committee 2012: 257). There is an increased demand for making the civil marriage ceremony mandatory for any marriage concluded in Sweden.[75] This shift of opinion can be traced back to both the challenges posed by the new gender-neutral marriage concept, which highlights a conflict between concerns of anti-discrimination and concerns of freedom of religion, and the more recent multicultural and multi-faith concerns, highlighting the differences between a civil marriage and a religious marriage.

Interestingly enough, an obligatory civil marriage requirement has become popular even among leaders of numerous faith orientations in Sweden. The reason is, primarily, that the state law notion of marriage has developed in a manner which they no longer can combine with that of their own faith; same-sex marriage was the 'final blow'. This also applies in relation to the national churches.[76] Humanist life-stance communities oppose the state delegation of powers to religious communities for reasons of principle, such as its incompatibility with a secular legal system and its allegedly discriminatory effects.[77]

The state's delegation of marriage-officiating powers to faith communities has, *inter alia*, served the function of accommodating faith communities into society. From a faith community's perspective, such powers can mean societal inclusion and respect. The figures above (Section 4.2) do not, however, support any multicultural thesis when dealing with faith orientations outside of Christianity (Jänterä-Jareborg 2011a: 866–7). Most striking is the very limited number of imams who are authorised by the state to officiate marriages.

---

73 This appears to be the practice followed by the Financial and Administrative Services Agency (Swedish Ministry of Justice Committee 2012: 258).

74 See above, Section 4.4.4.

75 Marriages concluded abroad are subject to the rules of private international law. A marriage is, normally, recognised in Sweden if it is valid in the state of conclusion. Restrictions exist if the parties had connecting factors to Sweden and have evaded the marriage obstacles of Swedish law.

76 It should, though, be kept in mind that the Scandinavian national churches remain divided on the issue. Many, in particular ordinary ministers, also wish to retain the current system due to concerns of the Church's continued attraction for people. Others (in particular many of the bishops of the Church) are convinced that supplementary religious ceremonies will be attractive enough for churches to remain involved.

77 In this respect, the focus has been on the faith communities' right to refuse to marry same-sex couples (see Jänterä-Jareborg 2011b: 74).

Having all these factors and later developments in mind, my conclusion is that the double-track system's continued existence and justification should, indeed, be thoroughly examined.

5. Concluding Remarks

5.1 A Cautious Accommodation

The Nordic states could be labeled as 'cautiously accommodationist regimes' as regards their outlook on issues of faith and religion and their willingness to cooperate with the faith communities active on their territories. Even if a dominant national majority church exists in each of the states, their official policy is neutrality of the state in matters of confession and treating faith communities equally. The 'accommodation' takes place through the states' efforts to enable faith communities to carry on with their core activities (organising divine services, providing spiritual assistance, education and care). State cooperation with faith communities serves, at the same time, as an 'instrument' for the state to control and to anchor such values which from the state's perspective are perceived as fundamental for societal peace and development, and to mark limits for any extremist ideologies. The 'cautiousness' is demonstrated by the fact that state support is conditional and, with some exceptions, does not extend beyond what from the point of view of the state is a faith community's main function, i.e., to pursue faith-related activities.

5.2 Being 'Blind' in Different Ways

It is often claimed that the Nordic states are so secular and so ignorant as regards religion that they have become blind towards a faith's importance in a believer's life and do not realise religion's societal potential. This allegation is not without grounds. Religion's societal role remains marginalised, as it has been for the last hundred years. Stereotyped prejudices about religions' contents are, furthermore, common, making people intolerant towards religion. It is even more serious that many people have no idea of *why* freedom of religion is protected at all, i.e., the reasons for respecting religion.[78] The state alone cannot be made responsible. It appears reasonable to expect of faith communities themselves that they too take measures to counteract prejudices and to acquire a place in society, by demonstrating where they stand and what they strive to achieve.

As a jurist I am concerned by a 'blindness' of another kind, towards law and the legal framework. 'Religious libertarians' can demonstrate a total lack of interest as regards the binding nature of (contemporary) law, how laws come about and how a country's laws must strike a balance between various kinds of interests. From a legal point of view, it is evident that no religion can expect to be protected as such, or to be acknowledged to constitute a 'safe harbour' for practices which contradict the laws of a state. This statement has a special relevance within family law. On the other hand, the lawmakers should realise that in order to accommodate all, the laws of a multicultural, multi-faith society should be made mandatory only to the extent that fundamental values are at stake.

---

[78] The foundations of freedom of belief appear more solidly anchored, as well as the 'negative freedom' of religion, namely to leave a faith or not to have any religion at all.

5.3 Identifying the Cultural and Multi-faith Challenges of Family Law

Considering that immigration into the Nordic states is expected to increase in the near future, not least from the presently turbulent Middle East, and the other pluralistic trends in society, it is high time to analyse where the most important challenges lie in a family law context. A united value-basis on the most important issues can, for example, no longer be taken for granted but must be reached. In this process, international human rights instruments should have the best potential for providing the model. Both the majority society and the minority groups must, however, be willing to distance themselves from the cultural constraints of their national, cultural or faith-based norm systems towards more universal values, or at least demonstrate a tolerance towards other ways of looking at issues. With this insight, the dilemma of who sets a faith community's value agenda (see Section 1), there being minorities among minorities, is reduced to at least some extent.

I wish to end by quoting from a recent Swedish report, by a Swedish Ministry of Justice Committee (2012: 43) which investigated how to protect children and women against involuntary marriages:

> A fear of xenophobia or stigmatization cannot be allowed to result in a lack of attention on the part of society to the individual's exposure ... At the same time it must be underscored that people, groups and cultures deserve basic respect even to the extent their traditions and approach include values that are unfamiliar to the majority in the country. To be sure, basic respect of this nature can never be allowed to mean any departure from fundamental rights and freedoms. But it should mean that amendments to laws that may be perceived to be directed against a group or a tradition be implemented in a tone of voice and with an approach in general that does not create unnecessary confrontation and which does not play into the hands of xenophobic forces. It must be admitted that in this instance the legislator is in an area that is unusually difficult to master.

References

An-Na'im, A.A. 2008. *Islam and the Secular State, Negotiating the Future of Shari'a*. Cambridge, MA: Harvard University Press.

Church of Sweden. 2009. *Information on a Possible Decision by the Church of Sweden Regarding Same-sex Marriages*. Report 17 September 2009, Uppsala: Church of Sweden.

Danelius, H. 2012. *Mänskliga rättigheter i europeisk praxis, En kommentar till Europakonventionen om de mänskliga rättigheterna*, fourth edition. Stockholm: Norstedts Juridik.

Edgardh, N. 2011. Sweden, in *Welfare and Values in Europe, Transitions related to Religion, Minorities and Gender, National Overviews and Case Study Reports, Volume 1 (Northern Europe: Sweden, Norway, Finland and England)*. Uppsala: Acta Universitatis Upsaliensis.

Göransson, Å. 2011. Trossamfunden en del av civilsamhället, *Frisinnad Tidskrift 2011*, 184–6.

Helmersson, E. 2012. Staten är ingen imam. *Dagens Nyheter*, 30 May 2012, 5.

Hirschfeldt, J. 2011. Inte är väl regleringen för ingående av äktenskap värderingsfri?, in *De lege 2011, Rätten och rättsfamiljer i ett föränderligt samhälle – rättshistoriskt och komparativt, Vänbok till Rolf Nygren*, edited by M. Jänterä-Jareborg and M. Kumlien. Uppsala: Iustus Förlag.

Jänterä-Jareborg, M. 2010. Sweden, in *Religion and the Secular State: National (Interim) Reports*, under the direction of J. Martinez-Torrón and W. Cole Durhan Jr. XVIIIth International Congress of Comparative Law, Washington D.C. 2010. Provo, Utah: The International Center for Law and Religion Studies, Brigham Young University.

Jänterä-Jareborg, M. 2011a. When 'marriage' becomes a religious battleground – Swedish and Scandinavian experiences at the dawn of same-sex marriages, in *Private Law, National – Global – Comparative. Festschrift für Ingeborg Schwenzer zum 60. Geburtstag*. Bern: Stämpfli Verlag.

Jänterä-Jareborg, M. 2011b. The legal scope for religious identity in family matters – The paradoxes of the Swedish approach, in *The Place of Religion in Family Law: A Comparative Search*, edited by J. Mair and E. Örücü. Cambridge: Intersentia.

Lindqvist, P. 2001. SST är en unik instans där världsreligionerna möts – ett samtal med Åke Göransson. *Signum*, 4/2001, 27–35.

Mehdi, R. 2007. Facing the enigma: talaq-e-tafweez, a need of Muslim women in Nordic Perspective, in *Integration & Retsudvikling*, edited by R. Mehdi. Copenhagen: Juristog Okonomforbundets Forlag.

Modéer, K.Å. 2005. Marriage and cohabitation in the history of law, in *Love, Cohabitation and Marriage*, The Theological Committee of the Church of Sweden, report from a public hearing September 6–9, Uppsala 2005. Uppsala: Church of Sweden.

Ramadan, T. 1999. *To Be a European Muslim*. Leicester: The Islamic Foundation.

Swedish Ministry of Education. 2009. *Staten och imamerna*. [Report by the Swedish Ministry of Education on the Investigation concerning Imam Education]. SOU 2009:52.

Swedish Ministry of Justice Committee. 2012. *Increased Protection Against Forced Marriages and Child Marriages* (*Stärkt skydd mot tvångsäktenskap och barnäktenskap*), summary in English, SOU 2012:35.

Swedish Ministry of Justice. 2007. *Äktenskap för par med samma kön. Vigselfrågor* (Marriage for Same-Sex Couples. Issues on Marriage Conclusion). SOU 2007:17.

Westerlund, K. 2012. *Frihetens sammanhang*. Nora: Nya Doxa.

Chapter 5
The Uniformisation of Family Law in Europe and the Place of Ethnic Minorities

Domenico Francavilla

Ethnic Minorities and Uniformising Trends in European Law

The interaction between the rules followed by ethnic minorities and official European legal systems in multicultural Europe is inevitably connected to a tension between uniformity and diversity. This tension between legal uniformity and legal diversity is a general feature of legal systems and one could argue that the entire history of law could be read from the perspective of different balances reached between these two 'forces'. In a sense, modern law in Europe has been the outcome of the making of uniform state laws, and medieval law, although not uniform, was characterised by a balance between local laws and a tendency towards universalism, which is at the basis of what is called *ius commune* (see in detail Cavanna 1982). On the other hand, clearly this is not just a European legal phenomenon. Ancient Indian law, for instance, may be seen as the result of a dynamic between local legal systems and general laws, as expressed in *dharmashastra* literature, made up basically of doctrinal opinions, which was universalistic in character, albeit universalism in this context was by no means the kind of state-directed uniformity which is assumed in modernity.[1] From a theoretical point of view, the couples uniform–diverse, monist–pluralist or, in simpler terms, one law–many laws are crucial and have been variously elaborated in several legal traditions and – even more significantly – continuously demand new conceptualisations.

In this sense, the current debate on legal practice and accommodation of cultural diversity in Europe is better addressed when linked to more general theoretical questions.[2] This also helps to avoid that sense of the analysis of the rules followed by ethnic minorities as a minority issue, as is often perceived by legal scholars. On the contrary, such difficult issues require investigation into general jurisprudential questions (see, e.g., Cotterrell 2006, 2007; Menski 2006) and, at the same time, can improve our understanding of other legal fields. This chapter aims to deal with legal practice and accommodation of unofficial laws in multicultural Europe from the perspective of general uniformising trends in European laws. In fact, if the tension between uniformity and diversity is real, as it seems to be, an investigation into these trends and, more generally, into the logic of uniformisation could help us to understand the nature and limits of accommodation.

Placing the focus on family law, several questions arise concerning European law as a whole: is there any uniform family law in Europe at the official level? How much cultural diversity exists between the family laws of the official systems of European countries? Are these systems converging? What problems could be experienced in writing a uniform

---

1 On the interaction between *dharmashastra* and local customary laws in India see Menski (2003) and Francavilla (2006).
2 On this debate see, for instance, Grillo et al. (2009).

European civil code in family matters? More generally, is uniformity of family laws in Europe desirable and/or feasible? In this framework, a further dimension could be added by considering the role and place of the rules followed by ethnic minorities in family matters in Europe. How do these harmonisation processes impact on ethnic minorities? How could ethnic minority family laws be accommodated in a uniform European family law, if not in a hypothetical European civil code?

Family law can be seen as a series of interconnected rules ranging from the age for marriage to maintenance, from adoption to divorce. This research endeavour should take into account the interaction between several kinds of law in the European context at different levels aiming at highlighting processes of uniformisation and pluralisation on the ground. In this chapter I focus on some issues that seem particularly worth considering. First, I briefly sketch the general rationale of uniformising trends in European laws. In this regard, European contract law is by far the most advanced field, even though work on European uniform family law is visibly increasing. This situation depends on the 'exceptional' character of family law, which is due to the fact that family law is more visibly connected to cultural and community identity. In fact, one could hold that uniform law may be good in contract law but bad in marriage law, and this attitude is widely diffused among scholars and policymakers as far as European laws are concerned. Nonetheless, when one comes to the rules followed by ethnic minorities in Europe this concern for diversity seems to be superseded. In addition, it is worth remembering that, although family law in Europe remains the central concern for ethnic minority issues, other parts of law, including contract law, are now more visibly involved, as the case *Khan v Khan* clearly shows.[3]

I then address some general issues concerning the logic of uniformisation and deal briefly with the general problem of feasibility and desirability of uniform law. In this context, I will make reference to some reforms in modern Hindu family law and to the debate on the Uniform Civil Code in India, which concerns family law, while contract, property, tort, and so forth are already uniform, at least in the sense that they are not applied on a personal basis. Finally, I provide an account of what an inclusive comparative approach would mean. At the end of the day, the theoretical question I address concerns the place of differences. Provided that diversity is a fact, at what level could and should it be effectively dealt with?

Towards a European Civil Code?

The uniformisation of European private law is presently carried out with reference to several legal fields. This process concerns EU law as such and national legal systems. More analytically, 'uniformisation' could be distinguished from 'harmonisation', which is typical of EU directives. A uniform European law is not necessarily the outcome of legislation but, in this context, a European civil code may be seen as the highly symbolic expression of a single private law governing all European citizens in all European states. The debate on a future European civil code has become a standard issue for comparative lawyers. Some are enthusiastic about this project, while others are sceptical (e.g. Legrand 1997; Cotterrell 2007). In any event, much scholarly research addresses this issue. This scholarly endeavour is at the same time highly theoretical and practice-oriented. In fact, legal research addressing difficult comparative issues across European laws is potentially the

---

3   *Khan v Khan* [2007] EWCA Civ 399. On this important case decided by the Court of Appeal of England and Wales, see the analysis by Ballard (2009).

basis for sustained legal reforms. The making of a uniform European law, and possibly of a uniform civil code in Europe, includes the activity of several research groups and projects. Among these, one can mention the activities of the Lando Commission, the Common Core of European Private Law project, the Acquis Group project, the Study Group on a European Civil Code and the activities of the Commission on European Family Law.[4]

As concerns ethnic minority issues, one of the most interesting aspects of this impressive movement towards uniformisation is that it is based on the idea of a preliminary ascertainment of what European law really is. The Common Core project in particular aims to 'unearth the common core of the bulk of European private law, i.e. what is already common, if anything, among the different legal systems of European Union Member States' (Bussani and Mattei 1997). The Acquis Group project is inspired by a similar perspective and the main difference is that it is concerned with EU law as such and aims at elaborating the principles of existing EC law, while the Common Core project is concerned with the national legal systems of European countries. The works of the Commission on European Family Law adopt the common core approach and combine it with the 'better law' approach, that is to say an approach that selects what could be seen as the best legal solution, independently from its being common.

All these approaches, and particularly those that are more assertive about the goal of a uniform civil code, are debatable, but what is interesting for the problem of legal practice and accommodation of cultural diversity in Europe is the attempt to define something like a common core of European law, what is common and what is different in all European laws, and therefore, in some sense, the boundaries of European laws. In fact, the supposed conflict between some ethnic minority laws and European law, meant as both the law of European states and EU law, is still largely ideological and not sufficiently empirical. A better understanding of the real boundaries of European laws, and of the range of possibilities, could help to discern where exactly some ethnic minority laws conflict or may be accommodated.

This debate concerns primarily contract law but family law is also becoming more and more analysed from the perspective of uniformising European laws. As mentioned, family law is often seen as a realm apart, being more cultural, and, as a result, comparative family law is a less established subject than comparative contract law. For certain, while same-sex marriage, divorce and polygamy have always given rise to hot debates and social movements, contract law and other parts of private law, such as property and torts, are much more technical, even though national legal traditions may contrast uniformisation in these fields also.

Coping with the issue of a hypothetical European uniform family law one could highlight that European laws here basically mean the official family laws of European countries, with their norms on marriage, adoption, divorce, patrimonial aspects and so on. Crucial to the argument here is that this debate should not avoid taking into account Muslim, Hindu and other originally non-European family laws. In my view these are now European laws in the extent to which they are followed in Europe by wide communities and significantly by individuals that are in many cases European citizens. In this sense, the debate on uniformisation could be an important opportunity for understanding the place of these laws side-by-side with other family legal regimes in Europe.

---

4 For a clear outline and critical analysis of convergence of private law in Europe, see Smits (2007). On different working groups and their methods see Bussani and Mattei (1997) and Antokolskaia (2007).

Furthermore, the comparison of European family laws opens a broader space than that existing within the boundaries of a single European state law. In other words, European diversity helps us to understand diversity as such and therefore could potentially make room for a more sensitive attitude towards ethnic minority cultural diversity. On the other hand, Ballard (2007) highlights that Europe has often dealt with cultural plurality and the novelty is now the unfamiliar, extra-European and non Judeo-Christian, character of new dimensions of plurality. In this sense, the awareness of European cultural diversity is not a guarantee of accommodation of further cultural diversity.

Therefore, the idea of a common core of European laws has much to say, in my view, about ethnic minority issues and, furthermore, ethnic minority issues would have much to say in this debate, and it is a lost opportunity that they are not fully considered from those perspectives. To be clear, in so saying, I do not want to engage myself here with the idea of the European civil code. I simply think that this debate is instructive, independent of the outcome of unification, in its descriptive aspects of the identity of European laws and, more generally, for the kinds of attitudes it may reveal. I am also interested in considering this possible European civil code from the perspective of accommodation in multicultural Europe as a speculative issue.

Actually, if this code is hypothetical, even more hypothetical is that this code would acknowledge ethnic minority laws. These laws are normally located in the shadow of official state laws. They may be recognised by official judgments or new specific legislation, but for certain these laws are generally recognised as official laws of almost no European country and no generalised system of personal laws comparable with the Indian one is operating in Europe. Therefore the debate on a uniform European civil code, specifically in family matters, is framed in terms that differ from the debate on the Indian uniform civil code, where the problem is whether to supersede the system of personal laws and adopt a uniform civil code for all Indians, irrespective of their being Hindus, Muslims, Parsis and so on. On the contrary, the starting point in Europe is the uniformisation at the European level of uniform state laws.

Nonetheless, the difficult enterprise of writing a European uniform family code could be an opportunity to consider the possible accommodation of ethnic minority law within a European code. In other words, once the door is opened to consider what norms should be written in this code, one should ask what one could do to accommodate plural Europe within this code. How inclusive would this hypothetical code be? I use the term 'inclusive' considering that European law, in its broader meaning, should be considered as also including non-original European laws that are presently followed in Europe even though at an unofficial level. As far as many ethnic minority members are European citizens, a uniform civil code should take them into account.

The Logic of Uniform Law

What would a uniform European family law be like? The answer to this question requires a better understanding of how uniformisation works. Starting from a situation of considerable pluralism on the ground, and assuming that one wants to move towards a single uniform law applicable to all those who up to then were subject to several different laws, what routes could one take? Specifically, is uniform law a new law? Or is uniform law one of the pre-existing laws that comes to be generalised? Who makes uniform law? Why is uniform law so attractive? Even more fundamentally, is it formal uniformity or substantial uniformity that counts?[5]

In this regard, we can usefully consider the debate on the uniform civil code in India. One of the reasons why it seems to be a failed attempt is that Indian Muslims fear that basically a sort of modified Hindu law would be applied to them. In other words, the fear is that uniform law would be nothing else than the generalisation of one of the pre-existing laws, the Hindu one. If we look at the reform of Hindu law after Indian independence, which aimed at amending and simplifying pre-existing Hindu law, it can indeed be observed that this reform was made in some areas by generalising some specific Hindu legal rules to all Hindus. The clearest example is provided by the case of monogamy, which was elevated to a general rule for all Hindus, in spite of the fact that significant Hindu communities were in fact polygamous. This means that the rule followed by a part of the society is generalised and extended to all those falling under the jurisdiction of the law of that society.

Another example could be provided by reference to dowry in Italy when family law was reformed in 1975. Dowry was an institution clearly recognised in the Italian civil code (1942) and was followed in many societal contexts, particularly but not only in the South of Italy, while it was not followed in other areas of Italian society. The reform promulgated in 1975 abrogated the norms on dowry, which ultimately became a forbidden practice. In this way, the rules that were already followed by some parts of Italian society were extended to all parts of society and institutionalised in the civil code. Formal written rules have, in many cases, precisely this role of extending by imposition some rules that have had their origin or are followed in some localised context. Interestingly, one could argue that those following dowry practices under the civil code continued to follow dowry practices against the official law after 1975. In other words, dowry became the unofficial law of some parts of Italian society. This also shows that methodologically one could consider unofficial European laws, for instance unofficial southern Italian dowry practices, as comparable to unofficial South Asian laws in Europe.

In any event, the point I want to make here is that uniformisation actually comes down to generalisation and this means that uniformisation disacknowledges diversity not simply because it is uniformising but, more significantly, because it reaches uniformity by setting aside some forms of life. In fact, in principle, one could imagine a different way to uniformisation, that is to say, uniformisation reached by producing a genuinely new uniform law that tries to accommodate several different pre-existing laws. But this new uniform law is hard to conceive of. In fact, what actually happens is that some pre-existing rules will prevail over others by reason of their prestige or following the application of a 'better law' principle. Diversity could be preserved only through a uniform framework that makes room for on-the-ground legal diversities by accepting the pluralisation of rules, so to say, at a second level. For instance, the Hindu Marriage Act, 1955, introduced some uniformity to pre-existing Hindu laws but renounced the regulation of all aspects of marriage and recognised, in some cases, local customs in two ways: by laying down a general rule that could be derogated by customs, as in the case of degrees of prohibited relationship, or by renouncing any general rule and making reference directly to customs, as in the case of the

---

5   The distinction between formal and substantial uniformity is used by Werner Menski (2008) in his analysis of the debate on the Indian uniform civil code and aims at demonstrating the existence of harmonisation patterns in Indian personal laws. On this issue see also Menski (2010).

solemnisation of marriages.[6] It is worth remarking that under official Hindu law, in order to be applied, customs must be certain, reasonable and not opposed to public policy. This test could be seen as a uniformising factor, setting aside those customs that are, so to say, beyond the boundaries of the legal system. On the other hand, much depends on the judicial application of these criteria to assess customs.[7] As a result we have a piece of legislation that makes some rules uniform, provides a general framework for other non-uniform rules and, in so doing, allows a certain degree of diversity. Judicial application may tend to uniformise this diversity or to pluralise those norms that seem to be uniformised, depending on the specific case. Needless to say, in spite of any kind of state legislation or judicial application, some rules will continue to be followed at the unofficial level.

Law is inherently plural and this depends on the very same legal process. In fact, rules have a localised origin in specific social groups and then are diffused to an entire society and institutionalised in a formal legal system. If legal diversity is a fact, the making of a legal system is basically a process of uniformisation and centralisation in contrast to competing processes of pluralisation. Even when there is no uniform law, uniformising processes happen and, on the other hand, even when there is formally a uniform law, pluralising processes continuously happen. Uniform law is also related to the making of wider integrated communities including originally separate groups. Interaction within these communities tends, in the long term, to select some rules, setting aside other originally coexisting rules. In other cases, on the contrary, some social groups can emerge as distinct communities and separate themselves from their original community because they elaborate new rules that cannot be integrated and legitimated in the original normative system. In this sense, social cohesion requires a certain degree of acknowledgement of different practices. But, as we will see, unity does not strictly require uniformisation.

Inclusive Comparative Approach

Law is a complex reality and what seems uniform may not be uniform, and vice versa. Where should similarities and divergences be searched for, when comparing two legal orders? The Common Core of European Private Law project explicitly relies on the concept of legal formants as introduced by Rodolfo Sacco (1991), meant as 'all those formative elements that make any given rule of law amidst statutes, general propositions, particular definitions, reasons, holdings, etc.' (Bussani and Mattei 1997: 344). This theory can be described in a very simplified form by saying that it is based on the observation that the rules embodied in legislation, in judgments and in the work of interpreters may be the same but in many cases they are different and conflicting.[8] The same could be said considering, for instance, customary law. One could ask where uniform rules should be searched for. All the attempts of uniformising law, for instance in contractual matters, should take into account that if one stops at one of the legal formants the conclusions could be undermined. One can hardly say that law is uniform just because legislation is uniform. And, reciprocally, one could argue that despite so many differences on the formal level, two legal orders could reach the same

---

6 A comprehensive analysis of the Hindu Marriage Act, 1955, explaining the role of customs in modern Hindu law may be read in Menski (2003).

7 On this complex issue see Menski (2003).

8 On the theory of legal formants and its relationship with other methodologies of comparative law, including the Cornell Common Core Project, see also Monateri and Sacco (1998) and Mattei (2001).

result starting from opposite positions. Comparative law, which is interested in ascertaining the real differences, must take this into account.

From our perspective on ethnic minority issues and European family law, the problem may be framed considering the interaction of different sources. But, while the idea of including all formants is accepted in current legal analysis of uniformising trends in European law, the idea of including all legal orders is not really accepted. If comparative law, at least in its basic sense, is comparing differences between legal systems, no doubt one has to articulate the analysis by considering several different kinds of law operating within a legal system. Specifically, one has to consider different legal orders, and their legal formants, along with the formal state legal order. The resulting picture would be much more complex but much more realistic and useful. For instance, one might discover that the official legislative rule of a European State may be in conflict with a Hindu doctrinal rule but not with a Hindu custom, which may well be conflicting with the doctrinal rule.

An inclusive comparative approach means, in my view, that European official laws should be analysed together with unofficial European and originally non-European laws. This is necessary from a dynamic point of view, interested in considering the law resulting from complex interactions in legal reality. In this sense, in analysing a specific legal institution in Europe, one should consider not only the rules resulting from legislation, judgments and doctrinal works of a specific European jurisdiction and compare all this with other European legal systems, within the framework of EU supranational law, but also those rules that operate in unofficial contexts, particularly ethnic minority customary law and written rules followed by ethnic minority communities in their interaction with these customary rules. The aim of this difficult task is to define the range of possibilities, the constraints of different legal traditions and the limits for further integration of new practices in European laws.

One could also highlight that the opposition between European laws and 'foreign' laws is misleading. For instance, in many cases Indian state law in its attempts to cope with some Hindu customs is in the same position as European laws.[9] In other terms, in Europe and elsewhere, what happens is a complex dynamic involving several normative actors, some who want to preserve the rules they follow and others who want to change them, usually by generalising other rules. This is a general phenomenon, not restricted to ethnic minorities. There is no perfect correspondence between a single European state law and all the European social communities living under that law, as abundantly shown by issues such as euthanasia and same-sex marriage. As a general rule, some parts of society are discontented with state enforcement of some rules that are at the same time supported by other parts of society.

Legitimation is a crucial topic when considering the process of integration of new rules in European laws. Through legitimation, others' practices can become 'our' practices. In other words, they are integrated within a legal tradition. This does not necessarily mean 'sameness' but rather 'togetherness'. Can some Hindu or Muslim practices, for instance, be legitimated in a European context? This depends very much on where one recognises the boundaries of legal traditions and what is assumed to be foundational for legal identity. But, boundaries are not fixed once and for all. For instance, gender equality is seen as foundational in Europe, and what does not meet the standard of gender equality can hardly

---

9 For a comparative analysis of different strategies to accommodate religious, cultural and ethnic diversity in Britain and India, see Menski (2010).

be accepted, that is to say legitimated.[10] Much depends on the force of the necessity of integrating new forms of life. Each standard rule is originally a negotiated rule. Therefore what the rule is very much depends on who are the parts involved. In this sense polygamy, which is firmly opposed by European laws, *had* to find its way through official Indian law, because it could not be ignored, being the rule followed by a huge part of the Indian population. This is the case for Indian Muslims, whose personal law can hardly be set aside for the sake of uniformising marriage laws in India. Should this happen, the rule would be monogamy in India also, considering that this is the statutory Hindu rule. Interestingly, as mentioned, Hindu law also allowed polygamy among several groups. These rules have been outlawed through the pursuit of uniformisation of Indian Hindu law, with the result that Hindus practising polygamy after 1955 had to follow the monogamy rule as far as official Hindu law was concerned, even though these communities remain polygamous at the unofficial level.[11] Arguably this happened because, differently from Islam, the dominant rule in Hinduism is monogamy and an opposition to Hindu polygamy was not felt as radically anti-Hindu. Therefore, quantitative factors have to be considered along with cultural aspects in considering the context where the rules are negotiated. On the other hand, the legitimation of same-sex marriages is much more discussed in Europe than in Asia, because in Europe the interests at stake are much more sensible, demand public recognition and are supported by some cultural movements, even though, of course, they have to face strong cultural opposition from other parts of European societies.

A general problem is whether uniform law is feasible and/or desirable. According to many, uniformity is unfeasible, precisely because while one may be successful in writing a uniform civil code, diversity will still find its way through other formants. As for desirability, each attempt to impose uniformity may be seen as a loss of something and as 'authoritarian'.[12] On the other hand, one should not underestimate what could be seen as uniformity from below, that is to say, uniformising trends operating in social reality independently of the intervention of state law. This might also involve the rules followed by ethnic minorities. Imitation might have a role in uniformising rules followed in social practice by different communities, even though principles are seemingly irreconcilable. Furthermore, rules followed in practice by ethnic minorities might be the same as those followed by individuals who are not part of ethnic minorities, irrespective of official state law. To sum up, multiple kinds of interaction may happen and should be understood by distinguishing several formants within a legal order and between legal orders.

---

10   This issue would require some clarification. First of all gender equality is recent in European legal history and this should suggest that foundational characters do not need to be permanent characters. Secondly, gender equality is a uniform foundational legal principle while, from a societal point of view, it is not at all uniform in European societies.

11   This dynamic has a great impact on living laws and Indian judges are compelled to articulate these different normative systems in order to provide just solutions in practice. For a detailed analysis see Menski (2003).

12   Considering recent perspectives on this issue one could consider, for instance, the work of Legrand (1997), Cotterrell (2007) and Sacco (2007). All pluralistic approaches to laws, including for instance of Ehrlich's theory of living law (1936), arguably embody the view and a warning that state-centred monopoly of law cannot but be authoritarian in character. In other words, pluralist analysis also unveils the competition between different social powers and social groups.

The Place of Differences

How many forms of life can coexist? Unity is different from uniformity. Every society has to organise different and often conflicting rules of behaviour and values in a coherent system. In this process the forms of life that a society considers binding are selected among the several that claim to be normative. In front of conflicting models of behaviour the system may preserve its unity through the elimination of one of the alternatives, or through their coordination. The first possibility is more compatible with an egalitarian society, but in this case the place of differences becomes external to the legal system. Uniform law implies the unity of the juridical subject and tends to set aside several forms of life, by selecting one as appropriate and imposing it on the overall society. But diversity emerges at other levels. In this sense uniform law does not seem to be an appropriate answer to complex societies and, at the same time, some uniformisation seems to be inherent to law, which in no case can accommodate all diversities and operates at a different level than individual worldview and expectations. In fact, legal rules must provide a suitable context for interactions that may occur between individuals who may be more or less different.

The articulation of differences in the laws of contemporary societies is a difficult but necessary task. This necessity arises from cultural diversity represented by ethnic minorities but not only by them. This issue is much more general. The real question is how many forms of life may coexist and be protected. Difference is a matter of fact and the problem is to find a theory and a practice of law that creates an appropriate place for diversity. European laws developed on the cultural basis of the desirability of a uniform law for all citizens, leaving little space to other realms of law based on other kinds of belonging. This makes them unready to integrate more cultural diversity within themselves. On the other hand, this simply means that differences remain outside the realm of official law. In this way, the norms that are an expression of this cultural diversity are dismissed as traditional habits. Nonetheless, they may preserve a high grade of institutionalisation and a binding character for those who adhere to that system of rules (Shah 2005).

The identification of law with state law hides the fact that competing systems of rules exist. The postulate according to which state law must be one and the same for all citizens runs the risk of being an ideological operation of exclusion of ethnic minorities. In fact, in this perspective the new Europeans having an immigrant origin should simply comply with existing laws and, even more importantly, their needs should not be taken into account in the making of law. This postulate masks the fact that European laws developed for centuries as an answer to new needs of protection emerging in the course of history. To pretend that ethnic minorities should simply comply with a law that was formed without their contribution goes far beyond asserting the principle of legality. In fact, the point is not simply to state that everyone has to respect the laws of the country but to understand who decides what for whom and the needs and values that have to be protected. On the other hand, the rules followed by ethnic minorities cannot demand official recognition, so to say, statically, as they are and as separate bodies in the society of which they are part, while they could more effectively demand recognition of their legal standing, needs and aspirations, as one of the many different components of European societies.

The building of citizenship and the integration of Europeans belonging to ethnic minorities require a politics of rights and duties where the relevance of original socio-legal structure is effectively recognised and defined. In principle, a system of personal laws following the Indian model could be laid down, and in this case the different systems of norms that are followed in Europe could receive official acknowledgement.[13] But this seems to go beyond one of the legal postulates of European laws. In fact, a system of personal laws does not seem viable presently, not only because of the well-known cases of real or potential conflict with European laws at the substantive level, but also for a more general reason, that is to say, the principle of formal uniformity that stands at the basis of modern European state laws.

On the other hand, European laws cannot simply rely on the dismissal of the rules followed by ethnic minorities because this might strongly undermine democracy and the functioning of the legal system as a whole. New forms of life must be recognised in some way, as difficult as it may be, in order to widen the space for differences. The outcome of this process is unpredictable but it will certainly depend on the quantity and quality of interactions. What seems crucial is not so much the recognition of single practices and forms of life and their accommodation, but the acknowledgement of the fact that new subjects, new actors exist in the making of law in Europe, and moreover of the fact that European laws concern persons who may belong to different cultural contexts and thus need to be interpreted and applied in a more culture-aware way, not as a matter of concession or derogation but in order to correctly apply the very same European laws and principles. This could be seen as the premise for elaborating increased cultural diversity without resulting in conflict or separation. In order to do so the issues raised by cultural diversity of ethnic minorities in Europe should not be analysed as a separate topic but as an aspect of the wider picture of uniformisation and pluralisation of law in the European context.

Bibliography

Aluffi Beck-Peccoz, R. and Zincone, G. (eds). 2004. *The Legal Treatment of Islamic Minorities in Europe*. Leuven: Peeters.

Antokolskaia, M. 2007. Comparative family law: Moving with the times? in *Comparative Law: A Handbook*, edited by E. Örücü and D. Nelken. Oxford and Portland: Hart Publishing, 241–62.

Ballard, R. 1994. *Desh Pardesh. The South Asian Presence in Britain*. London: Hurst & Co.

Ballard, R. 2002. Race, ethnicity and culture, in *New Directions in Sociology*, edited by Martin Holborn. Ormskirk: Causeway. Available at: http://www.casas.org.uk/papers/pdfpapers/racecult.pdf [last accessed 17 March 2013].

Ballard, R. 2007. *When, Why and How Far Should Legal Systems Take Cognisance of Cultural Diversity?* Paper prepared for the International Congress on Justice and Human Values in Europe, Karlsruhe, 9–11 May 2007. Available at: http://www.casas.org.uk/papers/pdfpapers/karlsruhe.pdf [last accessed 17 March 2013].

Ballard, R. 2009. *The Current Status of Coparcenaries in English Law*. Commentary on pluri-legal issues. Available at: http://www.casas.org.uk/papers/pdfpapers/coparcenaries.pdf [last accessed 17 March 2013].

Boele-Woelki, K. (ed.) 2005. *Common Core and Better Law in European Family Law*. European Family Law Series No. 10. Antwerp: Intersentia.

---

13 In this regard, it is worth noting that a system of personal laws involving the official acknowledgement of ethnic minority laws could start an evolutionary dynamic, like in India, where different customary Hindu laws, and also Muslim laws, are applied by state courts within the framework of public policy and constitutional principles.

Bussani, M. and Graziadei, M. (eds) 2005. *Human Diversity and the Law*. Brussels: Bruylant.
Bussani, M. and Mattei, U. 1997. The common core approach to European private law. *Columbia Journal of European Law*, 3, 339–56.
Cavalli-Sforza, L.L. 2004. *L'evoluzione della cultura*. Torino: Codice edizioni.
Cavanna, A. 1982. *Storia del diritto moderno in Europa. 1: Le fonti e il pensiero giuridico*. Milano: Giuffrè.
Chiba, M. (ed.), 1986. *Asian Indigenous Law: In Interaction with Received Law*. London and New York: KPI.
Cotterrell, R. 2006. *Law, Culture and Society: Legal Ideas in the Mirror of Social Theory*. Aldershot: Ashgate.
Cotterrell, R. 2007. Is it so bad to be different? Comparative law and the appreciation of diversity, in *Comparative Law: A Handbook*, edited by E. Örücü and D. Nelken. Oxford and Portland: Hart Publishing, 133–54.
Ehrlich, E. 1936. *Fundamental Principles of the Sociology of Law*. Cambridge, MA: Harvard University Press.
Ferrari, S. 2002. *Lo spirito dei diritti religiosi*. Bologna: Il Mulino.
Ferrari, S. and Ibán, I.C. 1997. *Diritto e religione in Europa occidentale*. Bologna: Il Mulino.
Francavilla, D. 2006. *The Roots of Hindu Jurisprudence*, Corpus Iuris Sanscriticum et Fontes Iuris Asiae Meridianae et Centralis, vol. 7. Torino: Corpus Iuris Sanscriticum Committee - Cesmeo.
Gambaro, A. and Sacco, R. 2008. *Sistemi giuridici comparati*, 3rd ed. Torino: UTET.
Grillo, R. et al. (eds) 2009. *Legal Practice and Cultural Diversity*. Burlington: Ashgate.
Jones, R. and Welhengama, G. 2000. *Ethnic Minorities in English Law*. Stoke-on-Trent: Trentham Books.
Legrand, P. 1997. Against a European civil code. *Modern Law Review*, 60, 44–63.
Mattei, U. 2001. The comparative jurisprudence of Schlesinger and Sacco: A study in legal influenc', in *Rethinking the Masters of Comparative Law*, edited by A. Riles. Oxford and Portland: Hart, 238–56.
Mattei, U. and Monateri, P.G. 1997. *Introduzione breve al diritto comparator*. Padova: Cedam.
Menski, W.F. 1998. Asians in Britain and the question of adaptation to a new legal order: Asian laws in Britain? in *Ethnicity, Identity, Migration: The South Asian Context*, edited by M. Israel and N.K. Wagle. Toronto: University of Toronto, 238–68.
Menski, W.F. 2003. *Hindu Law: Beyond Tradition and Modernity*. Delhi: Oxford University Press.
Menski, W.F. 2004. *Cherrypicking Customs: On What Happens when Custom is not Taught*. Proceedings of Windhoek Conference, 26–29 July 2004.
Menski, W.F. 2006. *Comparative Law in a Global Context: The Legal Systems of Asia and Africa*, second ed. Cambridge: Cambridge University Press.
Menski, W.F. 2008. The uniform civil code debate in Indian law: New developments and changing agenda. *German Law Journal*, 9(3), 211–50.
Menski, W.F. 2010. Law, state and culture: How countries accommodate religious, cultural and ethnic diversity, in *Cultural Diversity and the Law. State Responses from around the World*, edited by Marie-Claire Foblets et al. Brussels: Bruylant and Éditions Yvon Blais, 403–46.
Menski, W.F. (ed.) 1998. *South Asians and the Dowry Problem*. Stoke-on-Trent: Trentham Books.

Monateri, P.G. and Sacco, R. 1998. Legal formants, in *The New Palgrave Dictionary of Law and Economics*, edited by P. Newman. London: Macmillan, 531–3.

Poulter, S. 1986. *English Law and Ethnic Minority Customs*. London: Butterworths.

Sacco, R. 1991. Legal formants. A dynamic approach to comparative law. *The American Journal of Comparative Law*, 39(1), 1–34 and 39(2), 343–401.

Sacco, R. 2007. *Antropologia giuridica*. Bologna: Il Mulino.

Sagade, J. 2005. *Child Marriage in India*. Delhi: Oxford University Press.

Shah, P. 2005. *Legal Pluralism in Conflict: Coping with Cultural Diversity in Law*. London: The Glass House Press.

Smits, J.M. 2007. Convergence of private law in Europe: Towards a new ius commune? in *Comparative Law: A Handbook*, edited by E. Örücü and D. Nelken. Oxford and Portland: Hart Publishing, 219–40.

Sperber, D. 1996. *Explaining Culture: A Naturalistic Approach*. Oxford: Blackwell.

Chapter 6
Defending the Family Treasure Chest: Navigating Muslim Families and Secured Positivistic Islands of European Legal Systems

Federica Sona

Introduction

This article investigates mutual accommodation strategies among Muslim families and European legal systems, considering the interweaving and untangling of the marriage knot in Italy and the UK as case studies. 'Multi-sited' Muslim families navigate the contemporary global archipelagos of rule sources in family matters. Based on empirical research which began in 2005 in Italy and the United Kingdom, and is still ongoing, this chapter sheds light on the ways in which a European Muslim family, finding itself at the crossroads of several norms, determines its own course.

Increasingly conscious of the unrestrainable pluralisation of laws, European countries are nowadays reinforcing their claims to full legal control over society. With the covert incorporation of religious institutions into inclusive court decisions and legislation, hidden spaces for the assertion of Muslim personal law are created in Europe under the umbrella of secular uniform laws. European judiciary and legislators may indirectly cause the development of the European Muslims' navigation process across the sea of different legal systems. In particular, blanket provisions, blind-eye attitudes, discriminatory approaches, stereotypical assumptions and unfamiliarity with Muslim traditions and Islamic values lead European Muslim families to look for solutions on alternative legal islands. Additionally, religious legal systems often represent the unrenounceable legal source to which European Muslim believers feel compelled to adhere. As a result, underage marriages, polygamous unions, marriages of convenience, chained spouses and Islamic 'repudiation' can all find room and be concealed into the folds of European legal systems.

The first part of the chapter analyses the phenomenon of navigation regarding marriages of European Muslims, while the second part focuses on the dissolution of marriages of European Muslims and Islamically married couples.

The Legal Scenario: The Legal Archipelagos Sea

Adopting a dynamic and internal Muslim perspective, the legal scenario can be described as a sea in which we can find various archipelagos corresponding to diverse legal systems or legal orders. In each of these archipelagos different sources of law constantly interact, defining the hierarchy of internal rules of each legal island. When wearing the European Muslim's lenses the legal archipelagos assume a polycentric aspect. From this perspective, which tries to understand the law from the inside (Petersen and Zahle 1995: 8), we can shed light on and decipher the dynamic interaction among the legal cultures, formal rules and sets of institutions involved in the creation of the living law. This intellectual framework challenges the traditional analytical perspective with respect to the European Muslim presence. I suggest that the image of the legal archipelagos is the new legal arena, in other words, the post-modern geography of the current legal systems as perceived by European Muslims and their families.

European Muslims can navigate towards three major legal culture archipelagos: the islands of European legal systems, the legal islands of Muslim majority countries, and the Muslim/Islamic[1] legal isles. They determine their own course according to their needs.[2] European Muslims never act as European-only. They can choose to behave as European nationals and/or as Muslims and/or as citizens of a Muslim majority country, and these sets of behaviours may be adopted from legal, religious and customary perspectives. The possible harbours at which to dock thus multiply as the potential courses become more numerous.[3]

Family values, in particular, are perceived as a precious chest to be protected from the inclusive positivistic European model.[4] Accordingly, European Muslims have developed their own navigation strategies in the contemporary global archipelagos of rule sources in family matters. Muslim majority countries have not been silent about the development of the navigation process pursued by Muslims. On the contrary, they have been and still are actively involved in the expansion of navigation patterns among Muslim communities. It is evident that the embassies and consulates of those countries *de facto* constitute legal islands belonging to the Muslim/Islamic archipelagos where European Muslims can alight. Diplomatic premises either *de facto* recognise religious marriages or perfect marriages and divorces which are at the same time valid at religious level and civil level in Western legal systems. Additionally, experts within European Muslim communities build networks to offer effective solutions to their local communities.

Historically speaking, European states have adopted differing strategies regarding Muslim families. *Sharī'ah* has generally been perceived as contrary to Western public order. However, strategies to protect the most vulnerable part of the family have been developed, in a way that some coasts (if not the whole legal isle) of *sharī'ah*-compliant legal islands have been gradually acknowledged as legitimate foreign legal systems. To some extent, European legal systems and Muslim families have thus established a silent system of mutual accommodation. The British policy of turning a blind eye to the development of parallel Muslim/Islamic legal systems and legal orders,[5] which is now claiming effectiveness in the

---

1 I will briefly explain the terminology employed in this article since the adjectives Muslim and Islamic are often used as synonyms. The adjective Islamic is properly used when referring to Islamic sources. In effect, the word *Islām* derives from the Arabic verb *sallama li...* that means 'to submit to... [God's will]'. On the other hand, *Muslim* is the participle of the same Arabic verb *sallama li...*, thus the meaning of the word Muslim is 'the submitter'. Accordingly, the adjective Muslim identifies the believers and also the 'living Islamic law'.

2 On Muslims' navigation processes see Ballard (1994b: 30–31), Pearl and Menski (1998: 55) and Menski (2009: 445–6).

3 As a result, a European Muslim may have dissimilar statuses – even conflicting ones – in different groups of legal islands.

4 The history of European family law indeed shows that religious (Christian) principles regulating family relations were gradually incorporated by secular authorities. For a study of this historical dialogue between religious and lay sources in family matters, see among others Goody (1983), Witte (1997, 2001), Bonfield (2001, 2002) and Ronfani (2003).

5 The terminology 'Muslim legal order' has been suggested by Malik (2012).

state civil courts, for instance, seems to confirm this approach. Similarly, Italy is silently adopting a *quasi* personal status law system which grants autonomy to diplomatic premises in family matters and Italian judges implementing foreign laws, including some *sharī'ah*-compliant norms.

The Muslim Family Treasure Chest

The navigation processes pursued by European Muslims are probably best exemplified in the conduct of family matters. In psychological terms, family relations represent a treasure chest and reflect 'strong cultural values'.[6] As a consequence, families are often resistant to imported legal principles and uniformisation, instead expecting legal actors and politicians to translate their family values into laws.[7] Principles governing marriage solemnisation and nuptial dissolution, in particular, imply a change of status of the bride and the groom within their family structure and in the wider society, and the spouses or the divorcé(e)s are accordingly expected to adjust to an elaborated combination of new relationships and roles.[8]

With reference to Islām, marriage is regarded as the basis of human society ('Ali 1936: 268; al-Faruqi 1982: 160). The *Qur'ān* (30: 44) refers to the 'creation of mates' as one of the 'signs' of God, and the *Sunnah*[9] recommends Muslim believers to marry.[10] Furthermore, Muslims commonly recite the saying that 'marriage is half of the religion'.[11] Accordingly, it seems appropriate to focus the discussion on the creation and dissolution of the family, analysing the interweaving and untangling of the marriage knot in Italy and the UK as case studies.

---

6 From a socio-anthropological perspective, values are described as 'inferences from observation of behaviour', and this way of conduct remains persistent over time (Firth 1953). Regarding the metaphor of the treasure chest, I suggest that family traditions and values tend to be preserved from 'unacceptable legal intrusions of privacy'. Analogously, Dibbits (1996: 125–45) talks of lined cupboards as old pieces of family furniture representing the treasure of a family: its own status and memories and ties with the past.

7 Apropos the socio-legal debate and family law as a 'compendium of social realities' see Müller-Freienfels (1968), and also Lipstein (1959). With reference to contemporary individualistic tendencies in family law, see the thought-provoking essays of Heger Boyle (2000), and Fuszara and Kurczewski (2005).

8 For a sociological perspective see, for instance, Kornblum (2008: 399–402), Bryant and Chandler (1997).

9 The Arabic word *sunnah* means 'practice'. The *Sunnah* usually refers to the Prophet Muhammad's living habits reported through the *aḥādīth* (sing. *ḥadīth*), which narrate the Prophet's life as role model behaviour. The *Sunnah* represents the second Islamic source, following the *Qur'ān*.

10 See for instance the *ḥadīth* 'I fast, eat, pray and sleep and marry women, and who does not follow my *Sunnah* does not belong to me' reported as *al-Ṣaḥīḥ al-Bukhārī*, 7: 2 by Arabi (2001a: 150) and 67: 1 by 'Ali (1936: 602; 1944: 269).

11 This sentence is widely reported by scholars, but regrettably they tend to cite different sources for the same expression. For instance, Arabi (2001a: 150) regards it as a proverb. The very same expression is a *ḥadīth* reported in the *al-Mishkāt al-masābīḥ* by 'Ali (1936: 603), and referred to by al-Bayhaqī in the opinion of Maqsood (2003: 1). Some authors generally mention *al-Bukhārī* or *al-Ġazhālī* – see, e.g., Wiktorowicz and Farouki (2000: 690), and Blank (2001: 332, note 35) respectively; some scholars simply do not report the source of the *ḥadīth* – see, e.g., Lapidus (1976: 95) and Hoodfar (1997: 52). Islamic scholars and my fieldwork informants in Italy and in the UK almost unanimously reported this expression to me.

European Muslims may solemnise different types of marriages, according to which archipelago their ship is bound for. Each legal island of the archipelagos can recognise and record that marriage or not, in compliance with its own legal system or legal order. Muslims can marry in the European archipelago by civil and/or religious law. In Italy and in the UK, a civil marriage would be recognised by the state island. On the other hand, a purely Islamic and/or Muslim marriage would not be recognised *per se* as a marital union by both states, and the husband and wife who married only in compliance to *sharī'ah* would thus be regarded as cohabiting partners by the Italian and British legal islands. Nonetheless, they would be a married couple from Muslim and Islamic perspectives.

A European Muslim fiancé/e can also get married in the archipelago of the Muslim majority countries. Traditionally, the country chosen is the country of origin of the family of the bride or the groom (as my research confirmed). When a couple wishes to marry in Europe within the diplomatic premises of a Muslim majority country – if the embassy/consulate/High Commission offers this service – at least one prospective spouse must be a national of that country. These marriages are contemporaneously civil and religious, being based on the principles of Islamic law and also in conformity to the state law requirements. This is effectively the application of the law of the Muslim majority countries, which generally provide for official registration only as a facilitative option, but not as a mandatory requirement. In the greater portion of Muslim majority countries, the registration of the nuptial contract is compulsory from a positivist legal point of view, however it is not a condition for validity of the marriage itself.[12] Marriages solemnised on these legal islands are not recognised as valid by all European legal systems. Private international law principles enacted by the Italian legal system imply, however, a more navigable course compared to the regime adopted in the British Isles.

Muslims can also contract marriage in the Muslim/Islamic legal archipelago. The plurality of Islāms existing in contemporary Europe[13] induced me to write about an Islamic group of islands. Every Muslim community appears to practise an Islām that is enriched by traditions and customs rooted in the conventions of their countries of origin and in their personal family history.[14] These aspects are so intertwined with the 'Islamic category' – particularly when matrimonial issues are involved – that it is almost impossible to identify

---

12 Some examples may clarify this point. With reference to North African countries, for instance, both the Moroccan Family Code (*Mudawwanah*), 2004 and the Egyptian Procedural Personal Status Law, 2000 indirectly elucidate that unregistered marriages can have legal effects. In Morocco, courts 'may take into consideration all legal evidence and expertise' when 'the marriage contract was not officially registered' (art. 16), and in Egypt petitions for divorce or annulment 'shall be accepted … if the marriage is established by any written evidence', in case the marriage is not 'established by virtue of an official document' (art. 17). For a comment on *'urfī* marriages and divorces in Egypt see, among others, Aluffi Beck-Peccoz (2002), Arabi (2001b), Bernard-Maugiron and Dupret (2008). On Morocco, see for instance Bras (2007). In South Asia, for example, the Pakistani Muslim Family Laws Ordinance, 1961 and the Bangladeshi Muslim Marriages and Divorces (Registration) Act, 1974 both require marriage registration (s. 5 and s. 3, respectively); nonetheless, the validity of the marriage itself is not tied to its actual registration. For a discussion on the living laws in Pakistan and Bangladesh, see Pearl and Menski (1998: 46–50).

13 See, for instance, Dassetto and Nielsen (2003), Grillo (2004), Bowen (2004), Amiraux (2004), Parekh (2008).

14 This is what Pearl and Menski (1998: 58–9) identified as *angrezi shariat*.

an island that is Islamic only.¹⁵ The *shuyūkh*, *'ulamā'* and *a'immah*¹⁶ I interviewed, and the young generation of European Muslims who are trying to draw a clear line between religious teachings and customs, unanimously confirmed that they perceive as their everyday challenge the teaching of Islām purged from the local and social traditions of the Muslim community living in Europe. Younger generations of European Muslims tend to prioritise the 'Islamic element' over ethnic origin and national belonging. Parekh (2008: 101) explains this 'desire to return to the "true principles" of Islam' as a choice which is both politically effective and strategically motivated. Globalised Muslims forge a sort of 'common identity', and the Muslim women challenge the cultural gendered hierarchal power structure through their knowledge of the *Qur'ān* and the *Sunnah*.¹⁷ In this sense, twenty-first century European Muslims predominantly alight on Islamic legal islands of the Muslim/Islamic archipelago.

Marriage in the Muslim/Islamic archipelago – in other words, marriage solemnised in accordance with *sharī'ah* and habitually contracted also in compliance with the formalities of the spouses' Muslim island(s) – is not as such recognised as valid in terms of its civil effects in the European archipelago. An *'aqd al-zawāğ* or a *nikāhnama*¹⁸ may, however, be officially regarded as a legitimate nuptial contract by some Muslim majority states, locally or by their diplomatic premises in Western countries. Should this happen, a religious-only marriage is raised to the higher rank of a 'civil marriage', and it could thus be recognised in the European positivistic archipelago as well. The crossroads for multi-sited Muslim families are therefore innumerable. As a matter of fact, a European Muslim may be married in one legal island and yet be regarded as single or as a mere cohabitee in another. Furthermore, the same person may be married to different partners depending on the attitude taken in the different archipelagos.

My empirical research confirms that Islamic matrimony is widely regarded as 'the marriage' by Muslims who – according to a Western label – 'practise' their own religion, namely are not secularised or do not perceive Islām purely as an identity issue.¹⁹ Different patterns may nevertheless coexist. Presuming that a European Muslim wishes to marry in accordance with *sharī'ah* (and thus on a religious island) s/he could then map different courses, some of which I trace here.

---

15   This is the reason why I chose the expression Islamic and/or Muslim legal islands. See note 1 above.

16   The word *shuyūkh* is the plural of the Arabic word *shaykh*. This word derives from the verb *shākh* that means 'becoming old'. Accordingly, *shaykh* literally means 'elder'; nonetheless, this word is employed to identify an Islamic scholar. The word *'ulamā'* is the plural of the word *'ālim* and it denotes a learned person or a scholar. The word *a'immah* is the plural form of the word *imām* and it literally means 'being in front of': the *imām* is indeed the person who leads the prayers by staying in front of the other believers.

17   On this aspect, see also Naber (2005: 484–90).

18   The Islamic marriage contract is usually identified by these two expressions: *'aqd al-zawāğ* and *nikāhnama*. The first expression is more commonly used in North African and Middle Eastern countries, whilst the second word represents the ordinary letterhead of *sharī'ah*-compliant nuptial contracts issued in South Asia. Traditionally, and in everyday language, other expressions may also be used by Muslims.

19   With reference to the diverse typologies of Muslim identities in Europe see, for instance, Dassetto and Nielsen (2003), Grillo (2004), Roy (2004), Sabahi (2006).

Navigation Courses of European Muslim Spouses

In the European archipelago, Muslims can marry in a civil and religious manner. They can either choose both or only one of these options. European Muslims can also decide not to disclose their religious marital union to the state authorities, even when the Islamic marriage can be recognised and/or recorded by the state legal system. Some legal islands belonging to the Islamic religious archipelago are indeed partly seen and acknowledged by the British and Italian governments: Muslim and Islamic marriages can be recognised as valid in civil law when some requirements have been satisfied and procedures followed.

Regarding the United Kingdom, we must differentiate among its four constituent countries. In England and Wales, marriages compliant with Islamic provisions are recognised by the state authorities in two cases. Islamic marriages can indeed be celebrated in registered places of worship in the presence either of a civil registrar or before a celebrant, who is an 'authorised person' to solemnise marriages having civil effects in compliance with the Marriage Act 1949.[20] In Scotland, according to the Marriage (Scotland) Act 1977, a religious body may nominate to the Registrar General any of its members to be registered as empowered to solemnise marriages. Accordingly, Islamic scholars regularly appear listed among the 'celebrants' entitled to solemnise marriages with civil effects. In Northern Ireland, a marriage compliant with Islamic provisions may have civil effects when celebrated by an 'officiant' who is registered and recognised as a person authorised to conduct religious marriages by the Registrar General.[21]

As far as the archipelago of Muslim majority countries is concerned, a foreign embassy, consulate, High Commission or other diplomatic premises can be listed as an approved building for a civil marriage in the UK.[22] As for Muslim and Islamic marriages celebrated abroad, a transnational marriage is considered valid in the UK according to the UK Border Agency (UKBA) when the celebrated type of marriage is recognised in the country in which it took place; when the actual matrimony, properly executed (in relation to the requirements for the matrimonial ceremony itself), satisfies the requirements of the law of the country in which it took place and nothing in the law of either party's country of domicile (at the time of the marriage) restricts his/her freedom to enter the marriage.[23]

Consequently, to Western eyes, the preferable option seems to be a marriage celebrated on the coast of one of the Muslim/Islamic islands recognised by the British authorities. Nonetheless, Muslims appear to follow a different course in their navigation. In effect, Muslims in Britain increasingly alight on solely Islamic and/or Muslim islands. Muslim-only and/or Islamic-only marriages appear to outnumber the *sharī'ah*-compliant marriage ceremonies celebrated according to the formalities requested by the state authorities. Official figures do not exist. However, vivid discussions regarding unregistered Islamic-only marriages characterise public and governmental debates since the early 2000. Newspaper

---

20 Marriage Act 1949, ss. 43–44, 53. With reference to the provisions regarding the registration of buildings in England and Wales, see the Marriage Act 1949 (ss. 26, 41–42) the Marriage Acts (Amendment) Act 1958 (s. 1(1)(a)) and the Marriage (Registration of Buildings) Act 1990. In England and Wales, civil marriages can also be solemnised in approved premises provided that no religious blessing anticipates or follows the nuptial civil celebration. See s. 26(1)(bb) and s. 46B(4) of the Marriage Act 1949 as introduced by the Marriage Act 1994.

21 See the Marriage (Northern Ireland) Order 2003.

22 See UK Border Agency (UKBA), *Immigration Directorate Instructions (IDIs)*, Ch. 8, S. 1, Annex B, Feb 2010, para 1.1.

23 See UKBA, *IDIs*, Ch. 8, S. 1, Annex B, Feb 2010, para 2.

articles and politicians' debates both tend to focus their attention on the position of women engaging in religious-only marriages; in particular, the lack of protection suffered by these Muslim unofficial wives, the system that indirectly increases the power of mischievous polygynous husbands, and the insufficiency and non-enforceability of Islamic provisions to protect these women within British legal systems.[24] Lord Bach (2009) reported that in 2008, among the 809 mosques that were registered as places of worship, only 159 were registered venues for solemnising legally recognised religious marriages. In addition, only 36 of these registered venues had authorised persons appointed to conduct marriages with civil effects. A predictable outcome is that a small proportion of registered marriages take place among Muslims. My empirical research also corroborates that Muslim-only and/or Islamic-only marriages are constantly requested by European Muslims and thus solemnised, not only in England and Wales, but in Scotland as well. In addition, my evidence confirms that Islamic-only marriages are in some cases preferred by young Muslim couples in the UK.

In Italy, the Islamic archipelagos can be theoretically seen and recognised through the law on admitted cults.[25] In effect, a marriage can be celebrated before a minister of 'religions admitted within the state'.[26] The minister of these religions can also solemnise marriages having the same civil effects as marriages celebrated before the vital statistics officer,[27] as long as some compulsory rules are observed. Nonetheless, Muslim religious figures do not appear in the list of persons authorised to celebrate recognised religious marriages in Italy.[28]

My fieldwork reveals that leaders of Islamic/Muslim associations, organisations and mosques in Italy are disoriented when it comes to nuptial issues. This does not imply, however, that Muslim and Islamic marriages are not celebrated and indirectly recognised

---

24   See, for instance, Branigan (2003), John (2004), Khan (2008), Drabu (2008), Addison (2008; 2010), Balchin (2010) and Talwar (2010).

25   See the Law 24.06.1929 No. 1159, *Disposizioni sull'esercizio dei culti ammessi nello Stato e sul matrimonio celebrato davanti ai ministri dei culti medesimi*, in GU 16.07.1929 No. 164; and the Royal Decree 28.02.1930 No. 289, *Norme per l'attuazione della L. 24 giugno 1929, n. 1159, sui culti ammessi nello Stato e per coordinamento di essa con le altre leggi dello Stato*, in GU 12.04.1930 No. 87.

26   This expression is compatible with the art. 8 IC, whose first two paragraphs state that '[a]ll religious denominations are equally free before the law. Denominations other than Catholicism have the right to self-organization according to their own statutes, provided these do not conflict with Italian law'. Accordingly, Italy recognises the same freedom for all religions; nonetheless, this does not imply that all religions are equal in an absolute sense, and different norms can regulate their relations with the state.

27   The Italian figure of the *ufficiale di stato civile* is translated as 'vital statistcs officer' by the English version of the Italian Civil Code provided by Beltramo, Longo, Merryman and Beltramo (1969–2007). De Franchis (1996: 1426) confirms that an officer with analogous functions does not exist in common law countries, and clarifies that the vital statistics officer has a role similar to the registrar general. The *ufficiale d'anagrafe* can be translated to the English word 'registrar'.

28   No Muslim appears to be a minister of cult authorised to celebrate marriages with civil effects in Italy. Statistical data published by the Ministry of Interior confirm that from 2003 to 2009 no Muslims were appointed or revoked as ministers of cults and no refusal to an Islamic ministry was issued. See the data published by the Ufficio di Statistica del Ministero dell'Interno (SISTAN), now Scuola Superiore dell'Amministrazione dell'Interno (SSAI), available at http://politichepersonale.interno.it/dcds/compendio04/file06/culti-34.pdf (last accessed 5 April 2009); http://politichepersonale.interno.it/dcds/compendio04/file07/21_culti.pdf (last accessed 5 April 2009); http://politichepersonale.interno.it/dcds/compendio04/file08/15%20culti%20int34.pdf (last accessed 5 April 2009); http://ssai.interno.it/download/allegati1/annuario2010indice.pdf (last accessed 15 December 2013). See also Ufficio Centrale di Statistica and Scuola Superiore delle Statistiche Ufficiali dell'Amministrazione dell'Interno (2010: 217–22).

by the Italian government. In the Italian legal system, Muslim and/or Islamic marriages are religious-only marriages, unless they are celebrated or formerly recognised by Muslim majority countries or foreign diplomatic premises. Muslims living in Italy can thus easily alight on a solely Muslim/Islamic legal island, in the event an *imām*, a *shaykh* or a Muslim believer auto-entitles himself to perfect the couple's marriage contract. Nonetheless, my empirical evidence confirms that, in some cases, foreign diplomatic premises may recognise and record as legally valid an Islamic-only marriage (or, in some cases, even Muslim-only marriages)[29] solemnised in Italy. Consequently, the Italian state authorities can be indirectly compelled to recognise Islamic-only marriages celebrated on its soil by unauthorised ministers.

Muslims who wish to marry on a Muslim/Islamic island and to have their religious marriage recognised by the Italian authorities can thus follow different courses. They can marry in a Muslim majority country (also by proxy), they may contract their marriage in diplomatic premises, or they can even claim recognition of their religious-only marriage. Theoretically, purported spouses willing to contract a *sharī'ah*-compliant marriage could also marry before an officially registered minister of the 'Islamic cult', provided there were any in Italy. The requirements to be satisfied vary according to the circumstances: predominantly, they concern religious belonging and the citizenship or nationality of the purported spouses.

The Fear of Marriages of Convenience and the Muslims' Navigation Process

Landing on an Islamic island can also be indirectly imposed by the positivist British and Italian legal islands: the legislators used to follow a similar discrimination course in order to protect the coasts of their own legal systems from unwanted immigrant spouses. Whereas in the UK the discriminatory provision has been recently amended, the Italian legal system can still compel the nationals of Muslim majority countries to marry abroad.

In the UK, under the Asylum and Immigration (Treatment of Claimants, etc.) Act 2004 (ss. 19–25), a non-European Economic Area (EEA) national who wishes to marry in the UK must satisfy some requirements.[30] If the purported non-EEA spouse was bound for the UK from overseas to get married, before s/he could give a registrar notice to marry, s/he had to have a fiancé/e entry clearance or marriage visitor entry clearance. If the non-EEA spouse-to-be was already in the UK and did not have 'settled' status before giving a registrar notice to marry, s/he had to obtain a certificate of approval (COA) from the UKBA.

According to the Explanatory Notes to the 2004 Act (para 4), these provisions were explicitly aimed 'to tackle sham marriages'.[31] Advantages such as the improvement of their immigration position are indeed obtained by persons subject to immigration control when marrying British citizens and EEA nationals (Berry 2009: 43). Nevertheless, the rules provided a notable exception. In England and Wales, the foreign fiancé/e was able to avoid these norms when landing on the Anglican legal island: marriages celebrated according to

---

29 For instance, in some rare cases Muslim customary marriages – *'urfī* marriages – can be 'legalised' by Muslim majority countries' diplomatic premises.

30 These nuptial prerequisites were applied to non-EEA nationals requiring leave to enter or remain in the UK under the Immigration Act 1971 with effect from 1 February 2005.

31 Sham marriages are defined in s. 24(5) of the Immigration and Asylum Act 1999 (as amended).

the rites of the Church of England were not subject to the same provisions.[32] Other religious legal islands were not exempted, however. This dispensation for Anglican weddings only was regarded as unjustified given the aim of the law, discrimination against other religions and contrary to art. 12 ECHR (right to marry) by the High Court, the Court of Appeal and the House of Lords.[33] In the *O'Donoghue and Others v the United Kingdom* case[34] (para 99), the British Government clarified that

> ... they were reluctant to rush to remedy the Article 14 incompatibility until a final judgment on the whole of the scheme was available. Following the House of Lords' judgment, they entered into discussions with a view to bringing the Church of England within the scheme. In spite of the discussions, however, no agreement could be reached.

Accordingly, the British government was not able to bring the Anglican religious legal island within its own legal system and thus third country nationals who alighted on the Church of England island, rather than on a legal isle of another religious or a secular archipelago, enjoyed a more comprehensive right to marry compared to lay migrants or aliens belonging to other faiths.

As stated by the House of Lords, thus, the COA scheme established by the Asylum and Immigration (Treatment of Claimants, etc.) Act 2004 involved a 'disproportionate interference' with the exercise of the right to marry. However, the apparatus designed to combat marriage abuse remained in force, albeit being repeatedly adjusted.[35] In July 2010, a Remedial Order was laid in Parliament to abolish the COA under the Human Rights Act 1998, and the Draft Asylum and Immigration (Treatment of Claimants, etc.) Act 2004

---

32   UKBA website: 'Religious ceremonies – The rules on certificates of approval do not currently apply if you plan to get married at an Anglican church in England or Wales, after marriage banns or with a religious licence. To find out more, you should contact a member of the clergy at the church where you plan to get married. If you plan to marry in any other form of religious ceremony, you will need to contact the people who will be conducting the ceremony. The rules on certificates of approval do apply if you marry in any religious ceremony outside the Anglican church'. Available at: http://www.ukba.homeoffice.gov.uk/while-in-uk/marriageandcivilpartnership/eligibility/ (undated; last accessed on 20 May 2010).

33   In real terms, the High Court ruled that the section 19 regime infringes both art. 12 ECHR and art. 14 ECHR. The Secretary of State did not appeal against the declaration of incompatibility of s. 19 with art. 14 ECHR (prohibition of discrimination). See *Baiai and others v Secretary of State for the Home Department* [2006] EWHC 823 QB (Admin), 10.04.2006. See also *Baiai & Ors, R. (on the application of) v Secretary of State for the Home Department & Anor* [2006] EWHC 1035 (Admin), 10.05.2006 and *Baiai & Anor, R. (on the application of) v Secretary of State for Home Department* [2006] EWHC 1454 (Admin), 16.06.2006. For the House of Lords' decision see *R. (on the application of Baiai) v Secretary of State for the Home Department* [2008] UKHL 53, [2009] 1 AC 287.

34   See *O'Donoghue and Others v the United Kingdom*, Application No. 34848/07, 14.12.2010 – 14.03.2011, [2011] All ER (D) 46 (Jan).

35   The scheme was repeatedly challenged and the Government amended the rules of the COA as a consequence. For instance, in April 2006 non-EEA nationals with insufficient leave were not automatically refused a COA but were asked to provide further information about their relationship; in June 2007 the non-EEA nationals with pending applications for leave to remain were authorised to apply for a COA; from 9 April 2009 the fee for applying for a COA scheme was suspended; in July 2010 a system of refunding fees was introduced. These changes were described as 'nothing more than cosmetic' by the Equality and Human Rights Commission who had intervened in the *O'Donoghue and Others v the United Kingdom* case (para 80).

(Remedial) Order 2010 was approved in the spring of 2011. In December 2010, in effect, the European Court of Human Rights (ECtHR) found the COA scheme in violation of arts. 8, 12, 14 ECHR read together with arts. 8, 9, 12 ECHR. The ECtHR recognised that the domestic system of national states may need to prevent marriages of convenience provided that the individual full legal capacity of the right to marry with the chosen partner is granted. In particular, the Strasbourg Court identified the violation of the right to marry, the violation of the prohibition of discrimination read together with the right to marry and also with the freedom of religion, the violation of the right to respect for private and family life read either alone or in conjunction with the prohibition of discrimination (para 129). Accordingly, The ECtHR stressed that

> there is no justification whatsoever for imposing a blanket prohibition on the right of persons falling within these categories to exercise their right to marry. Even if there was evidence to suggest that persons falling within these categories were more likely to enter into marriages of convenience for immigration purposes (para 89).

In effect, the Court was 'inclined to consider that any difference in treatment was on the ground of immigration status and not, in fact, on the ground of nationality' (para 106).

The COA discriminatory scheme ended on the coming into force of the Remedial Order of the Asylum and Immigration (Treatment of Claimants, etc.) Act 2004 on 4 April 2011. For the time being, navigation across the sea of legal islands has thus been an indirect effect. Marrying an EEA national or contracting marriage in a European Member State that implements different rules regarding the marriages of third country nationals frequently represented a more efficient and less expensive option for Muslims who are non-EEA nationals and wish to reside in the UK.[36]

In Italy, Muslims can similarly be impelled to marry abroad. Nationals of Muslim majority countries willing to marry in Italy can indeed be compelled to alight on the Muslim/Islamic archipelago, independently of their willingness to do so. Aliens wishing to contract marriage in Italy are subject to the legal systems of two countries: their national laws and the Italian domestic legislation. Accordingly, they need to produce a certificate of no impediment called *nulla osta* to the Italian authorities in order to prove that no impediments to the marriage exist according to the law to which they are subject.[37]

The demand for *nulla osta* by the Italian authorities is controversial: the fulfilment of this legal prescription may indeed lead to religious discrimination against a Muslim fiancé/e. When a Muslim woman wishes to marry a non-Muslim man, embassies and consulates of Muslim majority countries insist on issuing the *nulla osta* on the condition that the purported groom converts to Islām. Diplomatic authorisation for an Italian civil marriage is thus provided only when the act of conversion to Islām of the non-Muslim partner is submitted. Furthermore, some diplomatic premises only recognise as valid

---

36 With reference to a broad application of the EC legislation circumventing the UK's immigration rules, see Pilgram (2009) and Wray (2006).

37 See art. 116 of the Italian Civil Code (ICC) and the Royal Decree 16.03.1942 No. 262, *Approvazione del testo del Codice Civile*, in GU 4.04.1942 No. 79. This provision does not necessarily mean the national law of the foreign citizen due to the principle of *renvoi* (Ballarino 2008: 136). They are also subject to some other conditions necessary for contracting marriages according to the ICC (arts. 86, 86, 87 (Nos. 1–2, 4), 88, 89). In case they are foreign nationals resident or domiciled in Italy, they may also proceed with the publication under art. 93 ICC.

declarations of conversion to Islām provided by some listed mosques in Europe or in Muslim majority countries.

Accordingly, a person who is a national of a Muslim majority country and whose parents are Muslim could be denied his/her right to marry by the Italian authorities on the ground that s/he cannot produce the certificate of no impediment to his/her marriage from his/her diplomatic premise. The foreign purported groom or bride could however bring his/her case before the Italian judicial authorities. The relevant Italian case law is quite consistent. In these cases, the Italian judge orders the vital statistics officer to proceed with the publication[38] without the *nulla osta* on the ground that the capacity to contract into marriage of the Muslim non-national has been made subject to the religion of his/her spouse-to-be.[39] To the Italian judiciary, this limit to the non-nationals' marriage is against Italian public order. To the Italian Constitutional Court, nonetheless, the requirement of a *nulla osta* does not *per se* infringe the inviolable rights of the person 'as an individual and in the social groups where human personality is expressed', as protected by art. 2 of the Italian Constitution (IC).[40] The mentioned Constitutional Court order indeed clarifies that the *nulla osta* is a 'document that in the majority of cases does not limit but rather facilitates the enactment of the freedom of marriage'.

An additional solution has been suggested by some other Muslim majority countries' diplomatic premises. The *nulla osta* is released without the non-Muslim partner's conversion to Islām; however, such marriage would never be acknowledged and registered in the Muslim and Islamic legal islands. In other words, the spouses would be regarded as a married couple only in the Italian legal island and, as a consequence, in the European legal archipelago.

On the Italian island, therefore, there has been no legislative intervention to prevent the case-by-case seeking of solutions. From 2009 to 2011, aliens wishing to contract marriage in Italy faced further complications aimed at tackling marriages of convenience. A blanket prohibition stated in art. 15(1) of Law No. 94/2009[41] required the non-nationals wishing to enter into a civil marriage in Italy to also provide a regular residence permit to the vital statistics officer. An Interior Ministry Directive[42] clarified that this requirement was to be

---

38 The publication (in Italian *pubblicazioni*) is a nuptial preliminary required by arts. 93–96, 106 ICC. This word echoes the publication of banns prescribed by marriage celebrated in compliance with the Church of England (part II, Marriage Act 1949); nonetheless, in Italy, the publication is a legal requirement for both religious and civil marriages. Accordingly, the Italian publication is similar to the purported spouses' intention to marry manifested to the competent registrar and then displayed in the marriage notice book by the district registrar as prescribed by English/Welsh law (ss. 27(4), 31(1), Marriage Act 1949), Scottish law (s. 4, Marriage (Scotland) Act 1977), and Northern-Irish law (art. 4, Marriage (Northern Ireland) Order 2003).

39 See, among others, Trib. Reggio Emilia 29.09.1986, DFP 1987, 268; Trib. Potenza 30.11.1989, DFP 2001, 558; Trib. Camerino 12.04.1990, RDIPP 1991, 750; Trib. Genova 4.04.1990, GM 1992, 1195; Trib. Torino 24.02.1992, RDIPP 1992, 985; Trib. Torino 24.06.1993, DFP 1993, 1181; Trib. Barcellona 9.03.1995, DFP 1996, 164; Trib. Napoli 29.04.1996, FD 5/1996, 454; Trib. Taranto 13.07.1996, FD 5/1996, 445. The majority of case law concerns Muslim non-national women wishing to marry non-Muslim men; however, in some cases foreign men have been denied the *nulla osta* by their diplomatic premises on the ground that they were non-Muslims wishing to marry a foreign Muslim woman.

40 See the Const. C. 16-30.01.2003 No. 14, in GU 5.02.2003; DFP 2003, 331.

41 Law 15.07.2009 No. 94, *Disposizioni in materia di sicurezza pubblica*, in GU 24.07.2009 No. 170 SO No. 128.

42 See Interior Ministry Directive 28.01.2010 No. 2.

applied only to non-EU nationals. As a result, the capacity of non-EU Muslims to contract a marriage in Italy was temporarily subordinated not only to the religion of his/her purported spouse, but also to his/her own valid permit to stay. My empirical research showed that this requirement implied an increase in the navigation process through the legal archipelagos and, equally, across the Mediterranean Sea. A marriage contracted in a Muslim majority country or in another European state characterised by a less demanding legal system in effect represented a more prudent option for a Muslim migrant illegally settled in Italy.[43]

In July 2011, however, the Italian Constitutional Court recognised the partial illegality of art. 116(1) Italian Civil Code (ICC) as amended by art. 1(15) of Law No. 94/2009.[44] After the Tribunal of Catania questioned the constitutional legitimacy of the valid residence permit required for the civil marriage of foreign persons in arts. 2, 3, 29, 31, 117(1) IC, the Constitutional Court eventually declared unconstitutional the provision of art. 116(1) ICC.

Three main points were stressed by the Italian court. First of all, the Constitutional Court elucidated that 'the inviolable rights of art. 2 Italian Constitution (IC) are owed to any person not because s/he may belong to a particular political community, but to human beings as such' (para 3.1). Relying on its former decisions,[45] the Italian 'legislation judge'[46] clarified that citizens and foreign persons differ since the alien merely has an 'acquired and temporary' relation with the Italian state, while the foreign legal status should not be regarded as 'a justification allowing diversified or pejorative treatment'.

The Italian Court also referred to the balance of interests criterion. On the one hand, the need 'to ensure defence and protection of the borders and the control of migration flows' is acknowledged; on the other hand, the imposed sacrifice of the matrimonial freedom should not be disproportionate (para 3.1). In effect, both the rights of illegally settled foreign fiancé/es and Italian citizens wishing to marry an alien person without a permit to stay are compressed by art. 116(1) ICC.

Thirdly, the Italian Constitution Court underlined the violation of constraints deriving from international obligations, as recognised by art. 117(1) IC. Quoting the *O'Donoghue and Others v the United Kingdom* case,[47] the Italian Court stressed that 'the States' margin of appreciation cannot be so wide to imply a general, automatic and indiscriminate restriction of a fundamental right granted by the [European] Convention' (para 3.2). Accordingly, a blanket prohibition on the exercise of the right to marry also violates art. 12 ECHR.

From the summer of 2011, an irregularly settled Muslim can marry on Italian soil without submitting to the vital statistics officer 'a document attesting the regularity of his/her stay in the Italian territory'.[48] Nevertheless, the *nulla osta* continues to be required. Muslims can thus still be compelled to navigate towards an alternative legal archipelago in order to marry.

---

43 Naturally, the conversion of the non-Muslim partner can still be an issue.
44 See Const. C. 20-25.07.2011 No. 245, GU 27.07.2011.
45 See Const. C. 19-26.06.1969 No. 104, GU 2.07.1969 No. 165; Const. C. 10-24.02.1994 No. 62, GU 2.03.1994; Const. C. 5-8.07.2010 No. 249, GU 14.07.2010.
46 The Italian Constitutional Court is also called the 'legislation judge' since it verifies the constitutional legitimacy of the Italian legislation.
47 See above, note 33.
48 See art. 116(1) ICC as amended by art. 1(15) of L 94/2009.

Underage Marriages: European Muslim Ships Heading towards other Legal Archipelagos

The course mapped out by Muslim families in the archipelagos of legal systems can also be utterly labyrinthine in cases of young Muslims wanting to get married. The Western legal archipelagos tend to confer capacity to contract marriages to a person when s/he achieves his/her civil-political capacity through the age of majority, whilst the Islamic islands grant capacity to contract marriage when a person reaches the age of puberty. Teenagers can thus validly marry accordingly to the *sharī'ah* in the Muslim/Islamic islands. Having said that, would the European archipelagos or even some Muslim majority isles recognise these marriages of underage spouses as valid?

In Italy, a purported spouse must be aged at least 18, and the marriage is voidable if one of the parties is not. Nevertheless, a tribunal can permit the marriage of a person over 16 years of age.[49] No differentiation is made between aliens and Italian citizens. Thus, when the marriage of either alien party over 16 is permitted and recognised as valid by the domestic legislation of the foreign country in which the marriage has been celebrated,[50] the foreign spouses' marriage is valid for the Italian legal island as well.

In the UK, a marriage is void if either party is under the age of 16.[51] A person domiciled in England or Wales cannot avoid this provision by marrying abroad in a country where marriages under 16 are permitted. Furthermore, with effect from 27 November 2008, the age at which a person may sponsor, or may be granted entry clearance (including visas), or limited leave as the spouse, civil partner, fiancé/e, proposed civil partner, unmarried partner or same-sex partner of another person was increased from 18 to 21 years.[52] Accordingly, when a Muslim spouse is a non-EEA national, s/he was not allowed to legally land in the UK as the spouse of a British citizen[53] until they both reached the age of 21.[54] This provision has been repeatedly challenged in the courts,[55] before eventually being amended. On 28 November 2011, three years after the amendment of paragraph 277 IR, the minimum age requirement for both non-EEA applicants and sponsors of spouse visas reverted to 18 years.[56]

However, do these rules prevent Muslim children from marrying in the Islamic islands? The fact that a Western system does not recognise an underage marriage as valid does not prevent the solemnisation of Islamic child marriages. Underage Muslims wishing to contract marriage can navigate towards the Muslim/Islamic archipelago. Some Muslim

---

49   See art. 84 ICC.
50   See art. 28 of L 31.05.1995 No. 218, *Riforma del sistema italiano di diritto internazionale privato*, in GU 3.06.1995 No. 128.
51   See s. 11(a)(ii) of Matrimonial Causes Act 1973.
52   The minimum age for sponsoring a spouse was already raised from 16 to 18 on 1 April 2003, and the minimum age for foreign spouses was raised from 16 to 18 on 21 December 2004. See House of Commons (2003; 2005; 2008).
53   This rule, however, does not apply to a foreign spouse of an EEA national.
54   See para 277 of the Immigration Rules. An exception does exist however, in the case where a party is a serving member of HM Forces, the age limit is 18 as of 6 April 2010. See House of Commons (2010).
55   See *Quila & Anor v Secretary of State for the Home Department* [2009] EWHC 3189 (Admin) (7.12.2009); *Quila & Ors v Secretary of State for the Home Department & Ors* [2010] EWCA Civ 1482 (21.12.2010); *R (on the application of Quila and another) (FC) (Respondents) v Secretary of State for the Home Department (Appellant)* and *R (on the application of Bibi and another) (FC) (Respondents) v Secretary of State for the Home Department (Appellant)* [2011] UKSC 45 and [2011] 1 FLR 1187.
56   See House of Commons (2012).

majority countries prescribe a minimum age to get married that does not correspond to the Islamic marriageable age. Muslims can likewise opt for an Islamic-only island. Under some circumstances, Islamic authorities may indeed solemnise a solely Islamic marriage, either in Europe or in Muslim majority countries.

I had the opportunity to study some of these contracts of marriage between very young spouses. The age reported on the Islamic marriage contract generally complies with the provisions of *sharī'ah*, independently of the legal rules of Muslim majority countries or Western states. An Islamic-only marriage is celebrated and the nuptial contract is recorded only when the spouses reach the minimum marriageable age according to the provisions of their Muslim majority country of origin.

In some other circumstances, the age of a spouse, as stated on other documents, is different from the age on the marriage contract. Apparently, a spouse can have dissimilar ages in different legal archipelagos. A spouse can indeed appear older in his/her recorded Islamic contract of marriage compared to the date of birth as stated on his/her passport or birth certificate. Interestingly, the spouse's date of birth as reported on the marriage certificate can cleverly match the minimum age prescribed for a valid marriage in the foreign country to which the couple would then migrate or claim family reunification in.

In effect, problems arise when these marriage contracts are brought to the diplomatic premises of a Western country to obtain an official document or the legalisation of the marriage certificate, in order to claim the family reunification in that European country. In these cases, the couple may be requested to submit additional documents such as family situation record or birth certificates and the problem with age then becomes manifest. A mistaken date of birth or a forgery of one document may be quite easily obtainable, but not a falsification of several certificates. In the first case, the spouse's age may not be regarded as appropriate by a European legal system, thus Muslims that find themselves in this situation cannot be recognised as a married couple.

This phenomenon confirms that in European Muslim communities the religious marriage is generally perceived as 'the proper one', despite the official legislation; the religious archipelago is somehow considered superior by the Muslim believer. Landing on a Muslim/Islamic island is also an effective tool: if Muslim couples map their course carefully, they can navigate towards the positivist legal islands of the EU as spouses. In practice, when a *'aqd al-zawāğ* or a *nikāhnama* is valid according to the *sharī'ah*, the marriage contract can, in some circumstances, even misinform regarding the age of the spouse(s). The European Muslims' ship can thus be heading to other archipelagos, initially towards the recognition and registration with civil effects of that Islamic marriage by a Muslim majority country or by its premises in a Western country, and subsequently towards the legal island of a Western country in which the couple can thus be regarded as husband and wife.

Dissolution of Marriages: Muddling Up Different Courses

Turning our attention to the dissolution of marriages, it becomes evident that the combination of both the interweaving and untangling of the marriage knot allows Muslim families to enact situations, like polygynous marriages, which are forbidden by the European legal archipelagos.

Multi-sited Muslims may indeed follow patterns similar to the courses traced regarding marriages. Belonging to the three different legal archipelagos – European states, Muslim majority countries, Islamic and Muslim laws – European Muslims can determine their own course, selecting the legal system(s) and legal order(s) in which they would like to be regarded as husband and wife. Of course, the contested dynamics of the marital dissolution process, and the potential presence of children, usually complicate navigation in this peculiar stage and the result is frequently the muddling up of two or more different courses. For instance, a Muslim husband may be willing to opt for a *ṭalāq*[57] given by proxy in a Muslim majority country in order to avoid the long and expensive Western procedures or, alternatively, a mischievous Muslim man may desire to prevent his wife from remarrying by withholding a *ṭalāq* from her. An Islamically married woman, particularly when she is a non-Muslim and the mother of young children, may wish to avoid a procedure in a Muslim/Islamic context and instead apply for a marital dissolution in a European court or tribunal.

Marital Dissolutions on the Italian Legal Island

A number of courses and combinations can be mapped out by Muslims living in Italy who wish to dissolve their marriage. Primary considerations concern the type of marriage(s) previously contracted by the couple. If husband and wife were married in the Muslim/Islamic islands, at least one spouse – usually the Muslim wife – may wish to be divorced in the Muslim/Islamic archipelago as well, in order to have the right to contract a new marriage. In some situations, for instance when the husband agrees with the wife to marry other women, the couple may prefer to continue to be regarded as a married couple in the Muslim/Islamic archipelago, independently from their marital status in other legal islands. If married in the eyes of the Italian legal system in which they live – as domiciled, resident or national – Muslims may desire to dissolve their marriage in the very same island; or they would rather continue to be regarded as husband and wife by that legal system, for instance so as not to compromise their permit to stay if they are migrants. Similarly, when they are also citizens of a Muslim majority country, European Muslims can opt for marriage dissolution as recognised by the legal system of their countries of origin, in order to be properly divorced in the eyes of their communities and to avoid inheritance disputes.

Muslims do not necessarily need to travel in the real world to navigate among the three legal system archipelagos. In effect, an Italian judge can dissolve a marriage according to the law of a Muslim majority country, when some conditions are satisfied. In compliance with Italian private international law, when husband and wife are nationals of foreign countries, their legal separation and/or their marriage dissolution are governed by the spouses' common national law. In the absence of a spouse's common national law, their separation and divorce are ruled by the law of the state where the couple's matrimonial life has been predominantly located.[58] Accordingly, married Muslim spouses who are both foreign citizens and nationals of the same Muslim majority country are allowed to petition an Italian tribunal for divorce in accordance with their own national legal system.

In addition, Muslim citizens of foreign countries can divorce in their diplomatic premises in Italy, thus obtaining a divorce simultaneously recognised as valid with religious and civil

---

57   The word *ṭalāq* derives from the Arabic verb *ṭallāqa, which* means 'to set free'. This word usually indicates the husband's unilateral divorce and is therefore also translated as 'repudiation'.

58   See arts. 13–19, 31(1) of L 218/1995. In other circumstances, Italian law is applied: the Italian Statute on Private International Law recognises the special position of Italian tribunals. See arts. 13–19, 31(2), 32 of L 218/1995 and art. 43 ICC.

effects by Muslim/Islamic and Muslim majority countries archipelagos. Analogously, a Muslim spouse can divorce by proxy in his/her country of origin – when permitted – while physically being in Italy; or s/he can actually travel and divorce in a Muslim majority country. These three types of dissolution can also be registered in and recognised as valid by the Italian legal island, as long as some requirements are satisfied.[59]

A dissolution of marriage in accordance with *sharī'ah* is not recognised as valid *per se* by the Italian legal system; it is nevertheless valid in the Muslim/Islamic archipelagos, once it has been perfected according to the rules of the *sharī'ah*-compliant legal system. An Italian Muslim can thus combine these courses and select the path that better suits his/her own desire and the needs of his/her family. Consequently, across the Mediterranean Sea, we can in fact meet Muslims, or also Islamically married couples, who have a dissimilar status in different islands of the legal archipelagos. The so-called 'limping' marriage can represent a voluntary choice, or be a consequence of misinformed positivist jurists, or hide a 'chained spouse' situation.[60]

Some examples would probably clarify this point. We can consider the *ṭalāq*, for instance. Scholars have clearly noted the principle according to which a *ṭalāq* would be regarded as being against public order and thereby not recognised by the Italian legal system.[61] The published case law is scarce and confused, but it can help us to shed light on some connected issues.

Ṭalāq Issues in Italy: Alternative Paths of Muslim Families and Islamically Married Partners

The problem of 'repudiation' was first discussed in the Italian courts regarding Jewish couples and, indeed, early commentators tend to compare the Jewish *get* to the Islamic *ṭalāq*.

In 1948, we find the first reported case of two Syrian nationals, whereby the husband 'unilaterally repudiated' the wife before the Sharī'ah Council of Damascus in November 1947. The Rome Court of Appeal laid out the Italian standards for refusing to recognise the *ṭalāq*. The Court held that repudiation is not a divorce and that the institution is against public order.[62]

The same approach became well established and fairly uniform. Thus, 20 years later, a 'chained' wife repudiated by her Iranian husband in Teheran, but still married to him according to the Italian legal system, mapped a new course. Mrs Kramer tried to get around the denial of the recognition of her *ṭalāq* in Italy by requesting a declaration of her 'unmarried status' before the Tribunal of Milan. Her application was, however, unsuccessful and the judge was rather emphatic in stressing that Mrs Kramer had not traced a practicable path.[63]

---

59 See arts. 64–65 of the L 218/1995 and arts. 95ff. of the DPR 396/2000. With reference to the Decree of the President of the Republic 3.11.2000 No. 396, *Regolamento per la revisione e la semplificazione dell'ordinamento dello stato civile, a norma dell'articolo 2, comma 12, della legge 15 maggio 1997, n. 127*, in GU 30.12.2000 No. 303 SO No. 223/L.

60 The expression 'chained spouse' derives from the Hebrew word *agunah* which means 'chained' and refers to the wife chained to her marriage since she is left without a *get*. For a detailed study, see Porter (1995).

61 See, for instance, Galoppini (2005), Mancini (2006), La China (2006), Albisetti (2008), Campiglio (2008).

62 CA Roma 29.10.1948, FP 1949, 348.

63 Trib. Milano 21.09.1967, RDIPP 1968, 403.

The Italian judiciary was so positively convinced of the impossibility of recognition of a foreign *ṭalāq* that in some cases[64] the Court did not pay enough attention to the submitted case, and a *khul'* divorce[65] was actually regarded as a *ṭalāq* divorce, and thus rejected on public policy grounds following reasoning that hardly fits the case. Consequently, the Italian wife of an Egyptian man who had agreed on a *khul'* procedure 13 years earlier was still regarded as married to him on the Italian legal island.

Given the judiciary's firm position, a solution to the problem of chained women had to be found within the Italian legal system, and indeed the law on dissolution of marriage[66] presented a good opportunity to do so. A special provision had been purposely included stating that one of the spouses may apply for the dissolution of their marriage or the cessation of the civil effects of the marriage when the other spouse – if a foreign citizen – obtained an annulment or a dissolution of the marriage abroad or s/he has contracted a new marriage abroad.[67]

Unfortunately, this norm was based on the assumption of catering for Italian women who had married Muslim men and who were then divorced by them. Foreign wives Islamically married to Muslim husbands remained victims of limping marriages within the Italian legal system. In effect, whilst Italian wives can apply for dissolution of marriage according to the rules of the Italian legal system,[68] alien wives, co-citizens of their husbands, can approach Italian judges by pleading the dissolution of the marriage, and the Italian judiciary can only enforce the national common law of the spouses. Consequently, paradoxical situations arose. Foreign women, who were free to remarry in the Muslim majority countries and Islamic legal archipelagos, were instead still married to their husbands within the Italian legal system.[69] The Court of Appeal of Milan,[70] for instance, refused to enforce the Iranian Civil Code on the ground that it was against the Italian and international public order. Foreign spouses having the same citizenship would, as a result, have to trace an alternative course to other legal archipelagos.

Following the same direction, the reform of Italian private international law[71] provided a kind of 'automatic execution' of foreign proceedings.[72] Nevertheless, because of the provisions contained in DPR 396/2000,[73] civil statistics officers frequently refuse to record a foreign divorce or annulment when they are not satisfied the prerequisites of arts. 64–65 L 218/1995 are met. Accordingly, the spouses whose marriage has been dissolved on a Muslim majority country legal island are frequently forced to file a petition for the recognition of their *sharī'ah*-compliant divorce or marriage annulment with the competent Italian local tribunal. As a result, the 'automatic execution' of foreign proceedings rule in

---

64   See, for instance, CA Roma 9.07.1973, DFP 1974, 653.

65   The *khul'* is a divorce obtained by the wife in return for remuneration to her husband. This nuptial dissolution is based on the following verse of the *Qur'ān* (2: 229): '… there is no blame on either of them if she gives something for her freedom'.

66   See L 1.12.1970 No. 898, *Disciplina dei casi di scioglimento del matrimonio*, in GU 3.12.1970 No. 306.

67   See art. 3(2)(E), L 898/1970.

68   See, for instance, Trib. Cremona 27.03.1973, RDIPP 1974, 307.

69   For instance, if the spouses are nationals of different countries and the husband's country of origin recognises as valid the Islamic divorce, the man was regarded as divorced, despite the non-recognition of the dissolution by the Italian legal system.

70   CA Milano 17.12.1991, RDIPP 1993, 109.

71   See L 218/1995.

72   See arts. 64–65 of L 218/1995.

73   See arts. 7, 95ff of DPR 396/2000.

Italy *de facto* does not apply to Muslim and Islamic legal systems. The Court of Appeal of Turin has more recently confirmed that a

> repudiation-divorce cannot be effective in the Italian legal system since the Italian judge is competent over divorce related matters, even when the marriage has been celebrated abroad, *ex* L 218/1995. The repudiation-divorce is also against our [Italian] internal public order ... thus it cannot be recorded.[74]

While the case law analyses and academic studies focus predominantly on the above-mentioned framework, the scenario is much richer in reality, as a recently published judicial decision concerning a *ṭalāq* pronounced in Egypt confirms. The Court of Appeal of Cagliari declared a 'judgment of divorce' between an Egyptian/Italian man and his Egyptian wife 'effective (in civil law) in the Italian legal system'.[75]

The unreported cases I have examined also deal with the suspension of Italian proceedings for dissolution of marriage on the ground of a *ṭalāq* proceeding pending in a Muslim majority country (to avoid international *litis pendentia*), and there are some cases in which Italian judges enact Muslim majority country laws in Italian courts. This is notwithstanding contrasting judicial and academic declarations, which tend to regard the laws of Muslim majority countries in family matters as invariably against the public order of Western legal systems. Furthermore, some diplomatic premises in Italy are fervently active in issuing *ṭalāq* certificates, regardless of international agreements and their scholarly interpretations, which appear to deny the possibility of so doing.[76]

Why is this happening? What does this mean? Muslim families and Islamically married couples have chosen alternative paths, and different sorts of parallel Muslim and Islamic legal systems already exist, independently of black-letter laws and their official interpretations. Some judges and legal experts, i.e. the ones who are more exposed to immigrant communities, appear to be more comfortable, although still largely lost, within this navigation process. A plurality of legal archipelagos and systems coexists and they are coping with that in their everyday activities.

Marital Dissolutions on the British Legal Isle

In the UK, we can identify the same three legal archipelagos coexisting from the Muslim perspective. European Muslims and Islamically married couples can dissolve their marriages in compliance with the European archipelagos or the Muslim majority countries' isles or the Muslim/Islamic islands, analogously to the families settled in Italy. European Muslims in Britain can thus similarly determine their own course, selecting the legal system(s) in which they would like to be regarded as husband and wife. The procedures to be adopted, however, may differ. For instance, section 16 of the Domicile and Matrimonial Proceedings Act 1973 implies that a *ṭalāq* pronounced in Britain is not to be regarded as a valid divorce.

---

74 CA Torino 9.03.2006, DFP 2007, 156.
75 CA Cagliari 16.05.2008, RDIPP 2009, 647.
76 For instance, Galoppini (2005: 984) notes that under art. 55(1) of the Vienna Convention 1963, diplomatic premises must not dissolve marriages between their nationals since the consulates and embassies have a duty to respect the laws and regulations of the receiving state.

Nowadays, therefore, consular officers *de facto* seem not to process *ṭalāq* divorces – at least divorces considered valid for civil law effects within the British legal system.

Islamically married couples and Muslim spouses in Britain can nevertheless dissolve their marriages, mapping a different course. Muslims can indeed opt for a transnational divorce in a Muslim majority country. Nonetheless, in order to be recognised by the British system, this divorce should be obtained by means of proceedings and/or comply with the provisions of the Family Law Act 1986, Domicile and Matrimonial Proceedings Act 1973 and Recognition of Divorce and Legal Separations Act 1971.[77] Muslims can also navigate towards a *sharī'ah*-compliant island only and thus opt for the Muslim and Islamic legal islands existing within the UK. These parallel and competing legal systems and legal orders, frequently conflated with Sharī'ah Councils, are composed of a much more structured and complex reality.

A widespread network of these so-called Sharī'ah Councils[78] does indeed operate across the country and they cater for various types of Islamic legal problems. My research reveals that the typology of these institutions varies from unconnected or semi-independent knowledgeable Islamic scholars to self-organised tribunals or councils with a court-like structure of clerks, councillors and judges with offices in different cities and countries, to European–Muslim mediation structures. Conciliation, mediation, arbitration are services offered to Muslims (and to non-Muslims in some cases) at several levels and with different expertise. Under the Arbitration Act 1996, their decisions in non-family matters can theoretically be enforced or questioned at the state level, if parties so claim, as it does routinely for the Jewish Beth Din decisions.[79]

In the UK, the possibilities of religious dispute resolution are so rich and variegated that the Muslim/Islamic authorities themselves describe the phenomenon as *fora* shopping. Muslims are navigating within the Muslim/Islamic European archipelago as well. My empirical research confirms the existence of a sort of internal hierarchy among the different Sharī'ah Councils almost imposed by the clients themselves, who also engage in double *fora* shopping among Muslim institutions and/or Muslim institutions and state courts, as a matter of choice.

Muslims in the UK can also opt for marital dissolution in compliance with state provisions. As Poulter (1986: 207–8) wrote, there is:

> only one way to obtain divorce in England. This is through a decree or order granted by a court of civil jurisdiction on the ground that the marriage has irretrievably broken down. Mutual agreement may provide the foundation for divorce, but the parties are not free to remarry until the order has been made by the court.

A different truth of overlapping matrimonial statuses and navigation in the sea of legal system islands is, however, revealed when taking a closer look at the real world of European Muslims.

---

77 See UKBA, *IDIs*, Ch. 8, S. 1, Annex B, Feb 2010, para 5.
78 See further note 90.
79 For a comparative study on religious courts in Britain, see Douglas et al. (2011).

Talāq Issues in Britain: Coexistent Diverse Legal Systems and Navigating Muslim Families

Regarding the *talāq*, the case law is more abundant than in Italy; it is similarly intertwined with legislation and originally linked to Jewish cases of *get*. As a matter of fact, the contemporary network of Sharī'ah Councils appears to somehow resemble the network of Jewish courts (Beth Din) in the UK.

The first reported case – the *Hammersmith* case[80] – dates back to 1917, almost 30 years before a case of *talāq* approached the Italian judiciary. A *talāqnama* pronounced in London by an Indian Muslim husband to his English wife was not recognised by British authorities on public policy grounds. Limping marriages were thus unavoidable. The international remedy was the XVIII Hague Convention on the Recognition of Divorces and Legal Separations 1970, implemented by Britain with the Recognition of Divorces and Legal Separations Act 1971. Nonetheless, on one hand, the rules of alien legal systems were respected; on the other hand, a foreign divorce would be recognised only when it did not contradict British public policy. In fact, the Act of 1971 imposed on judges a very limited window for recognising foreign divorces.[81]

The turning point for the recognition of a *talāq* was represented by *Qureishi v Qureishi*,[82] when the Court of Appeal acknowledged as a valid dissolution of marriage within the British isles a *talāq* executed in Britain in purported compliance with the Muslim Family Law Ordinance 1961 of Pakistan (MFLO). On April 1967, Mr Qureishi sent a letter to his wife containing the sentence 'I divorce you' written three times, and then a hearing at the London office of the High Commissioner for Pakistan explored the possibilities of a reconciliation between the spouses. Upon the expiry of 90 days (*al-'iddah*), the divorce was pronounced as absolute. The court held that 'the husband having established a Pakistani domicile ... the marriage has been validly dissolved ... no rule of English law precluded the recognition of talaq by reason of its non-forensic character' (para 174).

This decision provoked parliamentary action to protect women left without financial protection, and thus the Domicile and Matrimonial Proceedings Act 1973 was enacted. Its section 1 ended the rule of domicile dependency by virtue of marriage for wives, while section 16[83] ensured that no divorce or annulment obtained in any part of the British Islands would be regarded as effective in any part of the United Kingdom unless granted by a court of civil jurisdiction.[84] The Matrimonial Causes Act also extended the jurisdiction of English courts to habitual residents.[85] Consequently, the British legal system can easily refuse to recognise a foreign divorce and provide itself for the dissolution and its related matters. In addition, Part III of the Matrimonial and Family Proceedings Act 1984 was introduced to further limit the *forum* shopping of mischievous Muslim husbands. Accordingly, the competence of the British courts in granting ancillary relief to a spouse

---

80 *R v Hammersmith Superintended Registrar of Marriages ex. p. Mir-Anwaruddin* [1971] 1 KB 634.
81 See Pearl and Menski (1998: 87–9), who elucidate the manner in which English law struggled with private international law rules and 'the emerging scenario of resident immigrant or ethnic minority populations'.
82 *Qureshi v Qureshi* [1971] 1 All ER 323; [1972] Fam 173; [1971] 2 WLR 518.
83 Now, it is s. 44(2) of the Family Law Act 1986.
84 See Pearl and Menski (1998: 384–5), Poulter (1986: 113–4).
85 See s. 5(5).

was stated, even when a marriage was dissolved abroad through annulment, divorce or legal separation.[86]

This approach, however, did not prevent Muslims from dissolving their marriages in compliance with the *sharī'ah* and Islamic provisions as codified by Muslim majority states. Indeed, one might say that the British judiciary and legislators provoked the development of the navigation process towards the Muslim/Islamic legal archipelagos, where unofficial Muslim and Islamic marriages and divorce procedures could be enacted. Thus, the only practicable way was represented by the non-recognition of these marital dissolutions.

The problem of limping marriages and chained wives nonetheless, inevitably, followed, including some high profile cases – *Chaudhary v Chaudhary*[87] and *Ghulam Fatima*.[88] In the latter, a Pakistani fiancée was denied entry clearance to Britain on the ground that her purported husband had divorced his previous wife 'by post'. The court held that when a Pakistani national resident in Britain pronounces *talāq* and then sends a notification to the Chairman of the Union Council in Pakistan, it is not a valid divorce. In the former case, the Court of Appeal refused to recognise a 'bare *talāq*' of an English domiciled Kashmiri husband, as not to allow him 'to deprive the other party to the marriage of her rights'.

The English and Scottish Law Commissions issued a white paper on the *Recognition of Foreign Nullity Decrees and Related Matters* in September 1984, and in 1988 the Family Law Act 1986 came into force. Since then, the case law regarding Islamically married couples and Muslims has significantly decreased.[89] Nowadays, different legal systems coexist and thus Muslim families have learned how to navigate through these archipelagos.[90] The phenomenon of limping marriages continues and it seems to be an effective tool to perpetrate polygynous marriages in the UK and in European countries as well (Shah 2003; Yilmaz 2005).

The problem of chained women seems to be more effectively solved within the community itself through the so-called Sharī'ah Council network,[91] even if the British legal system left the door open to a possible indirect recognition of Islamic divorces with the Divorce (Religious Marriages) Act 2002. This provision indeed enables 'a court to require the dissolution of a religious marriage before granting a civil divorce'. The Act provides that on the application of either party, the court may order that a decree of divorce is not to be made absolute until a declaration made by both parties that they have taken such steps

---

86   For a discussion on divorced Muslim women in England see Carroll (1997). The position of British courts in having discretion to grant financial provision has been recently confirmed by the Supreme Court in the case *Agbaje v Akinnoye-Agbaje* [2010] UKSC 13. In addition, in the case *Syed v Ahmed* [2005] CSIH 72, where a couple debated whether or not a *talāq* had already been obtained in Pakistan whilst pending a divorce case in Scotland, the court remarkably clarified that '[w]hile the continued subsistence of the parties marriage is an essential fact to be proved in any action of divorce, the circumstance that, as established in subsequent and distinct proceedings, the marriage did not in fact subsist at the time of the divorce does not, in our view, render that decree an inherent nullity' (para 19).

87   *Chaudhary v Chaudhary* [1984] 3 All ER 1017; [1985] 2 WLR 350; [1985] FLR 476.

88   *R. v Secretary of State for the Home Department, ex parte Ghulam Fatima* [1985] QB 190.

89   Pearl and Menski (1998: 77–83, 87–117) explain this phenomenon in terms of a 'culture-blind' English legal system and the gradual involvement of Muslim local leaders in establishing formal British Muslim *fora*.

90   See Hamilton (1995), Pearl and Menski (1998), Khaliq (2002), Yilmaz (2002; 2005), Warraich and Balchin (2006), Shah (2007).

91   For an in-depth study on some Sharī'ah Councils see Shah-Kazemi (2001), Bano (2004), Keshavjee (2008), Bowen (2010).

as are required to dissolve the marriage in accordance with religious usages is produced to the court, and the parties to the marriage concerned should have been married in accordance with (i) 'the usages of the Jews' or (ii) 'any other prescribed religious usages'.[92] The law does not mention Islamic marriages explicitly, and Muslim communities, legal professionals and academics have approached this provision from rather different angles.

A recent case debated in the London Court of Appeal offered the opportunity to deal with *sharī'ah*-compliant divorces and to shed light on the enigmatic expression 'other prescribed religious usages'.[93] Mr Kandeel and Mrs Hands married Islamically in July 1991 and civilly in August 1991. When in June 2009 the wife sought a decree *nisi* of divorce, the husband claimed the application of section 10A(1)(a)(ii) Matrimonial Causes Act 1973. Mr Kandeel asked the court that the decree of divorce must not be made absolute until their religious marriage was dissolved; conversely, an infringement of arts. 9 and 14 of the ECHR would occur. Lord Justice Tomlinson agreed with Judge Styler that 'prescribed religious usages' could be identified solely by an order made by the Lord Chancellor through statutory instrument and quoted the Stoke-on-Trent County Court Judge when he pointed out that Mrs Hands 'also has human rights and she wishes that the stay upon a decree absolute should be removed'.[94]

In the present case, thus, the British courts appear more concerned with protecting a wife from a Muslim husband, who seems to be bound for the Islamic legal island in order to delay the proceeding, rather than willing to extend the time taken to pronounce the decree absolute on condition of a religious divorce. Nonetheless, the legal system remains blind with regards to the situations faced by chained women, in other words women who married Islamically and civilly and then divorced solely in compliance with civil law. A *sharī'ah*-compliant marriage dissolution is indeed of pivotal importance for a Muslim woman who wishes to remarry in the Muslim majority country and Muslim/Islamic archipelagos.

Islām persists in being a variegated reality and thus it is difficult to foresee any solution that may suit all Muslim communities. Presently, Muslims in Britain appear as skilled legal archipelago navigators,[95] and the system indirectly acknowledges that process.

Conclusions

In the contemporary legal scenario, international, European and national laws, religious norms, local customs and traditions seem to regularly overlap. Accordingly, the process of identifying an internal hierarchy appears to be almost impossible. Nonetheless, adopting the European Muslim perspective brings into focus the three legal archipelagos. European Muslims navigate towards diverse legal systems or legal orders, in other words legal islands, in order to accomplish their mission.

The Muslim journey is generally bound to the protection of what are perceived as Islamic and Muslim core values. Therefore, the circumstances of interweaving and untangling of the marriage knot represent ideal case studies to reveal that European Muslims regard family

---

92   See s. 10A added by the Divorce (Religious Marriages) Act 2002 to the Matrimonial Causes Act 1973.
93   See *Kandeel v Hands* [2010] EWCA Civ 1233.
94   See paras 4, 10 and 11.
95   See Ballard (1994: 30–31) on skilled cultural navigators, Pearl and Menski (1998: 55) on skilled legal navigators, and Bhamra (2010: 138–40) on skilled identity navigators.

values as a precious treasure chest to be protected from the inclusive positivistic European model. As a result, a new complex global and dynamic legal network is created from within every European nation state by European Muslims. Occasionally, a domestic legal island may perceive part of a Muslim navigation course, but the whole picture is often missed.

We might wonder whether in the near future European Muslims will try to further develop this network 'of their own' based on navigation techniques across the legal sea, in order to eventually exploit the domestic institutions of European states. Additionally, it might be interesting to discover if the reasons for the legal and cultural navigation skills implemented by European Muslims are to be found in the lack of trust towards secular institutions, or if it is a characteristic of the communities living as ethnic or religious minorities in Europe.

Bibliography

'Ali, M.M. 1936. *The Religion of Islām. A Comprehensive Discussion of the Sources, Principles and Practices of Islam.* Lahore: The Ahmadiyya Anjuman Ishā'at Islām.

'Ali, M.M. 1944. *A Manual of Hadīth.* Lahore: The Ahmadiyya Anjuman Ishā'at Islām.

Addison, N. 2008. Cohabiting and Islamic marriages. *The Sunday Times* [Online, 28 October]. Available at: http://www.timesonline.co.uk/tol/comment/letters/article5032544.ece [last accessed 3 May 2011].

Addison, N. 2010. Sharia is not the problem here. *The Guardian* [Online, 10 July]. Available at: http://www.guardian.co.uk/commentisfree/belief/2010/jul/08/religion-sharia-marriage-registration-islam [last accessed 31 May 2013].

al-Bukhārī, M.I.I. 1966–2000. *Saḥīḥ al-Bukhārī.* Vol. 1–11. al-Qāhirah: al-Majlis al-A`lá lil-Shu'ūn al-Islāmīyah, Lajnat Iḥyā' Kutub al-Sunnah.

al-Fārūqī, I.R. 1982. *Tawhid: Its Implication for Thought and Life.* Hemdon (VA): International Institute for Islamic Thought.

al-Ghazālī, M. 1975. *al-Islām fī wajh al-zaḥf al-Aḥmar.* al-Qāhirah: al-Mukhtār al-Islāmī.

al-Ḥamīd Qutb, I.Q.A. 1988–1991. *Khutab al-shaykh Muḥammad al-Ghazzālī fī shu'ūn al-dīn wa-al-ḥayāh.* Vol. 1–5. al-Qāhirah: Dār al-I'tiṣām.

Aluffi Beck-Peccoz, R. 2002. Islam e società in Egitto. Il matrimonio 'urfi'. *Daimon. Annuario di diritto comparato delle religioni*, 2002, 189–93.

Albisetti, A. 2008. A proposito del matrimonio islamico in Italia, in *Islam in Europa / Islam in Italia tra diritto e società*, edited by A. Ferrari. Bologna: Il Mulino, 121–8.

Amiraux, V. 2004. Restructuring political Islam: Transnational belonging and Muslims in France and Germany, in *Transnational Political Islam: Religion, Ideology and Power*, edited by A. Karam. London: Pluto Press, 28–57.

Arabi, O. 2001a. *Studies in Modern Islamic Law and Jurisprudence.* The Hague: Kluwer Law International.

Arabi, O. 2001b. The dawning of the third millennium on shari'a: Egypt's Law No.1 of 2000, or women may divorce at will? *Arab Law Quarterly*, 16(1), 2–21.

Bach, W. 2009. Letter dated 9 June 2009 on religious marriage and polygamy addressed to Baroness Cox. [Online]. Available at: http://www.parliament.uk/deposits/depositedpapers/2009/DEP2009-1647.pdf [last accessed 3 May 2011].

Balchin, C. 2010. Negotiating bliss. *Open Democracy* [Online, 8 March]. Available at: http://www.opendemocracy.net/5050/cassandra-balchin/negotiating-bliss [last accessed 31 May 2013].

Ballard, R. (ed.) 1994. *Desh Pardesh. The South Asian Presence in Britain.* London: C. Hurst & Co.
Ballard, R. 1994b. Introduction: The emergence of Desh Pardesh, in *Desh Pardesh. The South Asian Presence in Britain*, edited by R. Ballard. London: C. Hurst & Co, 1–34.
Ballarino, T. 2008. *Manuale breve di diritto internazionale privato.* III edition. Padova: CEDAM.
Bano, S. 2004. *Complexity, Difference and 'Muslim personal law': Rethinking the Relationship between Sharia Councils and South Asian Muslim Women in Britain.* Unpublished PhD thesis: University of Warwick.
Beltramo, M., Longo, G.E., Merryman, J.H. and Beltramo, S. 1969–2007. *The Italian Civil Code.* Dobbs Ferry (NY): Oceana.
Bernard-Maugiron, N. and Dupret, B. 2008. Breaking up the family: Divorce in Egyptian law and practice. *Journal of Women of the Middle East and the Islamic World*, 6, 52–74.
Berry, A. 2009. The right to marry and immigration control: The compatibility of Home Office policy with art. 12 and art. 14 ECHR in Baiai. *Journal of Immigration Asylum and Nationality Law*, 23(1), 41–50.
Bhamra, M.K. 2010. *The Challenges of Justice in Diverse Societies. Constitutionalism and Pluralism.* London: Ashgate.
Blank, J. 2001. *Mullahs on the Mainframe: Islam and Modernity among the Daudi Bohras.* London: University of Chicago Press.
Bonfield, L. 2001. Developments on European family law, in *Family Life in Early Modern Times, 1500–1789. The History of the European Family*, edited by D.I. Kertzer and M. Barbagli. Vol. 1. New Haven, CT and London: Yale University Press, 87–124.
Bonfield, L. 2002. European family law, in *Family Life in the Nineteenth Century, 1789–1913. The History of the European Family*, edited by D.I. Kertzer and M. Barbagli. Vol. 2. New Haven, CT and London: Yale University Press, 109–54.
Bowen, J.R. 2004. Beyond migration: Islam as a transnational public space. *Journal of Ethnic and Migration Studies*, 30(5), 879–94.
Bowen, J.R. 2010. How could English courts recognize Shariah? *University of St. Thomas Law Journal*, 7(3), 411–35.
Branigan, T. 2003. Islamic weddings leave women unprotected. *The Guardian* [Online, 24 November]. Available at: http://www.guardian.co.uk/uk/2003/nov/24/religion.world [last accessed 31 May 2013].
Bras, J.P. 2007. La réforme du code de la famille au Maroc et en Algérie: quelles avancées pour la démocratie? *Critique Internationale*, 37(octobre–décembre), 93–125.
Bryant, L. and Chandler J. 1997. Families in Europe, in *Britain in Europe: An Introduction to Sociology*, edited by T. Spybey. London and New York: Routledge, 201–18.
Campiglio, C. 2008. Il diritto di famiglia islamico nella prassi italiana. *Rivista di Diritto Internazionale Privato e Processuale*, XLIV(1), 343–76.
Carroll, L. 1997. Muslim women and 'Islamic divorce' in England. *Journal of Muslim Minority Affairs*, 17(1), 97–115.
Dassetto, F. and Nielsen, J. 2003. Conclusion. Past. Present. Future, in *Muslims in the Enlarged Europe: Religion and Society*, edited by B. Maréchal et al. Leiden: Brill, 531–42.
de Franchis, F. 1996. *Dizionario giuridico. Law Dictionary.* Vol. II. Milano: Giuffré.
Dibbits, H.C. 1996. Between society and family values: The linen cupboard in early-modern households, in *Private Domain, Public Inquiry: Families and Life-styles*

in the Netherlands and Europe, 1550 to the Present, edited by A. Schuurman and P.C. Spierenburg, Hilversum: Verloren, 125–45.

Douglas, G., Doe, N., Gilliat-Ray, S., Sandberg, R. and Khan, A. 2011. *Social Cohesion and Civil Law: Marriage, Divorce and Religious Courts*. Cardiff: Cardiff University [Online]. Available at: http://www.law.cf.ac.uk/clr/Social%20Cohesion%20and%20Civil%20Law%20Full%20Report.pdf [last accessed 31 May 2013].

Drabu, R. 2008. A marriage of convenience will not do. *The Guardian* [Online, 21 August]. Available at: http://www.guardian.co.uk/commentisfree/2008/aug/21/islam.religion [last accessed 31 May 2013].

Firth, R. 1953. The study of values by social anthropologists: The Marett lecture, 1953. *Man*, 53, 146–53.

Fuszara, M. and Kurczewski, J. 2005. Family values, friendship values: Opposition or continuity?, in *Family Law and Family Values*, edited by M. Maclean. Oxford and Portland, OR: Hart Publishing, 45–58.

Galoppini, A.M. 2005. Il ripudio e la sua rilevanza nell'ordinamento italiano. *Il Diritto di Famiglia e delle Persone*, 34(3/2): 969–89.

Goody, J. 1983. *The Development of the Family and Marriage in Europe*. Cambridge: Cambridge University Press.

Grillo, R.D. 2004. Islam and transnationalism. *Journal of Ethnic & Migration Studies*, 30(5), 861–78.

Hamilton, C. 1995. *Family, Law and Religion*. London: Sweet & Maxwell.

Heger Boyle, E. 2000. Is law the rule? Using political frames to explain cross-national variation in legal activity. *Social Forces*, 78(4), 1195–226.

Hoodfar, H. 1997. *Between Marriage and the Market: Intimate Politics and Survival in Cairo*. Berkeley and Los Angeles: University of California Press.

House of Commons. 1994. *Statement of Immigration Rules*. HC 395. Session 1993–94. London: HMSO.

House of Commons. 2003. *Statement of Changes in Immigration Rules*. HC 538. Session 2002–03. London: TSO.

House of Commons. 2005. *Statement of Changes in Immigration Rules*. HC 164. Session 2004–05. London: TSO.

House of Commons. 2008. *Statement of Changes in Immigration Rules*. HC 1113. Session 2007–08. London: TSO.

House of Commons. 2010. *Statement of Changes in Immigration Rules*. HC 439. Session 2009–10. London: TSO.

House of Commons. 2012. *Statement of Changes in Immigration Rules*. HC 1622. Session 2011–12. London: TSO.

John, C. 2004. It's not about the money. *BBC News* [Online, 21 February]. Available at: http://news.bbc.co.uk/1/hi/uk/3504485.stm [last accessed 31 May 2013].

Keshavjee, M.M. 2008. *Alternative Dispute Resolution in a Diasporic Muslim Community in the United Kingdom*. Unpublished PhD thesis: University of London.

Khaliq, U. 2002. The accommodation and regulation of Islam and Muslim practices in English law. *Ecclesiastical Law Journal*, 6(31), 332–5.

Khan, U. 2008. New Sharia law marriage contract gives Muslim women rights. *The Telegraph* [Online, 8 August]. Available at: http://www.telegraph.co.uk/news/uknews/2518720/New-Sharia-law-marraige-contract-gives-Muslim-women-rights.html [last accessed 31 May 2013].

Khaṭīb, M.I.A. 1960–1965. *Mishkāt al-maṣābīḥ*. Vol. 1–4. English translation with explanatory notes by James Robson. Lahore: Sh. Muhammad Ashraf.

Kornblum, W. 2008. *Sociology in a Changing World*. VIII edition. Belmont, CA: Thomson Wadsworth.

La China, S. 2006. Matrimoni misti al filtro dell'esperienza giudiziaria, in *Sposare l'altro. Matrimoni e matrimoni misti nell'ordinamento italiano e nel diritto islamico*, edited by I. Zilio-Grandi. Venezia: Marsilio, 119–37.

Lapidus, I.M. 1976. Adulthood in Islam: Religious maturity in the Islamic tradition. *Daedalus*, 105(2), 93–108.

Lipstein, K. 1959. The Hague Conventions on private international law, public law and public policy. *The International and Comparative Law Quarterly*, 8(3), 506–22.

Malik, M. 2012. *Minority Legal Orders in the UK: Minorities, Pluralism and the Law*. London: The British Academy.

Mancini, L. 2006. Il matrimonio islamico in Italia, in *Sposare l'altro. Matrimoni e matrimoni misti nell'ordinamento italiano e nel diritto islamico*, edited by I. Zilio-Grandi. Venezia: Marsilio, 105–18.

Maqsood, R.W. 2003. *Con il mio sposo… Giuda islamica la matrimonio*. Imperia: Al Hikma.

Menski, W.F. 2009. Justice, equity and good conscience, in *The Oxford International Encyclopedia of Legal History*, edited by S.N. Katz. New York: Oxford University Press, Vol. 3, 445–6.

Müller-Freienfels, W. 1968. The unification of family law. *The American Journal of Comparative Law*, 16(1/2), 175–218.

Naber, N. 2005. Muslim first, Arab second: A strategic politics of race and gender. *The Muslim World*, 95(Oct), 479–95.

Parekh, B. 2008. *A New Politics of Identity: Political Principles for an Interdependent World*. Basingstoke and New York: Palgrave Macmillan.

Pearl, D. and Menski, W.F. 1998. *Muslim Family Law*. London: Sweet & Maxwell.

Petersen, H. and Zahle, H. 1995. Preface, in *Legal Polycentricity: Consequences of Pluralism in Law*, edited by H. Petersen and H. Zahle. Aldershot: Dartmouth, 7–11.

Pilgram, L. 2009. Tackling 'sham marriages': The rationale, impact and limitations of the Home Office's 'certificate of approval' scheme. *Journal of Immigration Asylum and Nationality Law*, 23(1), 24–40.

Porter, J.N. (ed.) 1995. *Women in Chains: A Sourcebook on the Agunah*. Northvale, NJ: Jason Aronson.

Poulter, S. 1986. *English Law and Ethnic Minority Customs*. London: Butterworth.

Ronfani, P. 2003. Family law in Europe, in *Family Life in the Twentieth Century. The History of the European Family*. Vol. 3, edited by D.I. Kertzer and M. Barbagli. New Haven, CT and London: Yale University Press, 113–51.

Roy, O. 2004. *Globalised Islam. The Search for a New Ummah*. 2nd impression paperback 2006. London: Hurst & Company.

Sabahi, F. 2006. *Islam: l'identità inquieta dell'Europa. Viaggio tra i musulmani d'occidente*. Milano: Il Saggiatore.

Shah-Kazemi, S. N. 2001. *Untying the Knot. Muslim Women, Divorce and the Shariah*. London: The Signal Press.

Shah, P. 2003. Attitudes to polygamy in English law. *International and Comparative Law Quarterly*, 52, 359–400.

Shah, P. (ed.) 2007. *Law and Ethnic Plurality: Socio-legal Perspectives*. Leiden and Boston: Martinus Nijhoff.

Talwar, D. 2010. Wedding trouble as UK Muslim marriages not recognised. *BBC Asian Network*, [Online, 3 February]. Available at: http://news.bbc.co.uk/1/hi/8493660.stm [last accessed 31 May 2013].

Ufficio Centrale di Statistica and Scuola Superiore delle Statistiche Ufficiali dell'Amministrazione dell'Interno (ed.) 2010. *Annuario delle statistiche ufficiali dell'amministrazione dell'Interno*. Roma: SSAI.

Warraich, S.A. and Balchin, C. 2006. *Recognizing the Un-recognized: Inter-country Cases and Muslim Marriages and Divorces in Britain*. Women Living Under Muslim Laws publications. Nottingham: The Russell Press.

Wiktorowicz, Q. and Farouki, S.T. 2000. Islamic NGOs and Muslim politics: A case from Jordan. *Third World Quarterly*, 21(4), 685–99.

Witte, J. Jr. 1997. From sacrament to contract. Marriage, religion, and law in the Western tradition. Louisville, KY: Westminster John Knox Press.

Witte, J. Jr. 2001. The impact of the Reformation and Counter-Reformation, in *Family Life in Early Modern Times, 1500–1789. The History of the European Family*. Vol. 1, edited by D.I. Kertzer and M. Barbagli. New Haven, CT and London: Yale University Press, 125–54.

Wray, H. 2006. An ideal husband? Marriages of convenience, moral gatekeeping and immigration to the UK. *European Journal of Migration and Law*, 8, 303–20.

Yilmaz, I. 2002. The challenge of post-modern legality and Muslim legal pluralism in England. *Journal of Ethnic and Migration Studies*, 28(2), 343–54.

Yilmaz, I. 2005. *Muslim Laws, Politics and Society in Modern Nation States: Dynamic Legal Pluralisms in England, Turkey, and Pakistan*. Aldershot and Burlington, VT: Ashgate.

Chapter 7
Cross-border Family Cases and Religious Diversity: What Can Judges Do?

Maarit Jänterä-Jareborg

1. Confronting Religion and Tradition within Family Law

1.1 The Judge's Dilemma

The novelty of contemporary multiculturalism, a result of large-scale global migration during the last 40–50 years, is that it has introduced into many European states a kind of 'ethno-religious mix' (Modood 2007: 8), of which these states have had little – if any – previous experience. The 'legal actors', that is, the national courts, lawyers, legislators and legal scholars, have only recently come to realise the existence of a previously unthinkable and complex plurality within the field of family life,[1] namely that society includes minority groups who conduct their family lives in accordance with customs and traditions originating from another part of the world or another culture. These customs and traditions are often justified on the basis of the parties' religion. An increasing number of disputes are brought to courts in which a party wishes to rely on a right that a religious norm system allegedly accords to him or her. In court proceedings, religion and religious beliefs are likewise presented as defences or justifications for a person's action. In yet other cases, religious or cultural motives appear to have guided the parties' actions, even if such grounds are not pleaded in the litigation. The court is confronted with a new kind of diversity and new challenges.

First, the dispute's alleged religious dimension is likely to cause unease. The state courts of Europe are commonly seen as *secular courts*. As a result, European judges identify themselves as *secular judges* and tend to regard all matters of faith as falling outside both their professional competence and their jurisdiction. In England, this concern was exceptionally clearly expressed by the judge, Munby J., in the case of *Sulaiman v Juffali*.[2] Munby pointed out that he, as a judge, had sworn to do justice 'to all manner of people'. He added, 'Religion – whatever the particular believer's faith – is no doubt something to be encouraged but it is not the business of the government or of the secular courts'. I believe that European judges would generally agree with this statement.

Second, the court needs to find a *legal basis* in its own legal system (*lex fori*) in order to be able to adjudicate any request or defence. Claims that in the court's view are based

---

1 Earlier, upon migration, ties were gradually cut with the state of origin. In contrast, in the globalised context the world is in many respects borderless (easy travel prospects, the Internet and social media, television, etc.), enabling an individual to live simultaneously under 'different systems'.
2 *Sulaiman v Juffali* [2002] 2 FCR 427, at 439.

on purely religious practices, traditions or customs might not qualify[3] unless they are of legal relevance according to the applicable law. Equally, such grounds in support of a party's actions or defences might not count. Can justice be done, if no regard is given to these other norm systems?

Third, the parties to the dispute may turn out to be living under parallel norm systems, whether dictated by states, a religion, traditions or customs.[4] In cross-border cases, in particular when the persons have their origin in states with religion-based personal laws, the states of origin often demand full compliance with their religiously coordinated family laws, also when the persons concerned reside abroad.[5] The individual is left no choice in the matter, if he or she wishes to maintain legal or factual ties within that state.[6] On the other hand, the continued applicability of one's original personal law, or the submission to religious norms, may also be the preference of the individual concerned. Must the court under all circumstances force the applicability of mandatory forum law, even against the wishes of the individuals concerned?

Fourth, a person with economic means can make use of an 'overseas jurisdiction', normally in the state of origin. Alternatively, people seek to make use of faith-based dispute resolution within the forum state, where such is available. Where the parties have different preferences, there is a risk of parallel proceedings, whether religious or legal. These options increase the risk of limping legal relationships and conflicting decisions.[7] With all these factors in mind, how can a European court do justice to the individuals concerned?

Religion is a daily topic in the media in Europe, with the focus on tensions allegedly caused by religion, such as the wearing and banning of head scarves, political Islam, circumcision of boys, freedom of expression *versus* religion and, as a result, the extremely complicated content of the freedom of religion. Sociologists are seeking explanations to

---

3 An example is when a woman whose traditional or religious marriage does not qualify as a 'marriage' under forum law requests of the court a divorce or access to a benefit that depends on the validity of the marriage.

4 This can be labelled as a form of normative pluralism in a broad sense, covering not only legal sources of whatever origin but also moral values, ethics, diverse cultural understandings of the family, the expected roles of its members, etc. A point repeatedly made by, e.g., the Swedish Professor of Islamology, Jan Hjärpe, is that families exercise jurisdiction because the state itself in tribal societies is unable to protect the individual or the collective. This justification of the family's jurisdiction loses in strength in another kind of a surrounding.

5 In cross-border cases, from the point of view of Islamic law, sharia rules should always take priority over any other rules (see Menski 2006: 275). Confusingly, *foreign embassies* often exercise powers ('prolonged jurisdiction') in various kinds of matters related to family law, often without the authorisation or permission of the host state. The embassies, for example, may upon delegation of the state of origin appoint officials to celebrate marriages in the host state, certify divorces there as well as various kinds of agreements entered into there. Even if these acts are not recognised in the host state, they may be obligatory for legal validity in the parties' state of origin. See further Chapter 6 by Federica Sona.

6 Giving up that state's citizenship can have, inter alia, extensive legal consequences concerning ownership of property in that state. For example, under the law of Iran, an Iranian national renouncing his or her citizenship must transfer all of his or her immovable property to Iranian nationals (Ebrahani 2010: 516). It appears that very few Iranians who are habitually resident abroad renounce their Iranian citizenship. They acquire, instead, a new nationality, i.e. that of their new home state, while maintaining the citizenship of origin.

7 The persons concerned risk being the 'eternal losers', unless they are able to take measures ('fix it') in both jurisdictions, in agreement with one another.

religion's new visibility in society.[8] Judges and lawyers, in contrast, appear reluctant to participate in any public discussion on how religion relates to law (or law to religion) or how religion might challenge law (or law religion).[9] Whenever a judge has ventured to enter the debate, calling for the inclusion of multi-faith concerns within the legal system, the media reactions have been widely negative. Any vision of parallel legal systems provokes. In a much-debated and heavily criticised speech of July 2008, Lord Justice Phillips, following the example set by the Archbishop of Canterbury Dr Rowan Williams earlier that year, expressed sympathy for the idea of applying Islamic legal principles to Muslims in some parts of the legal system, for example matrimonial law.[10] The vision described by Phillips was not that this should take place in UK courts, but within the framework of agreed mediation or alternative dispute resolution.[11]

1.2 The Cultural Constraints of Family Law

Contemporary European states endorse secularism and the principle of confession-neutrality of the state.[12] For a long time, religion has been regarded as a private matter for the individual. The challenge is how to respond in particular to Islam, which, as Grace Davie explains, 'is essentially a public faith in which religion merges imperceptibly into other areas of society including the law'.[13] Another challenge is to strike a proper balance between the state's desire to interfere and people's right to live in accordance with their religion and traditions.

It is hardly surprising that these kinds of tensions appear daily within the 'culturally constrained' field of family law. Family law legislation is a primary tool of contemporary European society for promoting equal rights for men and women, as well as children's rights. The state also uses it for 'social engineering' purposes. Recent European legislation introducing same-sex marriages, registered partnerships or civil unions, for example, not

---

8 It is asked if this is a new kind of a 'class issue', whereby marginalised groups identify with religion, instead of sharing the values of the majority society. Or whether religious lifestyles are a way of claiming public recognition to what, in particular for minority groups, gives life a purpose, and the guidelines for a good way of living. On the other hand, is not religion something that one, according to the Western notion, *chooses*, with the result that we should avoid 'ethnifying' religions? But can the European secular emphasis stand considering that, globally, it constitutes an exception?

9 According to Professor of Sociology, Grace Davie (2012: 235), lawyers 'create and interpret legal frameworks, some of which deal with religion; they are less interested in the messy realities of lived religion as this is experienced in everyday life'.

10 'Equality Before the Law', Speech by Lord Phillips, Lord Chief Justice, East London Muslim Centre, 2 July 2008. 'Islam in English Law: Civil and Religious Law in England', Lecture by the Archbishop of Canterbury, Dr Rowan Williams, Lambeth Palace, 7 February 2008.

11 The stir created by the respective contributions of Williams and Phillips can at least in part be explained by existing controversies concerning the advantages and disadvantages of religious dispute resolution. According to critics, access to any such alternative takes place at the expense of women's rights, cementing discrimination and inequality in law. We are not living in a 'theocracy', but in a '*Rechtsstaat*'. Correspondingly, the justice system should respond to humanitarian and not religious needs. Others see religious dispute resolution as a way of combining different norm systems under which a believer lives, providing a method to prevent limping legal relationships from arising. Decisions by religious bodies might be enforceable in the parties' country of origin, contrary to decisions emanating from a state court. Both positive and negative experiences are reported. See, e.g., the special issue by Glazer (2012), and Chapter 10 by Douglas et al. herein.

12 The European models of secularism differ widely, however (see Ferrari 2010).

13 Davie (2012: 239).

only serves the purpose of protecting same-sex couples, but also steering societal attitudes in a direction that the state finds desirable. Since, from the point of view of the state, fundamental values of the legal order are at stake and there is little tolerance for any other outlook. It remains, nevertheless, unrealistic to expect that families living in diaspora are able, willing or interested in giving up their own family culture.[14] In the long run, however, no culture exists in isolation of external influences and with a fixed content. In a good society, we are voluntarily influenced by each other.

1.3 Secular Law versus Religious Law

In a contemporary European society, *secular family law* is associated with autonomy for the individual, promotion of equal rights for women in relation to men, children's rights and the prohibition of discrimination on such grounds as a person's gender, race, ethnicity, religion or sexual orientation.[15] It finds an ideological background in the ideas of the Enlightenment, further developed by the introduction of rights of various kinds, with or without the explicit support of international treaty law. It marks a landmark victory over 'the chains of religion'[16] and superstition, and is increasingly seen as a kind of a human rights regulation, applicable to everybody within the state's territory.

Religious family law, by contrast, is associated with supernatural 'divine' rules, governing all aspects of (everyday) life and, thus, with a broader scope of applicability than secular law. When regarded as 'fixed and immutable', it tends to reflect traditional patriarchal values with strict gender roles, women and children being subordinated to men, and homosexuality being regarded as a sin. Group rights prevail over individual rights. Others emphasise that religious law is 'the law of the believers', its authority being the divine will of God. Because its interpretation is 'the work of man', no agreement exists on its content.

The risk exists that those with power – religious leaders over the believers, clans over their members, parents over their children, men over their wives – have an interest in expanding religion (and religious law) to cover and sanction interpretations that they themselves prefer.[17] It is often pointed out that the deterioration of women's rights in many Islamic countries has nothing to do with these states' adherence to Islam, but with their patriarchal organisation (Mashhour 2005, Musawah 2011). Yet religious law has the potential to be just as 'progressive' as secular law.

In many European societies, religion is regarded as a 'dark force', conserving inequalities. Correspondingly, religious family law in Europe is viewed as anti-progressive and seen as a threat to modern European values of equality and other human rights standards.[18] There is a growing unease in every European society that the relatively newly established, progressive rights and values might not be shared by, in particular, the new 'ethno-religious' minority groups who might instead wish to follow conservative, religiously motivated rules, and

---

14   It is often assumed that religion, customs and traditions are strengthened in diaspora.
15   One of the largely ignored paradoxes of secularity in, e.g., regulations on family law, is nevertheless that the law continues to express values that are in line with the dominating religion in the state (see Jänterä-Jareborg 2011).
16   Professor Stephen Cretney (2005) uses the alternative expression, the 'shackles of culture and religion'.
17   This remains one of the major arguments against faith-based mediation in family law.
18   These rights are continually developing and their content and scope of application may be disputed, just as is the case with religion.

even cherish alternative loyalties to those of the state of residence. Leading European politicians, such as Angela Merkel, Nicholas Sarkozy and David Cameron, have signalled the importance of assimilating minority cultures into the mainstream culture, thus marking an end to society's recently more open attitude towards multiculturalism.

1.4 The Risk of Stigmatising Vulnerable Groups?

Measures have been initiated in several European states with the aim of putting an end to various kinds of (alleged) discriminatory practices, (allegedly) practised within minority groups. A criminalisation of forced marriages is currently under consideration in England. In Norway, provisions of criminal law that are specially tailored for forced marriages,[19] as well as marriages concerning a child under the age of 16,[20] have been introduced into legislation. Sweden is considering similar measures, but with a broader scope of application. According to the Swedish proposal, criminalisation should also cover religious and other *informal marriages*, if they are forced or concern a person under 18 years of age (Swedish Ministry of Justice Committee 2012: 45–7, and Chapter 4 by Maarit Jänterä-Jareborg). The current possibility of permission, by a competent authority, to marry before the general marriage age of 18, should be abolished according to the proposal. The aim of these proposals is to 'underscore society's reaction more clearly and in a more focused way' (ibid.: 45).

There is a visible European trend towards increasing the minimum marriage age for both parties to 18 years old. In European migration law, for example, a marriage conducted abroad with a person under this age does not qualify as a family unification ground, and many European states have increased the required marriage age in this context to 21.[21] The justification generally given in support of these restrictions is that society must dissociate itself from any inequality of treatment and from any kind of coercion, force or violence. Importantly, from the point of view of our topic, this development also *sets limits* to the recognition of religious and cultural diversity, as early marriages and arranged marriages commonly occur outside the majority society and are motivated by cultural and, possibly, religious concerns (see also Chapter 8 by Anika Liversage).

In a more elaborate language, the so-called *politics of universalism*, emphasising the importance of applying the same laws to all, are claimed to clash with the *politics of difference*, recognising the unique identity of an individual or a group, also at the level of the law (e.g. Taylor 1994). As Esin Örücü (2011: 5) puts it, 'there is pressure on the legal systems from individuals to be accepted for who they are'. Werner Menski (2011: 17) reminds us that people will not abandon their ways of life simply because they come to live with us. The legal system should not disregard this social reality but 'become more

---

19 Norwegian Penal Act § 222.2. The practical application of this provision has turned out to be complicated, and case law is limited. In the Norwegian Supreme Court judgment HR-2006-258-A-Rt-2006-140, the Court pointed out that the crime is fulfilled only when a legally valid marriage has been concluded in the state of celebration. In this case, the woman had been forced into a religious marriage in Iraq, but since the marriage had not been registered there it had not become legally valid in Iraq. The father and the brother of the woman were sentenced to prison for the attempt to carry out a forced marriage.

20 Norwegian Penal Act § 220. The age limit of 16 finds an explanation in that from that age onwards, a dispensation from the general marriage-age requirement in Norway of 18 can, exceptionally, be granted by the competent authority.

21 This applies, e.g., in the UK, Germany and the Netherlands, whereas Denmark follows the age requirement of 24 years.

perceptive of the need to account for such differences'. In Menski's opinion, however, we often 'instinctively desire more uniformity and certainty'. Menski asks whether such desires are part of the 'bone marrow', specifically of lawyers and legal scholars. But on the other hand, as emphasised by Abdullahi Ahmed An-Na'im (2009: 22), terms such as 'identity' are often misleadingly invoked to indicate something that is 'clearly defined, stable and fixed', whereas 'people organize their lives to be open and flexible enough to take advantage of alternative options, which they can justify in terms of their cultural or religious value system and meaning'.

The groups concerned and individuals themselves are diverse and there are no generally applicable standards of being, for example, a 'Muslim', a 'Jew' or a 'Catholic'. The legal system should, consequently, be careful in categorising people. Conflict levels should not be artificially raised and people should not be forced under rules that no party wishes to have applied.[22] In certain contexts, the normative plurality of people's lives may need to be taken into account – for example, the parties' need or wish to supplement a secular divorce decree with a religious decree on marriage dissolution.[23]

As demonstrated by the case of *R (on the application of Quila and another) v Secretary of State for the Home Department* ([2011] UKSC 45, judgment of 12 October 2011), finally decided by the UK Supreme Court, in the end it can be up to a court of law to decide whether a national enactment meets the proportionality test of the European Convention on Human Rights and Fundamental Freedoms (ECHR) or, on the contrary, is a violation of conventional rights. In its judgment, the Supreme Court found that the immigration rules of the UK, aimed at protecting against forced marriages, were not proportionate in relation to their effects.

Importantly, the pluralism of a contemporary European society includes a plurality of legal sources. Supranational law (the ECHR, EU Charter of Fundamental Rights and treaty law) sets limits to cultural constraints and popular tendencies in national law. Two supranational courts, the European Court of Human Rights and the Court of Justice of the European Union, have jurisdiction to decide, in a generally binding manner, how the common instruments should be interpreted and whether decisions by national courts live up to European human rights standards. Their interventions focus on sensitive issues, identifying fundamental European values.[24] In the first place, however, national courts are in charge of this test.

---

22 As the legal system is constructed, the right of the parties to dispose of the applicable rules varies from jurisdiction to jurisdiction. The stronger the public interest is, the less is the autonomy usually at the parties' disposal.

23 Persons who have married in the form of a legally valid religious ceremony may wish to divorce in a similar manner. They may feel that they are not otherwise properly divorced or they may even be prevented from remarrying under their religion and religious law. Catholics, on the other hand, may feel an urgent need to supplement a civil divorce with a religious marriage annulment.

24 From a nation-state's perspective, these interventions by the Court are not always welcomed. They may be regarded as 'too progressive' or 'not progressive enough', or destructive to the coherence of the national legal system, etc. They may also be regarded as mutually inconsistent, depending on the chosen emphasis and the legal system in question. Compare, e.g., the Court's judgment in *Munoz Díaz v Spain*, judgment of 8 December 2009 (Application No. 49151/07) with that in *Serife Yigit v Turkey*, judgment of 2 November 2010 (Application No. 3976/05). In the first case, refusal to recognise a Roma marriage was a violation of the conventional rights. In the second case, refusal to recognise a purely religious marriage as equivalent to a civil law marriage did not constitute a violation. See further Chapter 1 by Prakash Shah.

2. Private International Law as the Domain for Legally Relevant Religious Diversity in Family Life

2.1 Criteria and Relevant Questions to be Addressed

Cultural and religious constraints tend to pop up in cross-border family law cases, governed by the rules of private international law.[25] This discipline of law strives at promoting cross-border justice between individuals by coordinating legal systems' (alleged) claims to adjudicate the interests at stake. More recently, this discipline has also been described as a system of law governing 'conflicts between civilizations' (Basedow 2009, Kreuzer 2009) or 'conflicts between cultures' (Jayme 1995). To qualify as a case of private international law, the case at hand must, according to the Continental European understanding, demonstrate a legally relevant connection to another jurisdiction (or another state's law). This requirement is met where, for example, the parties are nationals of a foreign state but habitually resident in the state of the forum. Often, an event of relevance for the dispute has taken place abroad and the question is what effect – if any – this event can be given in the forum state. Questions of jurisdiction, applicable law and the legal effect of foreign decisions form the core of the discipline.

European case law concerning multicultural cross-border family cases demonstrates that numerous and, from the national court's perspective, unusual legal issues need to be addressed before the competent court can finally decide upon the subject matter of the dispute. Of particular relevance are such issues as how the parties' requests should be legally classified ('qualification'), in particular when forum law lacks a corresponding right. A well-known example is the Muslim institution of *mahr*, also known as the Muslim dower. If a foreign state's law is identified as being applicable to the dispute, how should the court ascertain the foreign law's content and apply it? How, furthermore, should the court deal with situations where the main issue of the dispute, for example the wife's right to *mahr* or maintenance, is dependent on the recognition of the spouses' civil status, for instance the legal validity of their marriage or divorce, when different states' laws might be applicable? Where should the court draw the line for the so-called 'public policy' (*ordre public*), aimed at protecting the fundamental values of the forum state's legal order and setting the limits to the right to enforce foreign laws? These issues are discussed in both this section and in Section 3.

2.2 Selected Case Law

I approach these issues with the assistance of examples that, due to my own geographical background, largely come from Scandinavia. They are supplemented by cases from other European jurisdictions. As the chosen examples indicate, encounters by European courts with Islamic law and culture have been problematic. Basically, in my opinion, at least four kinds of approaches are visible in the chosen examples, even if the approaches can also overlap. I have divided these approaches under three different categories.

---

25 Cultural and religious diversity is, nevertheless, an increasing concern also in situations that do not qualify as cross-border cases but are regarded as purely domestic by the legal system. These important issues are discussed further in Chapter 4 by Maarit Jänterä-Jareborg. See further on this distinction Chapter 3 by Mathias Rohe.

2.2.1 Category I

The Iranian wife's divorce claim in Sweden
An Iranian woman, who had arrived in Sweden as an asylum seeker together with her minor children, applied a few years later for a divorce from her husband who was still living in Iran. Having regard to the fact that the plaintiff's residence in Sweden was lawful, Swedish courts considered themselves to have jurisdiction and granted the wife the divorce after a reconsideration period of six months, in accordance with the provisions on divorce in the Swedish Marriage Code.[26] The courts disregarded the objections of the Iranian husband who claimed, inter alia, that there were no grounds for divorce according to Iranian law, and that the Swedish divorce decree would not be recognised in Iran. The courts (the case was finally decided by the Swedish Supreme Court) considered a spouse's unconditional right to divorce according to Swedish law to weigh heavier than any inconveniences for the parties (the children included) resulting from the non-recognition of the divorce in Iran.[27]

Denmark's forced dissolution of Iraqi polygamous marriages
For humanitarian reasons, Denmark decided to grant asylum rights for Iraqi interpreters who had assisted Danish troops in Iraq and, owing to this cooperation, risked their lives in Iraq. One of the interpreters concerned lived in polygamous marriages with two women; both marriages had been validly concluded in Iraq. Neither the man himself nor his wives were willing to dissolve the marriages. Evidence was provided that the wives' social and legal position in Iraq would be extremely vulnerable if they stayed in Iraq without their husband. Consequently, the man and both wives were granted asylum in Denmark, after which the competent Danish authority – *ex officio* – took actions to have the second marriage dissolved, its existence being regarded as manifestly contrary to the Danish notion of *ordre public*. The parties suffered nervous breakdowns and returned to Iraq.[28]

Muslim women's mahr *claims at Swedish courts*
Several cases on the Islamic institution of *mahr* are brought each year to Swedish courts by parties with an origin in a Muslim country. The explanation of the frequency of these cases is most likely that an affirmative Swedish case law,[29] confirming agreements on *mahr* and approving the wives' *mahr* claims, has encouraged other Muslim wives to bring similar suits to Swedish courts. I wish to report a couple of more recent cases.

In a case decided in 2011, an Iranian woman requested that her former husband, a national of both Iran and Sweden, be obliged to pay her Muslim dower, *mahr*, consisting of 114 gold coins of the type 'Bahar-e Azadi', agreed by the parties upon the conclusion

---

26 NJA 1991 A 2.

27 The starting point, according to Sweden's private international rules on the law applicable to divorce applications in Sweden, is the application of Swedish law as the *lex fori*. If, however, neither of the spouses is a Swedish national and the defendant objects to the divorce, account should be taken of the spouses' law of nationality. In the end, it is still up to the court's discretion whether it will grant the divorce, in accordance with Swedish law. See the Act (1904:26 s. 1) on Certain International Legal Relations regarding Marriage and Guardianship, Ch. 3 § 4.

28 See V. Greve (2009), and for reports on the case see, e.g., 'Denmark: Government to study polygamy', http://islamineurope.blogspot.co.uk/2008/03/denmark-government-to-study-polygamy.html [last accessed 17 December 2013].

29 Two of the judgments, both from an appellate (second instance) court, have been published in law reports, namely RH 1993:116 and RH 2005:66 (see Sayed 2008).

of their marriage in Iran. The husband contested the request and claimed that the wife had voluntarily, after her arrival in Sweden, remitted the contracted *mahr*, in an agreement signed by her at the Iranian embassy in Stockholm. The husband also claimed that the marriage was basically a 'sham marriage', and concluded only to make it possible for the wife to receive a visa to Sweden and to test the relationship between the parties. He had also made it clear to his wife, before the marriage, that he did not share the traditional Iranian outlook on marriage or the legitimacy of agreements on *mahr*. Their agreement on *mahr* was concluded only for the sake of appearances in Iran.

The first instance court[30] took special account of the circumstances of the case, particularly the (considerable) size of the agreed *mahr* and the circumstances when negotiating it in Iran, the position of women in the culture from which the parties originated and the wife's total dependency on her husband after her arrival in what was for her a previously unknown country. In the court's opinion, it followed that the wife's remittance of the agreed *mahr* could not have been voluntary but coerced under threats and thus was invalid, also according to Iranian law. The court of appeal[31] questioned the approach of the first instance court. In its opinion, it was for the wife to prove that the remittance was invalid according to Iranian law. In the appellate court's opinion, the wife had failed to show that she had signed the remittance agreement under coercion and threats. As a result, the court refused her claim. This outcome appears exceptional, in the otherwise affirmative Swedish case law.

In another, still pending case (2013), the spouses, who were both nationals of Iran, had agreed on a *mahr* consisting of 700 gold coins in connection with their marriage in Iran. The wife had been habitually resident in Sweden for 10 years. The couple separated soon after the husband's arrival in Sweden, and the marriage was dissolved through a Swedish divorce decree upon request by the wife, with the husband objecting to the divorce. After the Swedish divorce decree became final, the wife initiated court proceedings in Sweden requesting the payment of the agreed *mahr*. The husband denied her claim, inter alia, on the ground that she had orally agreed not to claim her *mahr*, and on the ground that the *mahr* agreement had only served a symbolic function without having been intended to be legally binding. The husband was neither religious nor traditional, and had made it clear to the wife in advance that he was opposed to the institution of *mahr*. The agreement had been entered into upon insistence by the wife and her family, but only after the husband and his family had been informed by the Iranian embassy in Stockholm that the agreement would not be enforceable in Sweden.[32] The wife, according to the husband, had in any case lost her right to the *mahr* after the marriage had been dissolved in Sweden upon her initiative.

According to the judgment of the first instance court, the husband had failed to prove both the existence of an oral agreement whereby the wife renounced her *mahr* and the agreement's alleged symbolic nature. The information on Iranian law available to the court provided, furthermore, that the Swedish divorce decree would not be recognised in Iran. With reference to its own understanding of the principle in private international law of *loyal application of foreign law*,[33] the court concluded that the wife was entitled to the agreed

---

30 Solna District Court, judgment 2010-03-05, Case T 2675.
31 Svea Court of Appeal, judgment 2011-10-19, Case T 2803-10.
32 This information had not been shared with the other party.
33 Whether the application of Iranian law qualifies as 'loyal' with reference to the circumstances behind the divorce decree and the content of Iranian divorce law could well be disputed. See also below, Sections 3.1 and 3.2.2.

mahr, since the parties according to Iranian law were still married to each other. By doing so, the court assessed the 'preliminary issue' to the *mahr*, namely the marriage's continued existence, in accordance with the law applicable to the claim on *mahr* (that is, Iranian law) and disregarded the Swedish divorce decree. This judgment has been appealed. In the meantime, the husband has taken various measures to have the case debated in the media, attempting to stir public opinion against 'medieval Muslim practices practised in Sweden'.

2.2.2 Comments

The impact of traditions, customs and religion are clearly visible in the disputes at stake, having regard to how the parties presented their claims. Even if the competent authority took its decision within a legal framework, mixing both private international law and substantive law of the forum or the foreign state, the outcome in none of the cases was obvious or predictable. Furthermore, references to religion or to human rights concerns are absent in the rulings.

The Danish case demonstrates a categorical refusal to recognise a polygamous marriage irrespective of the marriage's original legal validity and lack of connection to Denmark. The cultural constraints of family law, judged on the basis of Danish values,[34] are evident here. The judgment on the Iranian wife's right to divorce is more balanced, the initiative coming from her as a party to the dispute, even if it also meant disregarding Iranian divorce law and the husband's interests. The *mahr* cases indicate that Swedish courts are flexible enough to recognise a foreign legal institution lacking a counterpart in Swedish (European) law, but strive to adjust it in one way or another to the law of the forum. The favourable outcome for the wife in most of the cases might find an explanation through the general tendency in Swedish family law to protect the weaker party. The *mahr* does not appear as a bargaining tool for the wife's right to divorce[35] in Swedish case law, obviously because of Sweden's *lex fori* approach to divorce claims also in cross-border cases, as was demonstrated by the first example. The fact that a Swedish divorce will not be recognised in the parties' country of origin (or religious community in Sweden) has not been regarded as a sufficient ground to refuse a divorce claim in Sweden.

Above all, however, the outcome in the Swedish cases on *mahr*, as illustrated by the two examples above, shows the importance of the lawyers' skills regarding how the foreign claims are to be presented to the court. Court proceedings are subject to rules of their own, to a kind of 'procedural game', defined by the law of the forum state. All the actors must pursue their more or less strictly defined roles. It is the parties' lot to provide the facts that they consider to be of legal relevance for their claims, and it is the courts' duty to find the applicable rules to these facts. When foreign law is applicable, this divide becomes blurred, as the lawyers assisting the parties often are the ones to represent that system's content.[36] Thought-provokingly, in litigation and judgments, the *mahr* agreement is sometimes qualified as providing 'maintenance to [the] wife', sometimes as a 'contract'

---

34 Until recently, most world religions recognised polygamy (polygyny) with the exception of Christianity.

35 For examples on how the *mahr* can be used as a bargaining tool in a European context, see Jansen Fredriksen (2011), and on *mahr* claims and their treatment, see further Chapter 1 by Prakash Shah.

36 The framing of claims as legally protected human rights is an additional challenge, so far seldom employed in Swedish litigation (see Jänterä-Jareborg and Singer 2012).

or a 'gift', and sometimes as a matter of 'matrimonial property relations'.[37] In Swedish courts, the husbands are increasingly presented at court as 'modern men', opposed to Muslim legal traditions, whereas the wives are claimed to cherish Muslim traditions and even the religious dimensions of a Muslim marriage. A cynical observer might be tempted to state that it is all about money and nothing else.

2.2.3 Category II

Is it possible to identify judgments that are insensitive to allegedly fundamental values of the forum state in matters of the family? A couple of matrimonial cases from German and French courts, widely reported in international media, come to mind. In these cases, the court allegedly took into account cultural or religious factors, and upgraded them to factors of legal relevance. Wife beating, according to a German judge in a divorce case, was part of the parties' 'cultural milieu' and recognised by their religion.[38] A French court, in turn, acknowledged the outraged husband's right to annul his marriage, once he had come to the insight during the wedding night that his wife was not a sexually untouched 'virgin'.[39]

These kinds of rulings appear to confirm the otherwise heavily criticised argument of 'cultural defence', but in a manner that cannot be expected to be uncontroversial anywhere in society.[40] Even if secular law should be careful when intervening in religion and traditions, the legal system must do so under certain circumstances. I wish to quote once again Munby J., who in a judgment stated that religion can 'never of itself immunise the believer from the reach of secular law' and an 'invocation of religious belief does not necessarily provide a defence to what is otherwise a valid claim'.[41] In yet another judgment, Munby pointed out that 'the starting point of the law is an essentially agnostic view of religious beliefs and a tolerant indulgence to religious and cultural diversity'.[42]

One of the major difficulties in any discussion concerning family law and religious diversity is that of defining what qualifies as 'religion' and is covered by the special protection provided by national constitutions[43] or the ECHR, and what remains to be seen as an established tradition or custom within a certain group, not included within this protection. Religious freedom as a concept becomes particularly problematic when other peoples' rights risk being affected.[44] This fact alone may in certain cases call for a narrow

---

37 In general, this corresponds well to the Continental European case law on *mahr* claims and their qualification (see Mehdi and Nielsen 2011).

38 See *New York Times*, 23 March 2007.

39 *The Times*, 31 May 2008.

40 A Musawah report on CEDAW emphasises that 'family laws that perpetuate inequality in the family cannot be justified on religious grounds' (see Musawah 2011).

41 See Munby J. in *R v Derby City Council* [2011] EWHC 375.

42 *Sulaiman v Juffali* [2002] 2 FCR 427, at 439.

43 The Swedish Constitution's protection for freedom of religion, for example, is limited to the right to personal conviction, including the right to worship alone and jointly with others.

44 This is demonstrated by the much-debated decision of 2012 whereby a Cologne first instance court (Amtsgericht) did not consider (the parents') freedom of religion to justify the bodily harm to which a religiously motivated circumcision of boys subjects the child. Regard for the child's best interests, and the right to take any such decision himself at a more mature age, weighed heavier. The decision was incidentally reversed on appeal by the Landgericht but largely on grounds that there was an excusable mistake as to the law. Likewise, women's equal rights are given as justification for the banning of headscarves in, e.g. France, which others, on the contrary, wish to justify by reference to freedom of religion or freedom of religious expression.

understanding. It has been held that those actions required by a religion deserve better protection than those actions merely permitted by a religion. In the case of *Khan v United Kingdom*,[45] the European Human Rights Commission did not consider that the criminal law conviction of a Muslim man, due to his Islamic marriage ceremony with a 14-year-old girl, violated his freedoms of religion and to marry and found a family as protected by the ECHR, with Islam merely permitting early marriages. In *D v France*,[46] the award of damages against a Jewish man who had refused to grant his wife a 'get' after a civil divorce, thus preventing her from remarrying under Jewish law, did not qualify as a violation of freedom of religion, as Jewish leaders stated that the husband's refusal was not mandated by Judaism.

2.2.4 Category III

The third category consists of an approach of placing fundamental rights at the centre, as guaranteed in particular by the ECHR and its Arts. 6, 8, 9, 12 and 14, in addition to Art. 5 of the 7th Protocol to the ECHR (equal rights for men and women). The judgments show that human rights concerns can work 'both ways', namely both *in support of* religious and cultural values, as in the first two cases, and *against* such values, as demonstrated by the last cases. The judgments illustrate the courts' increasing consciousness of human rights, but they are also to be seen against a trend in European litigation to frame not least multicultural issues into claims of legally protected human rights (see Loenen, van Rossum and Tigchelaar 2010).

R (on the application of Quila and another) v Secretary of State for the Home Department[47]
This case, decided in October 2011 by the UK Supreme Court, focused on how the age requirement of 21 years for both spouses, in the immigration rules of the UK, in order for a marriage to qualify as a ground for family reunification, related to the applicants' right to private life and family life as protected by Art. 8 of the ECHR. The aim of the UK regulation was to prevent forced marriages. In the Court's opinion, the regulation did not strike a fair balance but interfered unlawfully with young married persons' right to family life in a cross-border context, beyond the scope of forced marriages and the interests of the community to prevent such marriages. The criteria developed by the court, in my opinion, provide useful guidance regarding how to approach potentially conflicting human rights concerns.

1. Is a *legitimate objective* (in this case, deterring forced marriages) *sufficiently important* to justify limiting a fundamental right (in this case, the right to private life and family life)?
2. Are the *measures* that have been designed to meet this objective *rationally connected* to it?

---

45 *Khan v United Kingdom*, Application No. 11579/85, 48 European Commission on Human Rights Decision (as reported by Evans 2003: 116).
46 *D v France*, Application No. 10180/82, 35 European Commission on Human Rights Decision (as reported by Evans 2003: 116).
47 [2011] UKSC 45, judgment of 12 October 2011. For thought-provoking criticism concerning decision-making in immigration cases in the UK, see Shah (2010).

3. Are the *measures proportionate*, that is, no more than is necessary to accomplish the objective?
4. Do the measures *strike a fair balance* between the rights of the individual and the interests of the community?

The Pastor Green case[48]

As another example of a judgment 'confirming diversity', with reference to the standards of the ECHR, I wish to refer the Swedish Supreme Court's judgment of 2005 in the so-called 'Pastor Green' case. This case made international headlines and focused on the protection of religious freedom of expression, as contrasted with the prohibition of agitation against homosexual persons as a group. The events leading to the criminal law charges in this case followed after Sweden had taken various kinds of legislative measures aimed at eliminating discrimination on the basis of sexual orientation, inter alia, by giving same-sex couples the right to formalise their relationship and to acquire joint parental rights. The case as such had no cross-border elements.

In a sermon delivered in 2003 in his church, in front of approximately 50 persons, a Pentecostal pastor (Green) labelled homosexuality as fornication, with the catastrophic effects of a cancerous tumour in society, spreading AIDS and other sexually transmitted illnesses, in manifest breach with the Bible's creation narrative and God's commandments. The sermon also insinuated that homosexuality was linked with sexual intercourse with children and animals. The pastor's sermon was entitled 'Is homosexuality an inborn instinct or the evil forces' trick upon people'. In support of his thesis, the pastor referred to numerous passages in the Bible. Afterwards, the pastor took comprehensive efforts to spread knowledge of his sermon to a broad public. The public prosecutor brought criminal law charges against him, on the ground that, in his sermon, he had disseminated statements of contempt for homosexuals on the basis of their sexual orientation and that his sermon had received extensive publicity. The pastor denied the charges and referred to his literal understanding of the word of the Bible. His actions were aimed at informing and guiding people, in particular young people, about the Bible's and the free churches' outlook on homosexuality, in addition to his wish to provide homosexual persons with pastoral care, but not to condemn or disgrace homosexuals. He had also wished to add another, in the Swedish debate hitherto absent, dimension to homosexuality.

In the end, the pastor was acquitted (by both the court of appeal and the Supreme Court). The Swedish Supreme Court paid special attention to the proportionality test of the ECHR and to the case law of the European Court of Human Rights, and concluded that a conviction of the pastor 'probably' would not meet the intended 'European standard'.[49]

---

48   NJA 2005 p. 805.
49   A later judgment, now by the European Court of Human Rights (after a Swedish Supreme Court judgment of 2006) in *Vejdeland and Others v Sweden*, 9 February 2012 (Application No. 1813/07), assesses the limits of freedom of expression in relation to hate speech concerning homosexuals and homosexuality. The offence (agitation against homosexuals) for which the defendants had been convicted by the Swedish Supreme Court consisted of distributing leaflets in a Swedish high school to which they had no connection. Their conviction was found reasonable with regard to the necessity in a democratic society for the protection of the reputation of others. In my opinion, this judgment is not in conflict with the outcome in the *Pastor Green* case, where the statements were made in a religious setting and not in a vulnerable school environment.

European judgments disqualifying religious law

European scholars, such as Marie-Claire Foblets, have drawn attention to a new trend in Continental European courts to refuse to recognise *talaq* divorces that have validly taken place in the parties' country of origin (see, e.g., Foblets 2007, and Chapter 1 by Shah). Whereas previously European courts decided on these issues on a case-by-case basis with regard to the specific circumstances of each situation, its links with the forum and the fairness of the outcome,[50] recent case law in France, for example, demonstrates a more or less categorical refusal with reference to fundamental rights recognised by the forum state (Foblets 2007: 152–4). This approach aims at promoting equal rights for women, in addition to safeguarding the right to a due process of law. Consequently, any legal measure in respect of which the woman did not enjoy an equal legal footing to that of the man is at risk of not being recognised.

Similarly, we can notice tendencies in Europe towards a complete dissociation with all polygamous marriages, all forced marriages, all proxy marriages and all child marriages, irrespective of their validity in the country of celebration, the parties' links to that state, the circumstances of the marriage conclusion and the time that has passed, the parties' interest in maintaining the marriage, etc.[51] Human rights concerns are interpreted as calling for a more or less total disregard of the laws, customs and even religious practices prevailing in the parties' country of origin.

European judges should know better. It appears justified to ask, in the light of the otherwise dynamic interpretation of the right to private life and family life in particular by the European Human Rights Court, why the family life in these cases should not qualify for protection when, for example, the parties themselves consider themselves as family and wish to be recognised as such? Having regard to the contents of the laws and customs concerned, this kind of a marriage – or divorce – was possibly the only option available.[52] A refused recognition in such a case can amount to discrimination against particular ethnic and religious groups contributing to the creation of limping legal relationships. A categorical 'non-recognition' of any foreign law, without regard to the circumstances of

---

50 The Swedish Supreme Court, for example, has held that a *talaq* divorce can be recognised in Sweden on condition that at least one of the spouses had a close link to the state where the divorce took place and that a public authority of that state had been involved in some manner, e.g. in the registration of the divorce. See the Supreme Court judgments, NJA 1989 p. 95 and NJA 1989 C 83.

51 Among the Nordic (Scandinavian) states, this trend is visible particularly in Denmark and Norway. Sweden has chosen a slightly more moderate approach. Since 2004, a marriage entered into under foreign law does not qualify for recognition in Sweden if, at the time of the marriage conclusion, one of the parties was a Swedish citizen or habitually resident in Sweden *and* there would have been an impediment to the marriage according to Swedish law. The impediments focus, primarily, on 'child marriages', i.e. marriages where at least one of the parties was under the age of 18, and bigamy. Forced marriages should always fall outside of recognition. Foreign marriages by proxy are not as such restricted.

52 In this respect the circumstances differ from those in the case of *Pellegrini v Italy*, decided by the European Court of Human Rights on 20 July 2001 (Application No. 30882/96). In that case, the Italian husband intentionally chose ecclesiastical marriage-annulment proceedings in the Roma Rota of the Vatican, to avoid the costly consequences (on maintenance) of a secular decree on judicial separation, granted by an Italian court upon initiative of the wife. The Vatican court, which annulled the marriage due to the spouses' being close relatives, did not give the wife the chance of a fair hearing. By recognising the Vatican decree, Italy violated Art. 6 of the ECHR.

the case, does not meet the standards to be required of the legal system in an increasingly pluralistic society.[53]

3. European Courts and Foreign Religious Law

3.1 Von Savigny's System of Choice of Law Resolution

In large parts of the Western world (common law excepted), cross-border conflict resolution follows a model originally created by the prominent nineteenth-century German scholar Friedrich Carl von Savigny.[54] The aim is to identify the *territorial legal system* to which an international (cross-border) legal relationship between private parties is most closely connected, by using established objective criteria, such as the nationality (citizenship) or habitual residence (domicile) of the persons concerned and, increasingly, the subjective test of the expressed preference of the persons concerned on the law applicable. The legal system thus identified shall govern the legal issue at stake, irrespective of whether it is the law of the forum state (*lex fori*) or the law of another state. The private law systems of different states are regarded as *equal and interchangeable*. Consequently, when the applicable conflicts rule refers to the law of a foreign state, the court should strive to apply the foreign law as it would be applied by a foreign court of the state of the law's origin. This, inevitably demanding, standard is labelled the principle of *loyal application of foreign law*.[55] Under this approach, foreign law can qualify for application only on condition that it qualifies as *the law of a nation-state*.

Originally, and as envisaged by von Savigny, this system was aimed at legal conflicts within the community of civilised, independent *Christian nations*, meeting on equal terms and bound together by communication, mutual needs and shared values (Jänterä-Jareborg 2003: 206ff., Kreuzer 2009). Von Savigny wished to dissociate his system from any system of personal laws, and emphasised each state's sovereignty over its territory.[56] In cross-border cases, a choice would have to be made between conflicting *territorial laws* of different states.

---

53 For constructive proposals regarding how human rights should be approached in cross-border cases, see Kinsch (2010: 272–5). Where the application of EU law is at stake, it can be expected that Art. 21 of the EU Charter of Fundamental Rights will be relied upon frequently.

54 The system was presented in the 8th volume, published in 1849, of von Savigny's magnificent work, *Das System des heutigen Römischen Rechts*. By 1869, it had already appeared in an English translation, by William Guthrie, under the title *A Treatise on the Conflict of Laws and the Limits of their Operation in respect of Place and Time*, Edinburgh: T&T Clark, Law Publishers. The common law systems have not followed this approach towards the application of foreign law.

55 The 'loyalty' in question is not towards the foreign sovereignty whose law is applicable, but towards the legislator of the forum by striving to do justice in accordance with the law applicable under the forum state's rules on conflicts.

56 Von Savigny was of the opinion that the religiously oriented rules, applicable to Jews in the Christian states of Europe, would gradually vanish (English translation, ibid., p. 16).

3.2 The Challenges of Religious Law

3.2.1 Only a nation-state's law qualifies for application

By the time the 'Savignyan conflicts model' became generally established on the European continent, at the turn of the nineteenth century, there was little need to explicitly limit its application to 'the laws of civilised Christian nations'. Regulations on private international law largely originated from international conventions adopted at The Hague Conference on Private International Law and were directly applicable only among the contracting states. The forum state's right to refuse the application of foreign law, if manifestly incompatible with its public policy, enabled states to extend the convention rules to cover relations with other states too.[57] In Continental European courts, encounters with the laws of a non-Christian state could have been expected to remain highly extraordinary.

In the Continental European system of private international law, when a choice of law rule refers to foreign law, the applicable foreign law, as a starting point in all procedural aspects, is to be treated as *law* by the courts, and not as a fact contrary to the common law approach. The applicable foreign law may be of a religious origin, for example, when it is closely linked with sharia and Islam or with the canon law of the Roman Catholic Church, or with Talmudic law and Judaism. To be applicable in a dispute, however, the foreign law must qualify as *the law of a nation-state*. The sharia, Talmudic or canon law does not in itself constitute applicable 'foreign law'. A religious law receives the label of state law only to the extent that it is recognised by the state, for example through codification, or is applied by the courts and other competent authorities of the state. If the applicable law, on the other hand, grants the parties a freedom to agree on other norms, the agreed norms should qualify for application irrespective of their label as 'law', 'customs' or 'religion'. Their enforcement takes place namely by authorisation of the applicable foreign law.

In the world of a believer, religious law supersedes any laws enacted by the state. A state codification of religious law remains, necessarily, *a selection* of solutions and interpretations, as pointed out by An-Na'im.[58] This explains in part the lack of consensus in the Muslim world regarding the true content of sharia law in different situations. It also demonstrates the difficulty of codifying any religious law and demanding obedience to the codified law. The constitutions of several Islamic states explicitly recognise that state law remains subordinated to sharia. Muslim states' reservations with regard to international human rights instruments, stating that the state shall not be bound by any violations of Islamic sharia law, must be seen against this background.[59]

---

57 In Sweden, for example, The Hague Conventions ratified by Sweden in the early 1900s were made generally applicable in relation to all states.

58 The codification and enactment of certain principles as interpreted within a certain Muslim school of law (primarily the Hanafi school) became the norm in the post-colonial Muslim world, at least in family law matters, and legitimised and institutionalised state selectivity among the competing views of sharia without genuinely opening the basis of family law legislation to debate as a matter of public policy. This created a tension. According to An-Na'im Na'im (2009: 16ff.), this tension has continued into the modern era, with sharia remaining the religious law of the community of believers and independent of the authority of the state, while the state seeks to enlist the legitimising power of sharia in support of its political authority. But 'since modern states can operate only on officially established principles of law of general application, Shari'a principles cannot be enacted or enforced as a positive law of any country without being subjected to selection among competing interpretations'.

59 Kreuzer (2009) mentions reservations to the Covenant on Civil and Political Rights (1966) and the Convention on the Elimination of All Forms of Discrimination against Women (1979) as

What the believer expects to be the content of the applicable 'law' does not necessarily find support in the authoritative legal sources of the law's state of origin. In that case, together with any other 'mistakes' on the content of law, it cannot count in a foreign court either. The treatment of foreign law as 'law' in the Continental European system also means that the parties' agreement on its content is not as such binding on the court.

3.2.2 Iura novit curia *and loyal application of foreign law*

The European court's obligation to know the law according to the principle of *iura novit curia*, which in the Continental system is frequently extended to also cover applicable foreign law, cannot reasonably include foreign religious law.[60] If the parties are not able to provide the court with reliable information on the religious law's content as approved by state law,[61] how should the court proceed? According to settled European case law, in situations of failure to sufficiently prove the content of the applicable foreign law, the claim is normally either dismissed or rejected (Jänterä-Jareborg 2003: 324–33). Alternatively, it is decided in accordance with the substantive law of the forum state (ibid.). A third model is the application of a 'closely related law', whether that of a very similar legal system within the same legal family or a presumably similar regulation of another state. When a religious law is at stake, it is not evident that any of these solutions is truly suitable. One might argue, nevertheless, that the application of 'a closely related law' within the same orientation of the religion and the same school of law provides the most appropriate way out.

Another challenge is posed by the principle of loyal application of foreign law. As pointed out by Michael Bogdan (2010: 113), 'a court applying foreign law should be cautiously conservative and it must resist the temptation to "improve" the foreign rules by interpreting them according to its own preferences'. But as the selected case law shows, national courts tend to interpret the foreign rules in line with forum law or to adjust them to fit the values underlying their own legal systems. An additional challenge posed by religious law is that its traditional interpretation, according to the sacred sources, is increasingly questioned. There exists, for example, no universal understanding of any Islamic family law that all Muslims would share (An-Na'im 2009: 19). A feminist Islam, for example, is under development. Yet to qualify for application in a European court, such interpretations must find support in the authoritative sources of law in the foreign state concerned.

3.2.3 *Considerations of public policy*

The public policy reservation of private international law is the ultimate defence for the protection of the fundamental values of the forum state's legal order. Public policy constitutes the 'policy of the day', meaning that it is subject to continual reconsiderations and influenced by political trends. Ultimately, unless 'overruled' by one of the supranational European courts by reference to supranational sources, it is for each national court to set the standard. The foreign rules' religious origin should not as such qualify as an infringement

---

examples. An additional example of relevance to our topic is the United Nations Convention on the Rights of the Child (1989); on these reservations, see, e.g., Baderin (2003: 155f.).

60 See Section 1.3 above regarding why religion is a complicating factor from the point of view of a court of law.

61 It appears to have become increasingly common in Continental European litigation that the parties not only request the application of rules belonging to a Muslim legal system, but also provide the court with information about that law, in the form of text of the codification, case law, experts' opinions and, increasingly, the hearing of witnesses in the country of origin through telephone conferences, etc. This is definitely the case in Sweden, not least in the light of the disputes on *mahr*.

of the public policy of the forum state. But it cannot be denied that, for example, Art. 10 of the EU's Regulation on the law applicable to divorce and legal separation[62] is targeted at religious law. According to this provision, which is a special and additional kind of public policy provision, the law of the forum shall replace the applicable foreign law when that law 'makes no provision for divorce or does not grant one of the spouses equal access to divorce or legal separation on grounds of their sex'. Laws not providing for divorce primarily refer to laws of a canon law origin (until recently this applied to Malta in Europe), whereas laws discriminating on the basis of a spouse's sex refer to, in particular, Islamic laws.

4 Concluding Remarks

4.1 Case Law or Legislation, or Both?

It is important to emphasise that the challenges brought forth by religious and cultural diversity are not only, or even primarily, to be solved by European courts. In a legal context, the first-hand tool should be legislation, to prevent and solve situations that are commonly experienced as problematic, to define what the mandatory fundamental values of society consist of and to bring the law in line with the needs of a modern pluralistic society. In the end, however, the application of any legislation is in the hands of judges who may need to demonstrate a greater degree of wisdom and sense of proportionality than the national legislator, acting under political and populist pressures.[63] In its decision-making, a national court must increasingly take into account supranational legal sources, in particular the ECHR. European courts can be expected to encounter ever more often situations where human rights are allegedly in conflict with each other or where human rights instruments appear to collide.

4.2 The 'Foreign Law Problem'

Cross-border cases are inevitably connected with the application of foreign law. This raises the so-called 'foreign law problem', consisting of the difficulties connected with the application of the law of a foreign state (Jänterä-Jareborg 2008: 341). There exists considerable uncertainty regarding the conditions for the application of foreign law, for example whether such law is to be applied *ex officio* or only upon a party's request, whether the court or the parties are to establish the foreign law's content, what quality is to be required of the information provided on the foreign law's content, and what solution is to be chosen when its content is not proved to the court's satisfaction. An additional problem is adjusting the applicable foreign law to the forum's rules on procedure, having regard that these rules are tailored to match the substantive law of the forum in each field. The

---

62 Council Regulation (EU) No. 1259/2010 of 20 December 2010 implementing enhanced cooperation in the area of the law applicable to divorce and legal separation, in force since June 2012 in 15 Member States of the EU.

63 Regard for the interests of the parties may call for creative solutions. An example, reported at the Religare judges' seminar (Brussels, 5–6 December 2011), is that of German divorce decrees, adjusted in formal respects not only to German law, but also, in addition, to Islamic practices in order to prevent any limping family law status from arising as regards divorce and child custody. It was also argued that European courts should make greater efforts to protect *bona fides* claimants, whereas a party's *mala fides* should not qualify for protection. See further Chapter 3 by Mathias Rohe.

particular links between the foreign law and a certain religion can be expected to increase the challenges facing the court.

Very different approaches are at present followed by European courts in all these respects (Jänterä-Jareborg 2003: 236–306, Esplugues 2011). Yet commonly, in the end much depends on the parties' own activities and the efforts they are prepared (or not prepared) to make in order to have foreign law applied to the case at hand. This state of affairs has not contributed to any 'unity of result', which common rules on the choice of law (where such exist) could otherwise achieve.[64] Where religious rules are at stake, it is nevertheless difficult to perceive any other solution than placing all these burdens on the parties, having regard to the European courts' lack of knowledge of such rules and, presumably, the religion itself. The final interpretation remains the court's responsibility.

4.3 Directing the Litigation

A final point to make relates to how the litigation should be directed by the court in a cross-border dispute. Also in this respect, jurisdictions follow very different approaches, from active court interventions and supervision of the parties to a much more passive role, adjusted to the parties' pleadings, in line with the general law of procedure applicable in the forum state (Jänterä-Jareborg 2003: 258–64). The current topical demand for cultural competence among judges only makes sense, in my opinion, if its aim is to enable the judge to identify what truly matters in the dispute for the parties concerned, also with regard to the parties' cultural or faith background. It follows that whenever a court has reason to suspect, on the basis of the requests made during the litigation or the evidence or documentation provided to the court, that such a link is of relevance in the dispute, a dialogue between the court and the parties should also take place on this aspect before the court decides on the case. Such a dialogue would additionally give the parties the opportunity to supplement and amend their claims to fit into the structure of the legal system of the forum, its conflict rules included.[65] In the end, however, it is not only the law applicable to the dispute but also the law of procedure of the forum that sets the limits to what the court may take into account in its judgment.

Bibliography

An-Na'im, A.A. 2009. *Islam and the Secular State, Negotiating the Future of Shari'a*. Cambridge, MA: Harvard University Press.
Baderin, M.A. 2003. *International Human Rights and Islamic Law*. Cambridge, MA: Oxford University Press.
Basedow, J. 2009. Multiculturalism, globalisation and the law of the open society. *Revue Hellénique de Droit International*, 62.

---

64 It remains to be seen what measures the EU will be prepared to take to bring forth more uniformity in the procedural application of the Union's choice of law rules. Such rules exist in the Rome I, II and III Regulations as well as in the Protocol on the Law Applicable to Maintenance Obligations and the recently (4 July 2012) adopted Inheritance Regulation.

65 Equally, a secular-minded person is safeguarded such that he or she is not involuntarily locked into a religious set of norms. The other party's legally protected claim may, nevertheless, result in giving such norms effect, as exemplified by the many affirmative *mahr* judgments in Europe.

Bogdan, M. 2010. Private international law as component of the law of the forum. *Recueil des Cours*, 348.
Crawford, E.B. and J.M. Carruthers. 2011. The place of religion in family law: The international private law imperative, in *The Place of Religion in Family Law: A Comparative Search*, edited by J. Mair and E. Örücü. Cambridge: Intersentia.
Cretney, S. 2005. Breaking the shackles of culture and religion in the field of divorce, in *Common Core and Better Law in European Family Law*, edited by K. Boele-Woelki. Cambridge: Intersentia.
Davie, G. 2012. Law, sociology and religion: An awkward threesome. *Oxford Journal of Law and Religion*, 1(1), 235–47.
Ebrahani, S.N. 2010. An overview of the private international law of Iran: Theory and practice. *Yearbook of Private International Law*, Vol. XII.
Esplugues, C. 2011. General report on the application of foreign law by judicial and non-judicial authorities in Europe, in *Application of Foreign Law*, edited by C. Esplugues, J.L. Iglesias and G. Palao. Munich: Sellier.
Evans, C. 2003. *Freedom of Religion under the European Convention on Human Rights*. Cambridge, MA: Oxford University Press (reprint).
Ferrari, S. 2010. Introduction to European church and state discourses, in *Law and Religion in the 21st Century – Nordic Perspectives*, edited by L. Christoffersen, K.Å. Modéer and S. Andersen. Copenhagen: Djof Publishing.
Foblets, M.-C. 2007. The admissibility of repudiation: Requirements in private international law, recent developments in France, Belgium and the Netherlands, in *Integration & Retsudvikling*, edited by R. Mehdi. Copenhagen: Jurist- og Okonomforbundets Forlag.
Glazer, S. 2012. Sharia controversy: Is there a place for Islamic law in Western countries? *Global Researcher*, 6(1), 1–28.
Greve, V. 2009. Hvornår er bigamy strafbart? *Festskrift till Suzanne Wennberg*. Stockholm: Norstedts Juridik.
Jansen Fredriksen, K. 2011. Mahr (dower) as a bargaining tool in a European context: A comparison of Dutch and Norwegian judicial decisions, in *Embedding Mahr in the European Legal System*, edited by R. Mehdi and J.S. Nielsen. Copenhagen: Djof Publishing.
Jänterä-Jareborg, M. 2003. Foreign law in national courts: A comparative perspective. *Recueil des Cours*, 304.
Jänterä-Jareborg, M. 2008. Jurisdiction and applicable law in cross-border divorce cases in Europe, in *Japanese and European Private International Law in Comparative Perspective*, edited by J. Basedow, H. Baum and Y. Nishitani. Tübingen: Mohr Siebeck.
Jänterä-Jareborg, M. 2011. The legal scope for religious identity in family matters – The paradoxes of the Swedish approach, in *The Place of Religion in Family Law: A Comparative Search*, edited by J. Mair and E. Örücü. Cambridge: Intersentia.
Jänterä-Jareborg, M. and A. Singer 2012. Folkrätten i familjerätten – familjerätten i folkrätten [Public international law in family law – family law in public international law], in *Folkrätten i svensk rätt*, edited by R. Stern and I. Österdahl. Stockholm: Liber.
Jayme, E. 1995. Identité Culturelle et Intégration: Le Droit International Privé Postmoderne. Cours Général de Droit International Privé. *Recueil des Cours*, 251.
Kinsch, P. 2010. Recognition in the forum of a status acquired abroad – Private international law rules and the European human rights law, in *Convergence and Divergence in Private International Law, Liber Amicorum Kurt Siehr*, edited by K. Boele-Woelki, T. Einhorn, D. Girsberger and Symeonides, S. The Hague: Eleven.

Kreuzer, K. 2009. Clash of civilizations and conflict of laws. *Revue Hellénique de Droit International*, 62.

Loenen, T., van Rossum, W. and Tigchelaar, J. 2010. Introduction: Human rights law as a site of struggle over multicultural conflicts – Comparative and multidisciplinary perspectives. *Utrecht Law Review*, 6(2).

Mashhour, A. 2005. Islamic law and gender equality – Could there be a common ground? A study of divorce and Polygamy in sharia law and contemporary legislation in Tunisia and Egypt. *Human Rights Quarterly*, 27(2).

Mehdi, R. and J.S. Nielsen (eds) 2011. *Embedding Mahr in the European Legal System*. Copenhagen: Djof Publishing.

Menski, W. 2006. *Comparative Law in a Global Context: The Legal Systems of Asia and Africa*. Second Edition. Cambridge, MA: Cambridge University Press.

Menski, W. 2011. Islamic law in British courts: Do we not know or do we not want to know?, in *The Place of Religion in Family Law: A Comparative Search*, edited by J. Mair and E. Örücü. Cambridge: Intersentia.

Modood, T. 2007. *Multiculturalism: A Civic Idea*. Cambridge: Polity Press.

Musawah 2011. *CEDAW and Muslim Family Law: In Search of Common Ground*. Selangor, Malaysia: Musawah, Sisters in Islam.

Örücü, E. 2011. Introduction, in *The Place of Religion in Family Law: A Comparative Search*, edited by J. Mair and E. Örücü. Cambridge: Intersentia.

Riles, A. 2008. Cultural Conflicts. *Law and Contemporary Problems*, 71(3), 273–308.

Sayed, M. 2008. The Muslim dower (mahr) in Europe – With special reference to Sweden, in *European Challenges in Contemporary Family Law*, edited by K. Boele-Woelki and T. Sverdrup. Cambridge: Intersentia.

Shah, P. 2010. Inconvenient marriages, or what happens when ethnic minorities marry trans-jurisdictionally. *Utrecht Law Review*, 6(2), 17–32.

Swedish Ministry of Justice Committee. 2012. *Increased Protection Against Forced Marriages and Child Marriages* (Stärkt skydd mot tvångsäktenskap och barnäktenskap), summary in English, SOU 2012:35.

Taylor, C. 1994 *Multiculturalism, Examining the Politics of Recognition*. Princeton, NJ: Princeton University Press.

Von Savigny, C.F. 1849. *Das System des heutigen Römischen Rechts*, translated by W. Guthrie (1869) [*A Treatise on the Conflict of Laws and the Limits of their Operation in respect of Place and Time*]. Edinburgh: T&T Clark, Law Publishers.

Chapter 8
Secrets and Lies: When Ethnic Minority Youth Have a *Nikah*

Anika Liversage

Introduction

For the past two decades, many researchers have conceptualised the lives of immigrants and their descendants as unfolding in transnational social spaces, spanning the boundaries of two (or more) nation-states (Basch, Glick Schiller, and Blanc 1994; Glick Schiller, Basch, and Blanc-Szanton 1992). In such spaces, ethnic minorities often maintain strong ties to their countries of origin (Levitt 2001; Levitt and Glick Schiller 2004). These ties raise the question of the consequences when norms and practices from two different continents are thus brought into close contact. Here, Peter Kivisto argues that '[t]ransnational migrants forge their sense of identity and their community, not out of a loss or mere replication, but as something that is at once new and familiar – a "*bricolage*" constructed of cultural elements both from the homeland and the receiving nation' (Kivisto 2001: 568, emphasis in original). However, while he offers an attractive image of conflict-free amalgamation, not all norms and practices lend themselves equally well to a straightforward merger, in part because some norms and practices are simply mutually exclusive.

Drawing mainly on cases from Muslim immigrants in Denmark, this chapter empirically investigates the issue of bridging hard-to-combine norms and practices in a transnational social space. The norms and practices investigated concern matters of sexuality, with specific focus on the link between sexual intimacy and marriage. According to Islam, as well as to norms in the countries of origin of many immigrants, premarital sex is a sin. Thus individuals should be married in a '*nikah*' – an Arabic word meaning 'wedding' and 'marriage' – before they have an intimate relationship. In contrast, in a destination country such as Denmark, premarital sex is routinely practised among the majority. For a young Danish woman to await her marriage to have her first sexual experience would indeed be considered highly unusual.

With this sharp contrast in the norms and practices of 'the homeland and the receiving nation' (Kivisto 2001), the empirical question becomes what 'at once new and familiar' practices develop in the transnational social spaces of Muslim immigrants and their descendants. After all, it is difficult for young Muslim women in Denmark to both be virgins and not to be virgins when they have a *nikah*.

The chapter draws on recent qualitative interviews with individuals in Denmark who all had a *nikah*. The majority of the material stems from Muslim ethnic minority couples, but also mixed couples are represented. With an empirical focus on the circumstances that relate to *nikah* ceremonies, the chapter looks specifically at how 'secrets and lies'[1]

---

1 Secrets (hiding a part of the 'truth') and lies (misinforming) are two central strategies involved in keeping family secrets (Brown-Smith 1998; Smart 2009). 'Secrets and lies' is also the title of an

may be central strategies for individuals and families trying to navigate conflicting norms and expectations. Creative *deceptions* of various kinds (and used *vis-à-vis* a variety of *audiences*) surface as ways of negotiating the contradictions about intimate conduct that may arise from ethnic minorities' – or their majority partners' – lives in transnational social spaces today. The chapter documents how such deceptions may be used as creative strategies to protect cherished family relations through bridging norms and practices which would otherwise be difficult to reconcile.

The chapter first draws on the dramaturgical model for analysing social interaction, as developed by Erving Goffman (1959). Second, the chapter discusses why sexuality is an issue of great importance in many ethnic minority communities, and also outlines how the norms of such communities may contrast with the general practices found in the Danish majority. Third, the chapter details the qualitative material that underlies the analysis before, fourth, coming to the empirical analysis of the secrets and lies that may underlie some *nikah* ceremonies in Denmark today. The chapter ends with conclusions.

Gofmann's *The Presentation of Self in Everyday Life* as Analytical Inspiration

The concepts of 'deceptions' and 'audiences' come from Goffman's book *The Presentation of Self in Everyday Life* (Goffman 1959), in which he develops a range of dramaturgical metaphors to further his analysis of social interaction. The basic tenet is that we can understand social life as a *performance* in which we all wish to 'present' ourselves in a variety of (usually favourable) ways. Such performances are not only individual undertakings but may very often take place in *teams*. Thus a team may collectively seek to manage the impression it gives its audiences. In terms of the present analysis, an entire ethnic minority family may act as a team. Their goal may, for example, be to give a performance of being a 'good family' who are doing the 'right thing' *vis-à-vis* audiences in co-ethnic communities, as well as audiences in their countries of origin.

In this chapter, Goffman's distinction that performances are framed by different kinds of bounded regions is useful. Goffman differentiates between the *front stage*, where a particular performance is, or may be, in progress, and the *back stage*, 'where action occurs that is related to the performance but inconsistent with the appearance fostered by the performance'. A third region is *the outside*, populated by outsiders for whom the goings-on of the performance are not relevant (Goffman 1959: 82). One element of skilful impression management is to keep different audiences apart, enabling the relevant performances to be given in the relevant contexts. But when '… audience segregation fails and an outsider happens upon a performance that was not meant for him, difficult problems in impression management arise' (ibid.: 85).

As Goffman writes, 'dark secrets' of various kinds must be kept away from the knowledge of the audience, so as not to undermine and discredit the performance. Thus a team 'must be able to keep its secrets and have its secrets kept' (ibid.: 87). Family members may negotiate their shared secrets at the *back stage*, while their *front stage* performance (where the *nikah* often occurs) belies the existence of such controversies for saving face. The audiences in question will often be local co-ethnic communities, while most majority Danes belong to the outside.

---

award-winning 1996 movie by Mike Leigh, about an adopted young woman seeking the truth about her biological parents.

I use Goffman's dramaturgical approach in the analysis of young Muslim women's entry into the *nikah*. My basic argument is that the coexistence of very discrepant norms and practices regarding entry into intimate relations in transnational social fields may create considerable tension. One way of dealing with such conflict and tension can be through deceptions of various kinds. In a Muslim family a daughter may, for example, be influenced by the practices of her majority peers – e.g., beginning dating in a way that does not square well with community expectations for 'proper' female behaviour. If parents learn of such 'deviant' behaviour, several responses can be envisioned. First, parents can seek to bring their daughter's behaviour into line with community expectations. If doing so is not possible, they can either distance themselves from her behaviour through cutting her off, or they can side with her at the risk of losing their position in the immigrant community. A fourth solution, however, one less tinged with loss, is to make the entire episode look like something else. A skilful deception may thus be a way of bridging otherwise unbridgeable differences, thereby preserving cherished social relations both within and across families. According to the empirical material underlying this chapter, such deceptions may be implicated in a variety of ways for young individuals' entries into *nikahs*. While such cases of deception connected to the *nikah* ritual are deviations rather than a dominant pattern, their existence can nevertheless yield valuable insights into the lived contradictions of transnational social spaces. As a background for this analysis, the next section deals with why ethnic minority female conduct in intimate matters is often such a sensitive – and central – issue.

Sexuality – A Central Topic in Transnational Spaces

In transnational social spaces, young ethnic minority women's behaviour in issues of sexuality and intimate relationships is often seen as central, as their actions in this life domain have implications for the reproduction of the entire ethnic group over time. Thus, such young women are often seen as the carriers of country-of-origin norms and values (Mooney 2006; Yuval-Davis 1997). In the present-day Danish context, the majority of these ethnic minorities originate from Muslim countries including Turkey, Iraq, Pakistan, Lebanon, Syria and Morocco. If young women from such minority groups do not live up to expectations and veer too far from normatively prescribed behaviour, social sanctions may in some cases be harsh, including violence and even death. Such crimes are primarily perpetrated by other members of such women's families (Borchgrevink 2004; Korteweg and Yurdakul 2009; Welchmann and Hossain 2005). It is thus not surprising that rule-breaking in this life domain may lead to secrecy. Such secrecy also occurs in majority populations. Albeit an issue notoriously difficult to research, studies here indicate that over half of family secrets are sexual, including such issues as pregnancy, abuse, homosexuality, rape and promiscuity (Mason 1993 in Brown-Smith 1998; Smart 2009).

With this chapter's focus on entry into *nikah* among ethnic minority groups from Muslim countries, Islamic prescriptions regarding sexuality become a relevant issue. According to Islam, intercourse should take place only within marriage. Thus, only after a *nikah* does a sexual relationship between a man and a woman become legitimate. While relevant for all young people, the norm against sex outside a *nikah* is generally enforced more strongly for young women than for young men (Dion and Dion 2001; Samad 2010). Furthermore, breaches of this norm may affect not only the individual in question but the entire family, due to collective notions of 'honour' being intimately tied to the sexual conduct of female family members (Borchgrevink 2004; Gill 2006). Attempts to keep one's family's honour from being damaged can thus be a central motivation for *impression management* in ethnic minority communities – honour in the public domain is not lost if no one knows that trespasses against established norms have taken place.

However, the established norm that women should be virgins upon marriage may come under considerable pressure in circumstances of migration. One element is the confrontation with the different norms and practices of the majority society. The practices of the majority Danish population are a case in point: on average, young majority women have their first intercourse around the age of 16 (Nielsen 2007), an act predating the average entry into marriage (about age 32) by a full 16 years (Danmarks Statistik 2012). As the birth of a first child on average occurs when women are 29 years old (ibid.), marriage in Denmark constitutes more a way of celebrating and consolidating an already established family than the sole legitimate context for sexual intimacy (Ottosen 2011). Muslim minorities living in Denmark are thus routinely confronted with a very different way of practising intimate relations.

Another factor challenging Muslim norms of entry into intimate relationships is the different life circumstances of the Danish welfare state. While the majority of Muslim immigrants and refugees arrived from less-developed countries, often having only limited educational qualifications with them (Trænæs and Zimmermann 2004), the second generation is increasingly taking advantage of the well-developed Danish educational system (Jakobsen and Liversage 2010). As more education is also often associated with higher levels of individual autonomy – also a cherished value in Scandinavia (Prieur 2004) – this altered context may in itself affect established practices, such as marrying at young ages to partners found with substantial parental involvement.

Moreover, economic dependence on parents is lower in Denmark than in immigrant countries of origin, through the availability of Danish welfare state provisions for groups such as students, the unemployed, the ill and for single parents. As a result, the underpinnings of parental authority – including the expectation that parents should arrange or at least condone a daughter's choice of partner – may be undermined, leading to negotiations and sometimes conflicts over levels of parental involvement in their adult daughter's conduct in intimate matters.

Methodology

Empirically, this chapter rests on a broad base of qualitative interviews, the majority of which stem from 2011 when the author led an investigation initiated by the Danish Ministry of Refugee, Immigration and Integration Affairs. The Ministry especially wanted more empirical knowledge on women's experiences of 'Muslim divorces' – i.e. the dissolution of *nikahs* – in Denmark (Liversage 2012a; Liversage and Jensen 2011). While this issue has especially been investigated in the UK, where such *nikah* dissolutions may occur at Sharia councils (Bano 2009; Keshavjee 2006; Shah-Kazemi 2001), knowledge about the situation in Denmark was restricted to the situation among Pakistanis (Mehdi 2007). In the spring and early summer of 2011 we conducted interviews with 156 respondents, all of whom had experiences relevant for the ministerial investigation. The vast majority of these respondents had family histories in Muslim countries, but some majority Danish converts to Islam were also represented. Furthermore, we interviewed 13 imams and 77 professionals (e.g. social workers, police officers and ethnic consultants). Due mainly to time constraints, most of these interviews were rather brief and neither tape-recorded nor transcribed but instead reported in a note format. The second part of the empirical investigation was conducted in 2012.² It consists of 10 in-depth interviews made with Muslim women, all of whom had been partially or fully raised in Denmark, and who in 2012 were between 21 and 33 years old. These women had all had at least one *nikah*. Nine of the women's parents came from countries with family law regimes based on Islamic principles (e.g. Morocco, Syria and Lebanon). One respondent was an ethnic Dane who had a *nikah* with a Muslim man living in Denmark.

These 10 interviews were all made using a life story approach, in which respondents were encouraged to tell their story, with specific attention to entering into and, in most cases, subsequently dissolving, a *nikah*. As compared to interviews following a standardised interview guide, this approach encourages respondents to introduce topics that they themselves consider central to their life stories, rather than focusing strictly on the researchers' preconceived understandings of what should be considered important (Bertaux 2003; Liversage 2009). The interviews, generally lasting between one and two and a half hours, were subsequently taped and transcribed. A number of secrets and lies emerged in these life stories, an observation that provided the inspiration for the chosen analytical approach. As the majority of all the empirical material in both the 2011 and 2012 data collections stems from ethnic minority women, female experiences dominate the chapter's empirical section.

As previously stated, the vast majority of respondents in both data collections had had at least one *nikah* dissolved. This selection criterion gives a specific bias to this empirical investigation of *nikahs*, as the entries into these *nikahs* were frequently fraught with contradictions and tensions that were often implicated when the relationship subsequently foundered. As a lesser number of secrets and lies would likely have been present had the respondents been selected differently, observations made in this chapter should not be generalised as representing the situation among Muslim ethnic minorities more broadly. Despite these cautionary remarks, however, I find that this material offers insights into the tensions and contradictions of living in transnational social spaces, and the creative ways in which individuals may seek to handle the difficult challenges they sometimes face.

The remainder of the chapter discusses empirical examples of how secrets and lies may be implicated in young women's entries into a *nikah*. Such secrecy may occur either when women seek to hide a pre-*nikah* relationship, be involved in a *nikah* ceremony itself, or both. The article ends with two extended cases in which *nikah* rituals are part of rather elaborate deceptions regarding young women's entries into intimate relationships.

Secrets and Lies regarding Pre-*nikah* Intimate Relations

One case in which secrets and lies could occur concerned young women who wished to make their trajectories into intimate relationships appear more acceptable from a parental and community point of view.³ As explained earlier, young ethnic minority Muslim women

---

2 These interviews form part of a larger project, investigating developments in the couple formation processes of ethnic minorities in Denmark during the last decade. I want to thank student Nora Neaman for her invaluable contribution in conducting these interviews.

3 Another situation where secrets and lies may be tied to *nikahs* involves situations of polygamous unions, where a man takes a second wife. Here, the secrecy may be *vis-à-vis* different

in Denmark are often expected to refrain from having intimate relations with men until after they have had a *nikah*, as they should be virgins when entering into marriage. Furthermore, a general norm is that their fathers should give their approval to the relationships. Many young women support these norms and practices (Als Research 2011).

When family agreement exists about following the normatively sanctioned path into marriage, young women's *nikahs* can be fully planned and made public, and can be celebrated as important markers of community cohesion. Not in all cases, however, do young ethnic minority women follow such a path. One deviation may be that they – in line with the majority Danish peers – find themselves a boyfriend and have premarital sex. Doing so, however, may occur clandestinely and may thus involve both secrets and lies when young women have to create cover stories.

The far greater focus on young women (as compared to young men) being virgins when they marry is a central element in patriarchal control over female sexuality (Mernissi 1982). Thus, secret deviations from prescribed norms may create problems when a young woman subsequently wishes to marry. The conundrum of both having premarital sex and refraining from it may surface in the form of demands for 'virginity restoration surgery', a type of surgery that occurs not only in the diaspora but also in immigrants' countries of origin. Among urban middle-class women in Turkey, for example, such surgery may occur for women who subscribe to an individualised, 'westernised' lifestyle of which having premarital sex with a boyfriend is a part, but who nevertheless face family and community expectations of being 'virgins' when they later marry (Cindoglu 1997). This type of surgery can be considered a physical 'prop' (Goffman 1959) supporting women's ability to misrepresent their pre-nuptial life (Cindoglu 1997; Ozyegin 2009; see also Eich 2010). Such operations are also documented as occurring among young ethnic minority women in Scandinavia (Aamund and Uddin 2007; Essén et al. 2010) and Holland (van Moorst et al. 2012). They epitomise the contradictions, and the ensuing secrets and lies regarding sexuality, which may sometimes be implicated in such young women's intimate lives.[4]

Impression Management regarding Entry into a *Nikah*

Where secret relationships and virginity restoration surgery exemplify secrets and lies that occur before a *nikah* relationship, the entry into a *nikah* itself may also entail elements of concealment for different audiences. One reason for such deceptions involves the expectations of some amount of parental control surrounding a daughter's entry into a *nikah*. While norms may dictate that fathers in particular can control their daughters' conduct, levels of parental control are often decreasing in post-migratory life. While a young woman in a Turkish village would, for example, generally have limited unsupervised contact with the opposite sex before she – at a young age – married (Delaney 1991; Hart 2007; Liversage 2012b), in Denmark such daughters could both spend many years in the gender-mixed educational system (Jakobsen and Liversage 2010) and (in part due

---

audiences as first wives, broader family networks and state authorities. In some cases the seclusion is exactly made possible due to the distances involved in transnational social space. For more information on such matters, see Charsley and Liversage (2013). For a case of intergenerational secrecy regarding whether a wife in a transnational marriage was a virgin or not, see Liversage (forthcoming).

4   While such operations occur in Denmark as well as elsewhere, none of the respondents in this study described having had one. Indeed, some respondents strongly distanced themselves from what they perceived as the 'hypocrisy' of such operations.

to educating themselves) remain single at increasingly later ages. The tendency to marry at increasingly later ages also occurs due to severe restrictions on marriage migration, in effect in Denmark since 2002 (Jørgensen 2012; Liversage and Rytter forthcoming; Schmidt et al. 2009). Daughters' increasing levels of both education and of ages of marriage affect the intergenerational processes involved in such women's trajectories into intimate relationships.

As other studies show, ethnic minority marriages in Denmark may increasingly be formed through young individuals first – discreetly – coming to know each other before they subsequently ask their parents to 'arrange' the marriage (Liversage, Ottosen and Mouritzen under review). While the initiative leading to the *nikah* may thus rest with the young couple, a performance of parental control is given to make the situation correspond better with the established norms supposed to shape partnership formation.

Occasionally, however, young ethnic minority women (and men) may find partners whom their parents do not accept. In such cases, the *nikah* itself may be drawn into a family dispute. The empirical material had a variety of examples of young couples having a *nikah* without their parents' knowledge, after which the young couple would present this *fait accompli* of their togetherness. In such cases, there was little the parents could do to affect the situation. A variation on this theme comes from a young woman who had fallen in love with a young man:

> When I was 18, I meet a guy. At that time I had had no boyfriends, I had never been in the nightlife, I had never tried drinking – I had never *anything*. And then I met this guy who gave me so much attention. And after a short while he proposed to me, and my parents they were just *so* much against it, and thought I was too young and all ... So my engagement wasn't really one – it was almost under-cover, because I couldn't talk with my parents about him at all. He was a taboo topic in our family. But then we had a huge Islamic wedding. It was huge, because my father should demonstrate to his friends and family that nothing was wrong in this marriage. That it was fully normal, so to speak.

This statement demonstrates that the relationship began as a secret one, against the parents' wishes, but when the parents realised that they could not prevent their young daughter from marrying her chosen partner, they publicly presented the situation as one of family harmony and thus of parental sanction and control. In this way the parents could prevent a loss of face – a primary reason for making and keeping family secrets (Brown-Smith 1998; Smart 2009).

A last example of a *nikah* involving secrets and lies in order to hide intergenerational conflict over the young relationship through a show of family harmony adds further complexities. These complexities arise due to the need for 'keeping up appearances' for audiences scattered across transnational space. In this example a young woman of Turkish origin fell in love with a man from the Danish majority. After first keeping the relationship secret from her parents, the couple decided to fight for their right to be together. The Danish man converted to Islam, after which the couple had a *nikah* in secret. This exemplifies how not only ethnic minorities but also individuals from the majority may be involved in secret *nikah* ceremonies. Subsequently, the daughter broke the news of their de facto relationship to her parents. While the parents at this stage were still very much against the relationship, they did not want to cut themselves off from their daughter, and they accepted the situation and (gradually) their son-in-law. After four years, the young couple wanted to have a child. The family in Turkey, however, still knew nothing of the relationship, and with a child soon on its way, something needed to be done. Thus ensued a cover-up, both of the initial intergenerational conflict (where the daughter had 'won') and the years that had since elapsed.

The family devised the following solution: they all went to Turkey, pretending that the daughter had recently found the convert majority suitor whom her 'open-minded' Turkish parents fully accepted. The couple was therefore going to have a *nikah* and a full-scale wedding party in Turkey to 'start' their relationship. As the family believed it to be a sin to have a *nikah* for those already married, they hired an actor who (unbeknownst to the guests) was to *perform* being an imam. Thus to the team (the young couple, the parents and the actor-playing-imam) as well as to an 'all-seeing God', the '*nikah* ceremony' was simply a theatrical performance. In the eyes of the audience of the Turkish family and the other guests, however, the wedding was a full-fledged ceremony consecrating the 'newly formed' relationship of the mixed couple. This example shows both the different ways in which *nikahs* can be strategically deployed for different ends and how one deception may lead to another for keeping up appearance *vis-à-vis* a variety of audiences.

Three points run across this example more broadly. First, the events are propelled by post-migratory changes in female expectations towards and practices of autonomous decision-making, leading to intergenerational conflicts over a young woman's passage into a relationship. Second, the first-generation parents wish to misrepresent the de facto autonomy of their daughter to their co-ethnic relations, so as not to be perceived as parents who have 'lost control'. Third, it is pertinent for the team to stay 'honest' in the 'eyes of God', as deceiving the deity is not an option.

These three elements are also centrally present – albeit differently configured – in the next example of another young couple's public celebration of their togetherness. A young couple of Kurdish refugee origin had lived most of their lives in Denmark. Both coming from families in which they had had high levels of individual autonomy, they had fallen in love and begun dating without any need for prior ritualisation. When the couple wanted to begin living together, however, the family (particularly the woman's) demanded that they first have a *nikah* for the cohabitation to become socially acceptable in the Kurdish community. Both young people, however, considered themselves atheists. Thus they did not want to have a *nikah* as they emphatically did not believe in God.

They therefore chose a different solution. Before moving in with one another, the couple had a big party in which good food, music and elegant clothing made the party *look* exactly like a wedding. These props made the guests assume that the couple had just undergone a *nikah*, even though there had been no such ritual. For the parents, the most important point was that the couple's relationship to one another had now become official and that 'everybody now knew' that they were 'married' – even though this was technically not the case. Furthermore, the young couple did not have to tell a 'bare-faced lie': the audience took a prior *nikah* for granted – it was not something which they, themselves, stated had occurred.

In this case, too, the deception involved serves to bridge a gap. On the one hand is the reality of the post-migratory changes (changes in intergenerational power structures, in couple formation processes and in the religious affiliations of the second generation). On the other hand are the normative expectations of the co-ethnic community, as well as family and network in the country of origin. Regardless of the situation on the family 'back stage', the 'front stage' performance seems to be one of the adult children's respect for and obedience to their parents, religion and established home country practices. In addition, all involved took care to align a 'back stage' understanding of their performances with their religious convictions.

While deceptions such as these cases may serve their purpose at a given time, they may also lay the foundation of what can subsequently be 'said' and 'known' *vis-à-vis* a variety of audiences. They thus run the risk of being exposed – a situation that may result in a considerable loss of face. As Goffman writes, when '… audience segregation fails and an outsider happens upon a performance that was not meant for him, difficult problems in impression management arise' (Goffman 1959: 85). How the passage of time may challenge such audience segregation and thus threaten to reveal prior family team performances is one of the issues in the next case. It offers a complex example of secrets and lies set in motion at one point in time but still holding importance years later. It concerns the conception and paternity of a child, a topic which holds a central place in family secrets more generally, not only among ethnic minorities but also in majority populations, and not only today but also historically (Laslett 1977; Smart 1992).[5]

Laila's Story

Laila's parents came from the Middle East, but she was born in Denmark. The oldest of three girls, she was raised in a very liberal way and could both attend parties and drink alcohol. In her late teens, she had a secret boyfriend from another ethnic group. Subsequently she entered a relationship with a majority Dane, with whom she had an unplanned pregnancy at the age of 20.

> I was afraid of telling my mother about the pregnancy, because it was against all she had taught me: 'You should not just sleep with a man, just to sleep with him – it is first and foremost your virginity which is at stake.' So I kept the pregnancy secret for nine months. I lived with my parents, and I hid it – it was really crazy … I didn't dare say 'shit, I did something stupid – I am pregnant.' I didn't dare, because I didn't want to disappoint them. I had also been thinking some really sick thoughts – that my family would cut me off and so on. And I didn't want my father to tell my mother: 'Look! What did I tell you! The way you have brought her up has been *far* too liberal!'

When her parents asked, Laila simply insisted that she was not pregnant, and as her stomach grew, she told them that she had seen the doctor and that she just had a benign problem with her metabolism. Her ability to make this bare-faced lie for months may in itself be linked to the intergenerational situation where Laila spoke better Danish than her parents so that her taking care of her own health situation with a Danish doctor appeared credible.

After nine months, Laila went to the hospital to give birth:

---

5 While, for example, the illegitimacy of a child born out of wedlock was something to be disguised in Western Europe a century ago, also due to such illegitimacy having major negative consequences for the legal status of the child (Brown-Smith 1998; Smart 1992), today's secrets of conception and paternity more often spring either from infidelity, or are due to parents' wishes to hide their use of modern reproduction technologies such as, for example, sperm donation (Smart 2009).

> The day I had the child, I thought: 'Shall I give him away for adoption or shall I keep him?' I remember that I first decided against adoption when I held him in my arms: I thought 'no, I can't do that [i.e. give the baby away]. They can cut me off, if they want to: I'm keeping this child.' Then my sister went to get my parents, and she told them that I had given birth. It came as a shock to them ... My father forgave me really quickly. For him, it was only about what people outside would think. It was not so much about my having lied. That, however, mattered to my mother: I had broken trust with her. The most important part of my life I had kept from her for nine months ... [But in the end both parents said:] 'Why didn't you just tell us, instead of lying for nine months?'

The birth of the baby could have been concealed through Laila's giving the child up for adoption – something that historically has been the case for numerous 'illicit' children of various kinds (Laslett 1977; Smart 1992). Deciding against this option, Laila found that her parents very quickly forgave her. Next, however, the family was faced with the challenge of how to explain the arrival of the baby boy in a way that would not be totally at odds with community norms. After all, an unwed pregnancy with a non-Muslim man from the majority population was a very radical departure from community perceptions of 'proper' female conduct.

The family – acting as a team – devised the following performance: first, they made up a story of Laila having gone to the country of origin nine months earlier, having here entered into a short-lived marriage with a distant relative. She had fallen pregnant, but as the marriage had not worked, Laila had divorced her husband, and left him behind when she returned to Denmark. To give credence to this story of a non-existent country-of-origin *nikah*, Laila shortly after having given birth entered into a *nikah* with a man from the same ethnic group already living in Denmark. Having this *nikah* in Denmark was central in making the rest of the community believe in the cover story:

> [This co-ethnic *nikah*] really made the people who were saying 'where did that child suddenly come from?' shut up. Because people thought that if [Laila had fallen pregnant outside of marriage], 'her new husband would know it, and then he would *never* have married her'. And so they thought: 'what Laila's father runs around saying – that she had married somebody from [X-country] – must be true.'

The believability of this cover story was somewhat complicated by the family's joint denial of their daughter's nine months of pregnancy, a complication that made Laila's father wish she had told him about the pregnancy earlier on. As Laila really was not ready for marriage and as the couple were not in love with one another, Laila and her co-ethnic husband had their *nikah* dissolved a few months later. At the time, however, the performance had served its purpose, as the family managed to have their made-up story stick.

Five years later, Laila was living as a single mother. However, the secrets and lies surrounding her child's conception were possibly about to surface, because the Danish father suddenly wanted to see his son on a regular basis. In the interview, Laila said that her support of her son's contact with his father could unravel the elaborate family story of the (non-existent) country-of-origin *nikah*:

> My mother says 'but [Laila's son] is a known face. What if people see him with a Dane, and see that they look alike?' Then I said: 'You know what? I'm just tired of being so egoistic. I don't want to be that any more. I don't care if "they" see him, or my uncles see him or whoever sees him – he is with his father and that's it.' And then my mother said no more – she became quiet, which meant she agreed. In the end, too many Muslims care too much about what people from the outside are going to say.

With the passage of time, Laila – also growing older and more independent – was now acting in a way where protecting the family secret of her son's parentage was becoming subsumed under the importance of her son getting to know his biological father. Such genetic family relations have been attributed increasing importance over the last three decades (Smart 2009). This case has resemblances to the experiences of some young homosexuals. Because their sexual conduct is considered outside of family and community norms in certain milieus, young homosexuals may also keep their intimate lives secret from their parents. If such young people 'come out', either on their own initiative or through being found out, only the close family may come to learn (as in Laila's case) about their 'deviant' sexual lives. Subsequently, such families may thus collude in misrepresenting this sexual orientation to the broader community. At later stages in life, however, such performances may be abandoned, as the problems and complications of living such a lie are seen as outweighing the possible repercussions.

A Mixed Couple

The final example of secrets and lies related to having a *nikah* concerns a mixed couple. The husband, Michael, had Muslim parents, as his father was a Muslim immigrant from East Asia and his mother was a Danish majority convert to Islam. When in his early thirties, Michael met 24-year-old Line, a woman of majority Danish origin. While her father was a believing Christian, Line considered herself an atheist. This subsection outlines this couple's complex process of ritualising their relationship. Their case demonstrates how a variety of secrets and lies may be implicated when individuals seek to construct their private lives in desired ways while still protecting important relations, both between generations and to family members in the country of origin. While the wife in this case was a majority Dane, through her choice of partner she, too, had to negotiate the expectations of ethnic minority family members, as well as of kin abroad.

Michael and Line had both had prior sweethearts when they met in 2007. After a year, they moved in together. As they both had finished studying at this time, they went backpacking – a common experience in the 'extended adulthood' of Danish youth (Liversage, Ottosen, and Mouritzen under review; Ottosen and Mouritzen 2013). On the trip, Line and her husband went to Sri Lanka where the following happened:

> [Michael] proposed to me. And of course I accepted. And then he asked me if we could just get married right away – while we were still in Sri Lanka? I had to think a bit about it, because I had always pictured a Danish [wedding] party, with parents and girlfriends and all, but I got the idea of it being romantic – and he wanted it to be *our* day, and *our* day only, with just the two of us. So we didn't tell anybody, and we had a

traditional Buddhist wedding with gold chains around our fingers and dancers and all. It was really fine.

Despite neither of the spouses being a Buddhist, we can view their Buddhist wedding as a way of circumventing the contradictory pressures of having to choose between a Muslim and a Christian (or a secular Danish) ritualisation of their relationship. Indeed, back in Denmark, Line's father was somewhat upset about her not having opted for a white church wedding, a reaction underscoring that their choice of having a secret wedding far from their own environment may well have spared the young couple from considerable family debate over how their marriage should otherwise have been conducted.

As to the couple's Buddhist wedding, Michael's Muslim father reacted in the following way:

> He got quite confused. He didn't understand it at all – why we would do it? He thought we were playing some weird game. Later, he told us that the family in [East Asia] had seen some pictures [from the Sri Lankan wedding] on Facebook, and had asked what that was about. And [Michael's father] had told them that we were just taking part in a theatre performance.

Electronic media can, for example through Facebook, make audiences otherwise separated by the distances of transnational space become privy to a performance not meant for their eyes. In this case, the Muslim father felt the need to misrepresent his son and daughter-in-law's wedding ritual as a 'theatre performance', thereby indicating that it was not anything serious – and certainly not a Buddhist wedding, an actuality that could otherwise have led to complications with the Muslim family in his country of origin.

However, as the couple had learned from the wedding planner they had used in Sri Lanka that their Buddhist wedding ritual was not legally valid in Denmark, the couple shortly afterwards had a civil Danish town hall wedding. This ritual was necessary to make them husband and wife in the eyes of the Danish state. Michael's father then began asking when they would go to [his country of origin] to get married – an event of great importance for him and something that he told the young couple he would give them as a gift.

When the young couple decided to accept the gift, for them to have a *nikah* in the country of origin raised further complications and made necessary yet other secrets and lies. Line tells the story of the time of planning their wedding trip to East Asia:

> By that time, we already had a daughter, and for us to go to [X-country] as a family, we had to be married – in a Muslim way – and we hadn't done that. So we first had to have a Muslim wedding here in Denmark. As I had studied the five pillars [of Islam] and learned the Muslim creed in Arabic, we went to my father-in-law's mosque. We sat talking with a *müfti*, and I wasn't allowed to say that I already had a child. I really felt bad about that – it was really boundary breaking. And afterwards, I told my husband 'you must *never, ever* tell our daughter that we lied, saying that she didn't exist.' I really didn't like that.

Whilst the *nikah* in Denmark occurred two years after their first Buddhist marriage ritual, the couple at this time considered themselves an established family – for the Danish majority, the birth of a child is generally what establishes or symbolises a family (Ottosen 2011). Yet from a Muslim perspective no intimacy should ever occur before the *nikah*, a reason why their daughter's existence had to be elided. The couple is now planning to go to the husband's father's country of origin for a fourth – and last – ritualised celebration of their relationship.

This couple's complex trajectory into family life springs both from how they (with their mixed backgrounds) negotiated issues of autonomy and relatedness, and from their ability to be globally mobile. Different layers of secrecy (for example, having a Buddhist wedding without their parents knowing) and lies (of telling family members that the Buddhist ritual was just 'theatre' or refusing that they have a child) are involved. Throughout, however, the purposes have been to protect individual integrity and broader relations. As a mixed couple, they were thus creating a new, hybrid way of celebrating their togetherness and had as their first, central ritual, one in which they purposely did not choose between one or the other of the established paths of their different religious/ethnic backgrounds.

Conclusion

Using recent qualitative material, this chapter demonstrates various ways in which secrets and lies may be involved when ethnic minorities living in Denmark – or majority individuals with ethnic minority partners – have a *nikah* to ritualise a relationship. The chapter points to at least five factors underlying this phenomenon. First, sexuality is a field in which the lines separating the 'proper' from the 'deviant', or the 'acceptable' from the 'unacceptable', may be attributed great importance in ethnic minority communities. Second, very different norms regarding sexuality coexist in transnational social spaces where a Muslim focus on female virginity upon marriage encounters the very different practices of sexuality among majority Danes. Third, this coexistence of different norms and practices affects the first and the second generations in immigrant families in discrepant ways, with the younger generation often changing practices to a lesser or greater extent, and the older generation seeking to arrest such moves. Fourth, the different structural conditions after migration affect the context of sexual conduct. This is the case when young ethnic minorities, for example, participate in education and here become part of an environment where males and females with different ethnic backgrounds – including majority Danish – meet and mix. Fifth, whilst parents and their (more or less) grown-up children may have discrepant understandings of how the sexuality of the younger generation should be played out, family members still have strong bonds between them. Such strong and important relations may have children's perceived 'dishonourable' conduct (if publicly known) reflect badly on their parents, but the importance of these intergenerational relationships may also fundamentally motivate family members to seek to protect their mutual relatedness.

Such protection may take place when young women individually use secrets and lies that then add a layer of deception *between* the younger and the older generations. In such cases young women may hide having had pre-*nikah* relationships – influenced, as they often are, by the less bounded sexual conduct of their majority Danish peers. Young women may also in some cases have virginity restoration surgery, which can be considered a physical misrepresentation of a young woman's pre-*nikah* conduct, and thus may be seen as an attempt to circumvent the patriarchal control which attaches such great importance to virginity.

Secrets and lies may also occur as family team performances, made to make what goes on in the younger generation look like something else. In these cases, teams may perform a level of 'parental control' at the front stage, which does not align with the 'back stage' situation. In other cases, the misrepresentations aim at concealing illicit (i.e. pre-*nikah*) sexual intimacy, to make it appear as something that conforms more closely to community expectations.

One audience of specific importance may be the perceived 'all-seeing eye of God'. Here, individuals and teams may take great care to create performances which at once can serve their purpose *vis-à-vis* the worldly audiences whilst not breaking too fully with 'acceptable' conduct from a religious point of view. Avoidance of telling 'bare-faced lies' can be important here, for example transforming a given ritual into a de facto theatrical performance through hiring an actor to play an imam.

While such secrets and lies should in no way be taken as general characteristics of *nikahs* conducted among (or including) Muslim ethnic minorities in Denmark today, the empirical material underlying this chapter nevertheless demonstrates how some of the tensions and contradictions arising from lives in transnational social spaces may be handled through sometimes surprising and creative strategies involving secrets and lies.

References

Aamund, K. and Uddin, A. 2007. *Mødom på mode. Beretninger om skik og brug blandt indvandrerne*. Copenhagen: Gyldendal.

Als Research. 2011. *Ung i 2011 – nydanske unges oplevelse af social kontrol, frihed og grænser er*. København: Social- og Integrationsministeriet.

Bano S. 2009. Shariah councils and resolving matrimonial disputes: Gender and justice in the 'shadow of law'?, in *Violence Against Women*, edited by A. Gill and R. Thiara. London: Jessica Kingsley Publishers.

Basch, L., Glick Schiller, N. and Blanc, C.S. 1994. *Nations Unbound: Transnational Projects, Postcolonial Predicaments, and the Deterritorialized Nation-State*. Amsterdam: Gordon and Breach.

Bertaux, D. 2003. The usefulness of life stories for a realist and meaningful sociology, in *Biographical Research in Eastern Europe – Altered Lives and Broken Biographies*, edited by R. Humphrey, R. Miller and E. Zdravomyslova. Hampshire: Ashgate, 39–51.

Borchgrevink, T. 2004. *Dishonourable Integration: Between Honour and Shame*. AMID Working Paper Series. Aalborg: 2004.

Brown-Smith, N. 1998. Family secrets. *Journal of Family Issues*, 19(1), 20–42.

Charsley, K. and Liversage A. 2013. Transforming polygamy: Migration, transnationalism and multiple marriages among Muslim minorities. *Global Networks*, 13(1), 60–78.

Cindoglu, D. 1997. Virginity tests and artificial virginity in modern Turkish medicine. *Women's Studies International Forum*, 20(2), 253–61.

Danmarks Statistik. 2012. *Statistikbanken*. [Online]. Available at: http://www.dst.dk [last accessed 18 December 2013].

Delaney, C. 1991. *The Seed and the Soil – Gender and Cosmology in Turkish Village Society*. Berkeley: University of California Press.

Dion, K.K and Dion, K.L. 2001. Gender and cultural adaptation in immigrant families. *Journal of Social Issues*, 57(3), 511–21.

Eich, T. 2010. A tiny membrane defending 'us' against 'them': Arabic Internet debate about hymenorraphy in Sunni Islamic law. *Culture, Health and Sexuality: An International Journal for Research, Intervention and Care*, 12(7), 755–69.

Essén, B., Blomkvist, A., Helström, L., and Johnsdottor, S. 2010. The experience and responses of Swedish health professionals to patients requesting virginity restoration (hymen repair). *Reproductive Health Matters*, 18(35), 38–46.

Gill, A. 2006. Patriarchal violence in the name of 'honour'. *International Journal of Criminal Justice Sciences*, 1(1), 1–12.

Glick Schiller, N., Basch, L. and Blanc-Szanton, C. 1992. *Towards a Transnational Perspective on Migration: Race, Class, Ethnicity, and Nationalism Reconsidered*. New York: New York Academy of Sciences.

Goffman, E. 1959. *The Presentation of Self in Everyday Life*. Harmondsworth: Penguin.

Hart, K. 2007. Love by arrangement: The ambiguity of 'spousal choice' in a Turkish village. *Journal of the Royal Anthropological Institute*, 13, 345–62.

Jakobsen, V. and Liversage, A. 2010. *Køn og etnicitet i uddannelsessystemet – Litteraturstudier og registerdata*. Copenhagen: SFI – the Danish National Centre for Social Research.

Jørgensen, M.B. 2012. Danish regulations on marriage migration – Policy understandings of transnational marriages, in *Transnational Marriage – New Perspectives from Europe and Beyond*, edited by K. Charsley. London: Routledge, 60–78.

Keshavjee, M.M. 2006. Alternative dispute resolution in a Muslim community: The Shia Imami Ismaili conciliation and arbitration boards, in *Migration, Diasporas and Legal Systems in Europe*, edited by P. Shah and W. Menski. Oxon: Routledge-Cavendish, 73–86.

Kivisto, P. 2001. Theorizing transnational immigration: A critical review of current efforts. *Ethnic and Racial Studies*, 24(4), 549–77.

Korteweg, A. and Yurdakul, G. 2009. Islam, gender and immigrant integration: Boundary drawing in discourses on honour killing in the Netherlands and Germany. *Ethnic and Racial Studies*, 32(2), 218–38.

Laslett, P. 1977. *Illegitimacy, Sexuality, and the Status of Women*. Oxford: Blackwell.

Levitt, P. 2001. *The Transnational Villages*. Berkeley: University of California Press.

Levitt, P. and Glick Schiller, N. 2004. Conceptualizing simultaneity: A transnational social field perspective on society. *International Migration Review*, 38(3), 1002–39.

Liversage, A. 2009. Vital conjunctures, shifting horizons: High-skilled female immigrants looking for work. *Work, Employment and Society*, 23(1), 120–41.

Liversage, A. 2012a. Muslim divorces in Denmark – Finds from an empirical investigation, in *Interpreting Divorce Law in Islam*, edited by R. Mehdi, W. Menski and J.S. Nielsen. Copenhagen: DJØF Publishers, 179–202.

Liversage, A. 2012b. Gender, conflict and subordination within the household – Turkish migrant marriage and divorce in Denmark. *Journal of Ethnic and Migration Studies*, 38(7), 1119–36.

Liversage, A. forthcoming. Gendered struggles over residency rights when Turkish immigrant marriages break up. *The Onati Socio-Legal Series*.

Liversage, A. and Jensen, T.G. 2011. Parallelle retsopfattelser i Danmark – et kvalitativt studie af privatretlige praksisser blandt etniske minoriteter. Copenhagen: SFI – the National Centre for Social Welfare.

Liversage, A., Ottosen, M.H. and Mouritzen S.S. under review. Changing times – Family formation processes amongst young Turkish women and their Danish majority peers.

Liversage, A. and Rytter, M. forthcoming. A cousin marriage equals a forced marriage: Transnational marriages between closely related spouses in Denmark, in *Cousin*

Marriages: Between Tradition, Globalisation and Genetic Risk, edited by A. Shaw and A. Raz. Oxford: Berghahn.

Mehdi, R. 2007. *Integration og retsudvikling*. Copenhagen: Jurist- og Økonomforbundets Forlag.

Mernissi, F. 1982. Virginity and patriarchy. *Women's Studies International Forum*, 5(2), 183–93.

Mooney, N. 2006. Aspiration, reunification and gender transformation in Jat Sikh marriages from India to Canada. *Global Networks*, 6(4), 389–403.

Nielsen, L.B. 2007. *Ung 2006; 15–24 åriges seksualitet – viden, holdninger og adfærd*. Copenhagen: Sundhedsstyrelsen.

Ottosen, M.H. 2011. Familien., *in Sociologi – en introduktion*, edited by H. Andersen et al. Copenhagen: Hans Reitzels Forlag.

Ottosen, M.H. and Mouritzen, S.S. 2013. Patterns of partnership and parenthood. Experience, approaches and readiness towards commitment and creating a family, in *Social Meaning of Children – European Perspectives on Fertility, Gender and Social Class*, edited by A.L. Ellingsæter, A.M. Jensen and M. Lie. London: Routledge.

Ozyegin, G. 2009. Virginal facades: Sexual freedom and guilt among young Turkish women. *European Journal of Women's Studies*, 16(2), 103–23.

Prieur, A. 2004. *Balansekunstnere*. Oslo: Pax Forlag.

Samad, Y. 2010. Forced marriage among men: An unrecognized problem. *Critical Social Policy*, 30(2), 189–207.

Schmidt, G., Graversen, B.K., Jakobsen, V., Jensen, T.G. and Liversage, A. 2009. *Ændrede familiesammenføringsregler – hvad har de nye regler betydet for pardannelsesmønstret blandt etniske minoriteter?* Copenhagen: SFI – The Danish National Centre for Social Research.

Shah-Kazemi, S.N. 2001. *Untying the Knot – Muslim Women, Divorce and Shariah*. London: Signal Press.

Smart, C. 1992. *Regulating Motherhood: Historical Essays on Marriage, Motherhood and Sexuality*. London: Routledge.

Smart, C. 2009. Family secrets: Law and understandings of openness in everyday relationships. *Journal of Social Policy*, 38(4), 551–67.

Trænæs, T. and Zimmermann K.F. 2004. *Migrants, Work, and the Welfare State*. Odense: Syddansk Universitetsforlag.

van Moorst, B.R., van Lunsen, R.H.W., van Dijken, D.K.E. and Salvatore, C.M. 2012. Backgrounds of women applying for hymen reconstruction, the effects of counselling on myths and misunderstandings about virginity, and the results of hymen reconstruction. *The European Journal of Contraception and Reproductive Health Care*, 17(2), 93–105.

Welchmann, L. and Hossain, S. 2005. *'Honour' Crimes: Paradigms and Violence against Women*. London: Zed Books.

Yuval-Davis, N. 1997. *Gender and Nation*. London: Sage.

Chapter 9
'Without Our Church We Will Disappear': Syrian Orthodox Christians in Diaspora and the Family Law of the Church

Annika Rabo

Syrian Orthodox Christians (from here on referred to as the Syrian Orthodox) belong to an ancient Eastern church and live mainly in Syria, Turkey and Lebanon but also in the Western diaspora. Today, Sweden constitutes the most significant European country for the Syrian Orthodox diaspora; large numbers settled in Sweden, particularly in the city of Södertälje, in the mid 1970s. They were Sweden's first large immigrant group considered to be significantly different from native Swedes. There were, for example, public debates about the 'Oriental' and 'patriarchal' character of their family organisation and critique of the role of the church in family and everyday life.

In this chapter I discuss how family, family law and the church are debated among the Swedish Syrian Orthodox in the diaspora.[1] Although many no longer define themselves exclusively in terms of their church, it is still of enormous importance for their group identity. In order to contextualise this discussion, I begin the chapter by providing a historical background of the Syrian Orthodox in Turkey and the Middle East and take a look at the establishment of the Syrian Orthodox community in Sweden and other countries in the West. I then explore family, kinship and transnational marriage links between the Syrian Orthodox in Syria and Sweden, and I address the role of the Syrian Orthodox church and pluri-legal family law.

Today, religiously motivated practices with legal repercussions are debated and scrutinised in Western Europe mainly with respect to Muslim immigrants' customs and not so much those of immigrant Christian communities. For the Syrian Orthodox in Sweden – as for many other migrants with persistent links to their 'home countries' – such practices are linked not only to beliefs but also to legal arrangements in both Sweden and their 'home countries'. I thus conclude the chapter by discussing how the image of the Syrian Orthodox and their lifestyles in Sweden have changed in the past three decades and if lessons of pluri-legality can be learned from this particular case.

---

1   This chapter is based on material collected on Syrian Orthodox Christians through interviews and participant observation in Syria in various periods between 2003 and 2009 – in connection with a project on family and family law among transnational Syrians – and through interviews in Sweden in 2005, as well as on published material on the Syrian Orthodox (*Suryoye/Syriaan/Assyrians*) in Sweden. (For more details see Rabo 2007a, 2007b, 2011b.) This research has been funded by the Swedish Research Council.

The Syrian Orthodox – A Background

The Syrian (Syriac) Orthodox church is one of the ancient Eastern churches. It was developed after the Council of Chalcedon in 451 by those who did not accept the idea of the dual nature of Christ. Today, the patriarchal seat of the church is in Damascus and Syria has the largest community in the region (Pacini 1998: 315) with around 90,000 members. In Syria this religious community is the fourth largest Christian one and is divided between those with Arabic as their native tongue and those whose mother tongue is *Suryoyo* ('Syriac'). The former trace a very long presence in particular villages and towns or regions in the central and southern parts of the country. The latter are mainly found in the so-called Jeziira region in the north, particularly along the present-day Turkish border. To a large degree these Syrian Orthodox trace their settlement in the Jeziira to the period around World War I when – in the wake of Turkish nationalism – massacres of Christians were taking place in what is today's Turkey. WWI was a period of enormous political upheaval with ensuing population movements from Ottoman provinces into what soon came to be French and British mandated Syria and Iraq. Kurds, Arabs, Armenians, 'Syriac' and 'Assyrians' were uprooted and resettled; many more than once.

Most of the Christians who settled in the Jeziira were members of the Syrian Orthodox church. Most Armenians eventually ended up in Aleppo and Beirut, and a very large number emigrated to Europe and the USA. Members of the Assyrian Church of the East (often called Nestorians) also settled in the Jeziira in this turbulent period. Some had their origins in present-day Turkey and others in present-day Iraq. The Assyrian Church of the East is the oldest so-called Eastern church. It developed after the Council of Ephesus (431) and underlined the two clearly separated natures of Christ. In Syria there were about 16,000 'Nestorians' in the 1990s (Pacini 1998: 314). There are also Uniate/Catholic varieties of the Syrian Orthodox and the Assyrian Eastern Church in Syria. Armenians, but also Syrian Orthodox and other Eastern Christians, used Syrian territory as a stopover before migrating to Lebanon or the USA. There have 'always' been Syrian Orthodox communities in Lebanon and migration to the USA started more than 100 years ago. There are about 150,000 Syrian Orthodox outside the Middle East and Turkey.

During the French mandate, all Christians who settled in Syria were given Syrian citizenship, in contrast to many Muslim Kurds. After independence in 1946, successive governments continued this policy of favouring Christians over Kurds. The Arab nationalism of the ruling Ba'th party (since 1963) exhibits a considerable fear that a large ethnic group like the Kurds may, given the chance, develop irredentist ambitions. The Christians in the Jeziira are at times regarded as 'foreign' but they have largely been allied to the present regime. Sato (2007) claims that the Syrian orthodox underplay their links to present-day Turkey and make claims – based on archaeological evidence and by building churches – of being natives of the Jeziira. Thus the general ethnic-religious composition in the Jeziira and the links between the Syrian state and the Christians living there is quite complex.[2]

---

2 At the time of writing – January 2013 – the humanitarian and political crisis in Syria shows no signs of a quick solution. The regime still claims it is the protector of minorities against Islamic extremism while the loosely organised opposition still underlines the non-sectarian and legitimate character of the protests. Although individual Syrian Christians and a few political organisations dominated by Syrian Orthodox in the Jeziira are part of the opposition, important representatives of the Syrian Orthodox churches have largely been silent or verbally supported the regime.

The Jeziira is stereotyped in other parts of Syria as only partly civilised due to the 'tribal', 'traditional' and not very educated perception of the Kurds, Arab and non-Arab Christians who live there. Few people in other parts of Syria remember the recent history of enormous population upheaval and very quick economic change. The Christians in the Jeziira were extremely important in the development of commercial agriculture in the 1950s when vast tracts of land were put under the plough with the help of mechanised production. The cities of Qamishli and Hassake were closely linked to other parts of the world because of the wealth that agriculture generated for some. Qamishli, for example, had direct flights to Paris and Beirut. Today the Jeziira is heavily connected to, for example, Sweden through networks of migrants. The development of oil production has also taken place in the Jeziira. In the last decade, however, there has been an enormous crisis in agriculture in the Jeziira which has affected both Kurds and Christians and patterns of migration from the region. All in all, this area – not least the border zone with Turkey – has been, and still is, of great strategic importance for the Syrian regime. This also plays out in the relationship between the state, the church(es) and Syrian Orthodox society.

Syrian Orthodox in Sweden

There are between 30,000 and 40,000 Syrian Orthodox in Sweden. Some generously calculate that there are between 70,000 and 80,000 (Cetrez 2005: 29). Like Syria, Sweden does not have statistics based on the religious or ethnic affiliation of a person. Only the country of birth of residents with foreign citizenship is registered. If the Jeziira can be seen as a 'homeland' of the Syrian Orthodox in Syria, and even the Middle East, then the city of Södertälje, 40 km south of Stockholm, is their home territory in Sweden, and even in Europe. In this city the around 18,000 Syrian Orthodox constitute almost a quarter of the population; it is often called 'Little Assyria' or 'Little Babylonia' as the presence of these Middle Eastern Christians is felt in many parts of the city. Syrian Orthodox are also found in many other larger cities in Sweden, where they often live interspersed with other migrants. But they are unique in being the only group with such a strong territorial concentration. Most non-European migrants in Sweden live in suburbs which are often depicted as deeply problematic and as a symbol of segregation. But such suburbs are typically very ethnically mixed. There are no ethnic enclaves in Sweden[3] except for the Syrian Orthodox in Södertälje. This town has been crucial in the development of diasporic and transnational networks, and in the development of identity politics in Sweden. 'Södertälje', writes Rakel Chukri in the newspaper *Expressen* (2005), 'is the closest our stateless people have to a capital'.

The first Syrian Orthodox who settled in Sweden came in 1967 as stateless refugees from Lebanon. After just a few years, Södertälje had become a centre for the Syrian Orthodox community as more and more people from Turkey, Lebanon, Syria and Germany[4] joined their relatives in Sweden. Although migration to Sweden came to a halt in the mid 1970s when the labour market had ceased to have a need for foreigners, the Syrian Orthodox were quite successful in gaining residence permits through a special refugee status: so called B-refugees. There was a great backlog of persons waiting for a decision on their applications

---

3 There are many enclaves of 'ethnic' white Swedes, but they are not classified as problematic areas.

4 Among the many Turkish citizens working in Germany there were also members of the Syrian Orthodox community, some of whom joined family and kin in Sweden.

as refugees. They were allowed to stay and were given permanent residence permits but their 'refugee'-reasons were not approved of by the authorities (Björklund 1981: 114). While Syrian Orthodox from Turkey claimed that their lives were threatened in their home country because of their religion, those coming from Lebanon stressed that the civil war made it impossible for them to return.[5] Most Syrian orthodox in Sweden (or their parents) come from Turkey, but many have their roots in Syria and some also in Lebanon.[6]

In the 1970s and during part of the 1980s the *Syriaan/Assyrians* were considered as very 'Oriental', patriarchal and traditional by the Swedish majority society. And since there were no jobs to be found they were instead subjected to a number of Swedish welfare programmes (Björklund 1981: 122). In general, migrants coming to Sweden for labour purposes or as political refugees in the 1970s talked, or dreamed, about returning home. The *Syriaan/Assyrians* were different. They declared that Sweden was their new homeland because as a Christian minority they had no future – at least no near future – in the villages and towns they came from. In Sweden, on the other hand, and especially in Södertälje, they had found suitable conditions to mobilise along religious and/or ethno-nationalist lines. Many Syrian Orthodox were very happy to be settled in what they thought was a 'Christian country' and could not understand that the Swedish society had so little respect for this commonality. They could not understand why Muslims were admitted to the country and allowed to stay when so many Syrian Orthodox had great difficulties in obtaining residence permits (Björklund 1981: 118). For many Swedish bureaucrats, on the other hand, the internal splits in the community were exceedingly confusing and something which caused many bureaucrats to see the Syrian Orthodox as troublemakers. What were they to be called, for example? While some insisted that they were *Syriaan/Suryoye*, others claimed that their proper name was *Assyrian/Ashouri*.

Assyrians or Syriaan?

The majority of the Swedish Syrian Orthodox with links to southeast Turkey or the Syrian Jeziira call themselves *Suroyo* in their own language. But how to translate this into Swedish? Assyrian or Syrian? Most of the spokespersons from the Syrian Orthodox church wanted the group to be called *Syriaan* (the pronunciation in Swedish and Arabic of this name is very similar) rather than *Assyrian* since this was the common name for members of the Assyrian Church of the East. Members of this church were also found in Sweden, but not as many as those affiliated to the Syrian Orthodox Church. But other Syrian Orthodox preferred to be called *Assyrian*, indicating a wish to launch another more ethno-nationalist identity outside the fold of the church. The struggle and the conflicts around what to call the group were intense in the 1970s and 1980s (Nordgren 2006). In Södertälje – the seat of the Scandinavian bishop – the conflicts and power struggles were particularly intense and included public threats, accusations of fraud and even an attempt to burn down the villa of the bishop. In simplified terms the main bone of contention concerned the different historiographies and the historical and contemporary role of the church. The *Syriaan* see themselves as linked to a Christian and Aramaic past, while the *Assyrians* link themselves

---

5 In the 1970s many of the Syrian Orthodox coming from Lebanon had Syrian citizenship.

6 Although interviews with Syrian Orthodox living in Södertälje used in this article are with persons with direct links to Syria, the general discussions in the article are valid also for Syrian Orthodox in Sweden with links to Turkey and/or Lebanon.

to a pre-Christian Assyrian territorial past (cf. Knutsson 1982). While the former emphasise the ethno-religious aspect of their group identity, the latter emphasise the ethno-nationalist aspect. There were enormous polarisations among the Syrian orthodox not only between *Syriaan* and *Assyrians* but also between various large families involving, among other things, the control of church resources (Deniz 1999). Although important families tended to take one position or the other, many families were split into two camps. Many of the older generation were also more ethno-religious than ethno-nationalist. But the 'combatants' and the positions taken cannot be neatly delineated.

In 1994 the Patriarch in Damascus decided to set up another bishop in Södertälje and the church in Sweden was in effect split into two administrative units, each with about 12 churches and a number of youth organisations (Cetrez 2005: 59). Since the 1990s, the fierce conflicts have subsided, but the question about what to be called and to call others in the group is still very sensitive for many. As a consequence of this sensitivity it has become common in Sweden to say and write *Syriaan/Assyrians*; i.e. both names together.

Family, Kinship and Marriage

The great importance of kin and family among the *Syriaan/Assyrians* in Sweden is underlined in all that is written about them. Researchers stress the strong social and economic links between members of families and large kin groups as well as the strong symbolic importance of blood links within the group. An official inquiry from 1975 underlined that the importance of family and kin, as well as the central role of the church, made *Syriaan/Assyrians* want to settle in close proximity to each other (Socialstyrelsen 1976: 46). Ulf Björklund, who did anthropological fieldwork in Södertälje at the end of the 1970s, gives examples of chain migration from Turkey to Sweden. A few members in one big kin group initiate this move and soon they are followed by other members (1981: 98ff.). Oscar Pripp (1994: 61ff.) describes Syrian Orthodox small businessmen and entrepreneurs, underlining how family members and relatives are crucial not only as a work force in these companies, but also how relatives lend money to each other and enter into economic partnerships. Fuat Deniz looks into the ways the Syrian orthodox both maintain and change their ethnic identity in Sweden, and describes how endogamy – marriage within the group – is very common also among those who have grown up in Sweden as a way for the young to avoid conflicts with their relatives and their parents (1999: 315). Önver Cetrez conducted a multigenerational study of Syrian Orthodox in Södertälje and claims that the importance of the smaller nuclear family has increased in Sweden, but large family groups are still very influential within ethnic organisations and within the churches.

In interviews conducted in Södertälje in 2005 within a project on transnational Syrians and family law, our respondents also underlined the great importance of family and relatives. Many interviewees have vast family networks spanning many parts of the world. Syrian Orthodox living in Södertälje had relatives in Syria, Lebanon, Turkey, Iraq, the Netherlands, Germany, Belgium, Austria, Switzerland, Australia, Venezuela, Canada and the USA. Many claimed that migration to Sweden had not changed their views on the central importance of family and kinship. But the majority did actually say that the meaning of 'family' and 'relatives' had changed in Sweden. 'People are not as family-minded here as in the Middle East' one woman said. She linked this to the wish of the Syrian Orthodox to become more like 'ordinary' Swedes. Others stressed that their lifestyle today in Södertälje is different from when they had just arrived. Then they had no jobs, lived on welfare and had plenty of time on their hands. Now they all work and work as the Swedes do, and thus have less free time. While many lamented the loss of 'thick' family ties, others said it was natural that young people spend more time on the computer than with the parents; some saw the same developments in the Middle East as well. The middle-aged informants typically had close contacts with their relatives in the Middle East, but some of the young were also keen to maintain these connections. All underlined, however, that close and strong contacts and mutual dependencies with family members and relatives are what make them Syrian Orthodox. This is what really distinguishes them from the 'Swedes'.⁷

A number of those who moved to Sweden as adults said that they do not really feel at home anywhere anymore. They are not so keen to move permanently back to the Middle East, either because they fear political or religious persecution or because their close family members are now all in Sweden. Most stressed that although they liked to visit the Middle East, Sweden was their new homeland. They lauded Swedish welfare but also said that this made people less dependent on their relatives. Middle-aged women seemed to like 'the Swedish system' more than men. They had gained economic independence and felt more in control of their lives compared to the men. In many of the interviews it is not so much 'Sweden' which is talked about as the new national home, but rather Södertälje. Although some underlined that there are drawbacks to living in 'Little Assyria', most claimed that the sense of security living there outweighs the drawbacks. '*Syriaan/Assyrians* who do not like this special atmosphere move to other places in Sweden,' someone said.

One woman said that the Syrian Orthodox who do not live in Södertälje have more freedom. She claimed that the girls have more opportunities to meet and to marry men who are not *Syriaan/Assyrians*: 'here in Södertälje everybody marries from within the group', and added that girls are much more controlled than the boys: 'The girls don't dare to go on dates, to smoke, drink or go out and have fun.' But although she wanted more freedom for young women she did not want too many changes. She wanted a 'good mixture' of Syrian Orthodox customs and Swedish ones. 'The greatest problem for the Syrian Orthodox,' one middle-aged woman said, 'is that they do not live their own lives, but the lives of others.'

Many of those interviewed agreed that men and women have different views on Syrian Orthodox traditions, but there was no agreement as to whether men or women were more 'traditional'. Some of our interviewees insisted that too many Syrian Orthodox keep traditions from the 'homeland', with great differences in the upbringing of girls and boys respectively. But others stressed that it is in the Swedish diaspora that one finds the most gender-divided lifestyles. A middle-aged woman said that her relatives in the Jeziira in Syria are more 'progressive' than her relatives in Södertälje. Others agreed that gender relations have 'regressed' in Sweden. Syrian Orthodox parents do not, in general, accept that their young adult children cohabit without marriage although this is a very common habit among 'Swedes'. Girls are especially discouraged from this. One young woman with a boyfriend who is not a Syrian Orthodox said that if they moved away from Södertälje they could cohabit, but that is not possible as long as they live close to all her relatives. She complained about this, but also insisted that she liked being so close to her kin: '[T]his is the point about living here in Södertälje. You don't think about yourself but you take the reputation of your father, mother, siblings and uncles into consideration.'

A number of the younger *Syriaan/Assyrians* spoke about a gap between themselves and their parents' generation. They saw this as wider than the differences between perceptions

---

7   There is a great deal of reification of 'culture', 'our culture' and 'Swedish culture' in these interviews.

of 'traditions' among women and men. Many of these young people spoke at great length about the warmth and closeness they feel towards their parents, but they also said that their parents 'live in past'. However, in our interviews with middle-aged parents, they – on the contrary – expressed great understanding for the problems facing the young, not least in striking a balance between being a 'good Syrian Orthodox' and finding a place in Swedish society as ordinary Swedish citizens. And when it comes to the question of whom to marry – somebody from the 'home country' or somebody from Sweden – there is great unity in the responses.

The vast majority underlined that it is much better to marry somebody who has been brought up in Sweden. 'Similar background' was a key term when discussing suitable marriage partners. But what do they actually mean when saying this? A number of interviewees talked about problems which may surface when a bride or groom is brought from the 'home land'. The mentality is different, they said, and they have different life experiences. Some young interviewees stressed that today there is a certain stigma in bringing a bride or groom from the 'home country': 'they are second choice. You only do that if you can't find a partner in Sweden.' Some implied that Syrian Orthodox brought up in Syria or Turkey were more old fashioned than those brought up in Sweden. But others – like the middle-aged woman mentioned above – claimed it was the other way around. Persons espousing both these views stressed, however, that shared expectations are essential for a successful marriage. For this reason a 'Swedish' partner should preferably be Syrian Orthodox. This is easier for the family and the group as a whole. 'Everywhere people want their young to marry from within the group. This is natural,' one older woman said. One middle-aged woman recalled that in the 1980s and 1990s it had been almost forbidden for the young to marry someone who was not a Syrian Orthodox. Now people are much more tolerant, many underlined, and marriages outside the group are increasing. But there is a very clear marriage boundary which should never be crossed: all except one (a young woman) underlined that it is impossible for *Syriaan/Assyrians* to marry Muslims.

No one elaborated on why marriage to a Muslim is out of the question. This is self-evident. The *Syriaan/Assyrians* see themselves as a threatened and persecuted Christian group in Lebanon, Turkey and Syria. Endogamy has been the very basis for ethno-religious survival. At the same time endogamy has constructed strong boundaries against other religious and ethnic groups. Can this boundary be maintained today in Sweden? Can the *Syriaan/Assyrians* regard themselves as part of this new society and at the same time as a specific minority within this society (cf. Nordgren 2006: 113)? For those with a strong *Syriaan/Assyrian* nationalist engagement, the boundary can be maintained through 'ethnic' labour in the many associations and clubs available in Södertälje.[8] For others it is the church which remains the most significant symbol of *Syriaan/Assyrian*-ness.

The Syrian Orthodox Church and Pluri-legal Family Law in Sweden and the Middle East

For a majority of our interviewees the church was extremely important. 'Our church is what remains for us,' one young man said, 'it is our only common denominator.' 'Without the church we would disappear,' somebody else expressed. Marrying in the Syrian Orthodox

---

8 In 2006, for example, *Suroyo sat* started to broadcast programmes to the Middle East, Turkey and many countries in Western Europe.

church is hence a way to reaffirm their ethno-religious identity in Sweden. But in Sweden a marriage in this church has no legal effect. In the eyes of the Swedish authorities the couple is simply cohabiting unless they also perform a civil ceremony. In sharp contrast to most other religious communities in Sweden, *Syriaan/Assyrians* have not acquired the right to be legally married in their own churches.

Marriage and Divorce in Sweden

Sweden may be considered (and officially depicts itself) as one of the most secular countries in the world. But this secularism is nothing like the laïcité of France or Turkey. Until 2000, Sweden had a State Lutheran Church into which all citizens were born. At the end of the eighteenth century foreign Catholics obtained a limited right to hold mass, but it took another 100 years before Swedish citizens could convert without having to leave the country. Only in 1951 did it become possible for a citizen to leave the State Church without joining another church. In the nineteenth century, the so-called popular religious movements – Baptists, Methodists, Pentecostalists and so on – gained recognition and followers, and later also obtained the right to marry their members with legal recognition by the state.[9] When Sweden became a country of immigration – rather than a country of emigration – this right was extended to 'immigrant' churches, and with the organisation of Muslim congregations in Sweden this right was also extended to Muslim imams. Today there are around 40 imams in Sweden with this 'licence', and more than 3,000 priests from congregations outside the former state church.

All clergy with this 'licence' are obliged to follow Swedish law concerning, for example, the age of bride and groom. Since 1 May 2009, Sweden has a sex-neutral marriage law.[10] While preparing for this law the Swedish parliament also decided that the former State Lutheran Church should not be privileged over others and that its clergy would have to apply for the right to legally marry its members, just like any other religious organisation. During the preparations for the sex-neutral marriage act, public debates about 'marriage licenses' were quite intense. Many argued that 'marriage' should legally remain as the union between a woman and a man. For the first time many 'ethnic' Swedes realised that state–church relations have a peculiar history in the Nordic countries.[11] Although civil marriage became lawful in 1908, most citizens had never thought about the strange cohabitation of state and church in the last 100 years. Now many argued that Sweden must join the ranks of the civilised countries in Europe and abolish the right for religious organisations to perform legally recognised marriage ceremonies. There was pressure on the former State Lutheran Church not to apply for the right to marry. In the end the Church decided to reapply, underlining that not doing so would hint that the church was against same-sex marriages.

In 2005, one of the Syrian Orthodox bishops in Sweden asked for the right to obtain a 'marriage licence' but this demand was withdrawn in 2009. One bone of contention between the Swedish state and the Syrian Orthodox church has been that the latter accepts a lower age for marriage than the former. In Sweden you have to be 18 to marry, but Syrian

---

9   It is actually not a church that has the right to 'legally' marry but individual clergy.

10 § 1 of the Swedish marriage code (1987: 230) has been changed (2009: 253). Rather than stating that 'marriage is a union between a woman and a man' it now states (in an approximate translation): 'The two entering into marriage become each other's spouses'.

11 In addition to Sweden, Norway also abolished the State Lutheran Church in January 2013.

Orthodox Canon Law accepts marriage between 16-year-olds or – at the recommendation of a priest – even younger. When I interviewed a bishop in Södertälje in the fall of 2005 he stressed the importance of the autonomy of the church. He did not want to be ruled by the 'Swedish Prime Minister'. He also said that having to follow Swedish law might force him to marry two homosexuals: 'This I cannot accept.' Until today, thus, all Syrian Orthodox in Sweden who marry in their church also have to perform a civil marriage if they want to ensure that they are married according to Swedish law. Some of those we interviewed in Södertälje who stated that cohabitation was not socially possible, admitted that they had only married in church and were thus cohabitants from a Swedish legal point of view. A few realised, during the course of this research, that if their spouse died or if they separated they would not be protected by Swedish law. Cohabiting couples in Sweden have to write a will to protect their partner in case of death. Swedish inheritance law is heavily 'spouse oriented'. The surviving spouse receives half the estate as 'marriage-estate', inherits a quarter and has lifetime usufruct rights to the remaining estate, unless there are children of the dead spouse only. They have the right to get their legal share on the death of their parents. This 'spouse orientation' is not found in Syria, Lebanon or in Turkey.

Our interviewees wanted their church to be 'legally' recognised. 'Why should we be the only Christians who have to marry twice?' Nobody wanted to get married in a registry office only. But some who had been living in other European countries where no church ceremony is legally binding for the state were quite used to 'double' marriages. While the bishop I interviewed wanted more power and legal autonomy for his church, this was not demanded by our interviewees. Divorce is an issue where the clergy and the lay-persons differ sharply. In the Syrian Orthodox church it is possible to divorce but only for certain very limited reasons. Many of the interviewees in Södertälje expressed that although 'Swedes' divorce too easily the *Syriaan/Assyrians*, on the other hand, are at the mercy of the clergy.

Under Swedish law divorce is a purely civil and not a religious institution. Like inheritance and custody it is regulated by state law. It is based on 'no-fault' and emphasises cooperation between the parents if there are children in the marriage.[12] Syrian Orthodox with a Swedish citizenship or residence permit can file for divorce; in fact this civil divorce is the only one legally recognised by the state. But a Syrian Orthodox divorced according to Swedish law and not according to Syrian Orthodox Canon Law will not be allowed to marry in his or her church again. And divorce is also where the transnational links to the Middle East become quite apparent.

Marriage and Divorce in the Middle East

In 1926 all reference to religion was taken away from 'family law' in Turkey through the adoption of the Swiss civil code. In one sweep laïcité was introduced and forced on citizens.[13] Since then marriage between, for example, a Syrian Orthodox living in Sweden with Swedish citizenship and a Syrian Orthodox Turkish citizen typically involves the national 'secular' laws of the two sovereign states. In terms of remarriage in a church ceremony the same applies as discussed for Sweden: the church will have to approve of

---

12 For comparisons between divorce law in Sweden and other EU countries see http://ec.europa.eu/civiljustice/divorce/divorce_ec_en.htm [last accessed 18 December 2013].

13 For a very interesting account of the fascinating history of the development of Turkish family law from the Ottoman period to the 1920s see Aydın (2010).

a divorce in its own court. If a Syrian Orthodox living in Sweden wants to marry a Syrian Orthodox from Syria and Lebanon, the situation, however, is very different. In Syria and Lebanon, unlike Turkey and Sweden, Syrian Orthodox Canon law is part of the law of the land and not only a question of 'informal' arrangements.

In Syria there is a Personal Status Law covering questions of marriage, divorce, parentage, custody, legal capacity, wills and inheritance. The Personal Status Law in Syria is mainly based on Hanafi jurisprudence. It is not a direct outgrowth of *fiqh* and applies to all citizens. Christians, Druze and Jews,[14] however, are allowed – obliged really – to apply their own religious rules for betrothal, marriage, divorce and the dissolution of marriage in their own religious courts.[15] This legal pluralism is inherited from the Ottoman period when various *millet* – different nationalities or religious minorities – had the right to regulate their own affairs (cf. Rabo 2005, 2011a). In Syria today the 11 different recognised churches have the exclusive right to marry their members, and all Christians must marry in church. A civil marriage contracted abroad will not be recognised by the Syrian state. In Lebanon there is no national 'family law' at all. Instead, the 18 different recognised Christian and Muslim sects have their own Personal Status Law and regulate their own affairs. But if a couple marries civilly abroad they can register their marriage in a civil court.

In both Syria and Lebanon a Christian couple wanting to divorce (or dissolve their marriage in case of Catholics) must go to their own church court. The procedure is typically long drawn out and complicated, but if the court decides to divorce the couple (or to dissolve the marriage) this is then registered with the civil authorities. A religious divorce/dissolution also enables the woman and the man to remarry. For the Syrian Orthodox in the diaspora a 'religious' divorce is needed if they want to remarry in their own church in their country of origin (or the origin of their spouse) or the country of settlement. A Syrian Orthodox couple who marry in Syria or Lebanon and later divorce in France or Sweden are thus still married in the Middle East. Remarriages and children born in these marriages are not legally recognised in the 'home countries'. For persons who make a clean break with their native countries this is perhaps not an enormous problem, but most Syrian Orthodox are deeply embedded within transnational networks of kin and family. This legal ambiguity creates stress and difficulties for many Syrian Orthodox in the diaspora. Muslims from Syria and Lebanon do not face such difficulties. Civil marriages or civil divorces abroad are easily recognised under private international law and quickly registered in the 'home country'. The difficulties transnational Middle Eastern Christians face in comparison to transnational Muslims are largely overlooked in European debates.

The Good Family and the Good Family Law

In 2003 a new marriage act was adopted by the Norwegian Parliament. Since then the bride and groom have to declare before they can get married that they are doing so by their own free will. They also have to sign a paper stating that they give their partner equal right to

---

14 There are almost no Jews left in Syria but they remain a category in the Personal Status Law. The Druze are a heterodox Muslim group found in Lebanon, Syria and Palestine.

15 Since 2010 Syrian Orthodox religious courts in Syria also handle inheritance issues. Sons and daughters now inherit the same share. The various Catholic sects obtained this right in 2006 by pushing for the equal inheritance of sons and daughters. In 2010 the considerably larger Greek Orthodox and Syrian Orthodox churches followed suit.

divorce, which is given to the civil registry (Thorbjörnsrud 2005: 17).[16] This new law was adopted very quickly without the usual consulting of experts and organisations typical of the Nordic countries. The new law came as an initiative by an organisation called Human Rights Services which had launched a campaign depicting so-called limping marriages (where a divorce is recognised in one jurisdiction only) as an enormous problem among Muslim women in Norway.[17] By making all couples sign a paper acknowledging the equal right to divorce they claimed that this problem would be solved. However, it was not Muslims but Christians and Jews in Norway who were most outraged by the new law. For many Christians, marriage is a sacrament and it is not possible for believing Catholics, for example, to sign a paper about a possible future divorce. The Catholic Church in Norway actually made a form where those marrying in church declare that the declaration given to the Norwegian civil authorities does not include their own marriage vow. The Pope called the Norwegian prime minister and protested by saying that this new law was an attack on the constitutionally sanctioned freedom of religion in Norway (Christoffersen 2006: 116). While members of the Norwegian parliament wanted to solve the problem of limping marriages they had not realised that informal plurality of family law exists in Norway (Thorbjörnsrud 2005: 17). The members also seemed ignorant of the fact that while divorce is allowed in all countries with a Muslim majority, this is not the case in all countries with a Christian majority. Malta is a case in point.[18]

'Limping marriages' are, of course, not a new issue in Europe, but a well-known legal and a social problem, exacerbated by the reluctance of many countries to sign the Hague Convention on the Recognition of Divorces and Legal Separations (cf. McGlynn 2006: 155ff.). Although the Nordic countries were 'early reformers' of family law (Melby et al. 2006), the authorities seem to have forgotten the slippery interface between national and private international law. We can, I think, talk about a legal amnesia in the Nordic countries when it comes to a serious discussion about 'formal' and 'informal' legal pluralism in national and international contexts. Today there is an urgent need to address this amnesia when many citizens can be considered to be part of transnational families. Sweden has not followed Norway in passing a law specifically directed against specific immigrant categories. Nor has Sweden followed Denmark in passing new and very tough restrictions on family reunion. Since 2002 'hundreds of Danish citizens have moved to Sweden' (Rytter 2007: 175) because of this new law.[19] But although Sweden might stand out as more 'liberal' and less nationalistic than Denmark and Norway, there is still a strong link between dominant discourses on the good and normal family and good family law (Rabo 2009).

'Swedish' discourses on the good family and good family law obviously threaten the morality of many Syrian Orthodox clergy, who imply that 'Sweden' encourages 15-year-olds to have sex but punish their church for accepting marriage before the age of 18. For the Syrian Orthodox in the diaspora these conflicting messages lead to more family problems, the bishop said. In my interview with him he stressed that the religious court was an instrument for family reconciliation. 'Many times we have been able to solve difficult

---

16 See the Marriage Act, Chapter 2 Section 7 l.
17 This organisation can only be described as Islamophobic. See http://www.rights.no/publisher/publisher.asp?id=1 [last accessed 18 December 2013]. See also Hagelund (2008: 76–8).
18 In May 2011 a majority of the Maltese voted for divorce in a non-binding referendum.
19 The very close legal harmonisation in family law between the Nordic countries has in this way been disrupted. This, I think, puts the discussions on 'national culture' and family law harmonisation within the EU in an interesting light. (See, for example, Antokolskaia 2007 and 2009.)

problems that the Swedish authorities have not been able to handle,' he said. But many of the lay persons in our study felt that the religious court was not impartial and some of the young were totally against the court: 'the church should not handle family problems. There are therapists and other lay people with professional skill to turn to. It is not good to bring such things to the priests.' Perhaps one can conclude that although many Syrian Orthodox endorsed the centrality of their church ('without it we will disappear'), the same cannot be said for how they view the church court.

From Patriarchal Orientals to 'Best in Class'

Much has happened in Sweden in the last three decades for the *Syriaan/Assyrians* and how they are regarded by the majority society (Rabo 2007a, 2007b). The 'Oriental' stigma attached to them in the 1970s has now been shifted to migrants and refugees from Kosovo, Somalia and Iraq, and a rather widespread Islamophobia has worked in favour of the Middle Eastern Christians. 'Today we are one of the minority groups which have been most successful in merging our traditions and our new homeland. In a few decades we have gone from being pizza-bakers[20] to becoming entrepreneurs and people with higher education,' Rakel Chukri (2005) states in her article in the newspaper *Expressen*. The title of the article is 'Best in Class'. Chukri underlines that the *Syriaan/Assyrians* have become mainstream in Swedish society. They have adapted to Sweden and also adopted Sweden as their new home country. Even those struggling for a New Free Assyria between the Euphrates and the Tigris underline that Sweden is and will be the most important territory for a long time to come. Many *Syriaan/Assyrians* in our interviews expressed how thankful they are because Sweden has provided a safe haven for them and a base from which their language has been developed and can be freely spoken, and a base from which their church(es) and organisations can flourish. It is, however, important to underline that this success is founded on strategies of both assimilation and ethnic closure. The Syrian Orthodox have mixed and mingled with majority society and patterned their organisations on 'the Swedish model'. However, they have simultaneously maintained their ethnic and religious uniqueness by largely choosing marriage partners from within their own group.

The example of the Syrian Orthodox community in Sweden is interesting from many points of view. Legal pluralism in some sense is obviously found in every society, but this case underlines that the awareness of its repercussions for family arrangements may be quite limited among both majority and minority groups. The Swedish majority population is generally unaware that for the Syrian Orthodox legal and religious aspects of family life are tightly linked. And although many Syrian Orthodox in Sweden are transnationally linked to the Middle East through marriage and kinship they are not always fully aware of how this might legally affect them. Marriages between members of the diaspora diminish some of the legal difficulties they are facing today. The case of the *Syriaan/Assyrians* furthermore shows that 'adjustment' is a two-way process and that strong diasporic organisations may indeed facilitate the sense of feeling at home in a new country. It also shows that very negative images spread about migrant communities can change, given time.

The complexities of contemporary international migration have been important in rekindling research interest in family and kinship relations in Sweden. But despite this,

---

20 Many *Syriaan/Assyrians* opened small restaurants making pizza or kebab (cf. Pripp 1994, 2001) and both these 'immigrants' have become Swedish national dishes.

and despite the lively debate about different possible ways to 'do family' in Sweden today, depictions of the Swedish family are still fundamentally based on ideas of ethnic and religious homogeneity. There is a deep division between research and public debates about *Swedish* families and research and debates about *migrant families in Sweden*. Although every fifth person in the country is born – or has at least one parent born – outside Sweden, they are seldom viewed as part of Sweden or as representing contemporary Swedishness. From that point of view not much has changed since the first Syrian Orthodox arrived in Sweden more than four decades ago.

Bibliography

Antokolskaia, M. 2007. Harmonisation of family law in Europe. A historical perspective, in *Convergence and Divergence of Family Law in Europe*, edited by M. Antokolskaia. Antwerpen: Intersentia, 11–24.

Antokolskaia, M. 2009. Family law and national culture. Arguing against the cultural constraints argument, in *Debates in Family Law around the Globe at the Dawn of the 21st Century*, edited by K. Boele-Woelki. Antwerpen: Intersentia, 37–51.

Aydın, M.A. 2010. Family law in Turkey. The journey from Islamic law to secular law, in *Familj, religion, rätt. En antologi om kulturella spänningar i familjen – med Sverige och Turkiet som exempel*, edited by A. Singer et al. Uppsala: Iustus förlag, 163–83.

Björklund, U. 1981. *North to Another Country. The Formation of a Suryoyo Community in Sweden*. Stockholm: Stockholm Studies in Social Anthropology.

Cetrez, Ö.A. 2005. *Meaning-making Variations in Acculturation and Ritualization. A Multi-generational Study of Suroyo Migrants in Sweden*. Uppsala: Acta Universitatis Upsaliensis.

Christoffersen, L. 2006. Intertwinement. A new concept for understanding religion–law relations. *Nordic Journal for Religion and Society*, 2, 107–26.

Chukri, R. 2005. Vi assyrier/syrianer är bäst i klassen, *Expressen* 20 September 2005.

Deniz, F. 1999. *En minoritets odyssé. Upprätthållande och transformation av etnisk identitet i förhållande till moderniseringsprocesser. Det assyriska exemplet*. Uppsala: Uppsala universitet.

Hagelund, A. 2008. 'For women and children'. The family and immigration politics in Scandinavia, in *The Family in Question. Immigrant and Ethnic Minorities in Multicultural Europe*, edited by R. Grillo. Amsterdam: Amsterdam University Press, 71–88.

Knutsson, B. 1982. *Assur eller Aram – språkligt, religiös och nationell identifikation hos Sveriges assyrier och assyrier/syrianer*, SIV Rapport nr 4/82. Statens invandrarverk.

McGlynn, C. 2006. *Families and the European Union. Law, Politics and Pluralism*. Cambridge: Cambridge University Press.

Melby, K. et al. 2006. *Inte ett ord om kärlek. Äktenskap och politik i Norden ca 1850–1930*. Centrum för Danmarksstudier: Makadam förlag.

Nordgren, K. 2006. *Vems är historien? Historia som medvetande, kultur och handling i det mångkulturella Sverige*. Umeå: Umeå universitet.

Pacini, A. 1998 (ed.). *Christian Communities in the Middle East*. Oxford: Clarendon Press.

Pripp, O. 1994. *Att vara sin egen. Om småföretagande bland invandrare – mönster, motiv och möten*. Tumba: Mångkulturellt Centrum.

Pripp, O. 2001. *Företagande i minoritet. Om etnicitet, strategier och resurser bland assyrier och assyrier/syrianer i Södertälje*. Tumba: Mångkulturellt Centrum.

Rabo, A. 2005. Family law in multicultural and multireligious Syria, in *Possibilities of Religious Pluralism*, edited by G. Collste, Linköping: Linköping University Electronic Press, 71–87.

Rabo, A. 2007a. 'Familjen betyder allt' eller 'Vi blir snart lika kalla som svenskarna'. Assyrier/syrianer i Södertälje, in *Globala familjer. Transnationell migration och släktskap*, edited by M. Eastmond and L. Åkesson. Riga: Gidlunds förlag, 205–29.

Rabo, A. 2007b. Gränslösa familjer – gräns(lös) kontroll, in *Transnationella rum. Diaspora, migration och gränsöverskridande relationer*, edited by E. Olsson et al. Umeå: Borea, 137–64.

Rabo, A. 2009. Den goda familjen och den goda familjerätten. Debatter om lag och moral i det mångkulturella Europa. *Socialvetenskaplig tidskrift*, 16(3–4), 300–319.

Rabo A. 2011a. Legal pluralism and family law in Syria, in *Legal Pluralism and the Problem of Justice*, edited by W. Zips and M. Weilenmann. Münster: Lit-Verlag, 213–34.

Rabo, A. 2011b. Syrian transnational families and family law, in *From Transnational Relations to Transnational Laws*, edited by S. Ali et al. Aldershot: Ashgate, 29–49.

Rytter, M. 2007. Giftermål över gränserna. Arrangerade äktenskap bland dansk-pakistanier i Malmö, in *Globala familjer. Transnationell migration och släktskap*, edited by M. Eastmond and L. Åkesson. Riga: Gidlunds förlag, 175–204.

Sato, N. 2007. Histoire et identité. Le cas des chrètiens syriaques orthodoxes dans la Jazira, in *La Syrie au présent. Reflets d'une societé*, edited by B. Dupret et al. Sindibad: Actes Sud, 131–9.

Socialstyrelsen. 1976. *I utlandet Sverige. En presenation av kristna flyktingar från Mellersta Östern och Turkiet*. Stockholm.

Thorbjörnsrud, B.S. 2005. Innledning, in *Evig din? Ektesaps- og samlivstradisjoner i det flerreligiösa Norge*, edited by B.S. Thorjörnsrud. Oslo: Abstrakt forlag, 7–33.

Waerstad, T.L. 2006. *Retten til ikke å bli diskrimineret ved skilsmisse. En rettsantropologisk studie av skilt muslimske innvandrerkvinner i Norge*. Kvinnerettslig skriftserie nr 64. Avdeling for kvinnerett: Universitetet i Oslo.

Chapter 10
Religious Divorce in England and Wales: Religious Tribunals in Action

Gillian Douglas, Russell Sandberg, Norman Doe,
Sophie Gilliat-Ray and Asma Khan

Introduction

Maleiha Malik (2012: 23) has given the term 'minority legal orders' to those minority groupings that possess both a set of distinct and concrete norms regulating social relationships and behaviour, and a coherent mechanism for identifying, changing and enforcing these norms. The question of how far such groupings should be 'recognised' or 'accommodated' by the state has become an important issue in civic society, triggered in particular by a highly publicised and controversial lecture given by the Archbishop of Canterbury at the Royal Courts of Justice in 2008 (Williams 2008), which was followed soon after by an equally important speech delivered by the Lord Chief Justice (Phillips 2008).

Particular concern has been expressed in relation to the possibility of religious tribunals – mainly Shariah councils – making what purport to be legally binding rulings on family or criminal matters, which would run counter to the ethos and values of wider society. So, for example, in order to forestall such a development, a bill – the Arbitration and Mediation Services (Equality) Bill (HL Bill 72) – was introduced by Baroness Cox into the House of Lords in 2011. This Bill would prevent any religious arbitrator from applying gender discriminatory rules (such as that a woman's evidence is 'worth' less than that of a man). It would criminalise any person who 'falsely purports to be exercising a judicial function or to be able to make legally binding rulings, or … otherwise falsely purports to adjudicate on any matter which that person knows or ought to know is within the jurisdiction of the criminal or family courts' and it would make it clear that 'any matter which is within the jurisdiction of the criminal or family courts cannot be the subject of arbitration proceedings.'[1] John Eekelaar has commented that it 'is by no means easy to discern the scope of these provisions' (2011: 1212), but the aim of the measure appears to be to reassert the preeminent authority of civil law in response to the demands by some religious representatives for greater autonomy to oversee the lives of their adherents, particularly in matters of family status and conduct within relationships.

Ayelet Shachar (2001, 2010) has noted that such demands increasingly revolve around the regulation of women and the family. She points out that family law occupies a space where identity, autonomy and privacy meet. On the one hand, in liberal society, the family represents and sits within the private sphere, with state 'intervention' requiring special

---

1 In response to pressure from lawyers who have recently established an arbitration service dealing with financial issues on divorce, Baroness Cox undertook, during the second reading debate on the Bill, to remove the reference to family courts but she stated that the non-discrimination provisions of the Bill would continue to apply. See Hansard, HL Debs, 19 October 2012, col 1684.

justification. On the other, it raises matters of status (marriage, legitimacy), ascription of legally enforceable rights and obligations (to support, for example) and concerns by the state regarding the well-being of its citizens (such as for the welfare of children, and the financial position of families and their individual members). So, the question of whether religious communities should be permitted to make decisions affecting the civil legal position of their adherents is particularly acute in relation to family matters, and especially regarding divorce, which entails both determining the marital status of those involved, and the consequences of the ending of their marital relationship regarding both finance and property and arrangements for their children.

The academic and political debates on these issues have taken place in the absence of much empirical information about how religious tribunals operate. While there have been some valuable studies of Shariah councils (Shah-Kazemi 2001, Bano 2007, Bowen 2012), there does not appear to have been any empirical study of the working of Catholic or Jewish tribunals in England and Wales until the study reported here. This chapter presents some findings from a small qualitative study (Douglas et al., 2011) into the workings of three tribunals from different religions, and the views of those who staff them, in handling religious divorces and annulments. The aim was to explore the relationship between civil and religious law, in order to help fill this evidence gap. This chapter concentrates on how the tribunals handled their work, focusing on their determination of religious marital status; the degree of their interaction with wider social norms and values; and their understanding of their relationship to the state and to civil law.

Elucidating what these religious tribunals actually do demonstrates that it is important to distinguish between two key functions – the grant of status (e.g. by terminating a marriage) and dispute resolution (e.g. the settlement of arrangements to govern the parties' post-marital life) – and that the former function is in fact the more significant activity presently engaged in by them. Evidence is also presented to show how these religious tribunals operate *within* and not apart from their wider social context and how their rulings and approach to their role are influenced by that context. Thus, some empirical support is found for Shachar's argument for a 'joint governance' approach under which constructive engagement between religious bodies and the state has the potential to encourage them to produce a more dynamic, context-sensitive and moderate interpretation of their religious tradition, rather than ignoring them and driving them underground, which may lead to a 'reactive culturalism' in which they retreat into greater fundamentalism and conservatism to preserve their difference from the majority culture (Shachar 2001: 35–7, Chapter 6). Finally, it is shown that, far from making claims to assert their jurisdiction over adherents, those working in the religious tribunals in the study were acutely conscious of the primacy of state law and sought no greater legal 'recognition' from the state. Rather, what they wanted was to continue to be able to provide a service for those of their faith which met a religious need and validated users' sense of their religious and communal identity. Given the chronic failures of the state 'family justice system' to deliver a service which meets the needs of its users, as shown by a long line of enquiries and commissions into the workings of the family courts, including most recently the Family Justice Review (Norgrove 2011), it is hard to argue that such a wish is unreasonable.

Models of Accommodation of Religious Tribunals and Norms

In discussing the accommodation of religious norms, this paper draws on Jeremy Waldron's discussion of 'accommodation' as embracing 'accommodation within a modern legal system of the norms and requirements of [a minority's] culture or religion or of the law associated with their culture or religion ... [occurring] within a framework of a comprehensive system of law in a modern democratic state.' He suggests it could embrace exemptions from generally applicable prohibitions or requirements, or giving legal effect to transactions (such as types of marriage) structured and controlled by norms other than those of the general law, but he would exclude the devolution of government in the sense of a separate legal system, and thus sees accommodation 'within the framework of a *single overarching* legal system associated ... with a single state in control of the legitimate means of coercion' (Waldron 2010: 103–4).

This is not what some have called for, especially those who advocate an overt system of legal pluralism under which those of differing faiths are governed by separate personal laws, such as in India, Malaysia, Singapore or Israel. In such jurisdictions, each (or some) religious group is given recognition by the state to provide and enforce laws regulating aspects of the lives of their adherents, although the state may require the institutions applying these laws to comply with particular requirements, for example, that all *nikah* marriages must be registered (see Pearl and Menski 1998: 36–43 and 149–53).

In addition to a system of separate personal laws, many commentators have described and/or advocated other forms of possible relationship between state and religious laws (Fournier 2010, Ahdar and Aroney 2010, Budziszewski 2010, Eekelaar 2013). Rather than identify ideal theoretical types, two other models can be empirically observed in England and Wales, which may be termed the 'cohabitation' and 'integration' models (Douglas et al. 2013).

Under the 'cohabitation' model, the state ignores the religious dimension of the activity for the adherent and simply applies the civil law equivalent to their situation, with no recognition of the religious code. This is the position with private *nikah* or other religious marriage ceremonies in England and Wales currently. People may go through the religious process and may believe that they are married in the eyes of the state, but they are not (see *Gandhi v Patel* [2002] 1 FLR 603; *A-M v A-M (Divorce: Jurisdiction: Validity of Marriage)* [2001] 2 FLR 6). Thus, not only do the systems 'cohabit' in the sense of occupying parallel spaces with each other, but religious systems are also in the position of non-recognised cohabitants (and indeed, literally, those who undertake such religious marriages are simply treated as cohabitants by the civil law).

By contrast, the 'integration' model is that which is provided by English marriage law in its acceptance of religious *rites* as giving rise to a legally recognised marriage (so long as certain prescribed preliminary requirements are fulfilled, such as the presence of witnesses and an authorised celebrant). The effect is one of 'integration' because, while enabling these and other religions to bring about a marriage which is recognised both by state and religious authorities, the *consequences* thereof remain governed by the civil law. Thus, as far as the civil law is concerned, what is being created and recognised is an English legal marriage – not a Jewish, Catholic or Muslim one (and so far as English law is concerned, then, Jews cannot divorce each other by mutual consent; Catholics cannot exclude each other from divorcing at all; and Muslim husbands domiciled in England and Wales cannot form actually polygamous marriages).

There have, however, been claims that Muslims should be given the same recognition of their religious norms as is enjoyed by other religions or cultural minorities, as if a type of separate personal law system already operated in jurisdictions such as England and Wales. In particular, there have been claims that Jews have been given such special recognition. For example, Tariq Modood (2010: 36) has commented on the Archbishop's speech that he 'was thinking about how the work of the existing Shari'a councils (which adjudicate on personal and civil matters such as divorce) could be extended and given legal recognition in the way that their Jewish equivalents have enjoyed for decades or longer.' Such claims appear to be based on a misunderstanding of the working of the Arbitration Act 1996 and especially the Divorce (Religious Marriages) Act 2002 (which inserted s 10A into the Matrimonial Causes Act 1973). In fact, recognition and enforcement of arbitral awards is open to any system of arbitration which conforms to the statutory requirements set out in the 1996 Act, and both the London Beth Din *and* the Muslim Arbitration Tribunal operate within its terms, *in relation to property and financial but not family* matters (Douglas et al. 2011: 16–21). And s 10A of the 1973 Act operates to delay the grant of a decree absolute of divorce until the requirements for a Jewish *get* have been completed, but does not 'recognise' that *get* as having any effect, in civil law, on the marital status of the parties.

This kind of error may reflect a failure to understand fully the experience and position of other religions – or to understand the law relating to them – but it is worth considering how such religions, which faced much greater legal disability and discrimination in the past, now operate within the broader society when debating the specifics of claims regarding Shariah law, and it was for this reason that this study examined the workings of a Jewish and Catholic religious tribunal alongside a Shariah council.

Methodology

The study focused on the work of three particular religious tribunals: the Shariah Council of the Birmingham Central Mosque, the London Beth Din of the United Synagogue and the National Tribunal for Wales of the Catholic Church. It is not claimed that these tribunals are typical or representative. Indeed, the Shariah Council, in particular, appears to be quite unusual in the 'liberal' approach that it takes to its work, not least by including a woman member on its panel. Moreover, there was difficulty in negotiating the degree of access to informants and, in the end, we were able to complete in-depth interviews with only three (rather than the intended five) informants from each tribunal. All interviews were fully transcribed and analysed using NVivo. We were also able to hold a workshop with representatives from all three tribunals to discuss their work with us and each other; we observed 27 hearings in the Shariah Council and we also analysed two years' worth of statistical data given to us by the National Tribunal. The nature of processes in the National Tribunal and the Beth Din meant, unfortunately, that we were not permitted to observe these.

Religious communities are heterogeneous and encompass a wide range of those who profess adherence or faith, from largely secular followers to ultra-fundamentalists. In this regard, it may be misleading to talk of the Muslim or Jewish or Catholic 'community'. The term is used to denote the body of adherents which the religious tribunal saw itself as serving. It is also important to note that the bulk of the data collected derives from interviews with officials and those working in the tribunals, and not from litigants themselves (or those from within the religious communities who did not choose to use them). It is quite likely that the informants sought to present a positive and 'official' picture of their workings, and a consumer perspective is necessary to produce a complete picture. So, the data discussed here are only indicative of how religious tribunals *can* work – not representative of how all such bodies *do* operate. Nonetheless, the study provides some important insights into how such bodies can operate and what values they may hold, particularly with regard to how they view their relationship with the state and the wider society.

The Working of the Religious Tribunals

Each tribunal is staffed by a number of judges, who, in the case of the Catholic Tribunal and the Shariah Council, may include lay members – and women – as well as priests. Each sits as a panel (of three or, in the Shariah Council, of four), although straightforward cases may be handled by a single judge in the Catholic Tribunal (with dispensation from the Rota in Rome) and the Beth Din.

The jurisdiction of each tribunal is not confined to marriage matters and all three tribunals will answer questions on details of observance and religious rules; indeed, 80 percent of the work of the Beth Din concerns matters other than divorce, including Jewish status, conversion, certification of Kashrut, and arbitration in commercial and property disputes.

The Shariah Council and Beth Din take cases from applicants across the United Kingdom (as well as from abroad), whilst the Catholic Tribunal has a geographical jurisdiction confined to those residing in the three Catholic dioceses in Wales and part of Herefordshire. Approximately 150 cases per annum are dealt with in the Shariah Council, around 110 in the Beth Din and about 40 in the Tribunal. Although not a high caseload for any of them, their facilities are stretched and dependent upon the resources which are made available to them by their governing religious authority. Their work on marriage and divorce has to be fitted in to the other roles that they fulfil, as priests, rabbis or professionals in other walks of life, and it may take time to bring a panel together.

The National Tribunal operates at the lowest tier of a hierarchy of tribunals reaching to the Rota in Rome, and all its 'sentences' of nullity are automatically referred to a Tribunal of Second Instance or are subject to appeal. By contrast, neither the Shariah Council nor the Beth Din is part of a wider network of tribunals and there is no appeal from their rulings. This has resulted in an element of 'forum shopping' whereby, for example in the case of Muslims, an applicant may choose to use a particular body in preference to another, in the hope of a ruling in line with their own views on the interpretation of Shariah. This is entirely in line with Abdullahi Ahmed An-Naim's explanation that the 'Quran and Sunna are where Muslims look for *guidance* in developing their social and political relations, legal and ethical norms; but *these sources are not legal codes as such.*' He goes on to argue that '[t]he religious nature of Islamic Law means that there is no person or institution authorised to decide for all believers the Islamic Law rule on any subject; each believer is responsible for his or her own belief in the matter' (An-Naim 2010: 5, 8). Thus, as one interviewee at the Shariah Council told us:

> Because there are different schools of thought and there are different views … they'd say well if somebody doesn't agree with a decision they'll say 'well what does he know?' … When you have different mosques I suppose people go to different places don't they? Where they feel comfortable with, where they feel they would accept the decision from and where they think they've been understood.

In the case of the Beth Din, forum shopping may occur because it is felt that the issue of a *get* from a more orthodox Beth Din will command wider recognition amongst other Jewish communities than one from a more liberal branch of Judaism:

> We often find that the non-Orthodox communities will refer to us even though, say, for example, the Reform won't necessarily say that they believe it is necessary for a get to be given, they do recognise and they will often tell their members that if you were married in an Orthodox way you must realise that if you want your marriage to be ended from an Orthodox point of view this is what you need to do.

Determination of Marital Status in the Eyes of the Religion

Religious tribunals should not be regarded simply as functional analogues of the civil courts, or of forms of 'alternative dispute resolution'. Those who make use of such tribunals do not do so because they find (or expect) them to be more congenial or accessible dispute resolution fora than the family courts and of course, they know – or find out when they do approach them – that the religious tribunal cannot determine or rule on their civil marital status. So for those who are civilly married, the religious tribunal represents an *additional*, not an alternative, juridical hurdle which they must surmount. They use them because, for them, obtaining the sanction of a religious body for a change in their marital status provides an important, indeed essential, judgment on their marital position *within their faith* and thus a key aspect of their identity as members of the religious community to which they adhere. Most importantly, it provides them with a licence to remarry within the faith, without which many adherents would refuse to take that step. This is particularly crucial in the Jewish religion, because the failure to obtain a *get* will jeopardise the legitimate status of the wife's future children and descendants.

Whether married under civil law or not, the authority of religious tribunals to rule on the validity/termination of a marriage does not derive from the parties' agreement to submit their 'dispute' to them in the same way as an arbitration clause in a contract or an agreement to try mediation. Indeed, for many couples, there may be no dispute – particularly in relation to the termination of the marriage, which they may agree is over. Instead, a determination and declaration of *status* is the main focus of the proceedings, and as Shachar (2001: 51–5; 2010: 128) has noted, this has both an internal and external dimension. Family law 'demarcates' the group's 'membership boundaries' in relation to the wider society as well as affecting the individual's position in the group.

Applying Religious Laws within the Social Context

The broader social context within which religious tribunals must operate was reflected in the approach they took towards determining whether the grounds for annulment or divorce had been satisfied. This broader context includes a shift in civil laws throughout Europe and other western states, away from a reliance upon fault as the basis for divorce (Antokolskaia 2006) towards first, a focus on irretrievable breakdown and, more latterly, a frank acceptance that, if one spouse wishes to end the marriage, there is really little that the state can or should do to prevent this. Thus, even in a system like that in England and Wales, where 'matrimonial fault' may still be relied upon as the basis of the divorce, the reality is that nearly all divorces are undefended, dealt with by post rather than a court hearing, and there is scarcely any scope to resist the grant of the decree even if a spouse wished to do so (there is no legal aid available to fight the case and the courts discourage the attempt).

The tribunals in the study varied in the extent to which they saw themselves as seeking (or even wishing) to 'hold the line' against such a shift in personal and public attitudes, but all were affected by it. Indeed, the fact that all three faiths in the study regard marriage as based fundamentally on the will of the parties (albeit overlaid by its sacramental quality for Catholics) could be said to facilitate it to some extent. Thus, in the Catholic context, if there was no true consent to the marriage, or in the Islamic or Jewish context, one or both parties no longer wishes to remain married, then the marriage may be regarded as either invalid, or open to dissolution. This leaves the religious institution scope to interpret its rules in ways which may reflect modern attitudes, although obviously there is a greater or lesser degree of tension between these and the religious tenets it must apply, according to its own position on the conservative/liberal continuum within the faith.

The Shariah Council operates in a religious context under which Islamic law permits the husband to divorce the wife by repudiation, by pronouncing a *talaq*. It also enables divorce by mutual consent, through a *khul* divorce where the husband agrees to the wife divorcing him. Where the husband refuses to divorce or agree to a divorce, the wife may apply to the Shariah Council (and thus, nearly all applicants to Shariah Councils are women) to terminate the marriage on a variety of grounds (Shah-Kazemi 2001: 6–8). Islamic law requires that the scope for reconciliation is investigated before the marriage is terminated, and so, in addition to the efforts of the spouses' families which are likely to have gone on for some time previously, when an application for a divorce is made, volunteers in a dedicated 'Family Support Service' see the applicant and, if possible, the respondent, to seek to achieve a reconciliation between them or to prepare a report to the Council that this has proved fruitless.

Samia Bano (2007) has noted that such attempts at reconciliation may operate detrimentally to the interests of women in putting pressure on them not to proceed (or to waive any financial claims). However, in the Shariah Council in this study, there was an acknowledgement of the need to recognise when the applicant was determined that the marriage was over, and to move on to a consideration of whether grounds existed to show that the marriage could not be saved. In so doing, it relied mainly upon 'fault' grounds, as the civil law of divorce would understand them, and the basic approach was to determine whether the marriage was 'un-saveable' – quite similar to the civil law doctrine of the 'irretrievable breakdown' of the marriage. And again similarly to the civil law, the finding that the marriage cannot be saved did not take long:

> Five, six minutes, depending upon the case – because most of the cases, all the preliminary work has been done and they've reached the stage when it's either nay or yay, and we do not intend to delay the process. If at any point in time we come to the conclusion that the parties are not going to budge from their position then it is not our attitude to delay the matter any further …

In stark contrast, the Catholic Tribunal was quite prepared to uphold the validity of the marriage, even though it insisted on the couple having been divorced under civil law before it would take the case.[2] In 2008 and 2009 respectively, for example, four out

---

2 On the problem of the 'limping marriage' that this created, see further below.

of 16 and four out of 11 'sentences' or determinations by the Tribunal confirmed the validity of the marriage. Of course, not only was it applying Canons laid down by the Church, it was also conceptually engaged in a different exercise to that of the divorce courts, since its task is to determine whether the marriage is *void*, not whether it can be terminated. It seems obvious, therefore, that it might well reach a different opinion and produce a different outcome to the civil law. But nonetheless, as the following quotations demonstrate, the impact of the wider world plays a part in the way in which the Canons are interpreted, and it is important to note that, despite the emphasis on consent at the time of the wedding, the Tribunal will look at evidence subsequent to that date, which may shed light on the 'quality of the consent'. Of particular interest is the concept of 'simulation', set out in Canon 1096.1:

> For matrimonial consent to exist, it is necessary that the contracting parties be at least not ignorant of the fact that marriage is a permanent partnership between a man and a woman, ordered to the procreation of children through some form of sexual cooperation.

One interviewee reported that:

> Coming up on the inside rails, as it were, is what we technically call 'simulation' which is in the area of people's intention – they could have an intention against their marriage being permanent … It's a growing area because of the divorce mentality in our culture. So you've got people entering marriage: 'Well, we'll try this for a few years' … I think it was presumed that a Catholic knew what a Catholic concept of marriage was in terms of permanence and faithfulness and openness to children … Now of course with varying influences on people, especially young people nowadays can we still presume that? … It's just they are surrounded with a culture, especially on the permanence one, where divorce is so common that it's [permanence] not part of their world view and so they are not including it.

Thus, the wider social acceptance of the free terminability of relationships may be setting a context in which the Tribunal may be able to find that a party has not truly understood what a *Catholic* marriage truly entails.

The position of the Beth Din was different again. In Jewish law as interpreted by the Beth Din in this study – although differing views can be taken on the Halachic authority for this stance (Jackson 2011) – a divorce depends upon mutual agreement, and as one interviewee explained:

> When there is a divorce the Beth Din doesn't actually divorce people. Formally, we ensure that they divorce each other correctly and so we ensure that all the documentation is drawn up in the right sort of way and the bill of divorce, the get, is drawn up and written correctly.

This stance means that the Beth Din is not particularly interested in the parties' reasons for seeking the divorce and reflects the modern European view that such matters are not justiciable and not the business of the state (or in this case, the religious institution). One informant put it thus:

> It's a no-fault system so we don't ask the couples 'why are you getting divorced?' I mean, we're not into wanting to know what went wrong with the marriage unless there's a possibility of saving the marriage … by very definition the fact that one person has written

to us wanting a get means that at least one of the two want the divorce; usually both want the divorce.

Attitudes towards the Civil Law

How religious tribunals handle the interaction between the civil and religious law is a sensitive and important issue, as the Cox Bill demonstrates, for this kind of response to the activities of religious tribunals is underpinned by the assumption that they may seek to impose rulings that are in conflict with civil law (or majority norms). It is therefore necessary to understand clearly how these tribunals saw themselves as relating to and operating alongside the civil courts.

Limping Marriages and Divorces

The grant of a religious divorce has no effect in civil law and this was abundantly clear in the operation of the three religious tribunals in the study, all of which reported that they advised those approaching them of the importance of resolving their civil marital status as well as undertaking the religious process:

> We are British citizens and we abide by British law and anything that's done from a Jewish perspective is in addition to civil law. (Interviewee at the Beth Din)

> We work within the law of the land we cannot go against the law of the land and we say that and that actually would be going against Islam as well because we have to honour our contracts according to the Islamic teaching. (Interviewee at the Shariah Council)

> In Britain we cannot start, we cannot give an annulment without the people being divorced otherwise we're in trouble with the state, people sometimes forget that we, if we try to dissolve something that the state hadn't dissolved then we would be in trouble. (Interviewee at the National Tribunal)

However, the problem of a 'limping marriage' arising where, in the eyes of the religion a couple remain married, but in the view of the state they are free to enter into a new union, or vice versa, appears to be an inevitable concomitant of having parallel 'jurisdictions', each, in effect, dealing with a different 'marriage' – religious or civil.

The best-known example of this arises in the Beth Din. Here, the *get* process may in fact be conducted prior to, or alongside, the civil divorce proceedings, but the certificate that the *get* has been granted is not issued until the parties have obtained the civil divorce. The need to carry out the process without necessarily waiting for a civil divorce is to avoid one of the consequences of the *agunah* problem. An *agunah* is a wife whose husband refuses to agree to a *get*. The Beth Din regards itself as unable to coerce the husband into agreement, or to override his refusal. If the parties were to divorce under civil law before going through the *get* process, which the husband then refused to give, the wife would be prevented from remarrying according to orthodox Jewish rites, and in addition, her children and descendants by a new partner would be regarded as illegitimate according to Jewish law. The Divorce

(Religious Marriages) Act 2002[3] was therefore enacted at the request of the orthodox Jewish community to enable the wife to ask the civil court to delay the grant of the decree absolute of divorce until the husband has agreed to the *get*. Should he refuse, he will remain married under civil law and thus himself not free to remarry. This is only a partial solution to the *agunah* problem. If the husband does not intend to remarry, he may be indifferent to his civil status, although an inability to resolve the financial consequences of the breakdown of the marriage may be more of an inducement to complete the process. However, the Beth Din informed the research team that the enactment has gone a considerable way to resolving the issue in practice. Once the husband does agree to the *get*, the divorce court can then complete the civil process. It is important to note that this is not a case of the state *recognising* the religious divorce: rather, the state is delaying the divorce until the party's position has been protected, in the same way that it may do so generally under the Matrimonial Causes Act 1973 sections 10 and 41 to ensure that arrangements for children, or the financial consequences of the divorce, are satisfactorily resolved.

It is open to other religions to seek inclusion within the terms of this provision, but none has sought to do so. For Muslims, as we have seen, Shariah Councils have the power under Islamic law to terminate the marriage notwithstanding the husband's refusal to pronounce a *talaq* or agree to a *khul*, and so the same problem of the 'chained wife' does not arise. Moreover, the Birmingham Shariah Council regards a civil divorce decree as the equivalent of a religious divorce, such that in its view, the parties would be entitled to remarry according to Islamic rites, without obtaining any form of religious divorce. This stance underscores the point made above regarding the significance of obtaining a religious divorce to the individual party – it sanctions and authorises her position in the community even though as a matter of interpretation of the relevant Islamic legal principles it may be strictly unnecessary. In fact, many applicants before Shariah Councils do not have a legally recognised marriage in any case and would be regarded only as cohabitants under civil law. This is a problem in itself but one which is not pursued further in this chapter. For those who are civilly married, however, the Shariah Council will usually advise the applicant to obtain the civil divorce before it will hear the case and, like the Beth Din, even if it grants the divorce beforehand it will withhold the certificate to this effect, until that is done. Of the 13 cases that were observed, which appeared to involve a civil marriage, eight were granted a termination *on the basis that* they had already been civilly divorced (in five other cases, the marriage was conducted abroad and its civil status was unclear to the research team).

As has been noted, the Catholic Tribunal will not accept an application for annulment until the parties have obtained a civil divorce, even though it may go on to withhold an annulment thus preventing the parties from remarrying in church. As with the problem of the Jewish woman who cannot obtain a *get* this creates an issue of conscience for the adherent, who must decide whether he or she is prepared to remarry outside the denomination.

Dealing with the Consequences of the Marriage Termination

While the marital status of the parties in the eyes of the religion has no bearing on their status in civil law, the position is rather different in relation to the other ancillary aspects of marriage termination – the financial consequences and the arrangements for the children. The jurisdiction of the civil courts cannot be 'ousted' and a party may always take their case

---

3   For Scotland, see the Divorce (Scotland) Act 1976 s 3A inserted by the Family Law (Scotland) Act 2006 s 15.

to the court for a finally binding ruling. However, the thrust of legal policy in the family justice system has long been to encourage private ordering and to discourage resort to the courts, both because of cost, and because of a prevailing view that the adversarial process is likely to increase the level of antagonism between the parties which is likely to prove detrimental to the welfare of their children. Indeed, civil legal aid for representation in family matters is to be withdrawn in 2013 under the Legal Aid, Sentencing and Punishment of Offenders Act 2012 unless a party requires protection, such as in cases of domestic violence or child abuse. Furthermore, it is not mandatory to obtain an order setting out the consequences of the divorce and it is estimated that only 10 percent of litigating *parents* resort to the courts to resolve disputes over their children's upbringing in any case (Blackwell and Daw 2003: 35).

The proportion will be higher in relation to the financial consequences because of the need to confirm, or ensure, the enforceability of the arrangements made by having the court embody the terms of the agreement in a consent order, but there is no requirement to do so. There are no reliable statistics demonstrating what this proportion is, however. In 2011, there were 119,610 decrees absolute of divorce granted, compared with a total of 80,601 orders for various kinds of financial relief, but since a settlement may well require more than one type of order being made, this total does not indicate how many divorces were involved. Of the total, 70 percent of orders were uncontested, i.e. presented to the court as agreed; and approximately 24 percent were settled during proceedings; thus, only 6 percent of orders were the products of full adjudication (Ministry of Justice 2012: Tables 2.5, 2.6). This is entirely in line with the procedural steps that the parties must go through in the court process, which include measures including full disclosure of assets and dispute resolution appointments in which the judge seeks to nudge the parties towards a settlement. Not only do we not know how many couples do not go to court, but we also have no way of knowing what financial settlements are reached by such couples, and even in the case of consent orders, the extent to which the court actively scrutinises the terms of the agreement to ensure that these are fair and appropriate is likely to vary from judge to judge.

In a recent ruling, *Radmacher v Granatino* [2010] UKSC 42 [2011] 1 AC 534, the Supreme Court held that a marital property agreement (colloquially known as a 'pre-nup') should be given effect unless, in the circumstances, it would not be fair to hold the parties to it. There is also strong encouragement of the use of out of court mediation or other forms of dispute resolution (including 'collaborative law' and private arbitration), and part of the strength of the appeal of such alternatives is the extent to which they may be more responsive to the parties' own values and norms (Roberts 2008: Chapter 1). These developments, together with the procedural hurdles the parties must go through within the court system, send a very clear message that agreements over the consequences of the termination of the relationship are to be encouraged, even if they fall short of what a family court would order. Given these circumstances, it is hard to see why religious tribunals should not be regarded as equally well-suited as any other potential mediator or arbitrator, to assist the parties in reaching a settlement that suits them, even if that settlement is one that reflects cultural or religious norms at odds with those of secular society.

Conclusion

The study reported here sought to add to the knowledge base of how religious tribunals can function in a largely secular society – although one must be alive to the extent to which

English law and its application are imbued with Christian understandings and norms based on a thousand years of history (Herman 2011). The case studies were drawn from different religions in part in order to consider their significance without becoming bogged down in the complications regarding ethnicity and politicisation which have marked discussion of Shariah Councils. The experience of other religions also added to understanding of how faith institutions can reach an accommodation with the state in dealing with family issues which are of importance to religious believers.

The main function of the religious tribunals in this study was the determination of marital status and the grant or withholding of a licence to remarry for the purposes of the faith. It was clear that all the tribunals in the study were mindful of the boundary between their role and that of the civil courts, and all were at pains to ensure that relevant civil legal requirements were undertaken before or alongside the religious process. The less significant (as far as the religious tribunals themselves were concerned) function of advising, mediating or even arbitrating on the consequences of the termination of a marriage was equally undertaken with full awareness of the limitations on religious tribunals imposed by the civil law.

Secondly, examination of how these tribunals functioned and applied their religious principles and rules showed that they do not operate in a vacuum cut off from the influences of the wider society in which they are situated. The interpretation of rules can be and was conducted with an awareness of the broader social circumstances in which their litigants live their lives.

Thirdly, contrary to the fears underlying the introduction of the Arbitration and Mediation Services (Equality) Bill, there was clear recognition of the primacy of the state and of its laws and a desire to interact with, not override, such laws. It was understood that religious tribunals are *religious* bodies delivering decisions which assist adherents to live their lives in conformity with their faith, which meet a religious need and validate users' sense of their religious and communal identity.

At present, religious annulments and divorces remain completely outside the civil legal system in England and Wales, and none, including Jewish divorces where the Matrimonial Causes Act is invoked to delay the civil decree absolute, is 'recognised' by the law. They thus fall within the 'cohabitation' model of accommodation of religion considered above, which in effect, offers no more than a passive tolerance of religious practice undertaken without expectation of state recognition. This appears to be readily accepted by these particular tribunals, which is understandable not least because it enables them to retain their own substantive and procedural rules which might otherwise require amendment if they were to seek to satisfy state norms of equality and due process.

It cannot, of course, be concluded from this study that all other religious tribunals similarly recognise the boundaries between their role and the power of the state. However, the findings from these particular institutions do suggest that there is a need for caution before seeking to restrict or prohibit religious tribunals in general from fulfilling a function to which their believers attach significance.

References

Ahdar. R. and Aroney, N. 2010. The topography of shari'a in the Western political landscape, in *Shari'a in the West*, edited by R. Ahdar and N. Aroney. Oxford: Oxford University Press, 1–32.

An-Na'im, A. 2010. The compatibility dialectic: Mediating the legitimate coexistence of Islamic law and state law. *Modern Law Review*, 73(1), 1–29.

Antokolskaia, M. 2006. *Harmonisation of Family Law in Europe: A Historical Perspective: A Tale of Two Millennia*. Antwerp: Intersentia.

Bano, S. 2007. Islamic family arbitration, justice and human rights in Britain. *Law, Social Justice & Global Development Journal*, [Online], 1. Available at: http://www.go.warwick.ac.uk/elj/lgd/2007_1/bano [last accessed 7 May 2012].

Blackwell, A. and Dawe, F. 2003. *Non-resident Parent Contact*. London: ONS.

Bowen, J. 2012. Sanctity and shariah: Two Islamic modes of resolving disputes in today's England. [Online]. Available at: http://anthropology.artsci.wustl.edu/files/anthropology/imce/bowen_sanctity_and_shariah_october_2012.pdf [last accessed 11 February 2013].

Budziszewski, J. 2010. Natural law, democracy, and shari'a, in *Shari'a in the West*, edited by R. Ahdar and N. Aroney. Oxford: Oxford University Press, 181–206.

Douglas, G., Doe, N., Gilliat-Ray, S., Sandberg, R. and Khan, A. 2011. *Social Cohesion and Civil Law: Marriage, Divorce and Religious Courts*. Cardiff: Cardiff Law School [Online]. Available at: http://www.law.cf.ac.uk/clr/research/cohesion [last accessed 18 October 2012].

Douglas, G., Doe, N., Sandberg, R., Gilliat-Ray, S. and Khan, A. 2013. Accommodating religious divorce in the secular state: A case study analysis, in *Managing Family Justice in Diverse Societies*, edited by M. Maclean and J. Eekelaar. Oxford: Hart Publishing, 185–201.

Eekelaar, J. 2011. The Arbitration and Mediation Services (Equality) Bill 2011. [2011] *Family Law*, 1209–15.

Eekelaar, J. 2013. Law and community practices, in *Managing Family Justice in Diverse Societies*, edited by M. Maclean and J. Eekelaar. Oxford: Hart Publishing, 15–32.

Fournier, P. 2010. *Muslim Marriage in Western Courts: Lost in Transplantation*. Farnham: Ashgate Publishing.

Herman, D. 2011. *An Unfortunate Coincidence: Jews, Jewishness and English Law*. Oxford: Oxford University Press.

Jackson, B. 2011. *Agunah: The Manchester Analysis*. Liverpool: Deborah Charles Publications.

Malik, M. 2012. *Minority Legal Orders in the UK: Minorities, Pluralism and the Law*. London: The British Academy.

Ministry of Justice. 2012. *Judicial and Court Statistics 2011*. [Online]. Available at: http://www.justice.gov.uk/statistics/courts-and-sentencing/judicial-annual-2011 [last accessed 11 February 2013].

Modood, T. 2010. Multicultural citizenship and the shari'a controversy in Britain, in *Shari'a in the West*, edited by R. Ahdar and N. Aroney. Oxford: Oxford University Press, 33–42.

Norgrove, Sir D., (Chair). 2011. *Family Justice Review Final Report*. London: Ministry of Justice, Department for Education and Welsh Government.

Pearl, D. and Menski, W. 1998. *Muslim Family Law*, 3rd edition. London: Sweet and Maxwell.

Phillips, Lord N., Lord Chief Justice. 2008. *Equality Before the Law*. [Online]. Available at: http://www.matribunal.com/downloads/LCJ_speech.pdf [last accessed 18 October 2012].

Roberts, M. 2008. *Mediation in Family Disputes: Principles of Practice*. 3rd edition. Aldershot: Ashgate Publishing.

Shachar, A. 2001. *Multicultural Jurisdictions: Cultural Differences and Women's Rights*. Cambridge: Cambridge University Press.

Shachar, A. 2010. State, religion and the family: The new dilemmas of multicultural accommodation, in *Shari'a in the West*, edited by R. Ahdar and N. Aroney. Oxford: Oxford University Press, 115–33.

Shah-Kazemi, S. 2001. *Untying the Knot: Muslim Women, Divorce and the Shariah*. London: Nuffield Foundation

Waldron, J. 2010. Questions about the reasonable accommodation of minorities, in *Shari'a in the West*, edited by R. Ahdar and N. Aroney. Oxford: Oxford University Press, 103–13.

Williams, R. 2008. Civil and religious law in England: A religious perspective, 7 February 2008, reprinted in (2008) *Ecclesiastical Law Journal*, 10, 262–82.

Chapter 11
Kurdish 'Unofficial' Family Law in the *Gurbet*[1]

Latif Taş

Introduction

This chapter focuses on alternative dispute resolution as practised by the Kurdish Peace Committee (KPC) in the UK. It discusses why and how, despite significant changes in many other parts of their lives, many Kurds still choose to rely on their customary practices via an unofficial legal system in combination with, or instead of, official legal processes, while living in a large western city like London. This chapter also considers responses to the re-development of the Kurds' customary laws and fora for dispute settlement from other relevant actors, including feminists and the British police. Three case studies are used to illustrate how the KPC has helped to resolve disputes, to develop Kurdish customs and traditions under different circumstances, and to act as a transnational bridge between official legal systems in both the UK and Turkey and Kurdish values and norms.

In this chapter, I focus on London-based *gurbet* (diaspora) Kurds who have emigrated from Turkey. *Gurbet* is the Kurdish and Turkish word approximating to 'diaspora', a place where someone is living for a short or long time, and that is not their original homeland. This Kurdish and Turkish word implies sadness, emotions related to the homeland, and the alienation felt in the 'temporary' host location, especially when it cannot be known how long the exile may last. *Gurbet* is not directly equivalent to 'diaspora', since the latter term refers more specifically to the community to which one belongs abroad. The concept of 'Diaspora' has been mainly used for Jews living outside of Palestine (Sheffer 2002), and subsequently to describe many displaced communities. Following Werbner (2002), who observes that 'each diaspora is unique', I use '*gurbet*' to better describe this uniqueness through a culture-specific concept.

As part of my recent doctoral literature review, I found that nothing had previously been written about specifically Kurdish customary legal practices either in the *gurbet* or in Turkey (Taş 2012). Indeed, there is very limited literature available on the laws and customs of Kurds and, given this, the research reported here is exploratory in nature. London was selected as the research site as it has so far the best-developed unofficial secular Kurdish legal system: the set-up in Germany, for example, is more fragmented and much less well organised.[2]

This chapter is based on research carried out between May 2009 and May 2012. As well as an analysis of primary and secondary documents, field observations and interviews, case study analyses and personal communications have also been reviewed. As part of

---

1 This chapter is the result of the workshop 'Law in the Everyday Lives of Transnational Families', held in Onati, Spain (24–25 May 2012) and coordinated by Betty de Hart and Wibo van Rossum. An earlier version of this chapter was also published in the Onati Law Journal (online), part of the Onati Socio-Legal Series.

2 A brief investigation into the practices of Kurds in Germany and Belgium was carried out by this author in 2008. More detailed fieldwork is currently being carried out (October 2012–August 2013).

this research project, I witnessed more than 400 cases brought before the KPC members. I also carried out in-depth, unstructured, mostly face-to-face interviews with 82 people (42 male, 40 female).

Many of these interviewees explained to me that Kurds arriving in the UK had experienced the imposition of a single set of assimilationist legal norms and policies, and the strong denial of Kurdish culture by successive Turkish governments. They had survived an often-challenging journey from the Kurdish regions and cities of Turkey. They expected the UK to be a rich and safe haven. However, as they discussed, many Kurds experienced a significant culture shock on their arrival in the UK. Although a few Kurds came as students, the large majority had been agrarian peasants, or inhabitants of small towns in the Kurdish regions of Turkey. They were used to living within a close-knit society with 'intensive social contacts in the framework of the extended family, neighbours and friends' (Sheikmous 1990: 103). Turkish repression and the Kurdish conflict meant that they had lost their land or sometimes even their whole village. Some of them experienced prison, or had lost members of their family. Many of them then moved to a global metropolis, never having lived in or perhaps even seen a large city. As Khayati (2008) has confirmed, Kurds in other countries, including Sweden and France, face similar issues to those in the UK. Their displacement created trauma, depression, alienation, homesickness and nostalgia for many Kurds.

When they arrived in the UK, many had no clear legal status. Struggling also with a new culture and especially language, they were therefore usually pushed into working within – and often being expoited by – the developing Kurdish community. These equivocal experiences, especially compared to unrealistic expectations of ease and freedom, hardened pre-existing attitudes of low trust in the state and in state institutions.

Kurdish organisations have been established in the UK to directly support community needs and help with the identity crisis of UK Kurds in the *gurbet*. Kurds in the UK continue an imagined and physical tie with their homeland (*welat*),[3] and their organisations use new communication technologies to establish and maintain transnational connections with other Kurds around the world, and specifically with those in the Kurdish regions in Turkey – referred to as north Kurdistan by many of my interviewees. According to most of my interviewees, Kurds in the UK continue to practise their traditional customs but also develop new cultural forms in the *gurbet* as they borrow from their new host culture. One key step has been to develop an alternative and unofficial dispute resolution process based on traditional mediation systems, but adapted to the new environment.

Their own and their relatives' experiences of life in Turkey have encouraged even *gurbet*-born Kurds to stick together, to be loyal to their own people and to work to re-establish their own ways of life. They have hybridised their customary practices, as they reorganise and re-strengthen their kinship networks in their new environment. According to those I interviewed, many Kurds living in the UK took power from their traumatic journeys and transformed themselves from victims or exiles, from being an 'oppressed nation', to

---

3   *Welat* is the word used exclusively by Kurds when they are talking about their legendary homeland. Some Kurds say *Welate şirin* (sweet homeland) for their actual homeland. They may also use *Welate xerib* (alien homeland) for the *gurbet* where they are living. Demir (2012) refers to the connection that Kurdish people in London have with their homeland, using the word *memleket*. However, *memleket* is not commonly used by Kurds for their homeland. It is a Turkish word used by people from all the ethnic groups in Turkey to refer to their small town of origin.

becoming actively powerful. As part of this, they connected with each other by re-enacting their customary practices in their new setting.

The Kurdish Peace Committee (KPC)

Why the Kurds Need Their Own Legal Approach

In Kurdish societies, as in other migrant communities, kinship and complex tribal relationships still exist and are very important. As Ballard (1994: 28) has pointed out for South Asian settlers in the UK:

> Migrants have helped each other gain access to jobs, housing and other scarce resources, and whenever they have sought to protect their gains (however limited) from encroachment, they have invariably found that kinship ties provided the most effective basis for collective mobilisation.

For Kurds, everyday life – economic issues, marriage, work – mostly operate through connections within extended families. As Sweetnam (1994: 152) observes, most Kurds can remember details about even their most distant relatives. There are three types of family connection: through blood, through marriage and those formed at a boy's circumcision. Since marriage within the extended family is still common, marriage promotes family ties. At circumcision a male guardian, a *kirve*, is appointed from outside the family to support the boy through the whole process, forming a close and important relationship, like the bond between a father and son. This support extends to the whole of the two families and provides a unique opportunity for Kurds to have close relationships with people outside their own immediate family. Even men from different religious and ethnic groups can be chosen to be *kirve*.[4]

In such a close social environment, it is not surprising that disputes over business, family, marriage and inheritance mostly take place within extended families. Historically Kurds have not had their own state and do not have a written body of law. Since, according to most of my interviewees, they have received unequal treatment from the majority governments they have lived under, they have very little trust in or knowledge about state laws or official legal infrastructure. According to members of the Kurdish community, most Kurds are either ignorant of written rules or do not want to learn about them; they think that written rules cannot harmonise with their traditions. Indeed, Kurds would generally consider it shameful and dishonourable to the whole family if any individual took their family problems outside the family and submitted them to the scrutiny of a legal system. There are, however, customary legal practices and although there is no written documentation of these, I was told by many Kurdish people that, for centuries, they had preferred to solve their problems within the family or community rather than involving state institutions.[5]

As well as the ongoing lack of trust of outsiders, Kurds have distinct social, economic and cultural practices, all of which shape a different approach to law. Some traditional Kurdish practices may be in conflict with state norms: family and criminal issues, marriage

---

4 M.H., N.S., interviews June 2009; B.E., interview May 2011.
5 For example, N.S., interview June 2009; B.E. and A.P., interview November 2011.

arrangements and inheritance work differently in Kurdish communities. According to my interviewees, Kurds do not use official written contracts. If they borrow or lend money or make a business agreement, they do so based on their 'word of honour' (*şeref, namus, haysiyet*) or oral promise (*söz*). These are important concepts in Kurdish society, conditioning the behaviour of leaders as well as the rest of the community. Because of shared moral values within the whole community, Kurds are likely to find it especially difficult to tell a lie in front of Kurdish unofficial judges. However, they might give different answers to a state court or simply avoid acting as a witness. According to interviews with many Kurds, state legal systems might not understand or accept these traditions and therefore might not be capable of finding solutions to typical Kurdish disputes.[6] The war between the Kurdish revolutionary movement, the PKK (Kurdish Workers Party), and the Turkish state – along with harsh official assimilation policies – has led to deaths, and even the destruction of entire villages. Kurds in Turkey have come to believe that the only justice they will receive will be at their own hands. According to most of my interviewees, this is one of the reasons why, wherever they move, they always stay close to their own community. Many Kurds have become determined to try to follow their own traditions even more steadfastly than before. After all, this – it is said – worked for hundreds of years. In the villages in the Kurdish homelands, disputes are sorted out by a group of respected older people. Smaller problems are resolved with the help of local leaders: an *ak sakallilar* ('white beard', respected person), or a knowledgeable person such as a teacher, doctor or religious leader. Mediation, in this tradition, can be seen as a better way for dispute resolution for most Kurds.[7] This echoes Galanter's (1981: 3) insight that a large proportion of disputes are best 'resolved by negotiation between the parties, or by resort to some "forum" that is part of (and embedded within) the social setting within which the dispute arose'.

As settlement numbers increased in the *gurbet*, and intra-community confidence grew, Kurds started to consider the more formalised organisation of a dispute resolution system run along customary lines. This was made more urgent in the late 1990s by the growth of mafia-type underground organisations which increasingly damaged the reputation of the Kurdish community, including by claiming to resolve disputes using their own (often violent) methods. Although most Kurdish disputes were with other Kurds, more and more disputes also took place with individuals of other ethnic groups, especially Turks, Cypriots, Iraqis and Iranians.

A very informal system had been operational in the north London Kurdish community centre. This centre, known as *Halkevi*,[8] was – and still is – a meeting place for various Kurdish interest groups, including for political activity. It is used for socialising and by womens' support groups, as well as for Kurdish language courses and folk dancing. Gradually, a practice had grown up whereby respected individuals were consulted informally about family and other legal disputes. As the need for mediation grew, to fill an apparent legal vacuum and so as to prevent people from using the mafia-like groups, the Kurdish community created the Kurdish Peace Committee (KPC, *Kürtlerin Barış Mahkemesi, Komisyonu*). This was formed as a secular or non-religious and unofficial dispute resolution system in 2001 in the same

---

6 For example, N.S., A.H., interviews June 2009; KPC judges, interviews June 2009, November 2010 and May 2011.

7 For example, A.H., interview, June 2009; KPC judges, interviews June 2009, November 2010 and May 2011.

8 '*Halk*' means public, and '*Halkevi*' literally means a house of people, a house for the public.

building as *Halkevi*.⁹ Thus, Kurds took another step in creating their own 'hybrid form of English law' (Menski 2008: 7), in a similar way to other different ethnic and religious group practices in the UK and around the world.¹⁰

Just two years earlier, in 1999, the PKK leader, Abdullah Öcalan, had been arrested and imprisoned in Turkey. After this, the PKK reorganised and developed a whole series of new policies. This helped them evade the rising pressure for a ban in their host states. In the UK, for example, the PKK and all organisations considered to be related to it were banned in 2001 under the Terrorism Act.¹¹ The new policies, more positively, were also designed to develop a new way to tackle the various imbalances of power across the social and legal system. Local institutions, including those in the UK, were empowered to fight for their Kurdishness rather than simply reacting against Turkish and other oppression by majority groups. This necessitated a kind of social and cultural training, an evolution for Kurds as they remembered or rediscovered their practices, customs and identity. KPC members explained that there were not many active Kurdish intellectuals alive and out of prison in the 1990s, and an emphasis was placed on learning about practices, traditions and laws, many of which had only survived in oral memory. Together with reclaiming the past in this way, it was also recognised that new approaches were needed to harmonise with the new situations that Kurds found themselves in. It has been thought to be especially important to move away from an individual form of feudal-based leadership and towards a system of elected leaders guiding a Kurdish community which is seen as a holistic entity rather than in fragmented terms.¹²

Kurdish community leaders and members took advantage of this self-education and training programme to try to organise their own community. They wanted to learn how to self-rule, both now and in a future where they hoped their autonomy would be gained within Turkey. An internationally recognised Kurdish autonomy was one of the important aims of the new Kurdish policy, with Kurds in all the involved European countries developing an 'imagined state'. They wanted to sort out their own disputes and problems in civic institutions manned by their own people, elected every year by members of the Kurdish community.¹³

According to Romano, the PKK had used their own court system from its inception, not just for their own fighters, but also for Kurds more generally. With an increase in civil disobedience and distrust of the state institutions, the PKK courts increasingly offered 'their services to local politicians and influential families in the [Kurdish] region', including helping villages to settle blood feuds (Romano 2006: 75, 87). The PKK even sometimes imposed taxes for their services to their people, thereby helping them to organise more effectively and improve their services. They reinvigorated and strengthened an idealised form of the old traditions, when leaders were bound by honour to take a benevolent interest

---

9   KPC judges, interviews June 2009, November 2010 and May 2011.

10   For research into the unofficial dispute resolution practices of other communities, especially South Asian and Muslim communities living in the UK, see Menski (1987, 1993a, 1993b), Ballard (1994), Pearl and Menski (1998), Yilmaz (2005), Keshavjee (2007) and Bano (2012). For other customary laws in different countries, see, for example, Makec (1988), Rosen (1989, 1995, 2000), Chowdhury (1993), Sheleff (1999), Goh (2002), Bowen (2003) and Hinz (2012).

11   For example, one of the first and best-known Kurdish television channels, Med TV, which had had a licence to broadcast from the UK from 2000, was banned in 2001. According to my interviewees, since the PKK was banned it has been more difficult for Kurdish people to claim asylum in the UK.

12   KPC judges, interviews June 2009, November 2010 and May 2011.

13   KPC judges, interviews June 2009, November 2010 and May 2011.

in promoting the interests of the whole Kurdish community. This model of dispute resolution became steadily more organised – with an overarching public court (*halk mahkemesi*) at the centre and local courts in each region in Turkey, as well as in each of the *gurbet*s. Fines and other penalties were imposed by calculating and balancing infringements between the various parties to any dispute. The ultimate penalty was always seen as rejection from the community.

After the arrest of Öcalan, Kurds in the UK were active in developing new policies and following the new system, and specifically in piloting the new approach to dispute resolution. Subsequently, the various Kurdish community organisations, including the PKK, met in 2005 on the Kandil Mountain as a Confederation.[14] This meeting noted how successful the new policies had been and agreed, among other things, to promote the more organised dispute resolution system that had been tried with such success in London.[15]

According to a male Kurdish lawyer working in London whom I interviewed, the informal, secular approach of the KPC might be seen as a new approach in the West, but Kurdish people had created their own unofficial bodies of self-governance and justice centuries ago, and these survived even under the harshest laws and most difficult circumstances. Most Kurdish disputes and problems can be sorted out within the parameters of unofficial or customary law by negotiation between the different parties involved. This lawyer pointed out that – as well as being autocratic, bureaucratic, expensive and slow – the state legal system is complicated and difficult to understand for professional legal practitioners, let alone ordinary citizens. Moreover, according to him, a state that is generally hostile to minorities like Kurds is unlikely to treat them as equal legally. He argued that people should question if one law is really right for everybody; whether the state has the right to impose a unitary law on everybody.[16]

Another of my interviewees, a female Kurdish lawyer, also talked about minority groups and explained that many members of these groups, including Kurds, think that

> [c]ourts do not care much about other people, about the moral values of different ethnic groups. Courts are a big show room, a theatrical place; and if you have the money to hire a big actor – a big lawyer – and if this actor acts perfectly for you, creating the right sort of show for the audience – the judge and jury – then even if you are a criminal, a murderer, a thief, you might escape prison because of this act, this show. And there's an idea that 'if you steal, you should steal big': since this will help you get out of prison, and even gain you respect. While if you steal something small, then you can spend all your life in prison.[17]

Several other Kurdish lawyers told me about the lack of trust among Kurds for the 'theatre' of courtrooms in the UK or in Turkey, and explained that this was one of the reasons why Kurds did not want to go to the police, let alone to court.[18]

In my interviews too, Kurdish people commonly reiterated that they believed the Western legal system was designed for rich people, not the poor. Some members of the

---

14 This is a high mountain place, on the borders of the Kurdistan Federal State, in Iraq, where active PKK fighters live.
15 A.E., A.P., interviews November 2010.
16 A.H., interview June 2009.
17 S.L., interview November 2009.
18 For example, A.H., F.K., interviews June 2009; A.Y., interview March 2011.

community had themselves had bad experiences at the hands of the British police and in the British courts, while others had heard negative stories or seen films showing negative experiences. According to many of my interviewees, Kurds were concerned that they might lose everything during a judicial process. This has created an increasingly insular approach in the community, with fewer and fewer Kurds confident about relying on state legal institutions or lawyers who only take a centralistic legal approach. A Kurdish community leader in London emphasised that

> [t]he police stop and search us many times more than the white British. They will arrest immigrants, including Kurdish people, for the smallest reason. If the official legal systems were equitable, many Kurdish people would not have been in prison in Turkey or in the UK. With these inequalities, we don't trust them and we don't expect them to help provide solutions to our problems.[19]

Confirming this, Bowling and Phillips (2002) and Povey (2011) have drawn on detailed Home Office reports to explain how the police exercise power differently over different ethnic groups. According to Topping (2011), the heavy-handed abuse of power further alienates communities, especially young people, who may perceive that they have nothing to lose in disobeying state-imposed social norms.

I observed that many second generation Kurds in the UK who are educated to university level have chosen to study law. Outsiders might think that Kurds are thereby taking part in the official legal system. When I asked young people and their families about this, they explained that they needed someone from their family or community to understand the legal system as a matter of bureaucratic necessity on matters of, for example, benefits, immigration or visas, accidents, tax or housing. Kurds want to be informed about these issues by educated members of their own community, who can act as a trusted bridge for them. Kurdish legal practitioners act as an advice bureau, and especially as a way of avoiding more in-depth legal contact. One young female Kurdish lawyer explained that when her family first arrived in the UK they paid huge amounts of money to lawyers to sort out their immigration status. When they bought a house and set up businesses they paid more money and had to wait lengthy periods. Then, when a family member went to prison they had to hire yet another expensive lawyer. That was why, she said, 'even when I was in secondary school my family told me I should become a lawyer, to solve all these problems easily, and keep all the money for myself and my family.'[20] Since being a legal practitioner is not only profitable but also prestigious, many Kurdish families want at least one of their number to study law.

'Unofficial' Kurdish Judges: Their Selection and Rationale

KPC members explained in my interviews that from late Ottoman times until recently one of the methods Kurdish people in Turkey utilised to avoid assimilation was to solve disputes with the help of their family elders, feudal leaders, religious opinion makers (*sheikh*, *dede*), landlords (*ağa*) or other locally respected or knowledgeable individuals. These people were sources of economic and political power and also acted outside the state system as judges. They were often respected in dispute resolution because of their age and extensive

---

19   E.L., interview June 2009.
20   A.Y., interview March 2011.

knowledge of Kurdish customary practices. Most of them were powerful leaders of their feudal communities. Although tribal leaders or landlords were not elected, when they made any decisions they usually also negotiated with other knowledgeable and respected local people – *ak sakallilar* or, collectively, *azallar birliği* (an unofficial commission of respected people). According to my interviewees, these people were, and still often are, considered to be real philosophers by many Kurds. They were especially known for not taking sides. In any dispute, decisions reached using their opinions were final. When a feudal leader died his oldest son usually took his place. If there was no son, then the *azallar birliği* would choose another family member to continue the tradition. Sometimes a Kurdish woman would take on the leadership responsibilities, especially if her husband or father had been the leader.[21]

Traditionally, some Alevi Kurds took their cases to the *Cemevi*. This is a place to meet and to practise Alevi rituals, including singing, dancing, socialising and praying, under the guidance of *dede*.[22] The elders offer advice or suggestions about how to find answers to disputes or conflicts in front of the community rather than in a state court (Şener 1991; Metin 1995; Ergene 2003). Van Rossum (2008) has carried out further research on the practices surrounding dispute resolution in a *Cemevi* in the Netherlands.[23]

From 2001 Kurds in the UK took a much more organised approach to the familiar methods of dispute resolution. There had been several old people who regularly came to *Halkevi* and spent almost all day there, talking and gossiping about other people's family, business and criminal issues, as well as about politics. One day, the head of *Halkevi* asked them why they did not use their time for useful things, helping to resolve problems instead of just sitting and drinking tea. This was the beginning of the KPC and the system of secular Kurdish judges in the UK. While the state, state institutions and the majority population might consider this an unofficial system, for many Kurds, these people have the authority to act as their judges. According to one of my interviewees, this system aimed

> to give people a platform, a chance to discuss their issues. If we did not create this, people might impose their own judgments without any trial. We do not want any crime to be punished without a fair trial. Our elders, our judges, are like our fathers. And a good father cannot be unfair to their children.[24]

The following year, members of the community wanted to elect their own judges and this election process now continues every year. Judges are elected for one year only and must stand for election if they want to continue in the post. There is no restriction on the number of re-elections a candidate can stand for. The elections for judges are included in the annual elections for all positions in *Halkevi*. A secret ballot is used with a pre-advertised list of candidates. There are more than 10,000 Kurdish community members of *Halkevi* and, although there is good attendance, not all of these can attend the annual election meeting. The pre-advertisement process in the various community facilities means that the community is pre-informed about the elections and the candidates, as well as encouraging potential new judges to put their names forward.

---

21 KPC judges, interview November 2010.

22 It may be difficult to find established *dedes* in London, and temporary *dedes* may come from Turkey. Different clans have different *dedes* and may not accept the same *dede*.

23 See also Güzel (2004) for a detailed discussion of the *Cemevi* court process. Alevi come from many different ethnic groups, so the religious *Cemevi* system is not specifically Kurdish.

24 D.L., interview November 2010.

Any Kurdish community member can stand for election – not just the traditional *azallar birliği*. No special education is required to become a Peace Committee judge. However, the judges need to be respected leaders, trusted by the community and with recognised wisdom, negotiating skills and authority, as well as having an unblemished personal reputation and a specific knowledge of Kurdish traditions and customs. They are also required to have a good understanding of the environment, culture and language in their host country. Members must be seen by the community to have developed all these attributes in their personal and work relationships if they are to earn the privilege of being elected. Care is also taken that the Committee fully represents the plurality of Kurds, embracing those from different geographical traditions with different languages and religions and of different ages, especially including women as well as men. KPC members believe that when women – judges and claimants – take part in meetings then the language and style of the meetings changes positively.[25]

During my fieldwork I observed three Peace Committee elections between 2009 and 2012. In 2009 all the previous judges (one woman and seven men) were re-elected unopposed. Some of these judges had been working on the KPC since its inception. Then, at the end of 2010, six of the eight previous members chose to step down. The individual judges gave a range of different reasons for stepping down: to open up space for new members, to concentrate on their own business, because they had been there for so long that they had begun to be tired of the work or following on some long-term unresolved dispute, when they felt they had perhaps started to lose the trust of some members of the community.[26] One of the KPC members explained:

> It is not an easy job; it is very stressful. Most of our members get mentally and physically tired ... After a while, the committee members might lose their ambition to help the community ... Creating space for others, young people to participate is important to develop a democratic culture in the community. If there aren't elections then the Committee is no different from all the centralised state institutions.[27]

In the election at the end of 2010 six new members (one woman and five men) were elected, with two re-elections (one woman and one man). In 2011 only two members (one woman and one man) stepped down, to be replaced by two new members. In 2012 eight members (two women and six men) worked as judges for the KPC.

Service on the Committee is totally voluntary and unpaid. Committee meetings take place every Monday, although if there is an important case an additional meeting can be arranged. This type of work is altruistic, with committee members receiving only respect and trust from their community. All committee members have their own businesses or jobs and are not part of rich or privileged families. This is an important part of the strength of the Committee: the Kurdish community, and the committee members themselves, do not want proceedings to be dominated by somebody from a powerful family, as in the bad old days. Disputants might also be inhibited from presenting their cases in front of high status individuals.

---

25 KPC judges, interviews June 2009 and November 2010.
26 KPC judges, interview November 2010.
27 A.P., interview November 2010.

According to members of the KPC, their main motive in participating on the Committee is to help their community, to help their people live without conflict by solving their disputes.[28] Tears came to the eyes of the oldest member of the KPC when he explained his feelings about the work of the KPC and why he wants to serve Kurds till his death: 'My contribution may just be a drop in the ocean, but if I make one individual justly happy and make space for them to live in peaceful conditions, then I will feel the happiest person in the world.'[29]

Another KPC member told me that he was not born into an environment of individualism but into a community where the needs of the Kurdish public were more important than the needs of any one person:

> It wasn't just my house that was burned down by the Turkish state. The identity of the whole Kurdish people was ignored or destroyed by that same state. Thousands of people lost their lives. For this reason, I am happy to travel every Monday from outside London to the KPC for work.

Current committee members range in age from 25 to 70: it is clearly no longer just a job for old people. Members of the Committee believe that making space for members from different age groups helps them to more easily understand the problems of people of different ages, as well as showing that the Committee is open to everybody and that everybody should feel welcomed.[30]

The Procedures of the Kurdish Peace Committee

For any specific dispute one party to the conflict usually comes to the KPC to lodge a complaint. They are asked to fill in a one-page form, including details of the disputants' names, addresses and phone numbers. At the bottom of the page is a space for a brief summary of the complaint and the reason for the dispute. These details and those in any subsequent proceedings are kept strictly confidential. A small fee of £10 is requested. This covers the entire process and has only recently been introduced to cover the cost of the Committee's phone bills. Almost every day, committee members make calls to both sides of a dispute, to start or to continue sorting out a problem over the telephone. After the complaint has been lodged, one of the Peace Committee members contacts the other side to explain that there has been a complaint about them and to appoint a day for the hearing. According to KPC members, all parties in a dispute have to verbally agree to have their case accepted by the KPC before any mediation can start. This minimises unacceptable behaviour during and after the sittings. Even if one side does not agree to take part, KPC members will still try to calm people down, and continue to talk to both parties to try to reduce any further damage.

Once a case is agreed as proceeding, if either side wants to call witnesses they have to declare this prior to the hearing. First-degree relatives are not usually accepted as witnesses unless there are no other possible options. Furthermore, witnesses have to be accepted by both parties to the dispute. On the day of the hearing both sides take their places in front of the Peace Committee judges. Both sides are usually given equal time, without interruption,

---

28 KPC judges, interviews June 2009, November 2010.
29 A.E, interview November 2010.
30 KPC judges, interview November 2010.

to make their case, and equal time to respond to each other. They have to use peaceful language and show no violence. The Peace Committee must hear cases with at least two of its members present, but for a decision to be made there must be at least three presiding members. These rules are unwritten and unrecorded but, according to my observations and interviews, are clearly understood by all those who approach the KPC. During the dispute resolution meetings, the Peace Committee uses everyday language that can be easily understood: simple Kurdish or Turkish, or even English (if necessary). They do not use any special words or legal terminology. During the meeting, as well as hearing the testimonies, the KPC members can ask for more evidence on specific questions. They write notes, and discuss their written notes with each other before making any final decision. Most of the members write notes in Turkish. One out of the 16 committee members I have observed during my field work preferred to write Kurdish Kurmanji and one member wrote in English. Usually one of the members acts to lead the meeting.

If both sides to a dispute are in agreement at the end of the procedure, they sign a document to that effect, including the arrangements for the payment of any fines. The document is signed by both parties and also includes the signatures of a minimum of three Peace Committee members. In some cases, if there has been serious conflict and trust has degenerated to the extent that neither side wants to even see the other again, a Peace Committee member will be asked to act as the bridge for the payment. If the dispute is about a debt, and one party owes the other a significant sum of money but does not trust the payee, he can ask that the money be paid via a Peace Committee member. I witnessed several cases in which payments were made in this way. Sometimes, parties to a dispute who had received a large sum of money owing to them, showed their gratitude to the KPC for their altruistic work (*hizmet*) by gifting a proportion of the money they received via the KPC to the Kurdish Community Centre (KCC).[31] I was told that, this money is usually then used for young people, specifically to encourage them to educate themselves as Kurds and their involvement in the community, including through language classes and by the promotion of Kurdish music and Kurdish folk dance.

If the decision of the KPC is not accepted by all sides, then any unsatisfied parties can appeal by bringing the case to the Kurdish Public Appeal Court (*Halk Mahkemesi*). This is a joint meeting involving a wider group from the community. Most people want to avoid the publicity that this would entail and so this option is only resorted to very exceptionally, for example in the most expensive business disagreements.[32]

According to Peace Committee members, between 2001 and 2012 more than 3,500 cases have been taken to the Committee. This number does not include cases that are settled on the telephone without the need for a formal hearing. Nearly all cases involve only Kurds although, as mentioned above, other ethnic groups are also involved. Apparently, around 80 percent of the cases are fully resolved with the complainants accepting and acting on Peace Committee recommendations. I observed that around two-thirds of the cases were sorted out with a solution agreed within only two or three weeks. I was told that 15 to 20 percent of cases either cannot be resolved or the agreement arrived at is not followed in practice. A few cases have been ongoing since 2006. This situation can occur when one of the sides

---

31 The largest and most important of these are the Kurdish Community Centre in Haringey, north London (KCC) and *Halkevi* (public house). KCC and *Halkevi* have several branches across the UK, including in north London, Croydon, Leeds, Portsmouth and Glasgow. The KPC and Roj Women Association work under the umbrella of KCC/*Halkevi* in north London.

32 KPC judges, interview November 2010.

has not followed the Committee's decision or has been out of the UK for a long time. On average, each case takes between 20 and 40 minutes to hear. Some complicated business, family and criminal cases will take longer.

Most of the cases I witnessed concerned businesses and partnerships, finance and family. I also witnessed some small criminal cases, including theft and assault. KPC members told me that 60 to 70 percent of cases are about business and commercial disputes. Fifteen to 20 percent of cases are about family problems and a further 15 to 20 percent of them about threats, fighting or petty crime. Cases involving murder or manslaughter are initially brought before the Committee, with the aim of helping all parties to accept and come to terms with the tragedy that has taken place in the community; but the police have to be informed and the perpetrator is urged to go to the police and admit his guilt.[33] A few other cases have to be referred to a British court of law, but were also heard by the Peace Committee. For some of these, perhaps 5 to 10 percent, this followed difficulties in arriving at an agreement via the Peace Committee. The KPC themselves recommended that some cases should be taken to an official court, although some of these cases were then taken back to the Committee when the parties were not happy with the outcome. Other cases were initially taken by the disputants to the police or other formal legal institutions, but then ended up at the KPC when one or both parties wanted either a different outcome or to prove themselves to the community. A threat to take a case to an official court is sometimes used tactically, or to put pressure on a disputant for a quick resolution. Less powerful protagonists can try and rebalance power relations in their favour in this way. Merry (1979), Huang (1996) and Ergene (2003) have described how similar approaches are used in other, non-Kurdish societies.

The Roj Women's Association

The Kurdish community, working through *Halkevi*, has established other institutions to respond to particular and sensitive issues – both to serve the community and also in response to criticisms by human rights and feminist organisations in both Turkey and the UK that, for example, the unofficial dispute resolution system actually prevents Kurds from 'modernising' and taking a full and equal place in UK society. One of the most important challenge areas is around women's issues, and the Kurdish Women's Organisation was set up to help with this. A subgroup of this, Roj Women's Association (*Roj Kadın Meclisi*), focuses on resolving sensitive family conflicts, including domestic and sexual violence, and forced marriage.

According to those working in Roj Women Association, there are several reasons why the Kurdish community needed to make a special space for women. The PKK movement fundamentally changed the position of Kurdish women, when they fought side by side with men against the Turkish state. Women became more liberated and were more ready to demand their rights. Despite this, some Kurdish women still struggle under patriarchal forms of family domination, being oppressed by religious and cultural constraints. Young girls, new arrivals and women who speak no English are especially vulnerable in the UK and some of these women are abused or bullied by their families or husband. Some are threatened by, or subjected to, honour-based violence, blood feuds or forced marriage. Specific facilities open a window for Kurdish women to discuss and solve their problems.

---

33 KPC judges, interviews June 2009, November 2010.

They also act as a response to criticisms from some feminist groups that the unofficial system does not respond to the specific needs of women.[34]

One member of Roj Women told me about the many and varied needs of Kurdish women. Those who have a problem in their family often do not want, or are afraid, to share this issue with men and prefer to use services delivered by and for women. The Roj Women is one such service that hundreds of Kurdish women approach annually.[35] It was established in 2002 and has been especially active since 2008. The Kurdish Women's Organisation has 57 active individual members,[36] four of whom focus on Roj Women work. The Roj Women tackles disputes in a very similar way to the KPC, but also provides any necessary practical support for vulnerable women, such as arranging shelter, food and money for women who have no place of safety. The Roj Women does not ask even for the nominal fees the KPC require.[37]

The Roj Women and the KPC are closely interconnected. They refer cases to each other and help each other with any sensitive family issues. Although, as mentioned above, there are some women on the KPC, most of the KPC members are men and there is a concern that some women may lack the confidence or feel ashamed or embarrassed to bring their personal or family problems to a Committee that might be perceived as male-dominated. Care is always taken to ensure that the most sensitive issues are tackled as confidentially as possible, and the small scale of Roj Women can help with this.[38]

According to members of Roj Women, their organisation, like the KPC, tries to create safe environments for women and men who may be in danger, reducing harm and even saving lives, not just for those initially involved but also for the extended families who might get involved as these issues spiral out of control. Roj Women works closely with members of the state-organised Multi-agency Consortium (MARAC). This includes the police, local councils (for housing as well as through their domestic violence advisors), the Special Domestic Violence Court (SDVC) and other women's organisations as necessary. MARAC are especially involved in cases of the highest risk, such as those with an 'honour' issue or concerning forced marriage. If a safe environment is to be created for a woman, her children and sometimes her sister(s) too, if the latter are also at risk, whole new identities need to be created, perhaps in quite different locations. 'Honour'-based issues do not fade over time. Families can commit crimes decades after an initial problem. Danger is always present until the family decides the issue is completely resolved. This is where Roj Women comes in. Women who approach the police or any other state institution may well be putting themselves in increased danger since this contact can itself be seen as damaging the family's reputation and honour. Women working for Roj Women are part of the Kurdish community, making sharing a problem much easier. Unlike most other women's organisations, they are also willing to work directly with husbands or other male family members to discuss the issue and to find joint solutions.[39]

The Roj Women works in parallel with the police, sometimes at joint meetings, or by providing training and education around cultural sensitivity and different value systems.

---

34 B.G, interview January 2010.
35 There are also some other women's organisations such as Kurdish Women's Rights Watch, the Kurdish Advice Centre and the Turkish Speaking Women Organisation.
36 Each member has different responsibilities, including the education of children and women, language, events organisation and housing.
37 B.P., interview May 2011.
38 B.P., interview May 2011.
39 B.G., interview January 2010.

The police provide help with community safety and even supported a recent bid by Roj Women for central government funding. They acknowledge that Roj Women reduces their own workload and costs. A member of Roj Women told me:

> They [the police] started to trust us recently. However the police still try to take domestic violence to the special courts, because these are new and need cases if they are to continue. SDVCs [Specialist Domestic Violence Courts] were established in Islington in 2009 and Hackney in 2010. The judges there have special expertise, but women still don't want to go there – they prefer us. Women know that if they go to an official court then they may be in danger from their family. So if organisations like ours don't take some responsibility for these vulnerable women, they are in danger.[40]

SDVCs are still developing. While best practice is suggested to address both justice and safety for the women and families involved, several reviews have pinpointed the special needs and 'systemic weaknesses' of the system for women from ethnic minorities.[41] Incidentally, the principles underpinning SDVCs have been described as providing 'a welcome move away from traditional adversarial principles' towards a consensus approach involving the whole community – very similar ideas to those underpinning the KPC.[42]

Feminist and Other Criticisms of 'Customary' Solutions to Disputes

Not all Kurds are happy with KPC processes. There are some Kurds who want to distance themselves from PKK influences and consequently the KPC. There are also Kurds who prefer to live outside London's Kurdish community and who are unaware of the existence of the KPC. Even those who have heard of the KPC may prefer to use the state legal system, while others may utilise religious dispute resolution methods, such as unofficial Sharia courts.

There have also been some significant criticisms over 'customary' solutions to disputes, especially where women's rights are involved. Some Turkish, British and also Kurdish feminist organisations have suggested that 'customary' practices can never produce equitable solutions for women. Indeed, these groups directly blame 'customary' cultural practices – with their continuity of village norms and values – for all the various sorts of gender-based violence that exist. They therefore feel that a 'culturally sensitive' and, as they see it, inevitably male-dominated mediation process can have no place in the resolution of these sorts of problems.[43] Instead, they say, women regardless of their ethnic origin want to talk to other women, and the state should therefore recognise and support women's organisations when they fill the current service vacuum.[44]

There are extremely strong and polarised views on this topic. For example, a representative of a leading Turkish women's organisation talked to me about how the views

---

40 B.P., interview May 2011.
41 For detailed information see, for example Cook et al. (2004), SDVC Review (2007/08) and Team Hackney (2011/13).
42 For detailed information see, for example, Cook et al. (2006) and Matczak et al. (2011).
43 For similar claims see, for example, Okin (1998, 1999, 2002), Pollitt (1999) and Phillips (2007).
44 F.B., interview May 2011. This is an especially contentious issue in the current debates on Sharia law. See, for examples of others espousing a similar position, MacEoin et al. (2009) and Namazie (2010).

of her organisation were criticised by others as coming from 'prostitutes, lesbians, and those who want to destroy families: we hear such things, but this does not stop us carrying on telling the truth as we believe it'.[45] She specifically remembered one occasion in 1989, when members of her group were trying to protect a Kurdish woman who had been subjected to domestic violence and men came onto the streets to try to attack all the women involved. According to her, many of the men she saw that day had important positions inside the Kurdish community.[46] Another feminist activist reported her more general concerns about how one law should be enough for everybody: 'People should follow similar values. And if they come here [to the UK], they should follow this country's rule of law.'[47]

On the other side of the argument, a member of the KPC was clear about his position:

> Most of these people [the critics] are from Turkish feminist groups. They did not want us to live freely and celebrate our customs and traditions in Turkey. When we tried to practise our culture, we were accused of being 'separatist' or 'terrorist'. And not surprisingly, people of the same mentality, under a different name and in organisations which are supported by the Turkish government, do not want us to practise our culture and tradition here either.[48]

Both sides claim (loudly) to provide the best services: with the best approach to risk management and to confidentiality. Both believe they should be given the space, power – and, most importantly, funding – to continue their work. Although the feminist groups are insistent that women's problems are best dealt with by women, one Kurdish woman, who has asked for help both from a feminist organisation and also from the KPC, told me that she was concerned that the feminist approach simply created more problems between a couple:

> Even for a small problem, these [feminist] organisations advise women to separate from their husband, and involve the police. They do not think about the children or family unity. They do not bring the couple together and talk with them both, which the KPC do. And many couples who went to the KPC, sometimes even those who had a big problem, are now living together happily. But there are some, who had a small problem but preferred to go to these feminist organisations, who have separated. Their children have suffered very badly. KPC respects the family and tries to keep it together, convincing people not to think of divorce as a first option.[49]

One member of the KPC reported that the Committee was concerned that some feminist groups just concentrate on women and divorce, without considering men or the importance of family unity:

> We do know that we should care for those that are most vulnerable and, especially, look after children and women well. But when you do that you cannot just treat the men as scum.

---

45 F.B., interview May 2011.
46 F.B., interview May 2011.
47 D.K., interview January 2010.
48 B.E., interview May 2011.
49 M.G., interview January 2010.

Men are part of the issue and should also be treated carefully to create a peaceful solution.[50]

Hybridisation of Kurdish Law in the Gurbet

One KPC member told me, 'the sign and character of humanity is to harmonise with the environment.'[51] He emphasised that it is therefore not possible to maintain that there are no changes when people move from an underdeveloped rural eastern country to big metropolis in a developed Western country. This move has naturally affected Kurdish people. Even though they still stay close together, close Kurdish communities have been disrupted. Individualism and the nuclear type of family have increased. Several of my interviewees told me that they agreed that city life had changed them profoundly. One of my interviewees summarised this thus:

> In our village, if somebody promised something and swore on his *namus* (honour), it would definitely be done ... But here it is different. People can easily lose their way in a crowded city. They might change their mind two minutes after they gave their promise. They might do business together, but on the second day, they may try to cheat each other. Not all, but some families are alienated from each other, from their culture. Some people lie easily, they are unfaithful to each other, sons and daughters steal money from each other. People stop trusting each other. This is how the big city turns innocent people into troublemakers. Of course, we have to change and update some of our customs if we are going to respond to these erosions, these troubles.[52]

When Kurds change to fit into their new environment, it is thought that they both leave something behind and take something new. One Kurd described this to me as follows: 'it is like bringing together half an apple and half a pear to create a new fruit. It looks strange, doesn't it?'[53] Many of my interviewees believe that many of these 'not here, not there' people may not behave properly in either the Kurdish or the majority British communities. They can therefore be dangerous to both the state and the community and the Kurdish organisations work to try to limit this danger.[54] According to many of my interviewees, the KPC and similar organisations can help keep the 'half and half' mixed-culture people out of trouble, out of prison. They want to 'stop any escalation of crime'. KPC members believe that they are helping state institutions with this parallel system.[55]

According to a KPC member, although Kurdish customs and moral values play an important role during the KPC process, 'some Kurdish customs have had to be reshaped in response to the capitalist system and the global world. Kurds do not necessarily do everything in the same ways as in the Kurdish regions of Turkey.'[56] For example, religion used to be strong and women used to be weak. One KPC member gave an example of

---

50 M.H., interview November 2010.
51 A.E., interview November 2010.
52 B.E., interview November 2010.
53 M.C., interview June 2009.
54 For example, M.H., N.S, interviews June 2009; C.C., interview March 2011.
55 For example, M.U, interview May 2009; N.S., S.A., interviews June 2009; KPC judges, interview November 2010.
56 B.H., interview February 2010.

how this has changed from when he worked in a hospital in a Kurdish region in the 1970s and 1980s:

> Because of Shafi [Sunni Muslim] beliefs, some women did not want to be treated by men. Some even refused to be operated on by our male doctors. But, later, the women fighting in the PKK affected all Kurdish society. It changed the character of Kurdish women. Women learnt their rights. They started to refuse to be treated differently from men. This affected *gurbet* Kurds too. They have become more tolerant and open to their new environment.[57]

Unlike in Sharia courts or the Muslim Arbitration Tribunals, during my fieldwork I did not witness any obvious sign of decisions being made in conformity with religious rules. One KPC member told me:

> If we look carefully, every legal system has been influenced by, has benefited from religion. Religion is one of the important values for people. Of course, some of our customary practices – like the state law – might have been affected by religions. But we do not make any decisions which are directly based on religion. We are not a Sharia court and our people are not religious fanatics.[58]

Alevi Kurds who I interviewed were especially unhappy if their processes for dispute resolution were confused or conflated with Sharia law or practices. According to them, there is nothing religious about their legal approach. The same KPC member who spoke to me about religion also provided more detail about how, in the Kurdish community, men and women are supposed to have equal standing:

> The experiences, feelings, ideas and words of men and women are equal in our proceedings. In Kurdish society, some women might have difficulties, but this does not mean we [the KPC] approve of this. No-one should mix the crime [of so-called 'customary' behaviour] with the solution [of a dispute resolution process drawing on customary practices]. Many Kurdish women choose to come to us, because they know that we will support them. They know that we do not take sides in any conflict or dispute; they know that we do not base our decisions on religion. We are a place where they can find a solution and peace for their dispute in an easy, cheap, traditional and private way.[59]

In practice, I observed many women bringing cases to the KPC. Women are allowed to speak first regardless of whether they are the complainant or defendant. Even if there were some advantages in the system for men in the past, in the *gurbet* there is now even a tendency for positive discrimination towards women. This showed, KPC members told me, that their traditions are not static but instead are open to hybridisation.[60] The feminist who had told me about how members of her group were assaulted in the street in the domestic violence

---

57 A.E., interview November 2010.
58 A.P., interview November 2010.
59 A.P., interview November 2010.
60 M.H., N.S., interviews June 2009; A.E., interview November 2010.

case in 1989 also conceded that the community has changed. She said the men who had punched her then were now more supportive of women's rights.[61]

Kurdish customary law has had to respond to all the new needs of the community. A KPC member explained:

> The problems have changed but there are still problems, just different sorts of problems. There is individualism. But, thank God, in our community this individualism is still a marginal position, at a very low level. Also there are new family and business problems. There is a transformation. But still many Kurds want their problems to be sorted out by their own people, in the traditional ways.[62]

According to KPC members, they do not want to be static rule makers. They strive to change their views and rules, especially those which might be seen as biased against women: 'We are open for learning new things. We are not inventing new customs or traditions; we are updating and understanding new issues. Nothing can continue the same throughout time.'[63] According to KPC members, although they act as representatives for Kurdish identity, for Kurdish culture and its deeply rooted value system, they do not ignore democratic Western values and the concept of universal human rights.[64] For all these reasons, a process of hybridisation is very active.

Since the KPC is not the only alternative justice system for Kurdish people, this hybridisation occurs not only with the official state legal system but with a range of sources of help. Kurds with a dispute to resolve might approach a powerful Kurdish family or any of the underground mafia organisations. If they are Alevi, they might go to the *Cemevi*. Women may use any of the Kurdish, Alevi, voluntary or state organisations aimed at women. I observed complainants in business and divorce cases agreeing a compromise solution to their problem based somewhere between the multiple answers they had received from multiple services they had consulted. Incidentally, this competition means that each mediation service is keen to be seen by the community as the best.[65]

The other important area of hybridisation is with the UK state legal system. During my research I saw representatives of law firms coming to the KCC every week to advise people about the English legal system. Members of the Peace Committee have themselves benefited from this help and advice. KPC members generally advise complainants who are not happy with their decisions to go to a state court, and some cases that the Peace Committee cannot resolve are referred to these law firms. According to a barrister from one such firm, there are gaps in the present legal system which are filled by the Peace Committee and such a system could be adapted to help many different ethnic groups sort out their problems.[66]

---

61 F.B., interview May 2011.
62 B.E., interview November 2010.
63 B.E., interview May 2011.
64 KPC judges, interview November 2010.
65 KPC judges, interview November 2010.
66 U.R., interview July 2009.

The UK State Reaction to Kurdish Organisations

Initially, the UK authorities had concerns about the *Halkevi* organisation and the dispute resolution system set up by the Peace Committee. This was even though, in all cases involving serious or organised crime, including unlawful killing or drug smuggling, contact with the police is insisted upon. Although, according to KPC members, there is no pressure within the community for anyone to use their dispute resolution system, the police still continue to approach business persons and other Kurds to tell them to report any pressure from *Halkevi*.[67]

Despite some setbacks in police–community relations, Peace Committee members report that, after their considerable successes in resolving various community conflicts the police started to have a more positive attitude to the Peace Committee. Members of the police force have even attended dispute resolution meetings. There have been some cases of family or domestic conflict in which the police have recommended that the cases be taken to the Peace Committee or Roj Women. Recently, recognising that minor criminal cases might be taken to the Peace Committee, the police specifically ask any Kurds who contact them if they are definitely going to continue with their official complaint before expensive court proceedings are commenced. In these ways, the Peace Committee and Roj Women act as a useful adjunct to the official legal system and save police and court time and money.[68]

In recognition of this, the Peace Committee received £5,000 from the Home Office at the end of 2004, as a grant to cover their expenses. Committee members believe that they could receive more financial help from the Home Office but have chosen not to do this. They are afraid of being controlled and inspected by state institutions and fear that Home Office involvement could deter some people from bringing their cases to the Committee, particularly those involving illegal immigrants. Some Kurds do not want to be visible to the state and some family issues are especially sensitive, including arranged marriages and the traditional marriage promises for baby boys and girls. Many oral business contracts are also seen as sensitive – businessmen are concerned about disclosing transactions that are not declared to the tax authorities. The Peace Committee is concerned they could lose community trust if they work too closely with the police or the Home Office.[69]

However, since the 7 July 2005 bombings in London, members of the Kurdish community have been affected by the increased implementation of the Terrorism Act 2000. According to Sentas (2010), the PKK was banned in 2001 but the continuing ban has criminalised not only PKK members but the whole community. Kurdish activists have been stopped and searched, intimidated, harassed and arrested for short periods before being released without charge. Those distributing Kurdish newspapers, preparing for festivals or simply putting up posters have been detained. Some Kurdish flags are banned under the Terrorism Act 2000 because they are seen to be connected to the PKK. I have myself observed Kurds being prevented from waving or even carrying flags at the *Newroz* celebrations in 2009 (in Trafalgar Square) and in 2010 and 2011 (in Finsbury Park).

Despite perceived or actual police pressure on the Kurdish community, most of my interviewees told me that they valued the freedoms they have in the UK compared to Turkey. They enjoy celebrating their festivals, practising their culture and speaking their own language. They appreciate the good health and education services they and their

---

67 For example, KPC judges, interviews June, November 2010; M.U., interview May 2009.
68 KPC judges, interviews June, November 2010.
69 KPC judges, interview June 2009.

children receive. They especially like not being unemployed, thereby contributing to the national economy as well as supporting their own families and community.

In the following section of the chapter I will discuss in more detail three cases that I observed during my fieldwork with the KPC. These cases are selected to illustrate Kurdish family practices, as well as various kinds of disputes and some of the ways in which a resolution is reached.

Case Studies

Case 1: Conflict Following an Underage Marriage

This case demonstrates how family support may be less about protecting a vulnerable individual and more about ensuring the preservation of reputation and family honour. It also indicates how important a speedy resolution is – the family here especially wanted the KPC to act before anybody might hear that there was a problem with their young daughter's marriage and suspect her of being at fault when her husband was violent.

On 11 April 2011 Fidan, then 16 years old,[70] came with her father to the KPC. The father made the following statement:[71]

> My daughter married Serhat in the customary way. She does not have any official marriage contract. Because he is a close relative we did not need it. But we are totally disappointed by his behaviour. He does not come home most of time. When he does come it's very late, but if my daughter asks the reason, he uses violence against her. Recently he has increased his violence, and so my daughter went to the police to complain about him. Later, he pushed her to change her statement and she had to do this. But Serhat still continues his unacceptable behaviour. Now, Fidan is not feeling well and as a family our reputation and honour has been damaged. My daughter's life is endangered by him. Please help us, and explain to him about our culture and values.

After this statement, a KPC member contacted Serhat and explained the case against him. Serhat said that he was afraid to come to any meeting with his wife's family but that he was ready to respect any decision of the KPC. Members of the KPC and Roj Women talked separately with both sides. After these consultations, Serhat apologised for his actions several times and promised not to repeat them. The wife, Fidan, was ready to continue her marriage, mostly to maintain her family's reputation and honour, but wanted the KPC members to bear witness and advise Serhat to stop being violent towards her. A member of Roj Women warned Fidan about the potential danger from her husband and offered to arrange a safe refuge for her. However, both sides chose to live together from 15 April 2011, just four days after the case process. This speedy

---

70 It is common for many Kurdish families to arrange marriages for their children when they are young. Early marriages sometimes cause problems, particularly in the *gurbet*, but families continue to support these arrangements in order to maintain the families' close ties and honour. See, for example, A (A Child) (No. 2) [2011] EWCA Civ 12.

71 All names of the individuals involved in the case studies described here are pseudonyms. The information for this particular case is based on the plaintiffs' written statement to the KPC members, my observations of the KPC meeting for this case and KPC judges, interview April 2011.

resolution was largely due to concerns within Fidan's family about gossip while the couple were separate.

Case 2: Divorce

This is a divorce case that the KPC considered after a family agreement had broken down. There were disagreements over the financial arrangements, but the real sticking point was linked to honour. This case illustrates the importance of the family in making and breaking marriages, the transnational nature of many KPC cases, and the risky situation that women can find themselves in. Some of the KPC documents are, with permission, included verbatim here, to illustrate both the court processes and also how community members think and act.

In the divorce case considered here, the official marriage took place in Turkey, while a *düğün* (customary wedding ceremony) took place later in the UK. Unfortunately, after only one and a half months, the husband decided that he wanted to end the marriage. Initially, elders of the two families agreed a separation and divorce arrangement, which involved equitably dividing the gifts and cash (£40,000) received from family and friends at the *düğün*. However, when the family of the ex-husband also insisted the wife return to Turkey, the agreement fell apart and the wife's brother approached the KPC to mediate a solution. The man's family said that they wanted the ex-wife to leave the UK because they felt that her presence might bring shame upon the ex-husband's family, especially if she were to begin a new relationship.

The KPC meetings involved representatives of the families, rather than the individuals themselves: the ex-wife's brother and her uncle represented the woman, whilst the man was represented by his father. After extensive discussions, the KPC decided to uphold the initial financial agreement prepared by the two families. However, they were very angry with the demands of the husband's family that the woman immediately return to Turkey. Upon hearing this, one of the KPC members said to the father of the man: 'if you have this concern, why did your son finish the marriage after one and half months? Your son wants to cover his dishonourable behaviour with another dishonourable action. It is totally up to her where she wants to live. It is not our duty or your duty either to decide where she should live.' The KPC decided that the woman did not have to return to Turkey, and that the husband would be responsible for filing for an official divorce in Turkey. Both families agreed not to claim any financial compensation as part of this official divorce. They both agreed to pay their own court fees. The KPC decided that the husband should repay the wife's family share of the wedding cash (£20,000), along with six pieces of gold.

This case illustrates the importance of the dual customary marriage and divorce processes: there are therefore two marriages and two divorces to consider, and the greater importance – in practice – of the customary system. Kurdish marriages (and divorces) are between two families within a community, rather than a purely private arrangement between two individuals. Kurdish marriages are, at least partially, business arrangements – with the couple given resources from the community to help them start their new life.

As in many of the other cases I witnessed, this example is of a transnational problem, with transnational solutions. Here, the members of the ex-wife's family already living in the UK were concerned for her not to be sent back to Turkey. Family members living in Turkey might blame her for the short marriage and perception of so-called 'family honour' could mean that her life would be in danger in Turkey. The wife's brother was in a strong position within her family, and could protect her not only from her own family but also try to prevent further gossip. Any gossip might put her at further risk – not only from a spoiled reputation within the Kurdish community, but also from her ex-husband and his family, who still clearly considered themselves as able to control her, even after the marriage had ended. It seems paradoxical that the husband, who has behaved so badly, seems the most likely to initiate a blood feud – and endanger not only his ex-wife, but any new partners she might have. On the other hand, the wife's brother was simply concerned to resolve the case, and get a fair share of the money that had been given to the couple, rather than getting any financial or other compensation for his sister's potentially spoilt reputation. Even though the KPC involvement has helped reduce the possibility of a blood feud, it is difficult to know what the future will bring for the wife. If her family, and especially her brother, is powerful enough in the community then hopefully she will stay safe.

Case 3: Property Dispute

This case involves a dispute between three brothers and their parents in Turkey. Two of the brothers live in the UK and the other lives in Germany. The dispute is over a property in Turkey, currently consisting of six separate apartments. An oral agreement was made within the family that each brother would have two apartments, and that an extra floor would be built in the future as another apartment for the parents to live in. All contributed financially in equal amounts. However, the ownership documents for the property were prepared in just one person's name, the eldest brother, who lives in London. This eldest brother refused to let work start on building the extra floor, or to let other family members use the extant property. This created conflict in the family. One of the brothers, who lives in Germany, brought the case to the KPC in April 2011. The eldest, London-based, brother was present and the parents were due to give telephone evidence to the KPC. The eldest brother, however, was not happy about the parents giving evidence and said: 'It is not a good idea if you call our father and mother. They are old and ill. They should not take part in our disagreement.'

The brother who lives in Germany interrupted him: 'Of course you do not want our parents involved. You know that they do not agree with you and they will say that you are a liar. They are our elders. They should take part in the decision.' After this, a KPC member telephoned the parents. The phone was put on loudspeaker so that everybody in the room could hear what the father and mother were saying. The father repeated what his son from Germany had said, claiming:

> We trusted our [eldest] son and put everything in his name. But, today, look at what he is doing to us. He does not have any shame and he has brought shame on our family. We cannot look in other people's eyes. Everybody knows that we have a problem in our family. This son is a greedy, grasping man. My other son worked very hard in Germany and gave him money for this building. My disabled son also gave all his savings. Their mother and I spent our time and energy to build this building. It is a family property. It does not just belong to one person. Because of our shameless son, we might even have to go to a state court to get what is due to us. But this would bring even more shame on us.

The mother also spoke on the phone, shouting at her eldest son: 'I fed you, I looked after you and I gave you my milk. Look at what you are doing to us. I will regret having given my milk to you if you do not sort this problem out immediately.' The eldest son immediately replied: 'Mother, I am sorry. I want to apologise to you and my father. Don't worry, we will sort all this out quickly.' An agreement was therefore reached such that: first, each brother was to have two apartments; second, the construction of the extra floor would start immediately; third, the three brothers agreed to contribute equally to the cost of building the extra floor. The KPC members also warned the eldest brother that his reputation as a local businessman was at stake if he continued to treat his family badly.

I have continued to follow this case. In August 2011, the whole family met in Turkey. The mother and father are now living in one of the six flats, and the others are being rented out to new tenants. Building of the additional floor has started, and the eldest son has received some additional monies from his brothers.

This case demonstrates several important generic points. Both the family involved, and the case itself, were transnational. However, the use of a customary approach was considered appropriate for a transnational conflict. The case illustrates how Kurdish families use oral agreements, based on trust, for significant financial and property matters. It shows how the official courts can be used as a threat to enforce agreements. The courts are, however, only an option of last resort, since they mean additional shame and damage within a family. Additionally, the case demonstrates the importance of family elders. Younger family members do not want to have these sorts of conflicts. It is especially important to avoid having a public intra-family conflict, since this may affect business and other reputations. The mother in this case must have already expressed her feelings to her errant son in private, so he initially tried to avoid her being given an opportunity to speak in public. When she did so, he was immediately repentant. Finally, this case demonstrates the value of detailed observational reporting – the only written record of the case is the initial two-sentence submission, and the (one-paragraph) annotated agreement.

Conclusion

The research reported in this chapter has aimed to understand and, if possible, to explain the work of the unofficial Kurdish dispute resolution system in operation in the UK. The prime importance of setting any mediational practice in its cultural context has been underlined. For Kurds in the UK, kinship ties, including marriages, frequent travel back and forth to other international Kurdish communities, and cheap telecommunications all maintain strong ties with a real and imagined transnational Kurdish community or *gurbet* (diaspora).

In the *gurbet* context, the state legal system may not be followed by many Kurds for various reasons. Arriving as traumatised outsiders from a repressive regime and then experiencing similar difficulties in the course of their settlement in a new country, Kurds may lose whatever limited trust they had in the state legal system of their new host country. In the course of discussions with KPC members and other members of the community, it became clear that Kurds also wanted to hold onto their customs and their sense of identification with a community that has been under threat and that they have had to fight to preserve. They said that for even the smallest of their rights they had to pay a price in Turkey, and now that they are in the UK they have no intention of giving any of them up.

In addition, almost all of my interviewees agreed that they did not really understand the UK state legal system. It seemed alien and appeared to exclude them in terms of language, education and so on. Some Kurds have experienced resentment by officials when they tried to use the translation services which are theoretically available in the courts and other legal institutions. According to most of my interviewees, the official legal system is too expensive, too complicated and too inflexible to cater adequately for the needs of the

Kurdish community. My informants told me that Kurdish customary methods of dispute resolution are generally cheaper, easier, swifter and more private, as well as being more appropriate to their own culture and individual circumstances. In this context, KPC and Roj Women's Association want to take advantage of a pluralising society to regulate and develop their own 'unofficial' dispute resolution system. They also want to avoid the escalation inherent in the harsh mafia-style processes.

As Kurds arrived in the UK, they had to make many changes in their customary way of life. The KPC and Roj Women's Association recognise the new and different family and other legal challenges which have developed – and that these need hybrid forms of legal solutions. These will continue to change, alongside the community. Many of my interviewees were eloquent on this topic, even if they have not yet fully resolved their response to the more subtle sort of assimilation that they witness taking place in the UK.

The KPC practices have been described as customary. They have therefore been criticised as, by definition, being 'unfit for purpose' in the modern world, especially for those women who were disadvantaged in the 'bad old customary days' of village life. However, many of my interviewees – both female and male – believe that the KPC and Roj women do not prevent Kurds from modernising. They repeatedly told me that the KPC offered what they thought of as justice – no less a justice than the state can offer. In fact, the hybrid and continuously developing nature of the KPC mediation processes acts to meet the needs of Kurds in a changing world. While the KPC is part of maintaining a dynamic Kurdish community in the *gurbet*, it is also a training ground for an imagined *welat*.

The Kurdish case-study shows how some ethnic groups can choose between a variety of options when they try to resolve their disputes – and that they tend to choose an option that delivers effective justice in a simple and economic way. Certainly, the 'unofficial' dispute process relieves pressure on the state courts: 80 percent of the 3,500 cases that the KPC considered between 2001 and 2012 were resolved. In this light, we might ask whether the state wants to deal with all these disputes; or whether it would not do better to accommodate this plurality, rather than ignoring or rejecting the existing successful practices of different ethnic groups.

References

Ballard, R. 1994. *The Emergence of Desh Pardesh. The South Asian Presence in Britain*. London: Hurst & Co.

Bano, S. 2012. *Muslim Women and Shari'ah Councils: Transcending the Boundaries of Community and Law*. London, Basingstoke: Palgrave Macmillan

Bowen, J.R. 2003. *Islam, Law and Equality in Indonesia: An Anthropology of Public Reasoning*. Cambridge: Cambridge University Press.

Bowling, B. and Phillips, C. 2002. *Racism, Crime and Justice*. Harlow: Longman.

Chowdhury, M.H. 1993. Popular attitudes, legal institutions and dispute resolution in contemporary Bangladesh. *Legal Studies Forum*, 17(3), 291–300.

Cook, D., Burton, M., Robinson, A. and Vallely, C. 2004. *Evaluation of Specialist Domestic Violence Courts / Fast Track Systems*. Crown Prosecution Service (CPS) [Online]. Available at: http://www.cps.gov.uk/publications/docs/specialistdvcourts.pdf [last accessed 30 April 2012].

Cook, D., Burton, M. and Robinson, A. 2006. *Enhancing 'Safety and Justice': The Role of Specialist Domestic Violence Courts in England and Wales*. British Society of Criminology [Online], 7. Available at: http://www.britsoccrim.org/volume7/008.pdf [last accessed 30 April 2012].

Demir, I. 2012. Battling with *memleket* in London: The Kurdish diaspora's engagement with Turkey. *Journal of Ethnic and Migration Studies*, 38(5), 815–31.

Ergene, B.A. 2003. *Local Court, Provincial Society and Justice in the Ottoman Empire: Legal Practise and Dispute Resolution in Çankırı and Kastamonu (1652–1744)*. Leiden, Boston: Brill.

Galanter, M. 1981. Justice in many rooms: Courts, private ordering, and indigenous law. *Journal of Legal Pluralism and Unofficial Law*, 19, 1–47.

Goh, B.C. 2002. *Law Without Lawyers, Justice Without Courts: On Traditional Chinese Mediation*. Aldershot: Ashgate.

Güzel, D. 2004. *Alevi Halk Mahkemeleri*. Ankara: ÜBL.

Hinz, M.O. 2012. The ascertainment of customary law: What is ascertainment of customary law and what is it for? The experience of the Customary Law Ascertainment Project in Namibia. *Oñati Socio-Legal Series*, 2(7). Available at: http://ssrn.com/abstract=2100337 [last accessed 9 February 2013].

Huang, P. 1996. *Civil Justice in China: Representation and Practise in the Qing*. Stanford: Stanford University Press.

Keshavjee, M. 2007. Alternative dispute resolution in a diasporic Muslim community, in *Law and Ethnic Plurality: Socio-Legal Perspectives*, edited by P. Shah. Leiden: Martinus Nijhoff, 145–75.

Khayati, K. 2008. *From Victim Diaspora to Transborder Citizenship: Diaspora Formation and Transnational Relations among Kurds in France and Sweden*. Linköping: LiU-Tryck.

MacEoin, D., Addison, N. and Green, D.G. 2009. *Sharia Law or One Law for All*. London: Civitas.

Makec, J.W. 1988. *The Customary Law of the Dinka People of Sudan: In Comparison with Aspects of Western and Islamic Laws*. London: Afroworld Publishing.

Matczak, A., Hatzidimitriadou, E. and Lindsay, J. 2011. *Review of Domestic Violence Policies in England and Wales*. London: Kingston University and St George's, University of London.

Menski, W. 1987. Legal pluralism in the Hindu marriage, in *Hinduism in Great Britain: The Perpetuation of Religion in the Alien Cultural Milieu*, edited by R. Burghart. London and New York: Tavistock, 180–200.

Menski, W. 1993a. Asians in Britain and the question of adaptation to a new legal order: Asian laws in Britain, in *Ethnicity, Identity, Migration: The South Asian Context*, edited by M. Israel and N.K. Wagle. Toronto: Centre for South Asian Studies, University of Toronto, 238–68.

Menski, W. 1993b. *Angrezi Shariat: Plural Arrangements in Family Law by Muslims in Britain*. London: SOAS (Unpublished paper), 1–10.

Menski, W. 2008. *Ethnic Minority Legal Studies: Managing Cultural Diversity and Legal Pluralism*. London: SOAS School of Law.

Merry, S.E. 1979. Going to court: Strategies of dispute management in an American urban neighborhood. *Law and Society Review*, 13(4), 891–925.

Metin, I. 1995. *Alevilerde Halk Mahkemeleri*. Istanbul: Alev Yayınevi.

Namazie, M. 2010. *Sharia Law in Britain: A Threat to One Law for All and Equal Rights*. London: One Law for All.
Okin, S.M. 1998. Feminism and multiculturalism: Some tensions. *Ethics*, 108(4), 661–84.
Okin, S.M. 1999. Is multiculturalism bad for women?, in *Is Multiculturalism Bad for Women?*, edited by J. Cohen, M. Howard and M.C. Nussbaum. Princeton, NJ: Princeton University Press.
Okin, S.M. 2002. Mistresses of their own destiny: Group rights, gender, and realistic rights of exit. *Ethics*, 112(2), 205–30.
Pearl, D. and Menski, W. 1998. *Muslim Family Law*. London: Sweet & Maxwell.
Phillips, A. 2007. *Multiculturalism without Culture*. Oxford: Princeton University Press.
Pollitt, K. 1999. Whose culture?, in *Is Multiculturalism Bad for Women?*, edited by J. Cohen, M. Howard and M.C. Nussbaum. Princeton, NJ: Princeton University Press, 27–30.
Povey, D. (ed.) 2011. *Police Powers and Procedures England and Wales 2009–10*. 2nd edition. London: Home Office.
Romano, D. 2006. *The Kurdish Nationalist Movement, Opportunity, Mobilization and Identity*. Cambridge: Cambridge University Press.
Rosen, L. 1989. *The Anthropology of Justice: Law as Culture in Islamic Society*. Cambridge: Cambridge University Press.
Rosen, L. 1995. Law and custom in the popular legal culture of North Africa. *Islamic Law and Society*, 2, 194–208.
Rosen, L. 2000. *The Justice of Islam*. Oxford: Oxford University Press.
SDVC Review. 2007/08. *Specialist Domestic Violence Courts Review*. SDVC. Available at: http://www.cps.gov.uk/publications/equality/sdvc_review.html [last accessed 30 April 2012].
Şener, C. 1991. *Alevi Törenleri*. Istanbul: Anadolu Matbaası.
Sentas, V. 2010. *The Impact of 'Terrorist Organisation' Laws on Diaspora Claims for Self-determination: Peoples in Motion: Self-determination and Secession* (Belfast, 5 June 2010). [Online]. Available at: http://www.eldh.eu/fileadmin/user_upload/ejdm/publications/documentation/Vicky_Sentas_-_speech_-_5th_June_2010.pdf [last accessed 16 June 2011].
Sheffer, G. 2002. *Diaspora Politics: At Home Abroad*. New York: Cambridge University Press.
Sheikhmous, O. 1990. The Kurds in exile, in *Yearbook of the Kurdish Academy*, edited by K. Fuad, F. Ibrahim and N. Mahwi. Ratingen: The Kurdish Academy, 88–114.
Sheleff, L. 1999. *The Future of Tradition: Customary Law, Common Law and Legal Pluralism*. London: Frank Cass.
Sweetnam, D.L. 1994. *Kurdish Culture: A Cross-Cultural Guide*. Bonn: Culture and Science Publication.
Taş, L. 2012. *Kurds in the UK: Legal Pluralism and Alternative Dispute Resolution*. School of Law, Queen Mary, University of London (unpublished PhD thesis).
Team Hackney. 2011/13. Hackney Domestic and Gender Violence Strategy (2011/13). Available at: http://www.hackney.gov.uk/Assets/Documents/Domestic_Violence_Strategy_booklet.pdf [last accessed 30 April 2012].
Topping, A. 2011. Looting fuelled by social exclusion. *The Guardian*, 8 August. Available at: http://www.guardian.co.uk/uk/2011/aug/08/looting-fuelled-by-social-exclusion [last accessed 7 November 2011].

van Rossum, W.M. 2008. Religious courts alongside secular state courts: The case of the Turkish Alevis. *Law, Social Justice & Global Development Journal (LGD)*. Available at: http://www.go.warwick.ac.uk/elj/lgd/2008_2/rossum [last accessed 11 March 2009].

Werbner, P. 2002. The place which is diaspora: Citizenship, religion and gender in the making of chaordic transnationalism. *Journal of Ethnic and Migration Studies*, 28(1), 119–33

Yilmaz, Ihsan 2005. *Muslim Laws, Politics and Society in Modern Nation-States: Dynamic Legal Pluralism in England, Turkey and Pakistan*. Aldershot: Ashgate.

Index

accommodation, legal xv, 2–3, 8, 21, 38, 51, 53, 56, 69, 99, 103, 105–6, 112, 115–6, 197, 206
    reasonable 56, 69
adoption 3, 4n, 104–5, 174; see also *kafala*
adultery 64n
advocates, see lawyers
Afghanistan 60
African legal systems 16, 19, 29n, 38, 43, 44n, 51, 55
Africans 6, 20, 36, 56, 83, 118n, 119n
alcohol 173
Alevis 216, 225–6
Algerians 17
alternative dispute resolution; see also arbitration xiv, 4, 8n, 15n, 20–23, 30, 43, 133, 144–5, 196, 200, 209–232
Antokolskaia 1, 41
arbitration; see also alternative dispute resolution 40, 43, 45, 133, 195, 198–9, 200, 205–6, 225
Archbishop of Canterbury, see Williams, Rowan
Armenians 182
Assyrian Church 182, 184
asylum seekers and refugees 83, 150, 168, 183–4, 192, 213n
attorneys, see lawyers
Australia 185
Austria 52n, 64, 185
autonomy, individual xiv, xv, 15, 50, 54, 56, 62, 81, 146, 148n, 168, 172, 177

Bangladesh 10, 34n, 42, 62, 118n
barristers, see lawyers
Belgium 1, 5–6, 11, 18, 21n, 63–4, 66, 70n, 185, 209n
Beth Din 22–3, 49, 94n, 133–4, 198–200, 202–4
Balkan states 52
Bowen, John 20, 30, 33n, 36
Britain 20–21, 23, 32, 38, 51, 61, 109n, 120, 132–6, 203; see also England, London, United Kingdom
Buddhism 80n, 86n, 176–7
Bulgaria 1, 6, 9n, 12
burials 81

Canada 14, 38, 44n, 185
caste 37
Catholicism, Roman 20, 22, 71n, 85–6, 90–91, 93n, 121n, 148, 158, 188, 190–91, 196, 197n, 201–2
    Catholic Tribunals 196, 197n, 198–9, 201–2, 204
children xii, 4n, 7, 11–12, 13n, 23, 53, 55, 56n, 68–72, 87, 89n, 129, 146, 150, 155, 168, 172–4, 176–7, 186, 189–90, 196, 200, 202–5, 221, 223, 228; see also adoption, custody, *kafala*
    abduction 71–2
    best interests of the child 34, 41–2, 46, 70–2, 87, 89n, 145–6, 159n, 196, 205, 223
    child marriage 89, 93–5, 97, 100, 127, 147, 156, 228
    Christian 71n
    custody of 53, 56–7, 61, 68–72, 160n, 189–90, 204
    Jewish 71n, 203
    Muslim 127, 129, 150
Christendom 157–8
Christian legal tradition 1, 10, 50, 52n, 55, 57, 91, 116n, 152n, 157, 189–90, 206
    canon law 2, 7–8, 15, 55, 158, 160, 189–90, 202
    ecclesiastical courts 20, 22n, 190–192, 198
Christianity 1; see also Catholicism, Church of England, Protestantism, Syriac Church
Christians 49, 52, 56–7, 68, 80, 86, 90, 175–6, 181–93
Church of Denmark 80, 87n, 92
Church of England and Church in Wales 5n, 122–3, 125
Church of Finland 80, 87n
Church of Iceland 80–92
Church of Norway 80
Church of Sweden 80–82, 85n, 86–7, 89n, 91–2, 95–7, 188
Churches, Nordic Folk's 80–82, 90–91, 98–9
church-state relations 2, 4–5, 32, 52n, 55, 80–82, 85–7, 89–91, 98, 157, 188–91, 206
circumcision (male) 39, 71n, 144, 153n, 211

citizenship and nationality xiv, 1–4, 10–12, 38, 56, 58, 66–8, 111, 122, 124, 131, 144n, 150, 157, 182–4, 189
cohabitation 9, 16, 55n, 82, 118–19, 172, 186, 189, 204, 206
colonialism 20
common law 72, 121n, 157–8
conflict of laws, conflict-rules; see private international law
conscience, freedom of; see freedom of religion
contracts xv, 14–15, 56, 58, 61, 64, 68–9, 72n, 104–5, 108, 200, 203, 212, 227; see also marriage
contractualisation 69
counsel, see lawyers
Court of Justice of the European Union 148

diet 33n
divorce xii, 1, 3–4, 10–23, 40–2, 49, 52n, 53, 55–68, 70, 82, 90n, 93–4, 104–5, 116–17, 118n, 129–36, 144n, 148–4, 156, 160, 168, 174, 188–91, 195–206, 223, 226, 229
    get 17–19, 49, 59, 62, 63n, 130, 134, 154, 198, 200–204
    Islamic 3, 17–18, 22n, 42, 49n, 62–5, 73, 115, 129–36, 156, 201, 204
    khul 18, 63, 131, 201, 204
    proxy 129–30
    talaq 3, 17–18, 22n, 42, 49n, 62–5, 73, 129–35, 156, 201, 204
    transnational 10
Dutch, see Netherlands, the

ecclesiastical courts 20, 22n, 190–92, 198
education 71, 81, 83, 85, 87, 99, 155, 168, 170–71, 177, 192, 213, 215, 217, 221, 227, 231; see also legal education
    religious 71, 80, 86, 94
Egypt xiv, 18n, 52, 55, 118n, 131–2
England and Wales 1, 5, 8–10, 12, 14, 16n, 18–19, 31, 37n, 40–42, 54, 63, 66, 71n, 104n, 120–22, 127, 133, 135n, 143, 145n, 147, 195–8, 200, 206; see also Britain, London, United Kingdom
English law 3–4, 9n, 10, 16n, 22–3, 31, 41–2, 134, 145, 197, 206, 213
equality 52, 57, 86, 89, 145–7, 153, 206; see also gender equality
    between spouses 16, 18, 61, 82
ethnicity 34–5, 146, 206
Eurocentrism 8, 39, 43

Europe xi–xiii, xv, 1–2, 13, 16, 20, 22–4, 29, 34, 49, 52, 55–6, 58–9, 63, 80, 103–4, 106, 110–12, 118–9, 128, 135, 137, 143–6, 156, 158, 181–3, 187n, 188–91, 213
European Commission 1
European Commission of Human Rights 154
European Convention of Human Rights (ECHR) 7–8, 63, 83, 84n, 148
    Eurocentrism and 8
European Court of Human Rights (ECtHR) 1, 7–9, 21, 124, 148, 155–6
European culture 16, 24, 30, 44, 50, 52–4, 57, 65, 67, 73, 103, 106, 109, 143, 145–9, 156, 173, 190
European Economic Area 122
European legal systems 1, 3–4, 11, 14–17, 23–4, 32–3, 41, 45, 50–55, 57, 59, 60–65, 68, 70–73, 103–112, 115–116, 119–20, 125, 127–8, 132, 137, 145, 149, 152–3, 157–9
    courts 3, 9, 11–12, 15–16, 23–4, 37, 61–2, 65, 129, 144, 149, 154, 156, 158–61
    judiciary 3, 7, 9, 14, 18, 62, 115, 143, 156–7
European Union (EU) 1–2, 105, 124, 148
expert witnesses 9–10, 17n, 40–41, 60, 118n, 159n
extremism 84–5, 89, 99, 182n

faith schools 86
families 3; see also children, marriage
    extended 34, 40, 201–11, 221
    kinship 23, 181, 185, 192, 210–11, 231
    nuclear 185, 224
family law xii–xv, 1–3, 13–16, 24, 29, 36, 43, 53, 56–8, 69, 71, 82–3, 99–100, 104–5, 117n, 143–5, 153, 181, 190, 195, 200
    academics 37, 40, 117n
    comparative 1
    Denmark 152, 191
    England 31, 63, 133–5
    European 1, 15, 29, 45, 55, 57–8, 62, 67–8, 71–2, 103–6, 109, 116n, 145, 191
    Hindu 104
    India 34n, 104
    international and transnational 67, 149, 185
    Iran 72n
    Italy 107
    Lebanon 190
    Middle East 187
    Muslim 2–3, 17, 18n, 22, 52, 54, 153–4, 159, 169
    Nordic 82, 85, 89–90, 92, 99–100, 191
    Norway 191

Pakistan 118n, 134
religious 59–63, 144, 146, 153, 181
Scotland 8, 204
secularisation 20, 92, 146
Sweden 80, 152, 187, 191
Turkey 189
uniformity of 2, 103–6
fathers 53, 60, 70n, 71–2, 147, 170–71, 173–7, 186, 211, 216, 228–31
female genital mutilation 72
feminism 159, 209, 220–23, 225
finance, Islamic 31, 45
France 1, 5, 6, 11–15, 17, 33n, 61, 64, 66, 153n, 154, 156, 188, 190, 210
freedom of religion xiii, xvi, 5n, 7, 19n, 52, 54–6, 70, 82n, 83–5, 88, 91n, 92–3, 95, 98–9, 124, 144, 153–5, 191, 204
funerals 81

gender equality 16–17, 53, 63, 82, 87, 109, 110n, 206
Germany 1, 13–14, 15n, 33n, 39, 61n, 66–7, 82n, 147n, 183, 185, 209, 230
Glenn, H.P. 32
globalisation 13, 24, 32, 34, 37, 43, 50, 115–6, 119, 137, 143, 177, 201, 224
Greece 2, 17, 58
Guardians 53, 70–72, 150n, 211
gypsies, see Roma

halal, see diet
Hindu law 17n, 22, 104–5, 107–110, 112n
Hindus and Hinduism 22, 80, 106
Holland, see Netherlands, the
Homicide 167, 212, 227
homosexual marriage 5, 189
homosexual partnership 72
homosexuality 5, 72, 92, 146, 155, 167, 175, 223
honour 167–8, 177, 203, 211–3, 221, 228–9, 224
  killings or violence 89, 220
human rights 18, 32–4, 36–9, 43, 46, 53–4, 57, 61, 63, 65, 68, 73, 80, 100, 123, 136, 146, 148, 152, 154, 156, 157n, 158, 160, 191, 220, 226; see also European Court of Human Rights (ECtHR), European Convention on Human Rights
Human Rights Act 1998 (UK) 123

imams 80, 94
immigrants 30, 33, 54, 57–8, 67, 123, 129, 211, 132, 134, 165, 167, 170, 191–3, 215, 227
  British 32n
  Christian 181, 183, 188

Illegal 227
intra-European 32, 67, 111
Iraqi 192
Kosovan 192
Kurdish 211
Muslim 20–21, 33, 126, 165, 168, 175, 181
Somali 192
Turkish 20–21
unemployment and 83
women 12
immigration controls and policies 6, 42, 66, 122–8, 168, 215
  European Union 13
  marriage and spouses 6, 12, 66, 122–8, 148, 154
  polygamy 12n, 66
India 13, 15, 20, 34n, 35, 37, 43–4, 51–2, 55, 103–4, 106–7, 109–11, 112n
Indians 13, 15, 35, 44, 134
inheritance and wills xii, 4n, 21, 23, 52, 129, 161n, 189–90, 211–12
Iran 18, 64, 72n, 131, 144n, 151–2, 212
Ireland 32
Islam 2, 6, 8, 22n, 23, 30, 32, 33n, 51, 53, 71, 79–80, 83–4, 88, 110, 124–5, 136, 144, 146, 154, 158, 165, 168, 171, 175–6, 182, 203
Islamic law 3, 4, 10–11, 13, 16, 18, 20–23, 31, 34, 40, 42, 45, 50, 52–3, 60–63, 65, 68, 71, 84, 110, 115–6, 118–22, 127–33, 135–6, 145–6, 149, 158–60, 165, 169, 199, 201, 204
  angrezi shariat 20, 118n
Islamophobia 79, 191n, 192
Israel 17, 52, 197
Italy 1, 3, 5, 9, 12–13, 18, 55, 56n, 57, 64, 66, 68n, 70, 71n, 107, 115, 117–8, 120–27, 129–32, 134, 156n

Jains 71n
Jehovah's Witnesses 56, 70
Jewish law 2, 17, 19, 49, 59, 62, 63n, 130, 134, 154, 198, 200–204
Jews and Judaism 2, 19–20, 49, 52, 57, 59, 68, 136, 157n, 190–91, 197–8, 209
judges and judiciary xii, 2–3, 6–11, 14–16, 18–19, 23n, 30–32, 34, 40–42, 44–6, 58, 60, 62n, 110n, 115, 117, 125–6, 129–36, 143, 145, 152–3, 156, 160–61, 199, 205, 212–28

kafala 4n; see also adoption
Kashmir 3, 135

kinship; see families
Kurds 23, 60, 172, 182–3, 209–232

laïcité; see secularism
lawyers 6, 15n, 22, 32, 38, 40, 44, 50, 57, 60, 69, 143, 145, 148, 152, 195n, 214–5
Lebanon 52, 55, 167, 169, 181–5, 187, 189–90
legal education 37–8, 46, 85
legal pluralism xiii, 2, 5, 29–30, 34, 36–40, 45, 55, 190–92, 197
London 4, 22–23, 36, 37n, 42, 134, 136, 198, 209, 210n, 212, 214–15, 216n, 218, 219n, 222, 227, 230

mahr or sadaq (Islamic dower) 4, 13–15, 18, 21, 40, 42, 60–62, 69, 149–53, 159n, 161n
Malaysia 197
Malik, Maleiha 38, 195
Malta 15n, 160, 191
marital property regimes 4, 15, 56n, 205
marriage xii, xiv–xv, 1, 3, 314, 19, 22, 32, 37n, 42, 49–50, 52–3, 55–63, 65–9, 71–2, 79, 81–4, 86, 88–98, 100, 104, 107–136, 144n, 145, 147–54, 156, 165–8, 170–71, 174, 176–7, 181, 185–92, 196–204, 206, 211, 220–21, 227–31; see also, children, cohabitation, divorce, honour killings, husbands, Islamic law, mahr, widows
  Church 5, 81, 91, 187–90, 204
  contracts xiv–xv, 10, 14–5, 22, 40, 42, 57, 60–62, 64, 66, 69, 118–9, 122, 128, 151–2
  forced 89n, 93, 95, 147–8, 154, 156, 220–21
  homosexual 5, 189
  human rights and 7–8, 13, 61, 125
  immigration and 6, 12, 66, 122–8, 148, 154
  monogamy 10, 107, 110
  Islamic or Muslim 8, 13, 22, 56, 115, 117–22, 124, 127–9, 132–3, 135–6, 150, 154, 165, 171, 201
  polygamy 4, 9–13, 65–7, 79, 94, 105, 110, 150, 152n
  presumption of 8–9, 37n
  proxy 10, 122, 156
  telephone 10, 98
Menski, Werner 1–2, 9–10, 20, 23, 52n, 107n, 147–8
methodological nationalism 11, 24
migrants, see immigrants, immigration control and policies
millet system 190

Morocco 4, 11n, 13, 67n, 118n, 167, 169
mothers 7, 53, 70n, 71–2, 129, 173–5, 182, 186, 230–31
multiculturalism 30, 33, 44–5, 93, 98–9, 103, 106, 143, 147, 149, 154
murder, see homicide
Muslims 2–3, 6, 8, 10, 13–15, 17–22, 32–5, 38, 40–43, 45–6, 49, 51–2, 56–7, 59–60, 63, 68–9, 71, 72n, 79–80, 83–4, 86n, 88, 91–2, 94, 145, 149–50, 152–4, 158–9, 165, 167–9, 174–8, 181–2, 184, 187–8, 190–91, 197–9, 204, 213n, 225
  Algerian 17
  Bangladeshi 10, 42, 62
  Egyptian 132
  European 8, 14, 71, 84, 115–20, 125, 127–9, 132–3, 136–7
  Iranian 18, 60n, 130, 150–2
  North African 6, 17, 20, 36, 56, 118n, 199n
  Pakistani 6, 10

Netherlands, the 1, 11, 14, 18, 64, 67n, 147n, 170, 185, 216
nikah, see marriage
Nordic Folk's Churches 80–82, 90–91, 98–9
North America 34
Northern Ireland 120, 125n
Norway 32, 80, 87, 92, 147, 156, 188n, 191

Ontario 23
Orthodox Churches 5, 86, 181–193
Ottoman Empire 2

Pakistan 10, 22n, 60, 118n, 134–5, 167
Pakistanis 6, 72n, 135, 168
Palestine 191n, 209
parallel legal systems xiv, 38, 51–3, 116, 132–3, 144–5, 197, 203, 224
parents xii, 10, 53, 70–72, 125, 146, 153, 166n, 167–9, 171–5, 177, 184–7, 189, 205, 230
paternity 173
personal status law xii, 2, 5, 19–20, 45, 52, 55, 58, 106, 107n, 110–11, 112n, 115, 117, 118n, 144, 157, 190, 197–8
police 79, 168, 209, 214–15, 220–23, 227–8
polygamy, see marriage
positivism 31, 33, 36–9, 41, 44, 46, 115–6, 118–9, 122, 128, 130, 137
Poulter, Sebastian 9n, 133
private international law xii–xiv, 3–4
  citizenship and nationality xiv, 3–4, 10–12, 56, 58, 66–8, 122, 124, 131, 150, 157,

connecting factors 4, 21, 56, 67, 98n
diplomatic premises 4
Hague conventions and process 3, 134, 158, 191
immigration and 67–8
long term residence xiv
transjurisdictionalism 4, 10
transnationalism 4, 10, 16, 22n, 24, 41, 43, 59, 120, 133, 165–7, 169, 170n, 171, 176–8, 181, 183, 185, 189–92, 209–10, 229, 231
public international law 3

Qur'an, see Islam

Ramadan, Tariq 83n, 84
reasonable accommodation 56, 69
religious freedom; see freedom of religion
Right to marry 13, 61, 125
rights, see human rights
Rohe, Mathias 1–4, 17–18, 21, 39
Roma 2, 7–8, 148n
Roman Catholicism, see Catholicism

Scotland 6, 8, 201–1, 125n, 135, 204n
secular law xi, xiv, 81, 146, 153, 189
secular state 59, 80, 85
secularisation xi–xiv, 1–2, 10–11, 20–21, 55, 62, 119, 145
secularism xi, 21n 53, 145n, 146n, 188; see also church-state relations
    laïcité 21n, 118–9
    separation of law and religion xi–xiii, 6, 80, 81n, 85n, 86n
sexual conduct 64n, 153, 155, 165–8, 170, 174–5, 177–8, 202
Shachar, Ayelet 38, 40–41, 44n, 195–6, 200
shari'a, sharia; see Islamic law
Sikhs 23, 37n, 71n
social security, welfare benefits, welfare state 7, 9, 11, 14, 42, 66–7, 82, 168, 184–6
social work(ers) 168
Somalia 192

South Africa 19, 38, 44n
Spain 1, 5, 7, 9–12, 55–7, 64, 66–7, 70n, 148n, 209n
    Roma 7
Strasbourg court, see European Court of Human Rights (ECtHR)
superdiversity 32
Sweden 5, 9, 79–100, 147, 150–52, 155–6, 158n, 159n, 181, 183–93, 210
Switzerland 21, 185
Syria 3, 167, 169, 181–7, 189–90
Syriac Church 5, 181–93

talaq; see divorce
transnationalism 4, 10, 16, 22n, 24, 41, 43, 59, 67, 120, 133, 149, 165–7, 169, 170n, 171, 176–8, 181, 183, 185, 189–92, 209–10, 229, 231
Turkey 1, 5–14, 15n, 20–21, 32n, 52, 60, 70n, 148n, 167, 170–72, 181–5, 187–90, 209–210, 212–5, 216n, 218–24, 227, 229–31
    Roma 8

uniformity and uniformisation of law 2, 4–5, 45, 52, 72, 103–12, 115, 117, 148, 161n
United Kingdom 6, 12, 15n, 16n, 20, 22n, 30, 32, 33n, 42n, 46, 49n, 52, 55, 57, 59, 63n, 69, 115, 117–8, 120, 121–4, 126–7, 132–5, 145, 147n, 148, 154, 168, 199, 205, 209–211, 213–6, 219n, 220, 223, 226–7, 229, 230–32; see also Britain, England and Wales, human rights, Scotland
United States 14, 30, 82n, 182, 185

Western Thrace 2, 17, 58
widows 7–8, 11, 37n, 66
Williams, Dr. Rowan 23, 30–31, 45, 54, 145, 195
wills; see inheritance and wills

Yemen 60